For the People

*A Documentary History
of the Struggle for Peace and Justice
in the United States*

For the People

A Documentary History
of the Struggle for Peace and Justice
in the United States

Charles F. Howlett
Molloy College

Robbie Lieberman
Southern Illinois University

INFORMATION AGE PUBLISHING, INC.
Charlotte, NC • www.infoagepub.com

Library of Congress Cataloging-in-Publication Data

For the people : a documentary history of the struggle for peace and justice
in the United States / book editors, Charles F. Howlett, Robbie Lieberman.
       p. cm.
  Includes bibliographical references.
  ISBN 978-1-60752-305-5 (pbk.) – ISBN 978-1-60752-306-2 (hardcover) –
ISBN 978-1-60752-307-9 (e-book)
  1. Peace movements–United States–History. 2. Peace movements–United
States–History–Sources 3. Social justice–United States–History. 4.
Social justice–United States–History–Sources. I. Howlett, Charles F. II.
Lieberman, Robbie, 1954-
  JZ5584.U6F67 2009
  303.6'60973–dc22

                                                            2009039168

Printed in the United States of America

To

Peter and Jennie, Theresa and Jennifer
and all members of the Peace History Society, past and present

Contents

Acknowledgments

Historians who have been instrumental in shaping our views and providing critical commentary on peace history subject matter are Harriet Alonso, Scott Bennett, Charles Chatfield, Wendy Chmielewski, Blanche Cook, Mitch Hall, Kip Kosek, Robert Shaffer, and Nigel Young. Alan J. Singer, noted professor of secondary education and editor of the *Social Science Docket*, provided support and encouragement with respect to developing document-based questions. Dr. Winston "Deke" Wilson deserves special commendation for making copies of Bowman Bubble Gum Cards numbers 41 and 153, which are part of the "Horrors of War" series and part of his personal collection. Many students assisted in this project, providing research support, critically reading the manuscript, analyzing documents, developing introductory narratives to the primary sources, and providing additional insights for the chapter essays. Mike Brecciano did a remarkable job going over the initial draft, making numerous suggestions throughout. Robert Windorf, Erin Geiger, Mary Berblinger, and Patrick Hoey, in particular, offered invaluable research assistance and fact-checked subsequent drafts as well as provided their own observations. Professor Audrey Cohan of the Division of Education at Molloy College has provided encouragement and support for this project. A Molloy College Faculty Research Grant is greatly appreciated. It assisted with payment of permission rights for those documents under copyright protection. The James Weldon Johnson Institute afforded a supportive environment for coeditor Robbie Lieberman. Teaching

For the People, pages xiii–xv
xiii

an introductory peace studies course with her colleague Jyotsna Kapur also inspired her and helped make clear the need for this sort of collection.

The editors are also indebted to Larry Wittner for writing the Foreword. A distinguished historian and committed activist for peace, Larry has been a moving force within the Peace History Society. Without his insights and leadership, our small, but deeply committed, organization would not be where it is today.

Permissions

The authors have tried diligently to obtain permission to reprint material currently under active copyright, except in cases of fair use. Even in this regard, efforts were made to contact for permission. If inadvertently we have made omissions, we will greatly appreciate being advised so that corrections can be made. We gratefully acknowledge the permission of the following publishers to reprint:

Basic Books, excerpt of "Mother's Day Proclamation" from Murray Polner and Thomas E. Woods, eds., *We Who Dared to Say No to War: American Antiwar Writings from 1812 to Now* (2008).

"Dekes Collection" for permission to use Bowman Bubble Gum "Horrors of War" Series Cards Nos. 41 and 153 for one of our documents.

Garland Publishers, excerpts from "War Resisters International Statement of Principles" and Jessie Wallace Hughan, "If We Should be Invaded" in Charles Chatfield, ed., *International War Resistance through World War II* (1971); excerpt from "War Resistance as War Prevention" in Chatfield, ed., *Devere Allen and a Radical Approach to War* (1971).

International Publishers, excerpt from W.E.B. Du Bois, *The Autobiography of W.E.B. Du Bois: A Soliloquy on Viewing My Life from the Last Decade of Its First Century* (1968).

James Baldwin Estate, "My Dungeon Shook—Letter to My Nephew on the One Hundredth Anniversary of the Emancipation" © 1962 James Baldwin. Collected in THE NEXT TIME, published by Vintage Books.

Kali Tal, Vietnam Generation, and Institute of Advanced Technology at the University of Virginia for excerpts from Port Huron Statement and SNCC's founding statement.

Kensington Publishing Corp./Citadel Press, excerpt from Joan Wile, *Grandmothers Against the War* (2008).

Joanne Landy, Tom Harrison, and Jennifer Scarlott, excerpt from "We Oppose Both Saddam Hussein and the U.S. War on Iraq" (2003). Readers are encouraged to check the website www.cpd.org.

Diane Lent for "Boots 2007" photograph.

A.J. Muste Memorial Institute, excerpts from Barbara Deming, "Revolution and Equilibrium" (1968).

Orbis Books, excerpts from Staughton and Helen Lynd, eds., *Nonviolence in America: A Documentary History* (1998).

Random House, excerpt from Margaret Washington, ed., *Narrative of Sojourner Truth* (1993) and James Baldwin, *The Fire Next Time* (1963).

Scribner, a division of Simon & Schuster, Inc., excerpt from Nat Hentoff, ed., *The Essays of A.J. Muste* (1967).

State University of New York Press, excerpt from John G. Neihardt, *Black Elk Speaks: Being the Life Story of a Holy Man of the Oglala Sioux, The Premier Edition* (2008).

Seven Stones Press, excerpt from Howard Zinn, *Terrorism and War* (2002).

Syracuse University Press, excerpts from the following: "The Custom of War"; "The U.S. Conquest of the Philippines"; "The State"; "War is Sin"; and "The Power of Nonviolence" in Charles Chatfield and Ruzzana Illukhina, eds., *Peace/Mir: An Anthology of Historic Alternatives to War* (1994).

Syracuse University Press, excerpts from the following: "A League of Peace"; "Peace Program of the Socialist Party"; "Patriotism and Pacifists in War Time"; and "War and the Social Movement" in John Whiteclay Chambers, ed., *The Eagle and the Dove: The American Peace Movement and U.S. Foreign Policy, 1900–1922* (1991).

Swarthmore College Peace Collection for the photos appearing in this work.

The Nation, excerpt from David Cortright, "What We Do Now: An Agenda for Peace," April 21, 2003.

Twayne Publishers/Cengage Learning, excerpt from Judith Porter Adams, ed., *Peacework: Oral Histories of Women Peace Activists* (1991).

Walter P. Reuther Library of Labor and Urban Affairs, Wayne State University, for the photo "Brookwood Labor Players Tour Bus."

Foreword

It is remarkable how little the American people know about their country's advocates of peace. Most Americans have little difficulty discussing the background and activities of leading athletes, movie stars, pop singers, and politicians. But how many Americans can identify David Low Dodge, William Ladd, Elihu Burritt, Jessie Wallace Hughan, John Haynes Holmes, Frederick Libby, Tracy Mygatt, Frances Witherspoon, Stephen Wise, Jeannette Rankin, Dorothy Day, A.J. Muste, Norman Cousins, and a host of other leading peace campaigners over the course of U.S. history? Just as striking, few Americans are aware that many well-known figures from their nation's past also have been sharp critics of war, including John Quincy Adams, William Lloyd Garrison, Susan B. Anthony, Henry David Thoreau, Abraham Lincoln, Charles Sumner, William Jennings Bryan, Mark Twain, Andrew Carnegie, John Dewey, Jane Addams, Robert La Follette, Albert Einstein, and Martin Luther King, Jr.

This historical amnesia probably reflects the fact that the cause of peace has not yet triumphed—or, to put it differently, that the American government and a large portion of the public are not yet ready to dispense with war. After all, for much of the past century the United States has been engaged in armed conflict, and today the largest portion of the U.S. government's budget remains devoted to military purposes. Furthermore, a substantial number of Americans and almost all the communications media seem to regard U.S. soldiers as more admirable than nurses, doctors, teachers, firefighters, policemen, and other civilian public servants. In

For the People, pages xvii–xix
Copyright © 2009 by Information Age Publishing
All rights of reproduction in any form reserved.

contrast to peace proponents, leaders of reform struggles that have been won or largely won—for example, the movements to abolish slavery, secure women's rights, and end racial discrimination—today receive recognition and respect.

Yet, ironically, American peace advocates—though not totally success-ful—have secured some important victories. They have not only built the American peace movement into one of the largest social movements in U.S. history, but helped force an end to a number of wars (including the Mexican War, the Vietnam War, and the Cold War), halt U.S. military inter-vention (in the Caribbean, Central America, and elsewhere), and curb the nuclear arms race. In addition, there are numerous wars that they helped to prevent. For example, the anti-imperialist crusade during the U.S. military conquest of the Philippines blocked the occurrence of later U.S. wars of this kind, while the critique of a looming U.S. military conflict with Mexico in 1916 helped to head off a war with that nation. There is also consider-able evidence that, after 1945, peace activism played a key role in prevent-ing the further outbreak of nuclear war. Indeed, thanks to peace agitation, numerous ideas championed by peace proponents became regular features of U.S. foreign policy, including the establishment of an international or-ganization (resulting in the creation of the League of Nations and, later, the United Nations [UN]), humanitarian relief and aid programs, a peace corps, and nuclear arms control and disarmament.

In addition, peace advocates played a central role in developing other social movements. Where would the civil liberties movement have been without Roger Baldwin, who, after heading up the Civil Liberties Bureau of the American Union Against Militarism and serving prison time as a con-scientious objector during World War I, founded and directed the Ameri-can Civil Liberties Union? Where would the civil rights movement have been without the key work of pacifists in developing nonviolent resistance, founding the Congress of Racial Equality, and serving as top advisors to Martin Luther King, Jr.? Where would the environmental movement have been without the pacifist campaigners against nuclear weapons testing who founded Greenpeace?

Of course, if peace advocates ultimately are successful in securing their long-range goal of a warless world, they probably will secure widespread recognition and praise.

But, in the meantime, we can learn much about their ideas and their work from *For the People.* In this broad survey of the struggle for peace throughout American history, Charles Howlett and Robbie Lieberman have rescued many important individuals, their ideas, and their writings from obscurity and have placed them in their historical context. In addition, they have pointed to numerous prominent figures who spoke out against war and to additional publications that students and others can read to secure further information about the American peace movement. For these achievements, we owe them our gratitude.

Moreover, after pondering the writings brought together in this book, we might also consider the immense debt we owe to America's peace advocates for their efforts, over the centuries, to move the world beyond the mass bloodshed and killing of the past. Others, of course, deserve our admiration as well—ethical leaders, peace activists in other lands, and a small number of farsighted statesmen. But let us not forget those Americans who, through their grassroots efforts for peace, blazed the trail toward a more humane and civilized world—a world without war.

Professor Lawrence S. Wittner
History Department, University at Albany

Introduction

$\mathbf{T}$his collection of edited documents examines the evolution of the struggle for peace and justice in American history from precolonial times to the Iraq War. The field of peace studies, and peace history in particular, has grown enormously since the Vietnam War era. Indeed, it has captured the attention of scholars studying various aspects of American military, diplomatic, and social history. Yet movements for peace and justice still receive little attention in secondary schools and college survey courses. This book addresses that oft-neglected yet integral part of history by exposing students to the many and varied American voices that have called for peace and justice over the years.

The volume is arranged chronologically. Each chapter includes an opening narrative that provides historical context, brief introductions to the documents, and questions for discussion The list of references at the end is intended to help those who want to do further research in U.S. peace history. Along with black freedom struggles and the women's rights movement, the peace movement is one of the most important social movements in American history, especially in the last one hundred years. The primary focus of this collection is on the role of peace movements and nonviolent action, based on the premise that the struggle for peace has almost always involved more than simply ending war. The story begins with an examination of the Native Americans of the Iroquois Confederacy and the Great Law of Peace and proceeds to address the role of the Religious Society of Friends (Quakers) and nonviolence, the rise of a nonsectarian, organized

For the People, pages xxi–xxiii
Copyright © 2009 by Information Age Publishing
All rights of reproduction in any form reserved.

peace movement after the War of 1812, advocates for the abolition of slavery, for the rights of women and Native Americans, the drive for international arbitration, support for labor, and opposition to imperialism. By the twentieth century, peace and justice advocates were promoting the importance of internationalism and investigative foundations in support of world peace. World War I witnessed the battle over civil liberties and the birth of a "modern" peace movement, which became more radical in its opposition to war and support for social and economic justice. Peace and justice activists also began promoting the tactics of direct action that flourished after World War II. The strategy for peace and justice activists was to move from passive nonresistance to directly challenging in a nonviolent way the centers of political and economic power in the United States. After World War II, activists protested the horrors of atomic and then nuclear weaponry, while developing a vibrant civil rights movement. The post–World War II era was also characterized by massive upheavals during the Vietnam War, highlighted by numerous examples of civil disobedience, and later the growth of citizen-activism in opposition to nuclear power plant construction, the call for a "nuclear freeze," efforts to end apartheid, movements to prevent U.S. intervention in Latin America, and global protests against the war in Iraq. These topics and many more are addressed in the documents that follow.

In this book, terms such as *nonviolence, nonresistance, passive resistance,* and *nonviolent resistance* are used somewhat interchangeably. In one sense, these terms all convey the desire to eliminate institutionalized violence using means that are themselves not violent. Initially, "nonresistance" was equated with colonial sectarian peace groups whose acts of individual conscience dictated their opposition to all forms of violence. By the early nineteenth century, as a nonsectarian peace movement emerged, these other terms surfaced in the writings of noted peace and justice activists, which essentially conveyed the same meaning. In addition, in the second half of the twentieth century, with the appearance of direct action that included physical acts of property destruction against the war-making machine, a new dimension to nonresistance, nonviolence, nonviolent resistance, and passive resistance was added to the equation.

The struggle for peace and justice is characterized by its own special history, leadership, enthusiasm, ideals, organizational bases, and traditions of social reform. We have chosen to highlight the rich diversity of peace activists and thinkers who have frequently been part of larger movements for social change. As these selections demonstrate, those involved in the peace and justice movement have often argued for a more organic world consciousness, proposing economic and social changes ranging from international regulation of the world's food supply to international control of the arms industry. Above all, they have consistently connected their actions to broader social and political concerns including civil rights, feminism, economic equality, and environmental awareness. They have insisted, time and time again, that war is an integral part of an unjust social order and that instruments of political control involve the hidden threat of violence, thus their work has often been geared toward expanding democracy and equality. Throughout America's past, they have formed ideal communities for the larger society to emulate and engaged in activities that promoted alternatives to oppressive and discriminatory political policies, economic and social institutions, and even cultural values that have stood in the way of establishing lasting peace.

Our intention as editors is to share the writings and speeches of those who devoted themselves to the struggle for peace and justice in order to make clear that this is an important part of U.S. history, integral to the much larger story of democracy in action. In addition to the words of well-known pacifists and antiwar activists, the documents bring to light lesser known figures who spoke out on a wide range of issues, from those who wanted to abolish slavery, oppose imperialism, promote the dignity of labor, and protest discrimination against women, Native Americans, African Americans, and other groups to those who challenged war, conscription, and the buildup of nuclear weapons and worked for gay rights and environmental sustainability. We hope that young readers, in particular, will come to appreciate the diversity of ideas and actions on behalf of peace and justice that have helped shape the country's history.

1

Early Forms of Peace and Justice from Precolonial Times to the Creation of a New Nation

Before the first Europeans "discovered" the New World, Native American tribes who had inhabited the Americas for many centuries worked to establish a way of peace. Some of the tribes adapted their way of life to the heavily watered, densely forested regions of what are now the eastern parts of Canada and the United States. The Iroquois Confederation, consisting of the Mohawk tribe, Oneida tribe, Onondaga tribe, Cayuga tribe, and Seneca tribe, decided after years of warring upon one another for food and territory to replace violence with peaceful relations. Living in harmony with the land defined their culture and way of life. However, the rampant violence had forced them to abandon their agricultural communities and hilly cornfields and resort to a more primitive existence in the forests. Bonded by their love for the land and desire to live in harmony, the first dwellers of America came to understand that their eventual survival could only be forged through a written instrument of peace.

For the People, pages 1–23
Copyright © 2009 by Information Age Publishing
All rights of reproduction in any form reserved.

1

Faced with this crisis the five Iroquois peoples adopted a "League of Peace," also known as the "Great Law of Peace." The Great Law consisted of three interconnected concepts, which if adhered to, ensured peace among the member nations of the Confederacy. The first concept, righteousness, called on people to possess a strong sense of justice and treat others as equals. All people must enjoy equal protection under the Great Law and shape their own personal conduct so as not to build up resentment or hatred toward one another. The second concept, health, encouraged soundness of mind and body; it also meant that a strong and determined mind will draw upon enlightened willpower to foster well-being among peoples and between nations. The third concept, power, relied on laws and customs in order to make justice prevail.

The most difficult part of the "Great Law" to comprehend was the meaning of the concept of peace. Peace was not simply the absence of battle. For the Iroquois Confederacy peace represented a state of mind. "One heart, one mind, one head, and one body" enabled the Confederacy to remain united in the face of conquest and European expansionism. More importantly, the concept of peace was based on the spiritual power of each individual. As one progresses through life's journey, the individual experiences different things, learns more, and connects to other forms of spiritual power; in the process the individual's spirit grows as well. The ultimate power of the "Great Law of Peace" rests in how well the individual person develops his or her sense of self and, in so doing, develops that sense with regard to the welfare of others in the clan, village, nation, and the entire Confederacy. Prior to the arrival of English colonists, the tribes composing the Confederation had worked out their differences and lived in harmony with nature and among one another. "The Great Law of Peace" serves as the first document in creating a peace tradition in American history (**Document 1**).

Meanwhile, as the colonies were being settled in the early seventeenth century, those in New England had to adjust to the rigors of the "New World." Colonists who attempted to establish peaceful relations with Native Americans often did so in the name of religion, and readers will notice many references to Christianity in the documents that follow. Among the settlers, one stood out for his brave stand against the Puritans' religious justification of war against the Native Americans in New England.

Perhaps the earliest opponent of war in America and supporter of justice and equality was Roger Williams, the rebellious Puritan divine who founded the colony of Rhode Island when he was expelled in 1635 from Massachusetts Bay (**Document 2**). As the late Harvard professor and authority on Puritanism, Perry Miller, observed, Williams was by no means a saint. He had many rough edges and embraced controversy to the chagrin of those who preached unquestioned obedience to church and state; however, he was brilliant in his own right and was certainly filled with righteous indignation relative to matters involving religion and politics. He was a separatist at heart and found it more comforting preaching among those who had settled in Plymouth. Much to the consternation of those in charge of the Bay Colony, he had no desire to reform the Anglican Church. While serving as minister to churches in Plymouth and Salem, he publicly denied the right of the civil government to enforce religious tenets and maintained that the colony's land was legally the property of the Native Americans. It is not hard to understand why, at a time when English common law determined property rights and Puritan settlers were staking a claim to the land, conflict erupted between the colonists and the Native Americans. America's first inhabitants did not share European concepts of land ownership and could not fathom how European settlers could erect fences to keep them out.

Paralleling this thinking, it was Williams's attitude toward the Native Americans that made him an opponent of war and defender of equal justice, for he did not acknowledge Puritan ownership of Massachusetts Bay by right of conquest. The men of Massachusetts, because of their theological orientation, required scriptural justification for all their actions. They sanctioned bloody slaughters of the Native Americans on the contrived grounds that the Indians were children of Satan, in whose extermination a solemn God rejoiced.

Williams, who had purchased land from the Narragansett Indians to establish the town of Providence, condemned the murder of innocent human beings as a gross immorality. He was particularly repulsed when told in 1636 to forward to Boston the hands of slain Pequots. Williams insisted that the Native Americans owned North America by virtue of their occupation and that the English must purchase the land if they were to settle it legally. He maintained that the King's grants to the Puritans were invalid; the King's royal proclamations had no legal jurisdiction since he did not own the land. To the dismay of the colony's leaders, Williams was striking at the heart of the Puritans' covenant theology, which regarded contracts, including colonial charters, as inviolable.

Residing in the wilderness with the Native Americans after his exile from Massachusetts Bay, Williams learned their language and garnered their complete support. Unlike French philosopher Jean Jacques Rousseau, Williams did not sentimentalize the Native Americans as "noble savages." In 1654, Williams successfully convinced his fellow colonists that it was far more conducive to use the Bible instead of rifles to win over the hearts and minds of the Native Americans, thus avoiding war that year with the Narragansett. His honest dealings with New England's first inhabitants and abhorrence of bloodshed helped postpone the battle of extinction until King Philip's War in 1675 dealt the final blow.

While Williams was a "voice in the wilderness" in New England proclaiming the virtue of peace, the first attempt to establish a colony in the New World based on the principle of nonviolence unfolded in Pennsylvania. By the 1660s, during a wave of persecutions in Great Britain initiated by the restored Stuart monarch, Charles II, the Quakers officially accepted pacifism as part of the "ever-present, ever-teaching Spirit of Christ." In practice, pacifism served to bridge the inward and outward emphases of the Quaker way. Itinerant Quaker ministers both lived pacifism for the sake of tranquility and as the pathway to Christ's kingdom here on earth. The Quakers and other religious pacifist groups in the seventeenth and eighteenth century represent what is known as the sectarian peace reform tradition.

The attempt among Friends to gain a colonial foothold with greater autonomy finally succeeded in 1681, when a well-born Oxford student turned Quaker convert named William Penn settled a family debt with King Charles II. Cerebral, yet astonishingly modest in terms of personality, he willingly accepted the proprietorship of a huge tract of land in the lower Delaware Valley, which he called "Penna," and it became home to many different settlers. The colony's leader invited honest, industrious settlers to come in exchange for religious toleration, representative rule, and, most importantly, cheap land. Settlers from all over poured in—Quakers from England, Wales, and Ireland; Scotch-Irish Presbyterians; Swiss and German Protestants from the continent; and Catholics and Jews from various European countries.

Penn established a model community that operated on voluntary and communal agreement and without physical coercion. He conceived of his colony as a profit-making enterprise, but also as a "Holy Experiment" in which Friends could test their visions of "brotherly love." Penn and his brethren viewed both man and society as perfectible. In support of peace, order, and popular self-determination, Penn drafted in 1682 a constitutional Frame of Government that provided unusually broad representative government and extensive religious toleration. Included in this proposal was a sincere effort to accommodate Native Americans.

Indeed, the focal point of Penn's experiment was the colony's relationship to the Native Americans, presenting an alternative to the violence of the past. Penn was infamous in England for his nonconformist views (inspired mainly by radical Whigs like Algernon Sidney), and he wrote of his beliefs to the Native Americans before arriving in the province (**Document 3**). The Quaker belief that "God within each man" met a counterpart in the Indians' concept of the "Great Spirit" helped pave the way for future peaceful relations between the Quakers and Native Americans.

For Penn, peace was an extension of justice, an extension that should be embraced by all earthly beings. In an "Address to the American Indians," November 1682, Penn said he considered the Native Americans as Christian equals composed of the same flesh and blood and of the same body as if it "were to be divided into two parts." In turn, the Native Americans were impressed with the fact that he insisted on purchase of the land, which both sides readily agreed to and endorsed by mutual consent. A "Great Treaty" was also signed with the Delaware Indians at Shackamaxon in 1683, and became a working reality for nearly seventy years. Thus, through patience and understanding, not hatred and bloodshed, Quakers and Native Americans carved out a record of peaceable relations that remains a model in the annals of migratory peoples. While nearly 12,000 English Friends made their way across the historically Native American land by the close of the seventeenth century, conflict was kept to a minimum and violence was rare. The Quakers' doctrine of nonviolence was a natural extension of their belief in social justice as well as respect for Native American rights and culture.

The most important representative of the Quaker doctrine of nonviolence was John Woolman. He is considered one of America's earliest social reformers, one who symbolized the peace movement's true objective: the attainment of justice and equality through nonviolence. A tailor by trade from Mt. Holly, New Jersey, he was really an itinerant preacher whose actual deeds spoke louder than words. In Woolman's eyes, violence and wars were bred by the spirit of possessiveness and the lust for riches. Appetites for profits are the "seeds of war that may quickly ripen." This identification of wealth-seeking with war and violence and his appeal to conscience caused Woolman to anticipate the Marxist interpretation of war on the one hand and Henry David Thoreau's critique of materialism on the other and led to his outspokenness on the issue of war taxes (**Document 4**). His views would become the focal point for action among many pacifists, especially during twentieth century wars.

Woolman's concept of peace was based on just social relationships and was a clear example of the Quaker ethos that pervaded the religious Anglo-American peace societies of the early nineteenth century. Their Enlightenment ideas helped inspire subsequent social reform movements such as women's rights, temperance, mental health, and abolitionism. Woolman's pacifism expressed a faith in rational and evolutionary progress based on the application of the absence of conflict to social organization. His liberal confidence in the benign power of peace—a view that would be shared by nineteenth-century reformers like Adin Ballou, Josiah Warren, and others—reflected the importance of social justice. Wars, Woolman believed, came about because some people had too much and wanted more, while other persons had not even the decencies of life.

Woolman's pacifism was also tied to an "implicit humanitarianism" opposed to slavery (**Document 5**). In colonial America, Woolman was not the first Friend to condemn the evils of slavery; as early as 1688, the Quakers of Germantown, Pennsylvania, spoke out against it, denouncing the owning and selling of human beings as property. Nevertheless, it was not until the mid-1700s, as the institutionalized system of slavery became embedded in southern culture and rationalized in some quarters of northern thinking, that Quakers such as Woolman took a more aggressive stand. In the 1750s Woolman emerged as a leading crusader on behalf of human rights and social justice. He journeyed through the colonies trying to persuade Quakers to free their slaves and educate them. He kept a careful record of his trips in his now famous *Journal,* in which he expressed ideas that continue to have resonance.

During the struggle for independence, though, Quakers were placed in an untenable position. According to Peter Brock, American Friends faced an unpleasant dilemma. On the one hand, as pacifists they could not take up arms for either side (some were sympathetic to the Tory cause). On the other hand, they regarded loyalty to the powers in charge (government) as a religious duty to be upheld even at the expense of human suffering and deprivation. Although leaders of the Revolution tried to respect their religious opposition to war, those refusing to take up arms were often persecuted. Their position of nonviolent neutrality put them at risk when it came to a compulsory draft.

In March 1777, when Pennsylvania enacted a mandatory draft law, for instance, even those Friends who had the money to pay for their exemption refused to do so. Draft resisters saw their property taken from them. For example, Thomas Passmore was forced to surrender his colt, valued at 20 pounds, and George Harlan's two mares and a blanket were seized, totaling 30 pounds and 16 shillings. Fines often exceeded what was required by statute. A number of draft-eligible Quaker conscripts were also punished, and many spent days or even months in jail. Nevertheless, most were willing to stand behind their conscience and speak out against the use of arms.

One of the foremost Quaker opponents of the Anglo-American conflict was Anthony Benezet. Born of French Huguenots, raised in England, and settling in America in 1731, Benezet had opened a school for African Americans in Philadelphia in 1750. He also wrote one of the earliest pacifist treatises in American history. In *Thoughts on the Nature of War* (1750), he condemned war as premeditated and solely aimed at destroying human lives, which were created in the image of God. Following Woolman's lead, Benezet held that greed provoked warfare. Preaching and practicing tax refusal, he badgered British and American military officers to reflect upon their actions, and demanded that Christians act in unison against the war menace. At best, Benezet hoped that *Thoughts* would demonstrate the utter futility of war.

During the American Revolution, Benezet wrote a letter to the Continental Congress reiterating the views he had expressed in *Thoughts* (**Document 6**), which were widely endorsed by fellow Friends (Quakers). Observing Benezet's stand, Quakers were precluded from assisting either of the conflicting armies with their labor. For example, farmers who volunteered horses and carts for military employment became liable for disciplinary action by their local meeting. The tax issue continued to cause much soul searching among Friends. During the war, the question—to pay or not to pay?—was debated vigorously. Many Friends refused to pay the war taxes; some advocated a complete tax boycott. Further complications arose when the American authorities imposed an oath of loyalty. Though the government recognized Quakers' long-standing objections to judicial oaths and was ready to agree to the substitution of a mere affirmation, the Society forbade its members to take the test. The very practice of conscientious objection earmarked the doctrine of Quaker pacifism. It was born in religious practice and carried out in life-affirming ways. The Revolutionary War made conscientious objection an effective philosophical instrument later known as passive nonresistance.

The creation of the new republic witnessed other peace activists promoting their own plans for a lasting and permanent peace. One such notable plan was proposed by Dr. Benjamin Rush in the early 1790s. Rush, a Philadelphia Quaker physician, former Continental Army Surgeon-General, and signer of the Declaration of Independence, was a fascinating figure who believed fervently in Christianity and possessed the scientific intelligence that enabled him to walk alongside such luminaries as Benjamin Franklin and Thomas Jefferson. After completing his medical training at the University of Edinburgh, he became one of the best-known doctors in America. He was an enthusiastic reformer who championed the causes of public education, women's rights, temperance, abolitionism, and, most especially, world peace. He was particularly outspoken on the need for an inclusive, democratic intellectual life. He was also a humanitarian who took the idea of peace seriously as part of one's civic responsibility.

Writing in 1793, Rush embodied Quaker ideals by urging the formation of a national peace office (**Document 7**). Aiming to substitute a culture of peace for the glamour of war—a problem perplexing peace advocates even to this day—Rush believed the peace office should establish throughout the country free schools that would promulgate pacific Christian principles, work to eliminate all capital punishment laws, and seek the elimination of military parades, titles, and uniforms. In Rush's estimation, all militia laws should be repealed because they generated "idleness and vice," thus producing the wars they were said to prevent. Military titles fed vanity and detracted attention from the unchecked brutality and misery of war. In the lobby of his proposed office, Rush suggested that painted representations of all the military instruments of death be displayed, along with a plethora of art examples depicting the sheer bloodshed and physical devastation wrought by war. Above these graphic scenes Rush suggested that the words "NATIONAL GLORY" be inscribed in red characters to represent human blood.

Clearly from the "Great Law of Peace" to the "Plan for a Peace Office of the United States" serious engagement with issues of peace and justice was part of the early American experience. These concerns would continue to be subject to intense discussion and action as the young republic entered a new century.

Document 1   *The Great Law of Peace* (1500s)

The Great Law of Peace is based on oral tradition and codified in a series of wampum belts. It was the founding constitution of the Iroquois Confederacy, and some historians suggest it inspired the framers of the U.S. constitution. The five nations of the Iroquois Confederation were governed by a Grand Council that laid down the ground rules for the various tribes to resolve disputes in order to maintain peace. The story is as follows:

> *A* boy is born to the virgin daughter of a Huron woman. Ashamed and depressed, the grandmother tries to destroy the baby three times, until she is told in a dream that the boy is destined to

bring forth a good message from the Creator. He grows rapidly and is honest, generous and peaceful.

The Peacemaker leaves in a white stone canoe for the land of the Mohawks where he finds war, killing, destruction and cannibalism. He announces that he is there to deliver a message from the Creator that war must cease.

The Mother of Nations [Jikonsahseh] takes in the weary Peacemaker and feeds him. He explains the principles of Peace, Righteousness and Power and the concept of the longhouse as a metaphor for the Great Law. She accepts the message, and in doing so, women are given priority in the League as Clan Mothers.

Looking into the smoke hole of a house, the Peacemaker sees a man carrying a human body to the cooking fire. About to eat the flesh, the man peers into the pot but sees the face of the Peacemaker and is magically transformed. The Peacemaker teaches him to bury the body and eat deer meat instead. The antlers of the deer will be symbols of authority. The former cannibal, Ayenwatha, accepts the message of peace. . . .

[Ayenwatha] visits a Mohawk community and is given an honored seat as a chief. He teaches them to make a signal fire at the edge of the clearing to announce the arrival of a peaceful visitor, how to make wampum, and how to use the wampum strings to deliver messages. He leaves to continue his search for consolation.

Using 8 of the 13 wampum strings made by Ayenwatha, the Peacemaker removes the pain and suffering of Ayenwatha and restores his mind so they can bring forth the message of the Creator. The Peacemaker decides that wampum will be used to carry that message. . . .

The Peacemaker established the symbols of the Great Law. The longhouse has five fireplaces but one family. Wampum will record the messages. The Tree of Peace was planted in the center of the circle of chiefs. An eagle was placed on top to watch out for enemies. The White Roots of Peace stretched out across the land. The weapons of war were buried under the Tree. A meal of beaver tail was shared. Five arrows were bound together. The council fire was kindled and the smoke pierced the sky. These are all symbols of power that comes from the unity of peace. . . .

Source: "Great Law of Peace," http://sixnations.buffnet.net (accessed January 29, 2007).

QUESTIONS

1. What is the significance of the Clan Mothers in upholding a tradition of peace?
2. What is the symbolic significance of the white stone canoe the Peacemaker used to deliver his message?
3. How does this law contradict earlier accounts of the Iroquois as cruel expansionists?

Document 2: Roger Williams
The Bloudy Tenant of Persecution (1643)

Roger Williams (1603–1682/3) sailed to Massachusetts in 1630 to escape the religious oppression of England. He was banished from Massachusetts in 1635 by John Cotton, Sr., for suggesting separation of civil and religious authority. He moved to Rhode Island and in 1643 wrote "The Bloudy Tenant of Persecution, for the Cause of Conscience, Discussed in a Conference Between Truth and Peace." Williams's insistence on religious toleration extended to his support for Native American tribes. Religious tolerance, he believed, was a basic means for establishing lasting peace among all peoples.

reface:

First. That the blood of so many hundred thousand souls of protestants and papists, split in the wars of present and former ages, for their respective consciences, is not required nor accepted by Jesus Christ the Prince of Peace.

Secondly. Pregnant scriptures and arguments are throughout the work proposed against the doctrine of persecution for cause of conscience.

Thirdly. Satisfactory answers are given to scriptures and objections produced by Mr. Calvin, Beza, Mr. Cotton, and the ministers of the New English churches, and others former and later, tending to prove the doctrine of persecution for cause of conscience.

Fourthly. The doctrine for persecution for cause of conscience is proved guilty of all the blood of the souls crying for vengeance under the altar.

Fifthly. All civil states, with their officers of justice, in their respective constitutions and administrations, are proved essentially civil, and therefore not judges, governors, or defenders of the spiritual, or Christian, state and worship.

Sixthly. It is the will and command of God that, since the coming of his Son the Lord Jesus, a permission of the most Paganish, Jewish, Turkish, or anti-Christian consciences and worships be granted to all men in all nations and countries: and they are only to be fought against with that sword which is only, in soul matters, able to conquer: to wit, the sword of God's Spirit, the word of God.

Seventhly. The state of the land of Israel, the kings and people thereof, in peace and war, is proved figurative and ceremonial, and no pattern nor precedent for any kingdom or civil state in the world to follow.

Eighthly. God requireth not an uniformity of religion to be enacted and enforced in any civil state; which enforced uniformity, sooner or later, is the greatest occasion of civil war, ravishing of conscience, persecution of Christ Jesus in his servants, and of the hypocrisy and destruction of millions of souls.

Ninthly. In holding an enforced uniformity of religion in a civil state, we must necessarily disclaim our desires and hopes of the Jews' conversion to Christ.

Tenthly. An enforced uniformity of religion throughout a nation or civil state confounds the civil and religious, denies the principles of Christianity and civility, and that Jesus Christ is come in the flesh.

Eleventhly. The permission of other consciences and worships than a state professeth, only can, according to God, procure a firm and lasting peace; good assurance being taken, according to the wisdom of the civil state, for uniformity of civil obedience from all sorts.

Twelfthly. Lastly, true civility and Christianity may both flourish in a state or kingdom, notwithstanding the permission of divers and contrary consciences, either of Jew or Gentile.

Chapter 9:

. . . Breech of civil peace may arise when false and idolatrous practices are held forth, and yet no breach of civil peace from the doctrine or practice, or the manner of holding forth, but from that wrong and preposterous way of suppressing, preventing, and extinguishing such doctrines or practices by weapons of wrath and blood, whips, stocks, imprisonment, banishment, death, &c.; by which men commonly are persuaded to convert heretics, and to cast out unclean spirits, which only the finger of God can do, that is, the mighty power of the Spirit in the word.

Hence the town is in an uproar, and the country takes the alarm to expel that fog or mist of error, heresy, blasphemy, as is supposed, with swords and guns. Whereas it is light alone, even light from the bright shining Sun of Righteousness, which is able, in the souls and consciences of men to dispel and scatter such fogs and darkness.

Source: http://www.worldpolicy.org/globalrights/religion/williams.html (accessed August 16, 2006)

QUESTIONS

1. What perspective, moral or practical, does Roger Williams employ to establish his thesis? Explain.
2. Identify and elaborate on one of Roger Williams's philosophical foundations.
3. What does Roger Williams believe results from religious intolerance?

Document 3: William Penn
A Letter to the Lenni Lenape (1681)

William Penn (1644–1718) became a Quaker, or Friend, while a student at Oxford University. He was imprisoned many times because of his faith. Nevertheless, in 1681 he was awarded the lands that eventually would become Pennsylvania as a proprietary province. The following letter was delivered by his aides to the Delaware Indians prior to his arrival. It reflects his belief in the importance of nonviolence and friendly relations with the original inhabitants in North America.

London, 18th of 8th Month, 1681

My Friends—There is one great God and power that hath made the world and all things therein, to whom you and I, and all people owe their being and well-being, and to whom you and I must one day give an account for all that we do in the world; this great God hath written his law in our hearts, by which we are taught and commanded to love and help, and do good to one another, and not to do harm and mischief one to another. Now this great God hath been pleased to make me concerned in your parts of the world, and the king of the country where I live hath given unto me a great province, but I desire to enjoy it with your love and consent, that we may always live together as neighbors and friends, else what would the great God say to us, who hath made us not to devour and destroy one another, but live soberly and kindly together in the world? Now I would have you well observe, that I am very sensible of the unkindness and injustice that hath been too much exercised towards you by the people of these parts of the world, who sought themselves, and to make great advantages by you, rather than be examples of justice and goodness unto you, which I hear hath been a matter of trouble to you, and caused great grudgings and animosities, sometimes to the shedding of blood, which hath made the great God angry; but I am not such a man, as is well known in my own country; I have great love and regard towards you, and I desire to win and gain your love and friendship, by a kind, just, and peaceable life, and the people I send are of the same mind, and shall in all things behave themselves accordingly; and if in any thing any shall offend you or your people, you shall have a full and speedy satisfaction for the same, by an equal number of just men on both sides, that by no means you may have just occasion of being offended against them. I shall shortly come to you myself, at what time we may more largely and freely confer and discourse of these matters. In the mean time, I have sent my commissioners to treat with you about the land, and a firm league of peace. Let me desire you to be kind to them and the people, and receive these presents and tokens which I have sent to you, as a testimony of my good will to you, and my resolution to live justly, peaceably, and friendly with you.

I am your loving friend,

William Penn

Source: Staughton Lynd, ed. *Nonviolence in America: A Documentary History.* Indianapolis, IN: Bobbs-Merrill Co., 1966, pp. 4–5.

QUESTIONS

1. How did Europeans treat the Native Americans prior to 1681?
2. What Quaker philosophy was Penn demonstrating?
3. Was Penn's cultural equivalency unique for the times? Explain.

Document 4:   John Woolman on War Taxes (1750s)

John Woolman (1720–1772), a Quaker, was a pioneer in the American practice of nonresistance. This excerpt from his *Journal* discusses the use of taxes to support militarism and war. Almost two centuries later many peace and justice activists refused to pay taxes in opposition to war. Woolman's views were the basis for that conviction and stance.

Journal

A few years past, money being made current in our province for carrying on wars, and to be sunk by Taxes laid on the Inhabitants, my mind was often affected with the thoughts of paying such Taxes, and I believe it right for me to preserve a memorandum concerning it. . . .

I all along believed that there were some upright-hearted men who paid such taxes, but could not see that their Example was a Sufficient Reason for me to do so, while I believed that the Spirit of Truth required of me as an individual to suffer patiently the distress of goods, rather than pay actively. . . .

True Charity is an excellent Virtue, and to sincerely Labour for their good, whose belief in all points, doth not agree with ours, is a happy case. To refuse the active payment of a Tax which our Society generally paid, was exceeding disagreeable; but to do a thing contrary to my Conscience appeared yet more dreadfull. When this exercise came upon me I know of none under the like difficulty, and in my distress I besought the Lord to enable me to give up all, that so I might follow him wheresoever he was pleased to lead me. . . .

As Scrupling to pay a tax on account of the application I hath seldom been heard of heretofore, even amongst men of Integrity, who have Steadily born their testimony against outward wars in their time, I may here note some things which have opened on my mind, as I have been inwardly Exercised on that account.

From the Steady opposition which Faithfull Friends in early time made to wrong things then approved of, they were hated and persecuted by men living in the Spirit of this world & Suffering with firmness, they were made a blessing to the Church, & work prospered. It equally concerns men in every age to take heed to their own Spirit: & in comparing their Situation with ours, it looks to me there was less danger of their being infected with the Spirit of this world in paying their taxes, than there is of us now. They had little or no Share in Civil

Government, neither Legislative nor Executive & many of them declared they were through the power of God separated from the Spirit in which wars were, and being Afflicted by the Rulers on account of their Testimony, there was less likelyhood of uniting in Spirit with them in things inconsistent with the purity of Truth. . . .

Some of our members who are Officers in Civil Government are in one case or other called upon in their respective Stations to Assist in things relative to the wars, Such being in doubt whether to act or crave to be excused from their Office, Seeing their Brethren united in the payment of a Tax to carry on the said wars, might think their case [nearly like theirs, &] so quench the tender movings of the Holy Spirit in their minds, and thus by small degrees there might be an approach toward that of Fighting, till we came so near it, as the distinction would be little else but the name of a peaceable people.

It requires great self-denial and Resignation of ourselves to God to attain that state therein we can freely cease from fighting when wrongfully Invaded, if by our Fighting there were a probability of overcoming the invaders. Whoever rightly attains to it, does in some degree feel that Spirit in which our Redeemer gave his life for us, and, through Divine goodness many of our predecessors, and many now living, have learned this blessed lesson, but many others having their Religion chiefly by Education, & not being enough acquainted with that Cross which Crucifies to the world, do manifest a Temper distinguishable from that of an Entire trust in God.

In calmly considering these things it hath not appeared strange to me, that an exercise hath now fallen upon some, which as to the outward means of it is different from what was known to many of those who went before us. . . .

Having many years felt Love in my heart towards the Natives of this Land, who dwell far back in the Wilderness, whose Ancestors were the owners and possessors of the [Country] where we dwell, and who for a very small consideration Assigned their Inheritance to . . . I felt inward drawings toward a Visit to that place. . . .

. . . And as I rode over the barren Hills my mediations were on the Alterations of the Circumstances of the Natives of this land since the coming in of the English. The Lands near the Sea are Conveniently situated for fishing. The lands near the Rivers where the tides flow, and some above, are in many places fertile, and not mountainous; while the Running of the Tides makes passing up and down easie with any kind of Traffic. Those natives have in some places for [small] considerations sold their Inheritance so favourably Situated and in other places been driven back by superior force. So that in many places as their way of Clothing themselves is now altered from what it was, and they far remote from us have to pass over Mountains, Swamps, and Barren deserts, where Traveling is very troublesome, in bringing their furs & skins to trade with us.

Source: Amelia Mott Gummere, ed. *The Journal and Essays of John Woolman.* New York: The Macmillan Co., 1922, pp. 160–162, 187–190, 204–207, 248–249, 254–256.

QUESTIONS

1. How does Woolman justify his refusal to pay war taxes?
2. What is his objection to the colonists' treatment of Native Americans?
3. How do "peaceable people" want civil government to act, according to Woolman?

Document 5:   John Woolman on Slavery (1743)

In this second writing from Woolman's journal, he actively intertwines the goals of pacifism, nonresistance, civil disobedience, and the sharing of wealth. He is the earliest proponent of the notion that peace depended on social equality and justice in Colonial America. Here he encourages people to speak out and act against slavery.

Journal

*A*bout the twenty third year of my age I had many fresh and heavenly openings, in respect to the care and providence of the Almighty over his creatures in general, and over man as the most noble amongst those which are visible, and Being clearly convinced in my Judgment that to place my whole trust in God was best for me, I felt renewed engagement that in all things I might act on an inward principle of Virtue, and pursue worldly business no further than as Truth open'd my way therein . . .

…My Employer having a Negro woman sold her, and directed me to write a bill of Sale, The man being waiting who had bought her. The thing was Sudden, and though the thoughts of writing an Instrument of Slavery for one of my fellow creatures felt uneasie, yet I remembered I was hired by the year; that it was my master who [directed] me to do it, and that it was an Elderly man, a member of our society who bought her, so through weakness I gave way, and wrote it, but at the Executing it I was so Afflicted in my mind, that I said before my Master and the friend, that I believed Slave keeping to be a practice inconsistent with the Christian Religion: this in some degree abated my uneasiness, yet as often as I reflected seriously upon it I thought I should have been clearer, if I had desired to be Excused from it, as a thing against my conscience, for such it was. [And] some time after this a young man of our Society, spoke to me to write [an instrument of Slavery], he having lately taken a Negro into his house. I told him I was not easie to write it, for though many [people] kept slaves in our society as in others, I still believed the practice was not right, and desired to be excused from doing the writing. I spoke to him in good will, and he told me, that keeping slaves was not altogether agreeable to his mind, but that the slave being a gift made to his wife, he had accepted of her. . . .

Conduct is more convincing than language; and where people by their actions manifest that the Slave trade is not so disagreeable to their principles but that it may be encouraged, there is not a Sound uniting with some Friends who Visit them.

The prospect of so weighty a work & being so distinguished from many whom I Esteemed before my self, brought me very low, & Such were the conflicts of my Soul, that I had a near sympathy with the prophet in the time of his weakness, when he said "If thou deal thus with me, kill me, I pray thee out of hand if have found favour in thy Sight," but I soon saw that this proceeded from the want of a full resignation to Him. Many were the afflictions which attended me and in great Abasement, with many tears, my Cries were to the Almighty for his Gracious and Fatherly assistance, and then, after a Time of Deep Tryals I was favoured to understand the state mentioned by the psalmist more clearly then ever I had before, to wit: "My Soul is even as a weaned child."

Being thus helped to sink down in Resignation I felt a deliverance from that Tempest in which I had seen sorely Exercised, and in Calmness of mind went forward Trusting that the Lord Jesus Christ, as I faithfully attended to Him, would be a Counselor to me and all

Difficulties, and that by his Strength I should be enabled...to leave money with the members of Society where I had Entertainment.... The Manner in which I did it was thus: when I expected soon to leave a Friend's house where I had Entertainment, if I believed that I should not keep clear from the gain of Oppression without leaving some money, I spoke to One of the heads of the Family privately, and desired then to accept of them pieces of Silver, and give them to such of their Negroes as they believ'd would make the best use of them; And at other times, I gave them to the Negroes myself, [according] as the way looked clearest to me. As I expected this before I came out, I had provided a large number of small pieces [of silver] and thus offering them to Some who appeared to be wealthy people was a trial both to me and them: But the [Exercise of my mind was Such and the] fear of the Lord so covered me at times, that way was made easier than I expected, and few, if any, manifested any resentment at the offer, and most of them, after some [little] talk, accepted of them....

Source: Amelia Mott Gummere, ed. *The Journal and Essays of John Woolman.*
    New York: The Macmillan Co., 1922, pp. 160–162, 187–190, 204–207,
    248–249, 254–256.

QUESTIONS

1. How did Woolman, by his actions, make his objection to slavery known?
2. What phrase would describe this form of resistance?
3. What hypocrisy concerning slavery and Quaker practices does Woolman reveal?

Document 6:   Anthony Benezet
A Letter to the President of the Continental Congress (1779)

Anthony Benezet (1713–1784), a Quaker, was a pacifist and abolitionist. A teacher, he founded schools for females and African Americans, a radical and unusual effort for the era. He refused to pay taxes to support the French and Indian War and opposed the American Revolution. The following is a letter to the President of the Continental Congress explaining his position and calling upon all peace-loving peoples to practice the art of persuasion and toleration.

Chestnut Street, 2d mo.

Feb. 7, 1779.

*W*ith affectionate respect I hereby salute thee, and take the freedom to send thee the enclosed pamphlet, containing some thoughts on war, slavery, &c. of which I earnestly request thy serious perusal. Indeed the subject is of the greatest weight to all, even as human beings; but much more so to those who indeed believe the great truths of the Christian religion, God becoming man, and dying for mankind, even for his enemies, "leaving us, says the apostle, an example that we should follow his footsteps." This, and other arguments therein deduced, from the doctrines and nature of the Gospel, will I trust tend to soften, if not remove, any offence which Friends' refusal to take part in matters of a military nature may have raised in thy mind, and induce thee to distinguish between such who are active in opposition, and those who have been restrained from an apprehension of duty, and a persuasion that our common beneficent Father who has the hearts of all men in his power, and has in former times so eminently displayed his goodness in favour of these countries, if properly sought unto, would in his love and mercy have averted the evil effects of any attempt which might have been made to impede our real welfare. By the deplorable effects which attend on these dreadful contests, it is evident that it cannot be agreeable to God, who the apostle denominates under the appellation of Love, as thereby every noxious passion of the human mind, instead of being calmed by the benign influence of grace, the end and aim of Christianity, are inflamed into greater wrath, and evil of every kind; as has been verified in that destruction of morals, that waste of substance, but more particularly in the hasty death of so vast a number of our fellow men, hurried into eternity, many it is to be feared in that distracted state of mind which generally attends on war.

These are considerations which cannot but strike every thoughtful mind with awe, and which, from the kindness considerateness of thy disposition, will I trust incite thee to advocate the cause of a number of innocent people of different religious persuasions, who from the above mentioned view of things, have not dared to give life or support to military operations, yet at the same time are indeed friends to, and really concerned for the true welfare of America, but willing to sacrifice their all, rather than do that whereby they apprehend they may offend that great and good Being, from whom alone they look for any permanent happiness for themselves of their afflicted country. With affectionate desires, that the blessings of the peace maker, the peculiar favourite of Heaven, may be thine, I remain thy friend.

Anthony Benezet

Source: Staughton Lynd, ed. *Nonviolence in America: A Documentary History.* Indianapolis, IN: Bobbs-Merrill Co., 1966, pp. 21–23.

QUESTIONS

1. What Quaker philosophy was Benezet demonstrating?
2. Did Benezet support the colonists' cause?
3. Was Benezet tolerant of other religions?

Document 7: Benjamin Rush
A Plan for a Peace Office of the United States (1792)

Benjamin Rush (1745–1813) was the preeminent physician of his day and would later serve as Treasurer of the United States Mint from 1797 until his death. Written shortly after the Revolution, but little known until he published it in his own *Essays* in 1798, "A Plan for a Peace-Office of the United States" was a passionate effort to establish pacifism as a foundation of government policy and the young nation's cultural identity. Clearly Rush lost out to those who promoted military defense and a standing army, but suggestions for a Peace Department in the federal government continue to be raised.

*A*mong the defects which have been pointed out in the federal constitution by its antifederal enemies, it is much to be lamented that no person has taken notice of its total silence upon the subject of an office of the utmost importance to the welfare of the United States, that is, an office for promoting and preserving perpetual peace in our country.

It is hoped that no objection will be made to the establishment of such an office, while we are engaged in a war with the Indians, for as the War-Office of the United States was established in the time of peace, it is equally reasonable that a Peace-Office should be established in the time of war.

The plan of this office is as follows:

Let a Secretary of Peace be appointed to preside in this office, who shall be perfectly free from all the present absurd and vulgar European prejudices upon the subject of government; let him be a genuine republican and a sincere Christian, for the principles of republicanism and Christianity are no less friendly to universal and perpetual peace, than they are to universal and equal liberty.

Let a power be given to this Secretary to establish and maintain free-schools in every city, village and township of the United States; and let him be made responsible for the talents, principles, and morals, of all his schoolmasters. Let the youth of our country be carefully instructed in reading, writing, arithmetic, and in the doctrines of a religion of some kind: the Christian religion should be preferred to all others; for it belongs to this religion exclusively to teach us not only to cultivate peace with men, but to forgive, nay more – to love our very enemies. It belongs to it further to teach us that the Supreme Being alone possesses a power to take away human life, and that we rebel against his laws, whenever we undertake to execute death in any way whatever upon any of his creatures. . . .

Let the following sentence be inscribed in letters of gold over the doors of every State and Court house in the United States. THE SON OF MAN CAME INTO THE WORLD, NOT TO DESTROY MEN'S LIVES, BUT TO SAVE THEM.

To inspire a veneration of human life, and an horror at the shedding of human blood, let all those laws be repealed which authorize juries, judges, sheriffs, or hangmen to assume the resentments of individuals and to commit murder in cold blood in any case whatever. Until this reformation in our code of penal jurisprudence takes place, it will be vain to attempt to introduce universal and perpetual peace in our country.

To subdue that passion for war, which education, added to human depravity, have made universal, a familiarity with the instruments of death, as well as all military shows, should be carefully avoided. For which reason, militia laws should every where be repealed, and military dresses and military titles should be laid aside: reviews tend to lesson the horrors of battle by connecting them with the charms of order; militia laws generate idleness and vice, and thereby produce the wars they are said to prevent; military dresses fascinate the minds of young men, and lead them from serious and useful professions; were there no uniforms, there would probably be no armies; lastly, military titles feed vanity, and keep up ideas in the mind which lessen a sense of the folly and miseries of war.

In the last place, let a large room, adjoining the federal hall, be appropriated for transacting the business and preserving all the records of this office. Over the door of this room let there be a sign, on which the figures of a LAMB, a DOVE, and an OLIVE BRANCH should be painted, together with the following inscriptions in letters of gold: PEACE ON EARTH— GOOD-WILL TO MEN. AH! WHY WILL MEN FORGET THAT THEY ARE BRETHREN?

In order more deeply to affect the minds of the citizens of the United States with the blessings of peace, by contrasting them with the evils of war, let the following inscriptions be painted upon the sign which is placed over the door of the War Office:

An office for butchering the human species.

A Widow and Orphan making office.

A broken bone making office.

A wooden leg making office.

An office for creating public and private vices.

An office for creating a public debt.

An office for creating speculators, stock Jobbers, and Bankrupts.

An office for creating famine.

An office for creating pestilential diseases.

An office for creating poverty, and the destruction of liberty, and national happiness.

In the lobby of this office let there be painted representations of all the common military instruments of death, also human skulls, broken bones, unburied and putrefying dead bodies, hospitals crowded with sick and wounded Soldiers, villages on fire, mothers in besieged towns eating the flesh of their own children, ships sinking in the ocean, rivers dyed with blood, and extensive plains without a tree or fence, or any other object, but the ruins of deserted farm houses.

Above this group of woeful figures—let the following words be inserted, in red characters to represent human blood, "NATIONAL GLORY".

Source: Arthur A. Ekirch, Jr., ed. *Voices in Dissent: An Anthology of Individualist Thought in the United States.* New York: The Citadel Press, 1964, pp. 17–21.

QUESTIONS

1. What are the results of military thinking and action in Dr. Rush's view?
2. Did Dr. Rush believe in an active, extensive role for government, or a moderate, restrained government? Explain.
3. What is your response to the inscriptions he wanted to see over the door of the War Office?

2

The Organized Movement and The Search for Justice in Antebellum America

The tradition established by the Quakers and other historic peace churches (Dunkers and Mennonites) in the seventeenth and eighteenth century gradually gave way to a new endeavor that was both religious and humanitarian, but not specifically tied to any one sectarian group. Between the War of 1812 and the outbreak of the Civil War, an organized peace movement grew to prominence largely as a result of the efforts of leaders such as Noah Worcester; David Low Dodge, founder of the New York Peace Society; and William Ladd, founder of the Massachusetts Peace Society and later first president of the American Peace Society—the country's first national peace organization. These builders of the early nineteenth-century peace movement were heroes just as truly as any leading military specialists in the art of death and destruction. So were those courageous souls who spoke out and organized to abolish the institution of slavery and promote equal rights for women. Many of these activists, inspired by Christianity, were concerned

For the People, pages 25–52

with compelling the United States to live up to the promise of equality expressed in the Declaration of Independence.

The peace movement as an organized effort gained considerable momentum through the initial efforts of Noah Worcester. A man of strong religious conviction, Worcester served as a fife-major in the Continental Army and was a veteran of Bunker Hill. Settling in the Brighton area of Boston shortly after studying for the ministry, he was deeply affected by the Federalist antiwar sentiment during the War of 1812. In 1814, at the conclusion of the war, he anonymously published his manifesto, *A Solemn Review of the Custom of War* (**Document 1**). Accordingly, he recommended the establishment of peace societies in every Christian nation for the expressed purpose of exorcising the war spirit within each follower of Christ. These educational efforts were to be carried out through newspapers, tracts, and periodical works, through churches and religious observances, and through educational institutions. He did not bring up the issue of either defensive war or conscientious objection, aiming instead at influencing as many readers as possible. Considered a "peace classic" by historians, *Solemn Review* insisted that war was incompatible with the Christian religion and the result of "collective delusion."

Inspired by Worcester's efforts in particular, nearly fifty societies appeared in the immediate postwar period, stretching from Maine to Philadelphia to Ohio. The early leaders of the nonsectarian peace movement were mostly notable citizens in their respective communities. As noted by America's pioneer peace historian Merle Curti, many were preachers, lawyers, merchants, and public servants. Personally conservative in both taste and politics, most were Congregationalist and Unitarian gentlemen committed to the goal of moral improvement through enlightened ideals. Like Worcester, Dodge, and Ladd, they were well-educated members of a northeastern urban middle class and their antiwar arguments made much of the fact that peace promoted trade and prosperity, that unchecked bloodshed resulted in physical destruction, and that it involved all kinds of financial deficits such as inflation, public debt, and excessive taxes. Their emphasis was on persuasion, and they appealed to the reason and sentiment of humankind. Little was said about the competition for markets and raw materials, trade rivalries, and the struggle for empire. Their views were a far cry from the more radical ideas that would mark twentieth-century antiwar protests.

Even as the formal peace movement continued to grow among "respectable" citizens, peace and justice advocates expanded the agenda, forcefully challenging slavery, women's inequality, and the oppression of Native Americans. In the first half of the nineteenth century, the ever-expanding frontier and abundant material resources of the young nation provided for a rapidly growing population. Feeling the effects of white settlement and patriotic confidence in the future were the land's first inhabitants. During the 1830s and 1840s, continuing a process that began much earlier, many Americans endorsed the claim that the Indians were doomed to extinction by the inevitable laws of progress. Justifying the removal of Native Americans from their land were individuals such as Lewis Cass, Governor of the Michigan Territory, South Carolina statesman and diplomat Joel R. Poinsett, who elaborated his views in *Inquiry into the Received Opinions of Philosophers and Historians on the Natural Progress of the Human Race from Barbarism to Civilization* (1834), and President Andrew Jackson, who defended the policy of Indian removal as an inevitable step toward progress in his Second Annual Message to Congress.

The classic case in point was the removal of the Cherokee, who were peaceful farmers, from Georgia in the early 1830s. In 1829, the state of Georgia appropriated all Indian land within its borders, declared all Cherokee laws null and void, disallowed them from testifying in court against state citizens, and distributed their lands to white settlers in a lottery system. After the passage of the Cherokee Removal Act in May 1830, tribal chiefs appealed to the Jackson Administration. But it was in vain. Even after Chief Justice John Marshall partially reversed himself in the case of *Rev. Samuel A. Worcester v. the State of Georgia* (1832), President Jackson dismissed the ruling and condoned Georgia's appropriation of seven million acres of land. When the Cherokee refused to move, General Winfield Scott led a 7,000-man force and removed some 1,700 Indians in the middle of winter without prior warning. On a path that became known as the "Trail of Tears," the Cherokee were first moved to Arkansas and then to Oklahoma. Along this terrible journey nearly 100 Native Americans, including many women and children, died each day from the cold, hunger, and disease that ravaged them during their forcible removal. In the end, thousands died a horrible death, although the government never provided an exact count.

The actions of the Jackson Administration were met with criticism by peace groups, especially the American Peace Society. Members such as Ladd and George Beckwith questioned the justification for such removal and the way in which it was carried out. In their view, the Cherokee were peaceful, civilized people who had even written their own constitution modeled after that of the federal government's. The Cherokee posed no threat to their white neighbors. The Society of Friends condemned the use of military troops to force the Cherokee from their homeland, while the American Board of Commissioners for Foreign Missions waged its own campaign condemning the removal. Rallying hundred of church groups, the American

Board submitted to Congress hundreds of memorials harshly criticizing the removal policy as a violation of Native American rights. Expressing the view that peace depended on justice was Jeremiah Evarts, the Board's secretary, who in a series of essays (composed under the name of William Penn), argued that the original treaties guaranteeing the Native Americans land rights must be upheld. A strong belief in equality underscored his message. Powerful criticism was also offered by the New Jersey attorney and later president of Rutgers College, the Reverend Theodore Frelinghuysen. Mixing his gospel oratorical skills with theological penmanship, Frelinghuysen condemned the removal as immoral and inhuman (**Document 2**).

Coinciding with efforts to call attention to the plight of Native Americans, a number of female activists began to play more prominent roles in movements for peace and justice. First involved in antislavery efforts, the Grimké sisters, Sarah and Angelina, began to challenge the idea that the public sphere was a male preserve. Born in Charleston, South Carolina, in the early 1790s and the first decade of the nineteenth century, the sisters became some of the earliest and most prominent advocates of abolitionism and women's rights. Experiencing firsthand the evils of slavery on their family's plantation, they traveled throughout the Northeast lecturing on its abuses. In the process, they linked their abolitionist work to equality for women.

Sarah Grimké, the older of the two, became involved in the Quaker movement when she took her father to Philadelphia for medical treatment during the War of 1812. Some years later Angelina Grimké converted to the Quaker faith, and both women remained in the north after 1829. That year Angelina Grimké wrote a letter to *The Liberator*, which William Lloyd Garrison, its editor, published without her knowledge. Immediately, the Society of Friends, which had disavowed political activism since the time of the Revolutionary War, demanded that the sisters either remain in good standing with their meeting house or give it up and devote their time to the abolitionist crusade. Their choice was to work actively in opposing slavery.

During the 1830s the sisters lectured throughout the Northeast, calling for an end to the system of slavery. At first, they spoke in private homes to members of the abolitionist movement, and then brought their personal experiences and knowledge of the plantation system to public audiences. In response to intense criticism from the Quaker community and male reformers who felt it improper for women to take to the public platform, the Grimké sisters began drawing parallels between the oppression of women and that of slaves. They were among the first women to speak publicly about these subjects. Noting that women were denied rights that were granted to men, they argued that it was impossible for females to address the wrongs of society unless they took power into their own hands.

By 1837, the sisters were in full swing. They went on a tour of Congregationalist churches in the Northeast. Not only did they denounce the practice of slavery, they also condemned racial prejudice. Their arguments were advanced as well as controversial. The particular view that white women had "a natural affinity" with black female slaves elicited attacks even from radical abolitionists, including Catherine Beecher. After Congregationalist ministers denounced the sisters for their radical views on slavery and women's rights, Angelina wrote a series of letters published as "Letters on the Equality of Sexes" (**Document 3**). In this tract, she vigorously defended a woman's right to speak on the public platform. The Grimké sisters received so much attention because of the attacks on their views that by 1838 thousands of people came to hear their lecture series in Boston.

These individual acts of courage on the part of the Grimké sisters highlighted the growing recognition of the relationship between peace and justice as the slavery issue came to dominate American politics. The link between organized peacemaking and abolitionism became reality in the early 1830s as the two reforms advanced with a common feeling of urgency, steadfastness, and likeminded activists. After 1830, the abolitionist movement spread with exceptional fervor throughout the villages of New England and the rural Northwest. The movement was composed of a spirit of religious perfectionism, a receptive upper-class female audience, and energizing, powerful orators. In western New York, Arthur Tappan gave voice to the cause, while Theodore Weld carried the banner in the Ohio Valley. In New England, William Lloyd Garrison led the way.

More than anyone, Garrison typified the pacifist as abolitionist, and he changed the latter movement in significant ways, rejecting gradualism and the idea that slaveholders should be compensated for their losses. He also represented the peace movement's sectionalism, which narrowed, along with the rest of romantic Protestant reformism, as a result of the slavery issue. Son of a Newburyport, Massachusetts, sailor, this unschooled radical pacifist entered the abolitionist movement in January 1831 by distributing the first issue of *The Liberator*. "I am in earnest—I will not equivocate—I will not excuse—I will not retreat a single inch—and I *will be heard*," he proclaimed. Garrison's social radicalism and pacifism merged as one conviction.

Under his leadership, the New England Nonresistance Society issued a Declaration of Sentiments, which resolved "to carry forward the work of peaceful, universal reformation" through "THE FOOLISHNESS OF

PREACHING" and the "Spiritual regeneration" of corrupt human institutions. Society members willingly pledged to oppose all military under-
takings (preparations for war, office, monuments, and dress) and "to live
peace with a universal sense of human equality" (**Document 4**). Until the
1850s, when passive resistance (or nonresistance, as explained in the Introduction to this collection) within the abolitionist community could not be
squared with the sectionalist politics wracking the nation, Garrison's *Sentiments* echoed the feelings of many antebellum reformers on behalf of peace
and justice.

The belief in inevitable progress exacerbated sectionalist tensions as
well as abolitionists' fears. By the 1840s, western expansion became inextri-
cably tied to the ideology of "manifest destiny," the idea that the U.S. had a
God-given right to expand its borders. A war with Mexico gave added cur-
rency to such claims, especially within southern quarters, which considered
the addition of more territory in the Southwest a golden opportunity to extend slavery. It also prompted supporters of peace and justice to speak out
against such a belief. Thus, in 1845, a brilliant Boston lawyer and later United States senator, Charles Sumner, boldly and publicly criticized America's
growing imperialistic designs. The turning point of Sumner's career was his
Fourth of July oration, in which he examined and condemned the whole
war system as a pitifully insufficient method of determining justice (**Document 5**). While uniformed military guests seated in the front row listened
in horror, Sumner, stern and resolute in his remarks, castigated the false
prejudice of national honor and drew powerful analogies to the Pelopon-
nesian War between Athens and Sparta and the Roman Empire of ancient
times. He cogently argued for the alternatives recommended by friends of
peace such as negotiation, mediation, arbitration, and a Congress of Nations, which had been proposed by William Ladd. This speech marked the
beginning of Sumner's influential role in the peace movement.

Although Sumner's July 4 oration set off a groundswell of enthusiasm
among peace disciples, it was scarcely enough to contain the ambitions of
President James K. Polk and the promoters of America's "manifest destiny."
After finally reaching a settlement with Britain over the Oregon boundary,
the President, in early 1846, turned his attention to Mexican–American relations—with the aim of making the Rio Grande the southern border of the
United States—and to U.S. aspirations for California. In May, open warfare
broke out between the United States and Mexico.

The mobilization of antiwar sentiment in its New England centers,
when New England also happened to be experiencing its first great literary renaissance, led to an unprecedented proliferation of dissenting tracts

against the Mexican War. Noted intellectuals such as Ralph Waldo Emerson, Theodore Parker, Henry David Thoreau, and Henry Wadsworth Longfellow spoke out against militarism in general and the war against Mexico in particular.

The most famous commentary on the matter was offered by the individualist and anarchist Thoreau, who produced one of the most thought-provoking and enduring criticisms of war and the power of the state. Thoreau rejected the war by defiantly refusing to pay the tax levied to support it. To demonstrate his protest, he spent one night in the Concord jail. From his brief incarceration was born his famous essay "Civil Disobedience," which profoundly influenced later pacifist thinkers such as Leo Tolstoy, Mahatma Gandhi, and Martin Luther King, Jr. (**Document 6**). His essay is an impassioned plea for moral commitment in the face of injustice and a justification for opposing the state when the demands of law and conscience conflict. Individual rights represent the highest form of authority from which the State derives its existence and ability to govern. Those who blindly serve the state and are "commonly esteemed good citizens" are, in reality, nothing more than mere animals or machines. Lacking a sense of individual integrity, their minds are nothing more than empty vacuums operating intellectual wastelands.

Upsetting as it was to some peacemakers and abolitionists who thought their own cause should come first, female activists continued their struggle for equality. Inspired by Sarah and Angelina Grimké, Lucretia Mott and Elizabeth Cady Stanton catapulted the issue of women's rights onto the national stage shortly after the conclusion of the Mexican War. The ferment of reform in the mid-nineteenth century continued, as Mott and Stanton organized the first national convention on women's rights. Many of the delegates at that convention, held in July 1848 in Seneca Falls, New York, were active in the antislavery movement. Attended by several hundred people (including more than thirty men), the two-day meeting produced a document called "Declaration of Sentiments and Resolutions." Taking the Declaration of Independence as a model, it spelled out the nature of women's oppression and the rights to which women were entitled (**Document 7**). Not to be overlooked was the attempt to promote the virtue of peace and nonviolence as part of the overall effort to quell acts of domestic abuse. While the delegates could not reach agreement on the issue of women's suffrage, every other resolution was passed unanimously.

Strengthening the position of women's rights activists and giving credence to the belief in equality for all human beings regardless of race, creed, or sex was Sojourner Truth, an African American woman born a slave in New York. In 1851, an aged Truth gave a speech that strongly protested the discrimination against her race and her sex (**Document 8**). Unlike most female reformers in antebellum America, Sojourner Truth had to withstand not only the experience of being black among white reformers and of being a female in a reform movement run by men, but also being a former slave and an abolitionist in a country that permitted slavery. Like the Grimke sisters she was not intimidated by shouting and jeering mobs, and she boldly spoke her mind. In numerous speeches, and later in her emancipationist actions, Sojourner Truth equated the liberation of slaves with the rights of women to have their own place in the public sphere. Until the Civil War broke out, Truth had hoped slavery could be abolished peacefully.

Such hopes were also initially shared by the most famous African American abolitionist of the time, Frederick Douglass. He worked hand-in-hand with the predominantly white antislavery societies. Black and white abolitionists had undertaken a number of novel and bold nonviolent actions by the time Douglass came on the scene. Apart from employing the technique of the boycott, they also used direct-action methods such as sit-ins, eat-ins, and walk-alongs. (This was long before Homer Plessy's individual act of heroism in Louisiana in the early 1890s; Rosa Parks's action in Montgomery, Alabama, in 1955,; and student protestors in Greensboro, North Carolina, in 1960.) African Americans sat in white sections of railroad cars and at tables reserved for whites, and even attempted to integrate steamboats along the Ohio and Mississippi Rivers. Walk-alongs saw whites and African Americans marching down streets arm-in-arm before entering a place to eat. Much like the resistance to such actions in the South during the heyday of the modern civil rights movement, these protesters were often met with violent attacks.

In 1841, Douglass joined the New England Nonresistance Society. An escaped runaway slave from Maryland, Douglass learned to read and write on his own. Articulate and passionate about his cause, Douglass traveled throughout the North providing personal accounts of the horrors of slavery. He was an excellent orator and skilled storyteller. His own recollections, *Narrative of the Life of Frederick Douglass, An American Slave,* published in 1845, represents one of the most compelling first-person stories of an individual determined to be free. In 1846, Douglass spoke out against the call for war as a means of emancipation, claiming that he would not risk a drop of blood for the complete abolition of slavery. Douglass insisted at this time that emancipation would only come about by a change of heart in white America that would guarantee lasting freedom. His 1852 oration, "What to the Slave is the Fourth of July," is filled with emotion, disappointment, and sarcasm (**Document 9**).

Although the women's rights and abolitionist campaigns occupied much of the antebellum reform movement's time, the peace crusade continued in its attempts to bring the message of harmony and goodwill to an international audience. The person most responsible for this effort was Elihu Burritt, perhaps nineteenth-century America's most important peace ambassador. Born in New Britain, Connecticut, in 1810, son of an eccentric shoemaker and farmer, Burritt was regarded as both brilliant and precocious. Referred to by Merle Curti as the "learned blacksmith," the self-educated, radical pacifist mastered more than thirty languages—a true commitment to his international sentiments. He anticipated many of the most effective modern propaganda techniques. From temperance circles, Burritt adopted the idea of a pledge of complete abstinence from every possible form of war. He also organized women into sewing circles where war and peace were the main topics of discussion. Additionally, he spent time urging the working class to overthrow the yoke of war's burden, despite the appeal to chivalry and the many martial songs glorifying the art of combat. Conscious of war's brutalizing effects, Burritt called upon the "workingmen of Christendom" to put an end to the worthlessness of human slaughter.

Though never sure where the next dollar would come from, Burritt founded a weekly newspaper, the *Christian Citizen*, in Worcester, Massachusetts, in 1844. This international pacifist publication dragged him deeply into debt before he was forced to abandon it in 1851. During the Oregon crisis between Britain and the United States in the early 1840s, Burritt, while editing the *Advocate of Peace and Universal Brotherhood*, besieged Congress with peace propaganda. He also cooperated with Friends in Manchester, England, in an exchange of "Friendly Addresses" between British and American cities, merchants, ministers, and laborers. Burritt himself carried the "Friendly Addresses"—with its impressive list of signatures—from Edinburgh to Washington, where John C. Calhoun and other senators expressed much interest in this "popular handshaking" across the Atlantic.

In the autumn of 1846, having established close ties with British Friends, he founded the largest nonsectarian pacifist organization yet known among Western peace seekers: the League of Universal Brotherhood. By 1850, this peace society had 70,000 British and American signatories to its pledge of complete disavowal of war. Burritt also induced the League to sponsor "The Olive Leaf Mission," through which peace propaganda was inserted in forty continental newspapers. A devoted believer in passive nonresistance, Burritt was one of the most active peace ambassadors on behalf of nonviolence and internationalism. Many of the lessons of peace that he taught were drawn from historical circumstances (**Document 10**). Between 1850 and 1856, he estimated that the *Olive Leaves* reached one million readers monthly. Burritt developed plans to prevent a civil war on American soil, urging the use of public funds for "compensated emancipation." He also devoted time to a related scheme of cheap international postage as an inexpensive means of maintaining transoceanic goodwill.

Despite powerful messages of peace and justice from the likes of Henry David Thoreau, Sojourner Truth, and Elihu Burritt, among others, the issue of slavery continued to cast a pall over attempts at political reconciliation between supporters of states' rights and those backing the Union cause. Without a doubt the Civil War presented nineteenth-century peace activists with their most daunting challenge to date: deciding between accepting violence to free the slaves and obedience to the teachings of nonviolence. It proved extremely disconcerting trying to temper an ethic of love with an acceptance of coercion. The vast majority of social reformers, though respectful of Christian nonresistance, ended up choosing the abolition of slavery and the survival of the Union over their commitment to nonviolence. This was most apparent in the violent utterance of some of Garrison's followers and in disagreement over bloody deeds such as John Brown's attempt to lead a violent slave rebellion at Harper's Ferry, West Virginia, and over retribution after the war ended. While some continued to promote nonviolence unconditionally, even a peace proponent such as Thoreau portrayed John Brown as a saint. The war itself generated intense patriotic and emotional loyalty on both sides, and in the end it became extremely difficult for anyone to stand apart from the conflict.

Undoubtedly, the Civil War left a legacy of martial enthusiasm, which gave credence to later appeals to arms. A scant 1,500 conscientious objectors who had refused to fight could hardly compete against Memorial Day, veterans' pensions, and the patriotic literature that swamped the popular periodicals of the day. At the same time, the war itself was so horrible and caused so much suffering—both in its enormous casualty rates and the pitting of brother against brother—that it left people hungry for a lasting peace. Revolting descriptions of battles, wounded veterans whose lives were destroyed, and fatherless children and husbandless wives were held up as examples to show why war should never be used as a means to resolve disputes and achieve peace. Moreover, while it brought an end to slavery, the war did not resolve the country's racial issues.

Torn between justice and use of arms many friends of peace chose the latter, only to be disappointed in the war's harshness. The human cost aside, the economic argument that the war was begun by greedy Northern industrialists had its subscribers, such as radical individualist Lysander Spooner. Others pointed out that the postwar depression, marked by widespread unemployment, was directly attributable to damage caused by war, which led to general economic distress. Still many more saw the burden of high taxes, rising debts, and unchecked prices as compelling reasons to work for lasting peace. Several military generals, including Thomas Hooker, Philip Sheridan, and William Tecumseh Sherman, admitted that modern warfare was more than the conscience could bear. Thus several new approaches emerged in the peace movement of the late nineteenth century, one concerned primarily with law and arbitration, and another with the economic roots of war.

Document 1: Noah Worcester
The Custom of War (1815)

Noah Worcester was the founder of the Massachusetts Peace Society. He played a prominent role in the early years of the organized peace movement in America. As editor of *The Friend of Peace*, he popularized his views against war in religious terms. A Unitarian minister, Worcester sought to unite absolute pacifists and those who supported the lawfulness of defensive wars in the name of peace.

*W*ar has been so long fashionable among all nations, that its enormity is but little regarded ... it is usually considered as an evil necessary and unavoidable. Perhaps it is really so in the present state of society, and the present views of mankind. But the question to be considered is this: cannot the state of society and the views of civilized men be so changed as to abolish a barbarous custom? ...

Some may be ready to exclaim, none but God can produce such an effect as the abolition of war; and we must wait for the millennial day, ... but God works by human agency and by human means ... if ever there shall be a millennium in which the sword will cease to devour, it will probably be effected by the blessing of God on the benevolent exertions of enlightened men ....

A war between two nations is generally produced by the influence of a small number of ambitious and unprincipled individuals; while the greater part of the nation has no hand in the business until war is proclaimed.

A vast majority of every civilized nation have an aversion to war, such an aversion that it requires much effort and management to work up their passions.... [Where peoples are civilized and Christians] more powerful exertions are necessary to excite what is called the *war spirit*.... If then, as great exertions should be made to excite a just abhorrence of war as have often been made to excite a war spirit...we may be very certain that rulers would find little encouragement to engage in any war, which is not strictly defensive. And as soon as offensive wars shall cease, defensive wars will of course be unknown.

...Every soldier ought to be impressed with the idea that offensive war is murderous, and that no government on earth has any right to compel him to shed blood in a wanton and aggressive war...

...[I]f the eyes of the people could be opened in regard to the evils and delusions of war, would it not be easy to form a confederacy of nations, and organize a high court of equity, to decide national controversies? Why might not such a court be composed of some of the most eminent characters from each nation, and a compliance with the decision of the court be made a point of national honor?...

Let every Christian seriously consider the malignant nature of that spirit which war makers evidently wish to excite, and compare it with the temper of Jesus, and where is the Christian who would not shudder at the thought of dying in the common war spirit....

Is it not possible to form powerful peace societies, in every nation in Christendom, whose object shall be to support and to secure the nation from war?...Let printing presses be established...to fill every land with newspapers, tracts and periodical works.... [Let education for peace have a place in] families, common schools, academies and universities....Let lawyers, politicians and divines, and men of every class who can write or speak, consecrate their talents to the diffusion of light, and love, and peace,...that "the sword shall *not* devour forever."

Source: C. Chatfield and R. Ilukhina. *Peace: An Anthology of Historic Alternatives to War.* Syracuse, NY: Syracuse University Press, 1994, pp. 88–89.

QUESTIONS

1. Explain what Worcester means when he states "but God works by human agency and by human means."
2. According to the author, why should every soldier be impressed with the idea that offensive war is murderous?
3. Describe how the author proposes the educated populace shall secure its nation from war.

Document 2: Theodore Frelinghuysen
Opposition to the Indian Removal Bill (1830)

Theodore Frelinghuysen was a distinguished lawyer, senator from New Jersey, and later president of Rutgers College. He was referred to as "the Christian statesman" because of his steadfast commitment to moral principles. He earned the respect of both Whigs and Democrats in Congress. In a six-hour speech before members of Congress he criticized the removal of the Cherokees from Georgia.

*B*y and by conditions are changed. His people [Native American] melt away; his lands are constantly coveted; millions and millions [of acres] are ceded. The Indian bears it all meekly. He complains, indeed, as well he may, but suffers on. And now he finds that this neighbor, whom his kindness had nourished, has spread an adverse title over the last remains of his patrimony, barely adequate to his wants, and turns upon him and says, "Away! We cannot endure you so near us! These forests and rivers, these groves of your fathers, these firesides and hunting grounds are ours by the right of power and the force of numbers. . . ."

Sir, . . . if the contending parties were to exchange positions; place the white man where the Indian stands; load him with all these wrongs; and what path would his outraged feelings strike out for his career?... A few pence of duty on tea—that invaded no fireside, excited no fears, disturbed no substantial interest whatever—awakened in the American colonies a spirit of firm resistance. And how was the tea tax met, sir? We successfully and triumphantly contended for the very rights and privileges that our Indian neighbors now implore us to protect and to preserve to them.

Sir, this thought invests the subject under debate with most singular and momentous interest. We, whom God has exalted to the very summit of prosperity—whose brief career forms the brightest page in history; the wonder and praise of the world; freedom's hope and her consolation—we, about to turn traitors to our principles and our fame, about to become the oppressors of the feeble and to cast away our birthright! Sir, I hope for better things . . .

Source: Register of Debates in Congress [Congressional Record], 21st Congress, 1st session, Vol. 6, part 1, pp. 311–312, 318.

QUESTIONS

1. How did Frelinghuysen's arguments against removal relate to moral justice and natural rights?
2. How did he equate the role of the colonists' struggle for independence to the crisis confronting the Native Americans?
3. What attitude does Frelinghuysen express with respect to the white society's view of the Native Americans?

Document 3: Angelina Grimké
Letter XII—Human Rights Not Founded on Sex (1837)

Angelina Grimké chose political activism over her religious community of Friends. Her pacifism led her into the abolitionist crusade. Deeply committed to the philosophy of sectarian nonresistance, she quickly recognized that the role of women continued to remain subservient to that of men in the various reform crusades of her era. After being rebuked for speaking out at antislavery meetings, she began demanding a place for women in the public sphere and tied the oppression of woman to that of the slave.

*D*ear Friend—The investigation of the rights of the slave has led me to a better understanding of my own. I have found the Anti-Slavery cause to be the high school of morals in our land—the school in which *human rights* are more fully investigated, and better understood and taught, than in any other. Here a great fundamental principle is uplifted and illuminated, and from this central light, rays innumerable stream all around. Human beings have *rights*, because they are *moral* beings: the rights of *all* men grow out of their moral nature; and as all men have the same moral nature, they have essentially the same rights. These rights may be wrested from the slave, but they cannot be alienated.... Now if rights are founded in the nature of our moral being, then the *mere circumstance of sex* does not give to man higher rights and responsibilities, than to woman....

The regulation of duty by the mere circumstance of sex, rather than by the fundamental principle of moral being, has led to all that multifarious train of evils flowing out of the anti-Christian doctrine of masculine and feminine virtues. By this doctrine, man had been converted into the warrior, and clothed with sternness, and those other kindred qualities, which in common estimation belong to his character as a man; whilst woman has been taught to lean upon an arm of flesh, to sit as a doll arrayed in "gold, and pearls, and costly array," to be admired for her personal charms, and caressed and humored like a spoiled child, or converted into a mere drudge to suit the convenience of her lord and master. Thus have all the diversified relations of life been filled with "confusion and every evil work." This principle has given man a charter for the exercise of tyranny and selfishness, pride and arrogance, lust and brutal violence. It has robbed woman of essential rights, the right to think and speak and act on all great moral questions, just as men think and speak and act; the right to share their responsibilities, perils and toils, the right to fulfill the great end of her being, as a moral, intellectual and immoral creature, and of glorifying god in her body and her spirit which are His. Hitherto, instead of being a help mate to man, in the highest, noblest sense of the term as a companion, a co-worker, an equal; she had been a mere appendage of his being, an instrument of his convenience and pleasure, the pretty toy with which he wiled away his leisure moments, or the pet animal whom he humored into playfulness and submission. Woman, instead of being regarded as the equal of man, has uniformly been looked down upon as his inferior, a mere gift to fill up the measure of his happiness....

... Whatever is morally right for a man to do, it is morally right for a woman to do. I recognize no rights but human rights—I know nothing of men's rights and women's rights; for in Christ Jesus, there is neither male nor female.

Now, I believe it is woman's right to have a voice in all the laws and regulations by which she is to be governed, whether in Church or State; and that the present arrangements of society, on these points, are *a violation of human rights, a rank usurpation of power,* a violent seizure and confiscation of what is sacredly and inalienably hers—thus inflicting upon woman outrageous wrongs, working mischief incalculable in the social circle, and in its influence on the world producing only evil, and that continually. *If* Ecclesiastical and Civil governments are ordained of God, then I contend that woman has just as much right to sit in solemn counsel in Conventions, Conferences, Associations and General Assemblies, as man—just as much right to sit upon the throne of England, or in the Presidential chair of the United States.

Source: "Letter XII Human Rights Not Founded on Sex," October 2, 1837, http://web.utk.edu/~mfitzge1/docs/374/HRNF1837.pdf (accessed May 16, 2009)

QUESTIONS

1. What was Grimké's notion of human rights, and how did this make the situation of women analogous to that of slaves?
2. What is her objection to the roles that men and women were expected to play?
3. How does she use religion in order to justify the rights of women?

Document 4: William Lloyd Garrison
Declaration of Sentiments (1838)

William Lloyd Garrison was in his early years a strict pacifist. He popularized the cause of abolitionism through his paper, *The Liberator*. Unlike the moderate American Anti-Slavery Society, Garrison argued that there should be no compensation for the emancipation of slaves. He promoted the doctrine of nonresistance as part of his effort to bring about an end to slavery. In splitting with the American Peace Society for not condemning slavery, Garrison and a few abolitionists issued the following declaration in 1838 at the founding of the New England Nonresistance Society.

---

*A*ssembled in Convention, from various sections of the American Union, for the promotion of peace on earth and good will among men, we, the undersigned, regard it as due to ourselves, to the cause which we love, to the country in which we live, and to the world, to publish a Declaration, expressive of the principles we cherish, the purposes we aim to accomplish, and the measures we shall adopt to carry forward the work of peaceful and universal reformation.

We cannot acknowledge allegiance to any human government; neither can we oppose any such government, by a resort of physical force. We recognize but one King and Lawgiver, one Judge and Ruler of mankind. We are bound by the laws of a kingdom which is not of this world; the subjects of which are forbidden to fight; in which Mercy and Truth are met together, and Righteousness and Peace have kissed each other; which has no state lines, no national partitions, no geographical boundaries; in which there is no distinction of rank, or division of caste, or inequality of sex; the officers of which are Peace, its exactors Righteousness, its walls Salvation, and its gates Praise; and which is destined to break in pieces and consume all other kingdoms....

Source: Staughton Lynd, ed. *Nonviolence in America: A Documentary History.* Indianapolis, IN: Bobbs-Merrill Co., 1966, pp. 26–31.

QUESTIONS

1. Identify the values to which Garrison is committed.
2. Why can the author neither acknowledge allegiance to nor oppose any government with force?
3. Explain why Garrison thinks war between nations and redrawing national boundaries would be pointless.

Document 5: Charles Sumner
The True Grandeur of Nations (1845)

Charles Sumner, Senator from Massachusetts, was an outspoken opponent of expansionism. Shortly before the Mexican War he delivered one of the most stirring July 4 orations in American history. (Frederick Douglass's speech, Document 9, was another.) A member of the American Peace Society, Sumner made clear his objections to war in general and, specifically, President Polk's desire to expand westward.

The world has supped so full of battles, that all its inner modes of thought, and many of its rules of conduct seem to be incarnadined with blood; as the bones of swine, fed on madder, are said to become red. But I now pass this by, through a fruitful theme, and hasten to other topics. I propose to consider in succession, very briefly, some of those prejudices, which are most powerful in keeping alive the custom of War. . . .

. . . Now I think that it has already appeared with distinctness, approaching demonstration, that the professed object of War, which is justice between nations, is in no respect promoted by War; that force is not justice, nor in any way conducive to justice; that the eagles of victory can be the emblems only of successful force, and not of established right. Justice can be obtained only by the exercise of the reason and judgment; but these are silent in the din of arms. Justice is without passion; but war lets loose all the worst passions of our nature . . . . The age has passed in which a nation, within the enchanted circle of civilization, can make war upon its neighbor, for any professed purpose of booty or vengeance. It does "naught in hate, but all in honor." There are professions of tenderness even which mingle with the first mutterings of the dismal strife. As if conscience-struck at the criminal abyss into which they are madly plunging, each of the great litigants seeks to fix on the other the charge of hostile aggression, and to assume to itself the ground of defending some right; some stolen Texas; some distant, worthless Oregon. Like Pontius Pilate, it vainly washes its hands of innocent blood, and straightway allows a crime at which the whole heavens are darkened, and two kindred countries are severed, as the veil of the Temple was rent in twain.

The various modes, proposed for the determination of international disputes, are Negotiation, Mediation, Arbitration, and a Congress of Nations—all of them practicable and calculated to secure peaceful justice. These may be employed at any time under the existing Law of Nations. But the very law itself, which sanctions War, may be changed- as regards two or more nations by treaty between them, and as regards all the Christian nations by general consent. If nations can agree together, in the solemn provisions of International Law, to establish War as an Arbiter of Justice between them, they can also agree together to abolish this Arbitrament, and to establish peaceful substitutes; precisely as similar substitutes have been established by the municipal law in order to determine controversies among individuals. A system of Arbitration may be instituted by treaties, or a Congress of Nations may be charged with a high duty of organizing an Ultimate Tribunal instead of "these battles" for the decision of international controversies. The will only is required in order to succeed in this work.

Let it not be said, then, that War is a necessity; and may our country aim at the True Glory of taking the lead in disowning the revolting system of International LYNCH LAW, and in proclaiming peaceful substitutes therefore, as the only proper modes of determining justice between nations! Such a Glory, unlike the earthly fame of battles, shall be immortal as the stars, dropping perpetual light upon the souls of men!

Another prejudice in favor of War is founded on the practice of nations, past and present. There is no crime or enormity in morals, which may not find the support of human example, often on an extended scale. But it cannot be urged in our day, that we are to look for a standard of duty in the conduct of vain, mistaken, fallible man. It is not in the power of man, by any subtle alchemy, to transmute wrong into right. Because War is according to the practice of the world, it cannot follow that it is right. For ages the world worshipped false gods; but these gods were not less false, because all bowed before them. At this moment the larger portion of mankind are Heathen; but Heathenism is not true. It was once the practice of nations to slaughter prisoners of war; but even the Spirit of War recoils now from this bloody sacrifice....

Source: Arthur A. Ekirch, Jr., ed. *Voices in Dissent: An Anthology of Individualist Thought in the United States.* New York: The Citadel Press, 1964, pp. 87–95.

QUESTIONS

1. What are the prejudices that Sumner believes are most powerful in keeping the custom of war alive?
2. Explain why Sumner believes that justice cannot be obtained through war.
3. What modes does Sumner propose to avoid war?

Document 6:   Henry David Thoreau
Essay on Civil Disobedience (1846)

Henry David Thoreau, a noted transcendentalist and student of nature, became a powerful example of an individual who followed his conscience. Refusing to pay a poll tax that supported war and expansionism, Thoreau chose to go to jail. Reflecting on his stay he penned one of the most famous essays on nonviolence ever written, which has had lasting influence. Although "Civil Disobedience" had little impact on the major issues of the day, it would later connect him forever to an international tradition of nonviolent passive resistance.

I heartily accept the motto, "That government is best which governs least"; and I should like to see it acted up to more readily and systematically. Carried out, it finally amounts to this, which also I believe—"That government is best which governs not at all"; and when men are prepared for it, that will be the kind of government which they will have. Government is at best but an expedient; but most governments are usually, and all governments are sometimes, inexpedient. The objections which have been brought against a standing army, and they are many and weighty, and deserve to prevail, may also at last be brought against a standing government. The standing army is only an arm of the standing government. The government itself, which is only the mode which people have chosen to execute their will, is equally liable to be abused and perverted before the people can act through it. Witness the present Mexican War, the work of comparatively few individuals using the standing government as their tool; for, in the outset, the people would not have consented to this measure....

But, to speak practically and as a citizen, unlike those who call themselves no-government men, I ask for, not at once no government, but at once a better government. Let every man make known what kind of government would command his respect, and that will be one step toward obtaining it. . . .

. . . Must the citizen even for a moment, or in the least degree, resign his conscience to the legislator? Why has every man a conscience, then? I think that we should be men first, and subjects afterward. It is not desirable to cultivate a respect for the law, so much as for the right. The only obligation which I have a right to assume, is to do at any time what I think right. It is truly enough said, that a corporation has no conscience: but a corporation of conscientious men is a corporation with a conscience. Law never made men a whit more just; and, by means of their respect for it, even the well-disposed are daily made the agents of injustice. A common and natural result of an undue respect for law is, that you may see a file of soldiers, colonel, captain, corporal, privates, powder- monkeys and all, marching in admirable order over hill and dale to the wars, against their wills, aye, against their common sense and consciences, which makes it very steep marching indeed, and produces a palpitation of the heart. They have no doubt that it is a damnable business in which they are concerned; they are all peaceably inclined. Now what are they? Men at all? Or small moveable forts and magazines, at the service of some unscrupulous man in power? Visit the Navy Yard, and behold a marine, such a man as an American government can make, or such as it can make a man with its black arts, a mere shadow and reminiscence of humanity, a man laid out alive and standing, and already, as one may say, buried under arms with funeral accompaniments, though it may be,

> Not a drum was heard, not a funeral note,
> As his course to the ramparts we hurried;
> Not a soldier discharged his farewell shot
> O'er the grave where our hero was buried

The mass of men serve the State thus, not as men mainly, but as machines, with their bodies. They are the standing army, and the militia, jailers, constables, posse comitatus, &c. In most cases there is no free exercise whatever of the judgment or the moral sense; but they put themselves on a level with wood and earth and stones; and wooden men can perhaps be manufactured that will serve the purpose as well. Such command no more respect than men of straw, or a lump of dirt. They have the same sort of worth only as horses and dogs. Yet such as these even are commonly esteemed good citizens. Others- as most legislators, politicians, lawyers, ministers, and officeholders—serve the State chiefly with their heads; and, as they rarely make any moral distinctions, they are as likely to serve the devil, without intending it, as God. A very few—as heroes, patriots, martyrs, reformers in the great sense, and men—serve the State with their consciences also, and so necessarily resist it for the most part; and they are commonly treated as enemies by it. A wise man will only be useful as a man, and will not submit to be "clay," and "stop a hole to keep the wind away," but leave that office to his dust at least:

I am too high-born to be propertied,
To be a secondary at control,
Or useful serving-man and instrument
To any sovereign state throughout the world.

He who gives himself entirely to his fellow-men appears to them useless and selfish; but he who gives himself partially to them is pronounced a benefactor and a philanthropist.

How does it become a man to behave toward this American government today? I answer that he cannot without disgrace be associated with it. I cannot for an instant recognize that political organization as my government which is the slave's government also.

Source: Arthur A Ekirch, Jr., ed. *Voices in Dissent: An Anthology of Individualist Thought in the United States.* New York: The Citadel Press, 1964, pp. 103–115.

QUESTIONS

1. Why does Thoreau believe in small government?
2. How does he believe most men serve the state?
3. According to Thoreau, when does civil disobedience become an obligation?

Document 7: *Declaration of Sentiments and Resolutions (1848)*

In July 1848, at the Woman's Rights Convention in Seneca Falls, New York, some seven hundred supporters met in support of women's rights. Among the delegates were hundreds of people involved in the antislavery movement. The two-day gathering to promote women's equality issued a document patterned after the Declaration of Independence. The declaration set the stage for a national movement for full equality and an end to laws and social habits that kept women second-class citizens in the United States.

*W*hen, in the course of human events, it becomes necessary for one portion of the family of man to assume among the people of the earth a position different from that which they have hitherto occupied, but one to which the laws of nature and of nature's God entitle them, a decent respect to the opinions of mankind requires that they should declare the causes that impel them to such a course.

We hold these truths to be self-evident: that all men and women are created equal; that they are endowed by their Creator with certain inalienable rights, that among these are life, liberty, and the pursuit of happiness; that to secure these rights governments are instituted, deriving their just powers from the consent of the governed. Whenever any form of government becomes destructive of these ends, it is the right of those who suffer from it to refuse allegiance to it, and to insist upon the institution of a new government, laying a foundation on such principles, and organizing its powers in such form, as to them shall seem most likely to effect their safety and happiness. . . .

Now, in view of this entire disfranchisement of one-half the people of this country, their social and religious degradation—in view of the unjust laws . . . and because women do feel themselves aggrieved, oppressed, and fraudulently deprived of their most sacred rights, we insist that they have immediate admission to all the rights and privileges which belong to them as citizens of the United States. . . .

Resolutions

Resolved, That all laws which prevent woman from occupying a station in society as her conscience shall dictate, or which place her in a position inferior to that of man, are contrary to the great precept of nature, and therefore of no force or authority.

Resolved, That woman is man's equal—was intended to be so by the Creator, and the highest good of the race demands that she should be recognized as such. . . .

Resolved, That inasmuch as man, while claiming for himself intellectual superiority, does accord to woman moral superiority, it is preeminently his duty to encourage her to speak and teach, as she has an opportunity, in all religious assemblies. . . .

Resolved, That the objection of indelicacy and impropriety, which is so often brought against woman when she addresses a public audience, comes with a very ill-grace from those who encourage, by their attendance, her appearance on the stage, in the concert, or in feats of the circus. . . .

Resolved, That it is the duty of the women of this country to secure to themselves their sacred right to the elective franchise. . . .

Resolved, therefore, That, being invested by the Creator with the same capabilities, and the same consciousness of responsibility for their exercise, it is demonstrably the right and duty of woman, equally with man, to promote every righteous cause by every righteous means; and especially, in regard to the great subjects of morals and religion, it is self-evidently her right to participate with her brother in teaching them, both in private and in pubic, by writing and by speaking, by any instrumentalities proper to be used, and in any assemblies proper to be held; and this being a self-evident truth growing out of the divinely implanted principles of human nature, any custom or authority adverse to it, whether modern or wearing the hoary sanction of antiquity, is to be regarded as a self-evident falsehood, and at war with mankind.

Source: Timothy McCarthy & John McMillan, eds. *The Radical Reader.* New York: The New Press, 2003, pp. 172–175.

QUESTIONS

1. How did women highlight the social, economic, and political inequalities of antebellum America?
2. What was the inspiration and philosophical justification for the Declaration of Sentiments?
3. Why do you think the resolution on suffrage (women's right to vote) was more controversial than the other resolutions?

Document 8: Sojourner Truth
Ar'n't I a Woman (1851)

Sojourner Truth spent nearly thirty years in bondage in upstate New York. She became instrumental not only in the abolitionist cause, particularly assisting runaway slaves through the Underground Railroad, but also in speaking out on behalf of women. Hoping for a nonviolent resolution to the issue of slavery, Truth in the end endorsed the Union cause during the Civil War. In this speech Truth offers an account of one African American woman seeking political and personal empowerment in a society dominated by white males.

*J*want to say a few words about this matter. I am a woman's rights. I have as much muscle as any man, and can do as much work as any man. I have plowed and reaped and husked and chopped and mowed, and can any man do more than that? I have heard much about the sexes being equal. I can carry as much as any man, and can eat as much too, if I can get it. I am as strong as any man that is now. As for intellect, all I can say is, if woman have a pint, and man a quart—why can't she have her little pint full? You need not be afraid to give us our rights for fear we will take too much,—for we can't take more than our pint'll hold.... I can't read, but I can hear. I have heard the bible and have learned that Eve caused man to sin. Well, if woman upset the world, do give her a chance to set it right side up again.... Man, where is your part? But the women are coming up blessed by God and a few of the men are coming up with them. But man is in a tight place, the poor slave is on him, woman is coming on him, he is surely between a hawk and a buzzard.

Source: Margaret Washington, ed. *Narrative of Sojourner Truth.* New York: Vintage Books, 1993, pp. 117–118.

QUESTIONS

1. How did the bible influence Sojourner Truth's commitment to abolitionism and women's rights?
2. How did Truth equate woman's power with that of a man?
3. As an emancipated slave and a woman, what effect might her words have had on the largely male audience?

Document 9: Frederick Douglass
What to the Slave is the Fourth of July? (1852)

Frederick Douglass, a former slave, became one of the most passionate orators in nineteenth-century America. Initially, Douglass supported and defended William Lloyd Garrison and the New England Non-Resistance Society. But as the prospects for civil war grew, Douglass developed his own form of radical abolitionism. This speech was delivered in Rochester. Douglass challenged white Americans to face the issue of slavery head on, arguing that black equality was consistent with the ideals of the American Revolution.

*F*ellow-citizens, pardon me, allow me to ask, why am I called upon to speak here today? What have I, or those I represent, to do with your national independence? Are the great principles of political freedom and of natural justice, embodied in that Declaration of Independence, extended to us? And I, therefore, called upon to bring our humble offering to the national altar, and to confess the benefits and express devout gratitude for the blessings resulting from your independence to us? . . .

But, such is not the state of the case. I say it with a sad sense of the disparity between us. I am not included within the pale of this glorious anniversary! Your high independence only reveals the immeasurable distance between us. The blessings in which you, this day, rejoice, are not enjoyed in common. The rich inheritance of justice, liberty, prosperity and independence, bequeathed by your fathers, is shared by you, not by me. The sunlight that brought life and healing to you, has brought stripes and death to me. This Fourth [of] July is *yours*, not *mine.* You may rejoice, *I* must mourn. . . .

Fellow-citizens; above your national, tumultuous joy, I hear the mournful wail of millions! Whose chains, heavy and grievous yesterday, are, today rendered more intolerable by the jubilee shouts that reach them. If I do forget, if I do not faithfully remember those bleeding children of sorrow this day, "may my right hand forget her cunning, and may my tongue cleave to the roof of my mouth!" To forget them, to pass lightly over their wrongs, and to chime in with the popular theme, would be treason most scandalous and shocking, and would make me reproach before God and the world. MY subject, then fellow-citizens, is AMERICAN SLAVERY. . . . Whether we turn to the declarations of the past, or to the professions of the present, the conduct of the nation seems equally hideous and revolting. America is false to the past, false to the present, and solemnly binds herself to be false to the future. Standing with God and the crushed and bleeding slave on this occasion, I will, in the name of humanity which is outraged, in the name of liberty which is fettered, in the name of the constitution and the Bible, which are disregarded and tempted upon, dare to call in question and to denounce, with all the emphasis I can command, everything that serves to perpetuate slavery—the great sin and shame of America! . . .

What, to the American slave, is your 4th of July? I answer: a day that reveals to him, more than all other days in the year, the gross injustice and cruelty to which he is the constant victim. To him, your celebration is a sham; your boasted liberty, an unholy license; your national greatness, swelling vanity; your sounds of rejoicing are empty and heartless; your denunciations of tyrants, brass fronted impudence; your shouts of liberty and equality, hollow mockery; your prayers and hymns, your sermons and thanksgivings, with all your religious parade, and solemnity, are, to him, mere bombast, fraud, deception, impiety, and hypocrisy—a thin veil to cover up crimes which would disgrace a nation of savages. . . .

Source: Timothy Patrick McCarthy & John McMillan, eds. *The Radical Reader: A Documentary History of the American Radical Tradition.* New York: The New Press, 2003, pp. 151–153.

QUESTIONS

1. How did Douglass equate America's revolutionary ideals to those of the abolitionist crusade?
2. In what way did he appeal to religion and the bible in justifying support for the elimination of slavery?
3. How does Douglass view the balance between adherence to non-violence and the demands of justice?

Document 10: Elihu Burritt
Passive Resistance (1854)

Elihu Burritt lived from 1810 until 1879. Believing that it was up to the masses to effect change, he called on the working class of the world to engage in a world-wide general strike against war. Burritt believed that nations should organize peace congresses and work on ways to improve global communication in order to encourage greater international understanding. The following passage was published in 1854 in his work *Thoughts and Things at Home and Abroad,* and it speaks to the importance of collective nonviolence rather than individual acts of conscience such as those expressed by Woolman and Thoreau.

The full power revealed and prescribed in that simple and sublime precept of the Gospel, *"overcome evil with good,"* has never been tested by any people, population, or community . . . subduing the evils and enemies that beset and oppress them.... To put into full operation, requires a capacity of good-will, of forgiveness of injuries, of abnegation of natural instincts, which the population of no town, or province, or state, has ever acquired. But, at long intervals and a little more frequently of late, a case has occurred here and there, in which a considerable community has acquired the ability of sustaining for awhile the lowest, feeblest, manifestation of this power, or a condition of *passive resistance* to oppression, armed with a force which could instantly crush any violent opposition they might attempt to array against it. Within the last two or three years, several of these cases have transpired in different parts of the world. In one of these, a little English colony at the Cape of Good Hope, *passively*, but successfully, *resisted* the great Government of the British empire, backed with all its navies and armies, in its attempt to make the home of their small population a receptacle of criminals, crime, and convicts from England. Then, almost simultaneously with this successful experiment with the force of Passive resistance, there comes the report of another, from the distant lands of the Pacific Ocean, tried under circumstances of more imminent peril and oppression, and crowned with illustrious triumph. The weak little Government of the Sandwich Islands, in order to diminish the use and effect of intoxicating liquors among their people, imposed a heavy tax upon French brandy and wine. This irritated the French, and they sent thither a great ship of war to compel the government to remove the tax.... But they absolutely refused to obey.... The French commander landed with his marines in battle array. Men with lighted matches stood at the great cannons of the ship. The hour of vengeance had come. Poor little people what will become of you now?... The gallant commander, therefore, landed his marines and took possession of the fort, custom-house, and some other Government buildings, *no resistance being offered*. All was still peaceful in the streets, business going on as usual. Here they remained for some days; when, finding that the government would not accede at all to their demands, though they offered to leave the whole question to an umpire, the chivalrous Frenchmen went to work to dismantle the fort, and destroyed everything within its walls. After having finished this Vandal-like work, they marched off with Flying colors. How full of illustration is this case of passive resistance? The simple, quiet force of *endurance* which the government opposed to the French wet their powder and turned their bayonets to straw. Against this unexpected force the marines were powerless. They had no arms to contend with such an enemy. All their weapons, and discipline, and bravery, were fitted only to overcome brute force; and of this they found none, except its shadow in the fort and its equipments; and with great valor they fell upon this shadow, and mutilated it terribly, and then marched back with flying colors! So far was this invasion of bayonet-power from inducing a settlement to the advantage of the French, that the government even refused their offer to submit the question to arbitration, or put the law at any hazard of modification, in face of all the brute force that France could marshal against it. . . .

Source: Staughton Lynd, ed. *Nonviolence in America: A Documentary History.* Indianapolis, IN: Bobbs-Merrill Co., 1966, pp. 93–108.

QUESTIONS

1. What does Burritt mean when he says we should overcome good with evil?
2. What social and political issues may have prompted Burritt's essay on passive resistance?
3. According to Burritt, why is true passive resistance so successful against those committed to war?

$$3$$

Standing Up for the Oppressed in an Age of Expansion

Between 1865 and the beginning of the new century, the peace and justice movement, in the context of the country's westward movement and its developing industrialization, became involved in a number of causes, both domestic and international. In an attempt to improve the quality of life at home, peacemakers continued to express concern about equality for women, freed slaves, Native Americans, and others, supported the rights of labor, and applauded the critique of contemporary U.S. society by utopian novelists. Some peace activists also focused on matters abroad, seeking a more organized, practical form of internationalism. These individuals called for a campaign supporting the use of arbitration in international disputes. Whichever channel peacemakers followed, late nineteenth-century peace and justice movements were charged with excitement and hope for the future of humankind.

One of the most important developments within the struggle for peace and justice was the growing influence of women. One example is poet, re-

For the People, pages 53–84
53

former, and American Peace Society officer Julia Ward Howe, who sought to unite the mothers of mankind to prevent future outbreaks of barbarity. In September 1870, the author of "The Battle Hymn of the Republic" issued "An Appeal to Womanhood Throughout the World." In public meetings in New York and Boston, Howe took steps toward forming a Women's International Peace Association and a World Congress of Women on behalf of International Peace.

Howe was the first female suffragist to take early feminist-pacifist ideology into a distinct and separate peace movement for women. She was also the first to propose a national day honoring mothers, a holiday that in its origins was linked to the cause of peace (**Document 1**). As a Universal Peace Union officer (UPU was founded right after the Civil War and represented a more radical version of Christian nonresistance), Howe proceeded to organize "Mothers Peace Festivals" in various places throughout the globe on June 2, 1873. Gatherings were held in Boston, New York, Connecticut, Pennsylvania, New Jersey, Delaware, Illinois, and Missouri, as well as abroad in Constantinople, Geneva, Rome, and London. At these festivals, mothers condemned war and military training in schools and urged that women be given a greater voice in politics, especially in regard to decisions about going to war. Each June, as late as 1909, the festivals attracted numerous participants worldwide.

While Howe tried to carry her peace message across the Atlantic, Quaker feminist Hannah J. Bailey remained at home and created a peace department within the Woman's Christian Temperance Union (WCTU). Bailey would become one of the most influential spokespeople on behalf of peace and internationalism of her time. She presented numerous speeches at international conferences calling upon world leaders to recognize the merits of arbitration and global harmony. Her specific efforts were directed at peace education (**Document 2**). Under her capable and efficient direction, the department operated in twenty-eight states—issuing the *Pacific Banner* and handing out thousands of Children's Leaflets in Sunday Schools. Encouraged by Bailey, local members of the WCTU peace department supplied antiwar material to women, who would then present papers to their literary clubs or civic organizations. They also worked to persuade ministers to preach against war, editors to publicize peace propaganda in their columns, and teachers to present the idea of international goodwill in their classrooms.

The efforts of Howe, Bailey, and other women were instrumental in keeping the peace movement alive while also expanding its focus on social justice. The period after Seneca Falls led to a widespread domestic revolution that freed many females to pursue other interests outside the home. Women who joined the temperance crusade, for instance, realized that achieving their reform goals required a broader social program for women's rights, peace, and justice.

The United States underwent tremendous material expansion in the late nineteenth century. The competitive economy based on profits that characterized industrial capitalism increased tensions between workers and those who employed them. One of the least explored areas in the history of the American peace movement has been its relationship to working people. Post–Civil War advances in industry swelled the ranks of the country's labor force. At the same time, the low wages, long hours, unsafe factory conditions, and an expanding labor pool fueled by the large number of immigrants coming to America diminished the efforts of workers to negotiate fair contracts. This era witnessed a number of strikes, resulting in bloody encounters between the strikers and strike-breakers backed by their allies— local law enforcement agents and state militias.

In this context, organized labor began to express broad concerns for economic justice. The establishment of the Knights of Labor in 1869, led by Uriah Stephens and Terrence V. Powderly, demonstrated one organization's belief in the power of a just cause. Calling itself a "fraternal order" rather than a union, during the 1870s and 1880s the Knights advanced cooperatives and used voluntary arbitration to achieve social and economic justice through nonviolence. By the mid-1880s, it was operating some 140 cooperatives and had mediated more than 300 labor disputes in New York alone. The Knights' Preamble specifically called for the substitution of arbitration for strikes. Its leaders considered strikes a last resort and told members not to use violence.

The Knights claimed a membership of 700,000 by the mid-1880s—the height of its influence. African Americans, women, and skilled and unskilled workers were all members of this one big union whose main objective was to gradually abolish the wage system. Promoting nonviolence through mediation, equality for all races and sexes among the laboring masses, and economic justice for all workers, the Knights spread ideas that were way ahead of their time (**Document 3**).

The Knights of Labor's altruistic policies proved inspirational to a number of important novelists concerned with the growing business civilization and its negative effects on society. Two who stand out for their concerns about economic inequality are William Dean Howells and Edward Bellamy.

Howells, who was born and raised in frontier Ohio, became one of the most influential American novelists, editors, and critics of his time. Focusing on the normal or commonplace, as opposed to the romantic notions of the ideal or sentimental, Howells was concerned about the views and ideals shaping the actual life of men and women. He was very much influenced by Russian novelist Leo Tolstoy's ideas about economic equality and nonviolence. This was conveyed in his 1886 novel, *The Minister's Charge.*

Building on the famous Russian novelist's nonresistance philosophy, Howells' intense feelings regarding social justice and democratic fairness became most apparent in his defense of the Haymarket martyrs. When a group of anarchists were accused of exploding a bomb at a rally in support of striking workers in Chicago on May 4, 1886, the response of the newspapers and most influential citizens was instant and bitterly retaliatory. Howells believed that the accused were set up due to anti-labor hysteria and conspiracy theories. After the Supreme Court of Illinois denied the anarchists' appeals on November 2, 1887, Howells sent a letter to the *New York Tribune* in which he urged readers to petition the governor of Illinois to commute their sentences. The letter appeared on November 6 under the heading, "Clemency for the Anarchists/A Letter from W.D. Howells." He immediately became the target of public scorn, but his sense of fairness and justice made him even more determined. After four of the men were executed (one had committed suicide in prison), Howells wrote a second letter to the *Tribune,* "A Word for the Dead." It was never published (**Document 4**). In what many critics consider his best novel, *A Hazard of New Fortunes* (1890), his feelings about the Haymarket executions are conveyed in his portrayal of the German socialist Lindau. The novel powerfully contrasts two prominent and incompatible worldviews held by two men, a narrow-minded capitalist and a cultured socialist. Howells's own distaste for war also finds expression through the actions and thoughts of Lindau, who fought in the Civil War and lost a hand while his capitalist foe bought a substitute.

While Howells's critique of industrial America was also clear in his lesser known utopian novel, *A Traveler from Altruria,* it was Edward Bellamy who inspired people to act on this critique. His *Looking Backward, 2000–1887* (1887) was the most widely read piece of utopian literature of its time (**Document 5**). The book was almost the number one bestseller of the nineteenth century. (Harriet Beecher Stowe's *Uncle Tom's Cabin* was first.) *Looking Backward* projected a future America in which the competitive aspects of capitalism were replaced by a culture of economic security, social harmony, and peace. Expressing the yearning for a cooperative commonwealth that was common in late nineteenth-century utopian thought, Bellamy called his philosophy of communal harmony Nationalism.

Shortly after *Looking Backward*'s publication, a number of Bellamy Nationalist clubs were formed. Many members of these clubs became involved with other political reform groups, including socialist labor leader and head of the American Railway Union Eugene V. Debs. The ideas of Bellamy and his followers also influenced the platform of the Populist Party in 1892.

Another writer who had a significant influence on the struggle for peace and justice was Ida B. Wells, a journalist who became best known for her crusade against lynching. Devoting her life to fighting injustice against women and people of color, she challenged segregation, argued for women's right to vote, and late in her life ran for public office, making her one of the first African American women to do so.

In 1880, after attending Rust College in Holly Springs, Mississippi, where she was born, Wells moved to Memphis, Tennessee. During the summer she attended school at Fisk University in Nashville. On one occasion, as she was traveling by train back to Memphis, she was ordered by the conductor to surrender her seat to a white man and move to the crowded "Jim Crow" car. When she refused, she was dragged out by the conductor and two other men. She promptly hired a black attorney to sue the railroad and also wrote a newspaper story about the incident.

Although the Tennessee Supreme Court overturned her $500 settlement in 1887, Wells had already achieved a degree of recognition for her writings about racial issues. In 1889, she became co-owner and editor of *Free Speech*, which was housed at the Beale Street Baptist Church. In 1892, an incident occurred that forced her to leave Memphis. Three African American owners of a Memphis grocery store were lynched for running a store that competed with white businesses. After a dispute broke out in which three white men were injured, the three black store owners were immediately jailed and accused of raping a white woman. A lynch mob stormed the jail and took the three men out and lynched them in an open field. Wells promptly wrote an article in *Free Speech* advising African Americans to leave town. When her newspaper office was destroyed as a result of her investigative journalism, she moved to New York and eventually settled in Chicago.

But she never stopped working against injustice in the South, and was particularly diligent in exposing the phony excuses given for the lynching of black men, which was a common occurence in this period. Wells documented 241 lynchings in 1892 and another 197 in 1894. In fact, during the 1890s, 187 black Americans were lynched each year. That amounted to two per week. In her 1894 investigative piece *The Red Record*, Wells exposed the real reasons behind the lynchings, which were crude, violent, and repulsive. Many blacks were beaten and tarred before they were executed. The commonly held belief that the crime of raping white women had led to the lynchings was inaccurate. In almost every case, Wells revealed, the reasons were for insubordination, talking disrespectfully, hitting a white man or child, writing an insulting letter, organizing sharecroppers, or just being too prosperous. While her rhetoric was fiery, what she asked for was that the rule of law be applied equally to people of every race (**Document 6**). Later in her life she worked hard to gain women the right to vote and became a founder of the National Association for the Advancement of Colored People.

Survival was a pressing issue for Native Americans in the late nineteenth century as well, with their culture and way of life in danger of being wiped out. The homesteaders' desire for good arable lands in the West, in conjunction with the development of the railroads and various business ventures, intensified the white man's pressure upon Native Americans. This would be the main cause of recurrent wars on the Great Plains from 1862 to 1877. To the frontiersmen, the Native American had always been an obstacle in the path of westward progress; to the Native Americans, that same "progress" spelled the doom of the buffalo and other game on which Indian tribes depended for food, and ultimately, the destruction of their way of life.

The new Colorado Territory was one scene of horrific bloodshed. Arapaho and Cheyenne who resented the intrusion of miners and ranchers on their sacred lands began raiding stagecoach stations and ranches and murdered a white family. In reprisal, Colonel J.M. Chivington surprised the Native Americans at Sand Creek, where he butchered and killed five hundred of them, including many women and children. Many of the bodies of those killed were mutilated, prompting Army General Nelson A. Miles to comment that the Sand Creek massacre, also known as the Chivington Massacre, was "the foulest and most unjustifiable crime in the annals of America." Throughout the 1870s, highlighted by the Battle at Little Big Horn on June 25–26, 1876—which the Indians called the battle of Greasy Grass and white historians dubbed "Custer's last stand"—Native Americans fought back against the U.S. military in a vain attempt to keep their lands and preserve their way of life. Their view is represented by a native American woman's account of that battle, one of the few the Indians won. In her account, She Walks with Her Shawl, who witnessed the battle, expressed the Indians' respect for life, refuting white people's claims that the Indians mutilated the bodies of white soldiers. Not one single soldier was burned at the stake, she proclaimed. Those already convinced that the Indians could not prevail turned their attention to mourning the dead. There was no victory dance that night.

It was on the northern plains that the final bloody chapter in the long and tragic history of Native American–white warfare was written. More than any other battle, the massacre at Wounded Knee symbolized the destruction of a civilization. Perhaps in retribution for "Custer's last stand" (Custer was killed at Little Big Horn), a unit of the Seventh Cavalry responded to the unfounded fears that white miners and settlers had of the "Ghost Dance." This dance became popular among Indians hoping to bring to life a vision in which their peaceful world had been restored. The cavalry, armed to the teeth and seeking a strong measure of retribution for the event that occurred fourteen years earlier, began arresting a number of Sioux men, women, and children who were traveling to the Pine Ridge Reservation in search of food and protection. The troops surrounded them and took away their weapons, using physical force in the form of rifle stocks and sabers to coerce them into submission. When a shot was heard, the troops opened fire with their rifles and Gatling guns into the disarmed Sioux. Some ninety men and two hundred women and children were mortally wounded or killed. Many Americans expressed horror and shame at the brutality. Sioux leader Black Elk later described the pain of seeing a "people's dream" die (**Document 7**).

Even those reformers who saw themselves as sympathetic to the Native Americans failed to comprehend the Indians' values, such as collective ownership of land and respect for nature, and their commitment to maintaining their way of life. Instead, reformers sought to "civilize" the Indians, which meant getting them to adopt Christianity, individual land ownership, and American forms of education. Within the peace movement, with the blessings of President Grant and other high officials sympathetic to the plight of the Native Americans, the Quakers' yearly meetings set up a Committee of Friends of Indian Affairs. This body watched over the work of two Quaker superintendents of agencies and the forty Friends associated with them in the work of demonstrating Christian love and kindness to 15,000 Native Americans.

Quaker agents succeeded in some ways, making substantial contributions to the education of many tribes, preventing at least one battle between rival Native American bands, and demonstrating the efficacy of the principle of nonviolence. Still, their role as friends of the Indians was limited by their view that "civilizing" Native Americans meant insisting they become Christians and independent farmers and give up their traditional ways.

The Society of Friends was not alone in promoting a nonviolent approach to Native Americans; the Universal Peace Union was quite vocal in criticizing military authorities for not adhering to the "peace policy" that the American government professed to follow. The Union argued before committees of Congress that various proposed Indian treaties were so unjust that they could only result in uprisings. On one occasion, the UPU helped save Native Americans captured in battle from the death penalty. With touching faith in good works, they sent agricultural implements and other gifts to Indian agents, and they consistently supported those working for a just and peaceful policy toward Native Americans.

While industrial workers, Native Americans, and campaigners against lynching promoted their own ideas of justice on the home front, growing global interdependence caused a number of American reformers to seek ways of establishing lawmaking machinery for settling international disputes. One of the peace movement's most active campaigns between 1865 and 1900 was seeking new ways to establish international harmony through law and arbitration. The increasing development of jurisprudence based on social interdependence reflected the changing status of law itself. Although the interest of lawyers in peace would become more important after the turn of the century, their concern for developing peacemaking machinery based on international law had already begun to take shape.

American business and reform leaders were well aware that improved communications and technology meant the U.S. would become more involved in a shrinking world. On the one hand, this gave new life to American peacemaking and the growing cosmopolitan approach to solving international disagreements through political, diplomatic, and legal means. On the other hand, such approaches were limited by social Darwinism—a view that Charles Darwin's biological discoveries about species were applicable to society and that supported the "survival of the fittest" argument. Along with racial assumptions, the search for profits, and the U.S.'s sense of mission, social Darwinism helped lead to and justify American imperialism.

Hoping to win public opinion by blending the rhetoric of evangelical Christianity with racial Anglo-Saxonism, leading British and American peace seekers promoted the general ideal of international arbitration. In 1887, British peace activist Randal Cremer and other British legislators traveled across the Atlantic, visiting many American cities, with a proposal for an Anglo-American treaty agreement to submit to arbitration all future disputes between the powers.

Anglo-American arbitration was finally given wide publicity in 1895 when two Quakers, Albert and Alfred Smiley, welcomed national leaders who supported the cause of international arbitration to their scenic Lake Mohonk resort in New York. This would be the first of twenty-two annual conferences to which selected guests were invited; the number of guests grew from fifty to three hundred. Topics most commonly discussed were peace education in the schools and colleges, the role of government in international arbitration, the impact of arbitration treaties, and arbitration as a matter of world politics. A considerable number of these sessions were devoted to peace education. A speech by the Reverend William Allen, for instance, was warmly received and given wide publicity (**Document 8**). Fundamentally, the argument was that before the public could appreciate the importance of internationalism and arbitration it was incumbent upon teachers to educate children about the necessity of world peace.

Within peace circles, the Lake Mohonk Arbitration Conferences became notable for popularizing the idea of a permanent international court, while also lending a glow of respectability to the peace movement itself. In his opening address to the first conference, Benjamin Trueblood set the tone for what would be a series of discussions about the proposed establishment of an international tribunal of arbitration. He emphasized "practical means" for settling disputes based on the increasing interdependence of nations, which he suggested had led to an "international conscience." Arbitration was just one expression of international cooperation; in his optimistic view, diplomacy had become a measure for peaceful cooperation rather than an instrument tied to war.

A respected figure at these conferences, Trueblood emerged as one of the most important peace leaders near the turn of the century. Fluent in a number of modern languages, he was selected secretary of the American Peace Society in 1892, a position he held until 1915. For most of that period, he was the only full-time salaried peace worker in the United States. Under his leadership, the Society's membership grew from 400 to close to 8,000 and subscriptions to its journal, the *Advocate of Peace*, climbed from 1,500 to more than 11,000.

Unquestionably, the limits of the cosmopolitan peace impulse were apparent in efforts to assist in America's rise to world power. Despite the earlier historical tradition of isolationism, the years between 1865 and 1900 were marked by notions of commercial destiny and political mission abroad. Although peacemakers did not favor a policy of colonization, promoting instead arbitration conferences giving the U.S. a greater presence on the world stage, American leaders seized upon such developments to insist upon a more commanding role in global affairs. Economic motives, not altruistic concerns about peace, were the primary factor behind American expansionism.

The growing need of American manufacturers for more resources and markets could only be satisfied by significantly increasing U.S. influence in other countries. To a considerable extent, this was precipitated by three decades—the 1870s, 1880s, and 1890s—of falling prices, financial panics, and periods of economic depression. Businessmen, in particular, urged an expansionist policy despite not insisting on territorial acquisitions. Many from this quarter strongly encouraged arbitral means to settle disputes in order to further peaceful trading relations.

In fact, the most vocal supporters behind the expansionist thrust were not businessmen but publicists, missionaries, politicians, naval officers, and professors, who blended the philosophies of manifest destiny, Anglo-Saxon racism, militarism, patriotism, and economic determinism into a unique justification for territorial acquisition. Supporters of territorial expansion argued that it was the duty of Anglo-Saxon nations to exercise political domination over "backward" areas in order to bring peace and spread the principles of Christianity and liberty. This rationale would be tested at the end of the 1890s.

The issue of territorial expansionism presented a serious challenge to peace seekers. In April 1898, the United States Government declared war on Spain and launched effective military attacks on Spanish holdings in Cuba, Puerto Rico, and the Philippines. This "splendid little war," as Ambassador John Hay called it, initially had popular support as it followed the failure of a three-year attempt by Spain to crush the Cuban independence movement. Within ten weeks, the United States had captured Cuba, Puerto Rico, and the Philippines, and facilitated the annexation of Hawaii. Later that year, Spanish and American negotiators worked out a settlement in Paris in which the United States compensated Spain monetarily in return for American occupation of Cuba (to be granted independence in 1902) and the cession to the United States of Puerto Rico and the Philippines.

The war ultimately led to the formation of the Anti-Imperialist League in Faneuil Hall, Boston, on June 15, 1898. The leaders were old-fashioned liberals, endowed with a New England conscience and a determination to keep an industrializing America free from imperial temptations. The league was concerned that, having won the war with Spain, the U.S. should not turn around and follow policies similar to the Spanish toward its newly acquired territories. Though branches were organized in Chicago, St. Louis, San Francisco, and other cities, Boston remained the heart of the movement. Anti-imperialists seriously believed all government derived its power from the consent of the governed and that Cuba and the Philippines had the right to self-determination. Respected professionals who were towers of strength in the League included Gamaliel Bradford (the 67-year-old descendant of the Bay Colony's first governor); Moorfield Storey (secretary to

Senator Sumner); pacifists Edward Atkinson, Ernest Crosby, and Jane Addams; urban reformers such as Hazen Pingree and Samuel "Golden Rule" Jones; African American activist Booker T. Washington; and educator David Starr Jordan. With political allies and influential supporters that included William Jennings Bryan, William James, Andrew Carnegie, Samuel Gompers, Carl Schurz, William Graham Sumner, and General Nelson A. Miles, the Anti-Imperialist League fomented much of the public opposition to American expansionism.

Supporters of the decision to acquire the Philippines, a result of the ten-week war with Spain, saw it as critical to United States interests in the Far East; however, history would demonstrate that it came at a heavy price. Two weeks prior to the February 6, 1899, Senate ratification of the Treaty of Paris, which ended the war with Spain, the Filipino–American War broke out. The war would last almost three and a half years; it cost the United States $170 million and caused the deaths of seven thousand Americans and hundreds of thousands of Filipinos. As the ill-equipped Filipino armies, led by Emilio Aquinaldo, were defeated by superior American-trained troops, they fled into the jungle to wage a vicious guerrilla war, with strong popular support. American troops resorted to torture and the slaughter of entire villages, and tales of unthinkable atrocities rocked the United States. American soldiers used the painful "water cure"—forcing water down victims' throats until they yielded information or died—and even established re-concentration camps similar to those used by the Spanish Army in Cuba. Fighting continued on and off throughout 1900 and 1901, until a cunning ruse led to Aquinaldo's capture.

Loudly challenging the government's policies was the Anti-Imperialist League. Originally, the League was organized to discourage the McKinley Administration from seizing the Philippines. It sought to convince the government and the people that war led to imperialism and imperialism led to war in a never-ending cycle, and that both ran counter to the principles of Christianity and humanitarianism. The brutality of the Filipino–American War quickly transformed the Anti-Imperialist League into a national movement with a mass constituency. Working with other anti-imperialist forces, League membership soared to more than 30,000 in a growth spurt that made it the largest antiwar organization per capita in American history. Finding receptive audiences, anti-imperialists distributed literature and placed speakers around the country. The League pursued two basic goals: an immediate suspension of hostilities in the Philippines and a Congressional pledge of Philippine independence.

Through the League's periodical, the *Anti-Imperialist*, and Edward Atkinson's *The Cost of a National Crime* and *The Hell of War and its Penalties*, the League exposed repulsive and ghastly brutalities despite official investigations that tried to cover up the actions of American military personnel. Stanford University president David Starr Jordon penned his own condemnation of the conflict (**Document 9**). He quickly dismissed any assertions that the Philippines would be better off under American control. He simply labeled it a form of "military commercialism." Critics also noted the increased power in the executive branch and the development of bureaucracy, which further demonstrated how imperialism was contrary to American constitutional traditions. Recalling the decline and fall of the Roman Empire, anti-imperialists urged Americans to remember that the initial path of conquest carried out by the Roman Legions also signaled the beginning of its decay. The effort to retain the Philippines, anti-imperialists were quick to point out, involved not only the race for naval supremacy but also international complications that led to war.

Men of letters also lent their pens to the anti-imperialist cause; perhaps the most famous was Mark Twain. His essays, "To a Person Sitting in the Darkness" and "The War Prayer," were satirical masterpieces that attempted to open the windows to the light of moderation and restraint. "The War Prayer" (**Document 10**) is particularly compelling in calling attention to the importance of personal convictions and how completely those whose appetites were whetted by misguided Christianity and the lust for commercial advantage had repudiated the nation's traditional belief in the right of self-determination of peoples. Written after the U.S. victory in the Philippines, the piece was too controversial for magazines to publish despite Twain's reputation. Along with Twain, other writers such as William Vaughn Moody, Harvard philosopher William James, and Judge Ernest Howard Crosby lent their pens and intuitions to the anti-imperialist cause.

The linkage between commercialism, colonialism, and a rapidly expanding naval power with the capability of expanding American influence overseas aroused passions on both sides. Those against a growing empire, like Twain, used the argument to highlight the nation's lost sense of purity. The acquisition of the Philippines came to represent the most significant development in American foreign policy with respect to past traditions. Many anti-imperialists were also afraid that America's outward thrust would distract from the more pressing needs of domestic reform. Those favoring a more aggressive overseas policy relied on an emerging virulent appeal to patriotism, which was used for sinister purposes—to label those opposed to war as disloyal.

The Anti-Imperialist League left an important legacy, growing from a small group of intellectuals and business leaders in Boston to a large nationwide movement in reaction to the mounting casualties in the Filipino–American War. Nevertheless, the rash of annexations accompanying the Spanish–American War quickly subsided as outright colonialism was replaced by indirect forms of political control. In that regard, the Anti-Imperialist League did have a latent effect on the conduct of U.S. foreign policy as it entered the twentieth century. By the start of the twentieth century newly endowed peace organizations were established in an effort to secure world order through the force of law. The peace movement became more "respectable" as leading citizens, educators, entrepreneurs, and church leaders lent money and ideas to the cause. A flurry of peacemaking efforts erupted only to be squelched with the onset of World War I. Out of these ashes emerged a "modern" peace and justice movement, one with a broad view of the causes of war and violence that would leave its mark on the twentieth century.

Document 1:   Julia Ward Howe
Mother's Day Proclamation (1870)

Julia Ward Howe was a noted abolitionist and women's rights advocate. Following in the tradition of her pre-Civil War sisters, she became involved in the peace movement as part of women's growing concern for political and social reform in America. She composed this poem in the burning ashes of the Civil War and the advent of the Franco–Prussian War in Europe.

---

*A*rise then . . . women of this day!
Arise, all women who have hearts!
Whether your baptism be of water or of tears!
Say firmly
"We will not have questions answered by irrelevant agencies,
Our husbands will not come to us, reeking with carnage,
For caresses and applause.
Our sons shall not be taken from us to unlearn
All that we have been able to teach them of charity, mercy, and
       patience.
We, the women of one country,
Will be too tender of those of another country
To allow our sons to be trained to injure theirs."

From the voice of a devastated Earth a voice goes up with
Our own. It says: "Disarm! Disarm!
The sword of murder is not the balance of justice."
Blood does not wipe our dishonor,
Nor violence indicate possession.
As men have often forsaken the plough and the anvil
At the summons of war,
Let women now leave all that may be left of home
For a great and earnest day of counsel.
Let them meet first, as women, to bewail and commemorate the dead.
Let them solemnly take counsel with each other as to the means
Whereby the great human family can live in peace...
Each bearing after his own time the sacred impress, not of Caesar,
But of God—
In the name of womanhood and humanity, I earnestly ask
That a general congress of women without limit of nationality,
May be appointed and held at someplace deemed most convenient
And the earliest period consistent with its objects,
To promote the alliance of the different nationalities,
The amicable settlement of international questions,
The great and general interests of peace.

Source: Murray Polner and Thomas E. Woods, eds. We Who Dared to Say No
    to War: American Antiwar Writing From 1812 to Now. New York: Basic
    Books, 2008, p. 297.

QUESTIONS

1. How did Howe envision the role of women as agents of peace?
2. Whom did she consider as "irrelevant agencies"?
3. What did she hope to achieve with a congress of women?

Document 2: Address of Mrs. Hannah J. Bailey (1895)

Hannah Bailey was one of the leading spokespersons in the Woman's Christian Temperance Union. Like many women in the temperance movement, her reform efforts went beyond this one issue. Working for world peace was an important part of the nineteenth-century reform mentality as women sought to connect domestic improvement to global harmony. At the inaugural meeting of the Lake Mohonk Conference on International Arbitration near New Paltz, New York, Bailey linked the call for international arbitration to the promotion of peace education among the nation's youth.

Honored Chairman, Gentlemen and Ladies,–The Woman's Christian Temperance Union has taken up forty-one lines of work, called departments. The construction of the machinery by means of which these departments are carried on, is very much like that of a wheel within a wheel....

I will tell you something (though but little, for want of time) of the aims, objects and work, of the special department of Peace. I will quote largely from my own report to the World's Convention that will assemble in London the fourteenth of this month and continue until the twenty-first....

This department aims to secure such training for children, in home, Sunday school, public school and loyal temperance legions, as will make them despise physical combat and will lift them to a plane where the weapons are arguments, parliamentary usage and law; all of these having above them the "sword of the Spirit," that weapon which is above all others, worthy of reasonable and responsible beings.

The department of Peace is one of love and forgiveness. It teaches people to regard one another as a common brotherhood, and not to judge each other harshly. The Woman's Christian Temperance Union is, itself, organized mother-love, and, as a part of the duty of a mother is to make peace in her family when contentions exist, or, better still, to prevent them by timely care, it is fitting that the W.C.T.U. have a department of Peace and Arbitration. The work of peace is especially adapted to women. They are expected to be in sympathy with every peace measure. When women shall have a direct voice in politics, and in determining the continuance of carnal warfare, doubtless the former will become more purified and the latter be abolished altogether....

We consider the most important work which has been or is being accomplished by your department, is that bearing directly upon the training of children. The Boy's Brigade, which so many Sunday schools are blindly adopting, and the military drill in the public schools, have been handled with earnest effort to prevent the spread of their pernicious influence.

The tendency of all military teaching is, of course, towards militarism, and it is passing strange that any should fail to discern this fact. A person interested in peace, recently visiting the family of one who had used great influence in favor of boy's brigades, claiming that they do not foster militarism, gave a sum of money to two lads connected with the family in order to see what they would do with it. They purchased mimic weapons and converted the dining room into the scene of a mimic battle. Our department has tried to exert an influence against prize fighting and all its attendant evils. . . .

The twentieth century will soon dawn upon us, and it is time, high time, that we prepare to enter upon a twentieth century civilization where human life will be held too sacred to attack, and true patriotism will everywhere prevail. . . . If the truth shall ever be universally recognized that to die for one's country is a service far inferior to living for one's country, women must bear a large share in its inculcation. So long the ideal of physical courage has been recognized in a willingness to meet death, and the highest ideal of moral courage has been associated with the willingness to meet death for a good and noble cause, that it has grown a difficult task to make people realize that it requires more physical courage to live three-score-years-and-ten than to die at an earlier date, and that it requires more moral courage to come up to four-score years, "by reason of strength" which has been devoted to the illustration, as well as to the advocacy, of high moral ideals, than to die for any, however noble, cause.

What the world needs is not men who can meet death, and women who can see their beloved die without terror and without revolt. Such men and such women it has had from the earliest historic times. But it needs men and women who together can meet life, who can unite in the solution of its problems, which, with the advancement of civilization, are constantly becoming more delicate, more intricate, and more exacting.

Perhaps the highest patriots thought the duty exacted in 1861 was death. Whether we think them right or wrong, . . . all must agree that death is not the duty exacted of the patriots of to-day. It is perhaps a harder one. It is quite impossible that men should solve these problems wisely who have grown up in homes where these great subjects were held in abeyance to the relatively trifling questions of what we shall eat, and what we shall wear, and what our neighbors say, or, indeed, what the last novel or the last poem says; subjects which the prevailing dilettantism takes quite seriously. . . .

Source: "Address of Mrs. Hannah J. Bailey," The Lake Mohonk Arbitration Conference, 1895, pp. 66–71.

QUESTIONS

1. Why does Bailey suggest that the work of peace is especially adapted to women?
2. Using a citation from the text, explain what links Bailey saw among temperance, suffrage, and peace.
3. What is Bailey's view of patriotism? Do you agree or disagree? Explain.

Document 3: *Preamble to the Knights of Labor Constitution (1878)*

The Knights of Labor was one of the most influential workers' organizations in late nineteenth-century America. Eschewing the notion of craft unionism, the Knights welcomed into its ranks laborers in all occupations. This all-inclusive membership and its leaders' endorsement of conciliation in the form of arbitration instead of strikes were among its most distinctive characteristics. The Knights' strength declined in the wake of the Haymarket Affair of 1886. Before that point, however, they proposed many reforms that would come to fruition in later years.

Preamble to the Knights of Labor Constitution (1878)

*T*he recent alarming development and aggression of aggregated wealth, which unless checked, will invariably lead to the pauperization and hopeless degradation of the toiling masses, render it imperative, if we desire to enjoy the blessings of life, that a check should be placed upon its power and unjust accumulation, and a system adopted which will secure to the laborer the fruits of his toil.... [W]e submit to the world the object sought to be accomplished by our organization, calling upon all who believe in securing 'the greatest good to the greatest number' to aid and assist us:

To bring within the folds of organization every department of productive industry, making knowledge a standpoint for action, and industrial and moral worth, not wealth, the true standard of individual and national greatness....

To arrive at the true condition of the producing masses in their educational, moral, and financial condition, by demanding from the various governments the establishment of bureaus of Labor Statistics.

The Establishment of co-operative institutions, productive and distributive. . . .

The abrogation of all laws that do not bear equally upon capital and labor, the removal of unjust technicalities, delays, and discriminations in the administration of justice, and the adopting of measures providing for the health and safety of those engaged in mining, manufacturing, or building pursuits. . . .

The enactment of laws giving mechanics and laborers a first lien on their work for their full wages. . . .

The substitution of arbitration for strikes, whenever and wherever employers and employees are willing to meet on equitable grounds.

The prohibition of the employment of children in workshops, mines, and factories before attaining their fourteenth year. . . .

To secure for both sexes equal pay for equal work.

The reduction of the hours of labor to eight per day, so that the laborers may have more time for social enjoyment and intellectual improvement, and be enabled to reap the advantages conferred by the labor-saving machinery which their brains have created. . . .

Source: "The Knights of Labor," http://www.uwm.edu (accessed February 21, 2007)

QUESTIONS

1. In the Knights' view, what is the measure of a great nation?
2. What were the Knights' most important goals? Did you find any of them surprising for that era?
3. How might workers today greet the Knights' goals, and why did many reformers of that period endorse them?

Document 4: William Dean Howells
A Word for the Dead (1887)

William Dean Howells is considered one of the great realist writers in American history. Responding to the new currents of the machine, industrialism, and big business, he vigorously criticized the new business order, eventually adopting a Christian socialist philosophy. Upset by the way in which newspapers and city authorities treated the accused anarchists in the Haymarket Affair, Howells penned strong objections to their execution.

It seems of course almost a pity to mix a note of regret with the hymn of thanksgiving for blood going up from thousands of newspapers all over the land this morning; but I reflect that though I write amidst this joyful noise, my letter cannot reach the public before Monday at the earliest, and cannot therefore be regarded as an indecent interruption of the Te Deum.

By that time journalism will not have ceased, but history will have at least begun. All over the world where civilized men can think and feel, they are even now asking themselves, for what, really, did those four men die so bravely? Why did one other die so miserably? Next week the journalistic theory that they died so because they were desperate murderers will have grown even more insufficient than it is now for the minds and hearts of dispassionate inquirers, and history will make the answer to which she must adhere for all time. They died, in the prime of the first Republic the world has ever known, for their opinions' sake....

... We have committed an atrocious and irreparable wrong. We have been undergoing one of those spasms of paroxysmal righteousness to which our Anglo-Saxon race is peculiarly subject, and in which, let us hope, we are not more responsible for our actions than the victim of petit mal.

... [P]erhaps the wildest of our humorists could not have conceived of a joke so monstrous as the conviction of seven men for a murderous conspiracy which they carried into effect while one was at home playing cards with his family, another was addressing a meeting five miles away, another was present with his wife and little children, two others had made pacific speeches, and not one, except on the testimony of a single, notoriously untruthful witness, was proven to have had anything to do with throwing the Haymarket bomb, or to have even remotely instigated the act. It remained for a poetic brain to imagine this, and bring its dream yesterday to homicidal realization. . . .

. . . [W]e had a political execution in Chicago yesterday. The sooner we realize this, the better for us. By such perversion of law as brought the Anarchists to their doom, William Lloyd Garrison, who published a paper denouncing the constitution as a compact with hell and a covenant with death, and every week stirred up the blacks and their friends throughout the country to abhor the social system of the South, could have been sent to the gallows if a slave had killed his master. Emerson, Parker, Howe, Giddings and Wade, Sumner and Greeley, all who encouraged the fight against slavery in Kansas and the New England philanthropists who supplied the Free State men with Sharp's Rifles could have been held morally responsible, and made to pay with their persons, when John Brown took seven Missourians out of their beds and shot them. Wendell Phillips, Thoreau, and the other literary men whose sympathies influenced Brown to homicidal insurrection at Harper's Ferry could have been put to death with the same justice that consigned the Anarchists to the gallows in Chicago. . . .

Source: Edwin H. Cady, *The Realist at War: The Mature Years 1885–1920 of William Dean Howells.* Syracuse, NY: Syracuse University Press, 1958, pp. 73–77.

QUESTIONS

1. Why was Howells so upset about the conviction and execution of the Haymarket anarchists?
2. Based on his letter, what evidence should have exonerated these individuals?
3. In terms of justice and the reform ideal, which historic figures did Howells evoke to support his contention that the right to dissent is a valued American tradition?

Document 5: Edward Bellamy
Looking Backward (1887)

Edward Bellamy's *Looking Backward*, published in 1887, was an instant best-seller and the most influential utopian novel of its time. It touched off a national movement in support of cooperative commonwealths and utopian socialist experiments. The son of a minister, Bellamy wanted his readers to consider a moral and peaceful alternative to the social Darwinist competition and brutality of the industrial age.

Excerpt from Chapter 28:

I dressed in a mechanical way, feeling lighted-headed and oddly uncertain of myself, and sat down to the coffee and rolls which Sawyer was in the habit of providing for my refreshment before I left the house. The morning newspaper lay by the plate. I took it up, and my eye fell on the date, May 31, 1887. I had known, of course, from the moment I opened my eyes that my long and detailed experience in another century had been a dream, and yet it was startling to have it so conclusively demonstrated that the world was but a few hours older than when I had lain down to sleep. Glancing at the table of contents at the head of the paper, which reviewed the news of the morning, I read the following summary:

FOREIGN AFFAIRS.—The impending war between France and Germany. The French Chambers asked for new military credits to meet Germany's increase of her army. Probability that all Europe will be involved in case of war.—Great suffering among the unemployed in London. They demand work. Monster demonstration to be made. The authorities uneasy.—Great strikes in Belgium. The government preparing to repress outbreaks. Shocking facts in regard to the employment of girls in Belgium coal mines.—Wholesale evictions in Ireland.

HOME AFFAIRS.— . . . The coal barons decide to advance the price of coal and reduce production.—Speculators engineering a great wheat corner at Chicago. . . . —Large failures of business houses. Fears of a business crisis. . . . —Pitiable destitution among the women wage-workers in the great cities.—Startling growth of illiteracy in Massachusetts.—Decoration Day addresses. Professor Brown's oration on the moral grandeur of nineteenth century civilization.

It was indeed the nineteenth century to which I had awaked; there could be no kind of doubt about that. . . . Coming after such a damning indictment of the age as that one day's chronicle of world-wide bloodshed, greed, and tyranny, was a bit of cynicism worthy of Mephistopheles, and yet of all whose eyes it had met this morning I was, perhaps, the only one who perceived it no more than the others. That strange dream it was which had made all the difference. For I know not how long, I forgot my surroundings after this, and was again in fancy moving in that vivid dream-world, in that glorious city, with its homes of simple comfort and its gorgeous public palaces. Around me were again faces unmarred by arrogance or servility, by envy or greed, by anxious care of feverish ambition, and stately forms of men and women who had never known fear of a fellow man or depended on his favor, but always, in the words of that sermon which still ran in my ears, had "stood up straight before God."

With a profound sigh and a sense of irreparable loss, not the less poignant that it was loss of what had never really been, I roused at last from my reverie, and soon after left the house. . . .

A dozen times between my door and Washington Street I had to stop and pull myself together, such power had been in that vision of the Boston of the future to make the real Boston strange. The squalor and malodorousness of the town struck me, from the moment I stood upon the street, as facts I had never before observed. . . .

Whether the pathos or the moral repulsiveness of the spectacle most impressed me, so suddenly become a stranger in my own city, I know not. Wretched men, I was moved to cry, who, because they will not learn to be helpers of one another, are doomed to be beggars of one another from the least to the greatest! This horrible babel of shameless self-assertion and mutual depreciation, this stunning clamor of conflicting boasts, appeals, and adjurations, this stupendous system of brazen beggary, what was it all but the necessity of a society in which the opportunity to serve the world according to his gifts, instead of being secured to every man as the first object of social organization, had to be fought for!

Source: Edward Bellamy, *Looking Backward,* http://xroads.virginia.edu (accessed February 21, 2007).

QUESTIONS

1. What particular events upset the narrator upon reading the paper that day?
2. What hints do you get in this excerpt of what Bellamy would like the future to look like?
3. What do you think made Bellamy's notion of cooperation so appealing for its time?

Document 6: Ida B. Wells
The Remedy (1895)

Ida B. Wells challenged injustice wherever she saw it, using her writings to arouse others to get involved in the struggle for equality. By documenting the many cases of lynching in this era and refuting the excuses, she brought attention to an issue that symbolized the continued subjugation of the African American population after slavery. The excerpt below from her book, *The Red Record*, is based on tabulated statistics involving the lynching of blacks in the South.

*I*t is a well-established principle of law that every wrong has a remedy. Herein rests our respect for law. The Negro does not claim that all of the one thousand black men, women and children, who have been hanged, shot and burned alive during the past ten years, were innocent of the charges made against them. We have associated too long with the white man not to have copied his vices as well as his virtues. But we do insist that the punishment is not the same for both classes of criminals. In lynching, opportunity is not given the Negro to defend himself against the unsupported accusations of white men and women. The word of the accuser is held to be true and the excited bloodthirsty mob demand that the rule of law be reversed and instead of proving the accused to be guilty, the victim of their hate and revenge must prove himself innocent. No evidence he can offer will satisfy the mob; he is bound hand and foot and swung into eternity. Then to excuse its infamy, the mob almost invariably reports the monstrous falsehood that its victim made a full confession before he was hanged.

With all military, legal and political power in their hands, only two of the lynching States have attempted a check by exercising the power which is theirs. Mayor Trout, of Roanoke, Virginia, called out the militia in 1893, to protect a Negro prisoner, and in so doing nine men were killed and a number wounded. Then the mayor and militia withdrew, left the Negro to his fate and he was promptly lynched. The business men realized the blow to the town's (sic) were given light sentences, the highest being one of twelve financial interests, called the mayor home, the grand jury indicted and prosecuted the ringleaders of the mob.... The day he arrived at the penitentiary he was pardoned by the governor of the State.

The only other real attempt made by the authorities to protect a prisoner of the law, and which was more successful, was that of Gov. McKinley, of Ohio, who sent the militia to Washington Courthouse, O., in October, 1894, and five men were killed and twenty wounded in maintaining the principle that the law must be upheld....

... [W]e demand a fair trial by law for those accused of crime, and punishment by law after honest conviction. No maudlin sympathy for criminals is solicited, but we do ask that the law shall punish alike. We earnestly desire those that control the forces which make public sentiment to join with us in the demand. Surely the humanitarian spirit of this country which reaches out to denounce the treatment of the Russian Jews, the Armenian Christians, the laboring poor of Europe, the Siberian exiles and the native women of India—will no longer refuse to lift its voice on this subject. If it were known that the cannibals or the savage Indians had burned three human beings alive in the past two years, the whole of Christendom would be roused, to devise ways and means to put a stop to it. Can you remain silent and inactive when such things are done in our own community and country? Is your duty to humanity in the United States less binding?

What can you do, reader, to prevent lynching, to thwart anarchy and promote law and order throughout our land?

...You can be instrumental in having churches, missionary societies, Y.M.C.A.'s, W.T.C.U.'s and all Christian and moral forces in connection with your religious and social life, pass resolutions of condemnations and protest every time a lynching takes place; and see that they are sent to the place where these outrages occur.

Bring to the intelligent consideration of the Southern people the refusal of capital to invest where lawlessness and mob violence hold sway. Many labor organizations have declared by resolution that they would avoid lynch infested localities as they would the pestilence when seeking new homes.... "Equality before the law," must become a fact as well as a theory before America is truly the "land of the free and the home of the brave."

Think and act on independent lines in this behalf remembering that after all, it is the white man's civilization and the white man's government which are on trial. This crusade will determine whether that civilization can maintain itself, or whether anarchy shall prevail; whether this Nation shall write itself down a success at self government, or in deepest humiliation admit its failure complete; whether the precepts and theories of Christianity are professed and practiced by American white people as Golden Rules of thought and action, or adopted as a system of morals to be preached to, heathen until they attain to the intelligence which needs the system of Lynch Law....

The belief has been constantly expressed in England that in the United States, which has produced Wm[William] Lloyd Garrison, Henry Ward Beecher, James Russell Lowell, John G. Whittier and Abraham Lincoln there must be those of their descendants who would take hold of the work of inaugurating an era of law and order. The colored people of this country who have been loyal to the flag believe the same, and strong in that belief have begun this crusade. . . .

Source: Ida B. Wells-Barnett, *The Red Record: Tabulated Statistics and Alleged Causes of Lynching in the United States* (1895), cited in http://www.gutenberg.org (accessed February 13, 2009).

QUESTIONS

1. How does Wells propose to use American law as an instrument of justice in the South?
2. In making her case against lynching, how does she compare the nation's position regarding fair treatment of peoples from other parts of the world to what was going on in the South?
3. What must readers of her work do to bring about an end to lynching? What patriotic plea does she invoke and what notable Americans does she name in the interest of justice?

Document 7:   Black Elk
At Wounded Knee (1890)

Black Elk was born into the Oglala Lakota tribe. He became an important Sioux visionary and religious leader. Native Americans did not write down their history, but Black Elk passed on his vision to writer John G. Neihardt, giving us a rare glimpse of the Indian view of the late nineteenth century. In 1932 Neihardt published Black Elk's oral narrative as *Black Elk Speaks*. The excerpt below highlights the horror and significance of the incident that took place at Wounded Knee.

*W*hen we drove the soldiers back, they dug themselves in, and we were not enough people to drive them out from there. In the evening they marched off up Wounded Knee Creek, and then we saw all that they had done there. Men and Women and Children were heaped and scattered all over the flat at the bottom of the little hill where the soldiers had their wagon-guns, and westward up the dry gulch all the way to the high ridge, the dead women and children and babies were scattered. When I saw this I wished that I had died too, but I was not sorry for the women and children. It was better for them to be happy in the other world, and I wanted to be there too. . . .

. . . I did not know how much was ended. When I look back now from this high hill of my old age, I can still see the butchered women and children lying heaped and scattered all along the crooked gulch as plain as when I saw them with eyes still young. And I can see that something else died there in the bloody mud and was buried in the blizzard. A people's dream died there. It was a beautiful dream. . . .

Source: John G. Neihardt. *Black Elk Speaks: Being the Life Story of a Holy Man of the Oglala Sioux, The Premier Edition.* Albany: State University of New York Press, 2008, pp. 210, 218.

QUESTIONS

1. Does Black Elk describe a battle or a massacre? Explain your answer.
2. In Black Elk's view, why were these events so decisive?
3. Why does Black Elk say he wished he had died at Wounded Knee?

Document 8:   Address of Rev. F. B. Allen (1902)

Among the many ministers who delivered addresses at the Lake Mohonk Conferences, Rev. Allen was among the most effective. He took a creative approach, satirically taking on the romantic attachment to veterans' groups like the Grand Army of the Republic. He also questioned the true meaning of Decoration Day (now Memorial Day) and how that day should really be celebrated.

Mr. Chairman, Ladies and Gentlemen:

I have here the account of a catechism or primer of patriotism prepared by the Grand Army of the Republic in Massachusetts. It has been sent to two or three hundred schools. Thirty or forty thousand copies of this primer have been printed, and they are to be used tomorrow in the Decoration Day exercise. This is a "Primer of Patriotism;" and what do you suppose is the first question which all these boys and girls are to be asked, and are supposed to answer? I will read it to you, with a few of the subsequent questions and answers.

> *Ques.* What is the first "position" of a soldier?
> *Ans.* Erect, feet firmly placed, heels touching, toes spreading slightly outward, the shoulders thrown back, eyes to the front.
> *Ques.* Why are these things required?
> *Ans.* That he may be in the best form to give attention.
> *Ques.* What is the first "duty" of the soldier?
> *Ans.* Obedience.
> *Ques.* What kind of obedience?
> *Ans.* Quick and unquestioning obedience.
> *Ques.* Why is this demanded?
> *Ans.* Because good order can be had in no other way.
> *Ques.* What is patriotism?
> *Ans.* Love of one's country and willingness to make sacrifices for it.
> *Ques.* Why should American boys and girls be patriots?
> *Ans.* Because they have a better chance to make the most of themselves than any children in the world.
> *Ques.* What organization today makes a specialty of teaching patriotism?
> *Ans.* The Grand Army of the Republic.

Now, my friends, there is not one of us here but would be glad tomorrow to lay his laurel wreath upon the graves of the brave soldiers who fought in the great War of the Rebellion. There are none of us but hold in honor the dwindling survivors of the great army of the North that fought for the Union, and yet among those survivors there are some men of even like passions with ourselves; and when we remember the record of the Grand Army of the Republic toward the question of pensions, we may hesitate to take them as the exclusive teachers of disinterested patriotism.

But what I wish to say especially is this: When it comes to teaching boys and girls we must remember the fascination of the flag and the uniform and the drum beat, and we are to think how to teach them patriotism in peace. I believe that the instinct of fight, the competitive instinct, is something not to be eradicated; I believe God plants no great passion, no primary instinct, in our humanity merely to be wiped out. I believe it is to be spiritualized, it is to be consecrated, and we are bound to train this very fighting instinct and aim it against the forces of evil.

We must not talk of passive virtues or of peace as if that were everything. The very same valor which our honored President showed at San Juan he showed for very many years in the great Civil Service Reform contest. We must teach our boys and girls to fight the forces of evil within our own boundaries. Even our peace-loving host is not ashamed to borrow a military bugle to summon us to breakfast. We are to take what has been the charm of militarism and we are to consecrate it to peace and to internal conflicts which are more constant than those of the battlefield. . . .

I am perfectly sure that there needs to be trained, not for bloodshed, but for determined, strenuous, constant conflict against the forces of evil,—there needs to be trained a certain fighting instinct. I hope we shall in our schools train our children to know that there is a battle for them to fight against the spoils system, against municipal corruption, against race hostility and class prejudice; a battle against intemperance and lust.

We have plenty of foes to fight, and we have got to teach our children to feel that that is the *great* battle, and that is where that glory of fighting is going to be; that our flag stands not for carnage and bloodshed, but for purity and duty and honor and all that is noble and high in our country's career.

Source: "Address of Rev. F.B. Allen." The Lake Mohonk Arbitration Conference, 1902, pp. 54–56.

QUESTIONS

1. How should children be taught about peace, according to Rev. Allen?
2. How do Rev. Allen's views about patriotism contrast with those he presents in "the primer of patriotism prepared by the Grand Army"? Be sure to use examples from the document to support your answer.
3. Compare Rev. Allen's ideas with those of Hannah J. Bailey and Henry David Thoreau.

Document 9:   David Starr Jordan
The U.S. Conquest of the Philippines (1899)

David Starr Jordan, the first president of Stanford University, was a noted spokesperson for the peace movement at the turn of the twentieth century and would later play an influential role in the World Peace Foundation. Like many of his colleagues in the Anti-Imperialist League, he questioned the moral reasoning behind the U.S. government's suppression of the Filipino drive for independence. For him, the United States was simply supplanting Spain and imposing its own imperialist designs on the Far East.

I wish to maintain a single proposition. We should withdraw from the Philippine Islands as soon as . . . we can. It is bad statesmanship to make these alien people our partners; it is a crime to make them our slaves. . . .

Why do we want the Philippines? What can we do with them? What will they do to us?

. . . By the fortunes of war the capital of the Philippines Islands fell, last May, into the hands of our navy. . . . Our final treaty of peace has assigned to us the four hundred or fourteen hundred islands . . . to these we have yet no real title. We can get none till the actual owners have been consulted. We have a legal title of course, but no moral title . . . for the right to finish the conquest of the Philippines and to close out the insurrection which has gone on for almost a century we have agreed on our part to pay $20,000,000 in cash for the people . . . and the land which they have cultivated. . . . The price is too high . . . when we observe that the failure of Spain placed the Islands not in our hands but in the hands of their own people, a third party, whose interests we . . . have as yet failed to consider. Emilio Aguinaldo, the liberator of the Filipinos, the "Washington of the Orient," is the *de facto* ruler of most of the territory. In our hands is the city of Manila, alone, and we cannot extend our power except by bribery or by force. . . .

We know nothing of Philippine matters, save through cablegrams passed through government censorship . . . the Filipinos are not rebels against law and order but against alien control. . . . We may easily destroy the organized army of the Filipinos but that does not bring peace. In the cliffs and jungles, they will defy us for a century as they have defied Spain. . . .

I cannot see one valid reason why we should want them, nor any why they should want us.... Our philanthropy is less than skin deep.... I am sure that their possessions can in no wise help us, not even financially or commercially....

The idea that every little nation must be subject to some great one is one of the most contemptible products of military commercialism.... If we behave honorably towards the people we have freed, we shall set a fashion which the powers will never dare to violate.

Source: Charles Chatfield and Ruzanna Illukhina, eds. *Peace/Mir: An Anthology of Historic Alternatives to War.* Syracuse, NY: Syracuse University Press, 1994, pp. 127–128.

QUESTIONS

1. What are Jordan's main objections to U.S. conquest of the Philippines?
2. Jordan states that "the idea that every little nation must be subject to some great one is one of the most contemptible products of military commercialism." What does he mean by this?
3. Does Jordan look down on the Filipino people or see them as equals?

Document 10: Mark Twain
The War Prayer (1904)

Mark Twain, author of such noted works as *Huckleberry Finn* and *Tom Sawyer,* is considered one of America's greatest writers. Twain's optimism vanished in the era of industrialization and expansionism. At the end of the century, when the United States began to create an overseas empire, Twain became a member of the Anti-Imperialist League. His "War Prayer," written after the end of the war in the Philippines and time spent in Europe, was not published until after his death in 1904.

*I*t was a time of great and exalting excitement. The country was up in arms, the war was on, in every breast burned the holy fire of patriotism....

Sunday morning came—next day the battalions would leave for the front; the church was filled . . . ; The service proceeded; a war chapter from the Old Testament was read; the first prayer was said; it was followed by an organ burst that shook the building, and with one impulse the house rose, with glowing eyes and beating hearts, and poured out that tremendous invocation—

"God the all-terrible! Thou who ordainest,
Thunder thy clarion and lighting thy sword!" . . .

An aged stranger entered and moved with slow and noiseless step up the main aisle, his eyes fixed upon the minister, his long body clothed in a robe that reached to his feet, his head bare, his white hair descending in a frothy cataract to his shoulders, his seamy face unnaturally pale, pale even to ghastliness. With all eyes following him and wondering, he made his silent way; without pausing, he ascended to the preacher's side and stood there, watching. With shut lids the preacher . . . continued his moving prayer, and . . . uttered in feverent appeal, "Bless our arms, grant us the victory, O Lord our God, Father and Protector of our land and flag!"

The stranger touched his arm, motioned him to step aside . . . and took his place. During some moments he surveyed the spell-bound audience with solemn eyes . . . ; then in a deep voice he said:

"I come from the Throne—bearing a message from Almighty God!" The words smote the house with shock; if the stranger perceived it he gave no attention. "He has heard the prayer of His servant your shepherd and will grant it if such shall be your desire after I, His messenger, shall have explained to you its import—that is to say, its full import. . . ."

"When you have prayed for victory you have prayed for many unmentioned results which will follow victory—*must* follow it, cannot help but follow it. . . . He commandeth me to put it into words. Listen!

"O Lord our Father, our young patriots, idols of our hearts go forth to battle—be Thou near them! With them, in spirit, we also go forth from the sweet peace of our beloved firesides to smite the foe. O Lord our God, help us to tear their soldiers to bloody shreds with our shells, help us to cover their smiling fields with the pale forms of their patriotic dead; help us to drown the thunder of the guns with the shrieks of their wounded, writing in pain; help us to lay waste their humble homes with a hurricane of fire; help us to wring the hearts of their unoffending widows with unavailing grief; help us to turn out roofless with their little children to wander unfriended the wastes of their desolate land in rags and hunger and thirst, sports of the sun flames of summer and the icy winds of winter, broken in spirit, worn with travail, imploring Thee for the refuge of the grave and denied it—for our sakes who adore Thee, Lord, blast their hopes, blight their lives, protract their bitter pilgrimage, make heavy their steps, water their way with their tears, stain the white snow with the blood of their wounded feet! We ask it, in the spirit of love, of Him Who is the Source of Love, and Who is the ever-faithful refuge and friend of all that are sore beset and seek His aid with humble and contrite hearts. Amen...."

Source: Bernard DeVoto, ed. *The Portable Mark Twain.* New York: Viking Press, 1966, pp. 579–584.

QUESTIONS

1. Why did Twain choose to use a religious metaphor in his discussion of war?
2. Does his use of satire seem an effective method of getting people to think more critically about the meaning of patriotism?
3. Draw a picture that could accompany the "unmentioned results" discussed by the stranger.

4

Early Twentieth-Century Peace Efforts and a "Modern" Movement

By the close of the nineteenth century the country was at a critical turning point. More and more Americans were now living in cities and earning their bread in factories, mines, and mills. Yet ninety-nine percent of the nation's wealth rested in the hands of only one percent of the population, according to Henry George's popular work *Progress and Poverty*. The bitter class conflict of the 1890s demonstrated that growing numbers of American workers were not happy with the effects of rapid industrialization, which pitted workers against each other in a struggle for economic security. Intense efforts to promote social and economic justice from the ranks of labor—including immigrants and racial minorities—made up one wing of the peace movement. This group worked from the premise that vast inequality was a recipe for ongoing violence.

In this age of expanding commercialism, social Darwinism, and imperial domination, wealthy elites promoted international peace to protect their own interests. Thus it was that another wing of the peace movement, concerned mainly with international affairs, was marked by its pragmatic approach. The leadership of this group came from businessmen and philanthropists such as Andrew Carnegie, influential lawyers like Elihu Root, and educational administrators such as Columbia University president Nicholas Murray Butler. Under their direction, international peacemaking became devoted to the legal settlement of disputes and the scientific study of war and its alternatives. Between 1901 and 1914, forty-five new peace organizations appeared, representing a strong interest in this approach. Among the most influential were the American Society of International Law, the Carnegie Endowment for International Peace, and the World Peace Foundation. These specialized agencies aimed to transmit the experts' knowledge of peace to others and encourage more conciliatory relations among governments.

By the first decade of the twentieth century, international peacemaking had gained considerable recognition as a respectable calling, having secured the allegiance of many of the country's academic, religious, business, and political leaders. Yet very few members in this wing of the movement subscribed to the more far-reaching position that sought the eradication of all forms of violence within the socioeconomic structure. The vast majority of these peace supporters considered war prevention a matter of international relations, and they ignored workers, socialists, and pacifists who argued that rival imperialisms were a primary cause of war and that there was a strong relationship between peace and economic justice.

In the eyes of the wealthy and social elite who dominated the drive for world peace for a short period, the peace movement was not an antiwar crusade either. They were not campaigning against the idea of defensive war, or, for that matter, against the use of force as an instrument of national policy. Instead, they couched their arguments for world peace in terms of a pro-law movement—one seeking to promote the nonidealistic mechanisms of arbitration, courtroom justice, and, if possible, world federation backed by the rules of international law.

A variety of motives brought these elites to the peace movement. In line with historian Richard Hofstadter's characterization of progressive reformers as "status quo Revolutionists," some joined as a matter of civic responsibility. Others saw it as a means to greater social stature. And then there were those who considered the peace crusade a placid, uncontroversial commitment without serious obligations aside from a generous donation or two.

Others were attracted out of a desire to defend the country's recently acquired position in the world. Between the conquest of the Philippines and the start of World War I, U.S. overseas investments multiplied fivefold;

for the first time, the American government was extending rather than receiving credit in large amounts. American elites sought a stable international order. Long convinced of the moral superiority of the United States, they doubted the capacity and goodwill of the international order's chief custodians—the European powers with their cabinet politics and secret diplomacy. They distrusted the balance of power system, believing it to be inherently unstable. How could the United States retain its purity and at the same time enjoy wealth and power, all without becoming involved in the crises generated regularly by the international system? As a vehicle for expressing their concerns and in terms of practical policies, the peace movement, rightly conceived, held the promise in their view of permitting Americans to have the best of both worlds.

The years prior to 1914, largely inspired by The Hague Peace Conferences of 1899 and 1907, were filled with ambitious and energetic peacemakers willing to compromise with ideological opponents in the quest for international order. Business leaders, in particular, were most supportive of peacemakers trumpeting the call for world peace based on international law (**Document 1**). Among the new peace societies that emerged were the American Association for International Conciliation and the American Society for the Judicial Settlement of International Disputes. Aided by society's upper crust, these new organizations reflected the peace movement's new dimensions, respectability and a judicial approach to international disputes. One of the more notable supporters of the idea of an international police force was Lucia Ames Mead, a leader in the women's peace movement. In her view, peace depended on educational awareness and the enforcement of law through the World Court (**Document 2**).

Inevitably, the rapid expansion of peace societies produced demands for improved organizational coordination. Most practical peace leaders, distinguished by their solid social credentials—northeastern metropolitan lawyers, government officials, and industrialists—were determined to avoid moral preachments and establish more efficient peace-seeking machinery. Sensitive to the spirit of organizational efficiency that characterized this era, these "practicalists" began calling for ways of aligning the activities of the burgeoning peace movement with their own views and dispositions.

One of the most recognizable efforts in this regard was undertaken by steel magnate Andrew Carnegie, who contributed $10 million in United States Steel Corporation bonds in December 1910 toward the formation in New York of the Carnegie Endowment for International Peace (**Document 3**). Carnegie had made part of his fortune by the sale of naval armor plate— some actually of an inferior quality produced during the Cleveland Administration. At the same time as he mercilessly exploited workers in his steel mills, resorting to violence to prevent them from organizing unions, he directed Carnegie Endowment officers to quickly bring an end to world war, which he considered the "foulest blot" on civilized society. The Carnegie Foundation was ably led by Elihu Root as president, Nicholas Murray Butler as head of the Division of Intercourse and Education (he succeeded Root as president in 1925), John Bates Clark as head of the Division of Economics and History, and James Brown Scott as head of the Division of International Law.

Carnegie, who already had spent more than $2 million for the Church Peace Union and $1.5 million toward the building of the great Peace Palace at The Hague, was anxious to immortalize his own name under the banner for peace. "What am I good for, anyhow?" he once asked his British friend Lord Morley. "If I'm not willing to sacrifice myself for the cause of peace, for what would I sacrifice?" The Carnegie Endowment became his philanthropic sacrifice for peace. He was delighted to witness the way the endowment was organized. The three divisions were testimony to the professionalism of peace "experts."

Each division had its own special task. The Division of Intercourse and Education was created to maintain agencies throughout the world in order to gather information about international policies and to promote international goodwill; under Butler's direction, the division arranged for the exchange of eminent scholars and writers among nations. The Division of Economics and History sponsored studies of the conditions—political, social, and economic—that fostered peace and war, and suggested methods of action. Clark's division encouraged intellectuals to draw upon its findings in accumulating more evidence for their writings against war. The Division of International Law tried to extend the law of nations to all disputes that arose between countries. This division disseminated information on the rights and responsibilities of nations under existing international law and promoted periodic international conferences to amplify and codify that law.

Carnegie's well-managed foundation best typified the practical, elitist, establishment-oriented approach to peace. Reluctant to subsidize peace societies per se, the endowment spent its money on only the safest peace proposals, and its twenty-seven trustees were very conservative in domestic affairs. Nevertheless, the Endowment was guided by a scholarly desire to encourage international goodwill and world peace through an appeal to the intellectual elite of all lands. Seeking to establish a "veritable Faculty of Peace," the popular endowment not only sponsored interchanges of American and foreign professors, but built up an admirable research library, collecting all the scholarly works on the development of international law, the causes of war, and past records of peace efforts.

Businessmen were not alone in seeking out practical roads toward a more peaceful world. One of the most significant peace proposals of this era was philosopher William James's "Moral Equivalent of War" (**Document 4**). James argued for creating a peaceful society by turning the energy of young men toward more constructive pursuits than war. Rather than being conscripted for military service, male youths would serve in an army of economic and industrial builders. James, a Harvard professor and pioneer in the field of pragmatism, believed the impulse for heroism through "individual sacrifice for the tribal good" was a basic instinct that guided men's behavior. (He did not concern himself with women.) Reacting to the manliness and physical vigor demanded by war, James "developed a counterweight" by providing what he called the "moral equivalent of war," encompassing the military virtues of "intrepidity, contempt of softness, surrender of private interest, [and] obedience to command." As a substitute for military conscription, he urged the drafting of all youth to form for several years an "army enlisted against nature," which would labor in coal and iron mines, build roads and tunnels, and construct the frames of skyscrapers, among other chores. James's essay was a topic of hot debate, and his idea later formed the basis for the creation of the Civilian Conservation Corps during the Great Depression of the 1930s.

Another approach to peacemaking, which generally receives less recognition, came from socialists in the labor movement. Industrialization brought people to urban areas to work in factories, and this coincided with the emigration of hundreds of thousands of workers from Europe, who came to America in search of a better life. Low wages, dangerous working conditions, and lack of job security led to conflicts between groups of workers but also to efforts to organize unions. Employers resisted such attempts to organize immigrant and native workers, oftentimes by force, due to the ingrained cultural belief in the system of private ownership and the "gospel of wealth," which justified vast inequality. Confrontation between labor and the captains of industry had been ongoing since the late nineteenth century. In a twenty-four-year period, 1881 to 1905, there were more than 37,000 recorded strikes. Many were bitter and bloody. Employers met attempts to unionize workers by firing employees, blacklisting them so they could not get another job, and employing private armies to use violence against them. Brute force was carried out not only by well-armed company guards but also by police deputies and National Guardsmen. A number of workers lost their lives or were imprisoned during such confrontations as the Homestead and Pullman strikes in the 1890s. Thoughtful observers believed the great concentration of wealth threatened individual liberties and denied opportunity to hard-working people. Many were fearful of a growing militarization of society as captains of industry employed guards armed with rifles and machine guns to put down strikes and unions. Immigrant and homegrown socialists sharply criticized the ruthlessness of American capitalism and some developed their own plan for peace, which they saw as an evolutionary process toward greater equality that would come via the ballot box and the organization of workers into unions.

Socialists reached the height of their influence in the United States between 1900 and 1914, succeeding in electing many state and local officials and in challenging low wages and dangerous working conditions that prevented industrial workers from supporting their families, much less living dignified, full lives. While some believed a violent revolution would be necessary to change their conditions and overthrow an oppressive system, many others fought for justice using nonviolent methods. Thus, one of the most famous strikes of this era took place in Lawrence, Massachusetts, where textile workers from a large variety of ethnic groups fought against cuts in wages and a "speed up" in their work. Many of the mill workers were women and children, who worked under difficult conditions, suffered many accidents, and died young. One reason this strike stood out was the deliberate attention to nonviolence. Strike organizers trained workers in the use of nonviolence, organizing them in their native languages whenever possible. Women played a central role in making the strike a success. Even police beatings of pregnant women did not break their solidarity and determination. It was a testament to the women that the song "Bread and Roses" came to be associated with this strike (**Document 5**).

Acquiring political power and using it to benefit workers was an important part of the socialists' vision. The Socialist Party of America was founded in 1901, but its origins date back to the 1880s and 1890s with the rise of labor and social protests by workers sympathetic to socialism. In the aftermath of the Pullman Car Strike in Chicago in 1893, union leader Eugene Debs successfully merged his followers from the American Railway Union and the Social Democrats of America with disaffected members of the more radical Socialist Labor Party. With the collapse of the Socialist Labor Party, Debs managed to solidify his hold over labor socialists and in 1900 ran for president of the United States. Although Debs and his fellow socialists were wrong in their belief that capitalism would be overthrown via the ballot box—in his five runs for president, Debs polled the most votes in 1912, six percent of the national total—they did succeed in establishing a homegrown political party with socialist roots.

Debs and the Socialist Party carried forward the nineteenth-century idea of the "cooperative commonwealth," believing that peace would be one result of class solidarity and economic justice, which would cross national borders. Debs, in particular, personified native protest against the forces of industrial capitalism that dehumanized the workplace and undermined individual self-worth. To socialist leaders like Debs, socialism and democracy were not incompatible. Their immediate focus was on advancing the rights of American workers, while giving them more of a voice in politics. While philosophically opposed to the whole system of private ownership, Debs did not envisage violent revolution. In fact, he spoke out against individual terrorism and acts of sabotage. His commitment to justice symbolized best the socialists' effort to create an environment receptive to international worker solidarity. The Socialist Party's efforts to prevent U.S. entry into World War I failed, but party members continued to lead opposition to the war and the draft, though they were attacked from without and wracked by dissension within (**Document 6**).

Despite labor's criticisms of a capitalistic war, growing nationalism, militarism, imperial conflict, and an alliance system enabled the assassination in 1914 of Archduke Franz Ferdinand, heir to the throne of Austria-Hungary, at Sarajevo to spark what we now call World War I. Europe experienced the worst bloodbath humankind had ever encountered. Almost ten million people lost their lives. With the use of tanks, 75's (large cannons first introduced in France), submarines, machine guns, and poison gas, modern technology proved its effectiveness in killing soldiers in unprecedented numbers.

Clearly the forces of nationalism had proved more effective in mobilizing people than the weight of moral opinion against war. World War I placed American peace apostles in an untenable position, as citizens were mobilized to support their country's war effort. Ultimately, a great majority of prewar peace workers abandoned their interest in practical peacemaking mechanisms and followed the flag into defending a war allegedly fought "to make the world safe for democracy."

Still, a number of activists and intellectuals attempted to keep the peace vision alive. When the limitations of the practical peace organizers became apparent, a new coalition was formed—opposed to the preparedness campaign being waged in America during the years 1914 to 1916. This coalition of feminists, social workers, and Social Gospel clergymen (led by turn-of-the-century Protestant ministers such as Walter Rauschenbusch who contrasted the teachings of Jesus with the materialism of modern society and urged a nonviolent socialist movement) joined to form an antipreparedness, or antimilitarist, campaign. John Haynes Holmes—a noted Unitarian minister who later would play a role in the Outlawry of War crusade during the 1920s—was in the forefront condemning war as sin and supporting a campaign against possible conscription (**Document 7**).

From this debate would emerge the modern peace movement, a movement that unequivocally understood peace in terms of social justice rather than surface order. Leaders of the new movement understood international justice in terms of ameliorating social wrongs rather than court adjudication, valued cultural diversity rather than Anglo-Saxon exclusivity, and saw war as a byproduct of militarism, nationalism and imperialism rather than an outburst of mass ignorance. They sought a reformed and democratized international system in which responsible policymakers would manage peace through applied social justice.

One of the most important leaders in the "modern" movement was teacher and settlement house reformer Jane Addams. Her commitment to the twin causes of peace and social justice is evident in her lectures and writings as well as her activities. Before the outbreak of World War I, she had already published several books and articles on subjects ranging from unemployment insurance to child labor. Her first book, *Democracy and Social Ethics* (1902), became the clarion call to all progressive reformers. She suggested that business leaders and politicians could display social ethics by developing plans for meeting the social and economic needs of the lower classes in modern industrial society. This meant a redistribution of profits for the general welfare. Addams received high acclaim when her autobiography, *Twenty Years at Hull House*, appeared in 1910. In this work, she examined her own efforts to eliminate barriers between classes that were caused by industrialism and to promote harmony among all nationalities and races. Her notion of social ethics reverberated to the international sphere as well. It was her constant belief that all national leaders had a moral obligation to resolve economic and territorial disputes that could lead to war. The average citizen was not responsible for starting wars but was always called upon to fight them. She also insisted that war, supported under the false pretense of patriotic allegiance, would inevitably lead to adverse reactions at home (**Document 8**). During World War I, some government leaders questioned her patriotism, while her worst detractors labeled her "the most dangerous woman in America."

Addams was in the forefront in establishing a viable women's peace organization. On January 10, 1915, the Woman's Peace Party was launched in Washington, D.C., inspired by Addams, Anna Garlin Spencer, Carrie Chapman Catt, Lucia Ames Mead, and Charlotte Perkins Gilman. Prompted by

University of Wisconsin English professor Julia Grace Wales's proposal for a Conference of Neutral Nations, Addams led the way for a meeting of top pacifist women at The Hague that sought to end the war through neutral mediation. This action led to the formation of four women's peace groups growing out of World War I—the Women's International League for Peace and Freedom, the Women's Peace Union, the National Council for the Cure of War, and the Women's Peace Society.

Pacifist women argued against war from three distinct ideological positions that sometimes overlapped. First, they insisted that human life must be preserved. As nurturers of human life, they believed women were more sensitive than men. New England–based writer Agnes Ryan, as well as Jane Addams, strongly supported this conviction. Second, female peace activists like Lucia Ames Mead, Congresswoman Jeannette Rankin, and Florence Tuttle emphasized the humanitarian aspect of life. Countering the social Darwinist position of "survival of the fittest," these women asserted that each individual deserved the best quality of human life. The commercial appeal to war was base and denigrated the fundamental importance of humanitarianism. Third, and most importantly, the women in these peace societies asserted the ethical and moral distinctions between killing and preservation of life. The principle of respect for life was imperative above all else and any qualification to that belief would not be tolerated. For organizers Dorothy Detzer and Lillian Wald, the male argument favoring war or its preparation in order to protect the home—security for wife and children—had little to do with actual results in war. War, in fact, destroyed the happiness and security of families whose husbands were killed in battle. Thus, in disagreeing with the modern worldview as established by male rulers, and in delineating the women's peace movement in terms of political and cultural reform, female pacifists were more committed to the quality of life and well-being of all peoples. In their view, it was up to the women of the world to change men's minds regarding the necessity of war. Just as families settle disputes, so should nations. The actions and ideas of pacifist women, determined to have their voices heard, helped define the meaning and content of the modern peace movement.

Before the United States entered World War I, female peace activists spurred other attempts to keep America away from the fighting in Europe. Anti-preparedness efforts, for example, received a boost in April 1916 when members of both the Anti-Preparedness Committee and Anti-Enlistment League—including Tracy Mygatt, Jessie Wallace Hughan, Lillian Wald, and radical feminist Crystal Eastman—established the American Union against Militarism (forerunner of the American Civil Liberties Union). With close to 1,000 members in 22 cities and led by David Starr Jordan and Oswald

Garrison Villard, editor of *The Nation,* the Union raised $50,000 in a year-long campaign to fight plans for conscription. The organization distributed literature, petitioned legislators, and dispatched speakers across the country to rally adherents to the antiwar campaign.

Success was only temporary, however. In May 1916, Congress approved all administration requests for military preparedness. In the early stages of the European war, Wilson shared the widespread disposition of most Americans that the conflict was the inevitable result of the earlier years of militarism and imperialism of the great powers. Clinging to the American tradition of democracy, Wilson, at first, had opposed the demands for a re-armament program. He had been anxious to preserve American neutrality. But, by 1915 he began yielding to the pressure of preparedness advocates and called for a stronger army and navy. During his 1916 reelection campaign, his posture was clearly ambivalent. When he spoke for more arms, he did so in the language of pacifist progressives, and his slogan was "he kept us out of war." Yet when he marched in preparedness parades, he was in the front of the line. Leaders in the crusade for peace and social justice had put their trust and hope in Wilson's increased preparedness as a way to avoid U.S. entrance into the war. Only the most radical pacifists and socialists criticized Wilson's preparedness program as being incompatible with pacifist neutrality.

Even when the U.S. entered the war in 1917, many Americans continued to have doubts. A number of antiwar groups quickly surfaced once the declaration of war was approved by Congress. Along with other antiwar groups that had previously campaigned against drafting men into the military, the AUM became even more active in conducting a vigorous campaign against universal compulsory military training. Its efforts were now directed at slowing down the implementation of the Selective Service and Training Act of 1917.

Others who loudly protested and resisted conscription were socialists as well as the radical syndicalist Industrial Workers of the World. While some prominent socialists supported U.S. entry into the war, many more took the position that the war was a conflict waged by capitalists for capitalists, yet fought by workers who received no measure of economic justice. Socialists and IWW members carried out a vast majority of antiwar actions, even in the face of violent opposition to their protests. From a socialist perspective, workers were being forced to fight each other for a system that oppressed them. It was simply a matter of justice for which they cried out in their condemnation of this war.

Intellectuals and educators were even more divided in their opinions on the war. Of the more notable liberal thinkers in American society who supported the war, no one captured the public's attention more than John Dewey. Before American intervention, Dewey declared all forms of militarism "undemocratic, barbaric, and scholastically wholly unwise." Now he was looking for his own suit of armor. As a practicing pragmatist, widely recognized for his "child-centered" views on education and schooling, he reasoned that war might serve as a useful and efficient means for bringing about a democratically organized world order. Given the circumstances in 1917, he reasoned that war could not be separated from the system of power politics in international relations nor disconnected from the ends it sought to achieve. Although war, on the whole, was undesirable, it might nonetheless be made useful and educative, or so he thought.

Dewey and other progressive supporters of war underestimated the war's impact on the American psyche and the power of antidemocratic forces at work. If the war was being fought for social reform in Dewey's estimation, he was totally unprepared for the scathing attack Randolph Bourne leveled against his overly optimistic and misguided reasoning. For Bourne it was a time when innocence abruptly came to an end and idols who had trumpeted the virtues of progressive reform reached their twilight.

Bourne, one of Dewey's most brilliant students, turned the pro-war internationalist logic upside down. He was virtually alone in calling attention to the fact that many who shouted loudly in behalf of the freedom and democracy for which the Allies stood were contemptuous of democratic strivings in their own backyard. How was one to channel the "fierce urgencies" of the war into positive democratic outlets? To Bourne, the pro-war liberal internationalists overestimated the power of intelligence and underestimated the force of violence and irrationality (**Document 9**). Indeed, "war is the health of the state," Bourne asserted, giving people a sense of belonging and convincing them to cede independent thinking to the government even as it worked against their own best interests.

Despite the pressure to go along with the war (discussed below), there were many who accepted Bourne's indictment of it. Hard-core antiwar socialists, some urban intellectuals, and liberal pacifists continued to oppose the war. Their opposition took the form of both individual and organized resistance. Approximately four thousand draftees received conscientious objector status. Most of these went into noncombatant military service; 500 were court-martialed and imprisoned, 17 were sentenced to death but never executed, and 142 were given life terms but released by 1921. World War I prisoners of conscience included civil libertarian Roger Baldwin, who helped found the American Civil Liberties Union (1920), and socialist leader Eugene V. Debs. Jailed twice for war opposition and in prison during the election of 1920, Debs received nearly a million votes as the socialist candidate for president that year.

The heart and soul of antiwar (especially pacifist) opposition was, of course, conspicuously exemplified by the conscientious objectors. Apart from the 4,000 classified as conscientious objectors, approximately 20,873 were granted noncombatant classification by their local draft boards. Among them were various types of opponents of war: religious objectors—opposed to all wars and human killing; humanitarian or liberal objectors who believed that all men were brothers and that fraternal blood should not be shed; and political objectors—socialists, anarchists, and syndical-ists—who promoted an international revolution of the working class but who objected to participating in a "capitalist" war.

To be sure, the problem of conscientious objection was an old and difficult one. It raised the important question of the relationship between the state and an individual's conscience (**Document 10**). Unfortunately, the military was unprepared at first to handle the issue with humanitarian compassion. When the COs arrived at an army camp, the general practice was to get as many of them as possible to accept combatant duty by labeling them as cowards and shirkers and using all kinds of pressures to break their convictions. In some camps, they were jeered, hosed, and called cowards or yellow backs. Being beaten, starved, and placed in solitary confinement was a daily occurrence. Army officers often looked upon physical punishment and pressure as the best means of testing the genuineness and sincerity of a man's convictions. One of the more egregious examples of mistreatment involved Molokans, Christian pacifists who had emigrated from Russia, who were sent to Fort Leavenworth in October 1918. They were thrown into a hole where they were manacled to cell bars and forced to stand for nine hours each day. They were not allowed to receive or send mail. At Alca-traz, some nonresisters were placed in straitjackets and locked to a ball and chain in a dark, damp, dreary cell for five consecutive days. Two of them, brothers, eventually died after being transferred to Fort Leavenworth.

Many held firm. At Camp Upton, Long Island, an objector refused to obey orders and was struck and cut across the knees and shins repeatedly with a bayonet. For two hours, he was also beaten by guards with both their fists and their rifles. From other camps came similar reports of the objector versus the military. Those suffering the greatest indignities were absolute pacifists. A normal prison sentence for absolutists was from twenty to twenty-five years. One CO avoided execution by volunteering to retrieve wounded soldiers from the battlefield. It was not until November 1920 that all objectors were released from prison.

The government was slow to respond to pacifist criticisms. John Nevin Sayre, brother-in-law to one of President Wilson's daughters, an Episcopal priest, and a member of the Fellowship of Reconciliation, called upon the president to intervene on behalf of better treatment for COs. He provided the president with a list of abuses committed against imprisoned COs. After reading Sayre's documentation, the president immediately ordered all military personnel to cease and desist the application of inhumane treatment meted out by soldiers at federal prisons. Emphasizing the democratic nature of American society and its support for differing viewpoints, socialist clergyman Norman Thomas proclaimed that fair treatment and justice to conscientious objectors strengthens, not jeopardizes, democracy's security. In most instances, pacifists from the historic peace churches took it upon themselves to establish their own forms of noncombatant relief work. For example, Rufus Jones and Philadelphia-area Friends formed the American Friends Service Committee in April 1917. It was specifically created for engaging Quaker noncombatants in volunteer work in the areas of war relief and reconstruction. Numerous AFSC volunteers grew crops and rebuilt villages in war-torn France; after the war, they fought disease and famine in central Europe.

Meanwhile, organized resistance was carried out by antiwar socialists who were also interested in changing the basic values and power relations of their society. An important part of such advancement would be the abolition of war. Such feelings were elaborated upon in eloquent fashion by Debs. From almost the beginning of his career, Debs argued that modern wars were nurtured by economic competition and commercial rivalry among nations. The struggle for industrial world power feeds upon the drive for new markets, which, in turn, leads to further subjugation of workers. For Debs, war was medieval, barbaric, and nourished by superstition and patriotic paranoia. Workers, rather than letting the government and capitalists make cannon fodder of them, should band together and overthrow this unfortunate and terrible blight on mankind. Workers are the bleeding victims of war who possess enormous power as the one force capable of bringing about world peace. For speaking his conscience in an antiwar speech in Canton, Ohio, Debs drew a ten-year jail sentence for violation of the Espionage Act. In his address to the jury, he expressed his abhorrence of war, solidarity with the downtrodden, and belief in free speech (**Document 11**).

The notion of workers as particular victims of war also became the battle cry of the People's Council of Americans for Democracy and Peace. Tentatively organized on May 30, 1917, in New York City, and officially established in September of that year, this coalition of radicals, labor leaders, and bohemian intellectuals insisted that workers despised war, recognized it as a conspiracy against their own fundamental interests, and, sought brotherhood and cooperation with workers in other parts of the world. Some 20,000 people attended the People's Council's organizing rally held at Madison Square Garden. The Council's program was a direct response to the Russian Revolution: Russian workers threw down their weapons and refused to continue fighting against German workers.

The basic argument of the People's Council was socialist in tone. Its base of support came from various trade unions and the Socialist Party's left wing. It endorsed the Socialist Party's pledge to "continuous, active, and public opposition to the war." Modern wars, the Council argued, were spawned by the capitalist system. Under capitalism, industrial oppression is manifest; the worker is incapable of commanding wages for the full value of his labor. The accompanying unequal distribution of income meant that the owning class produced more goods than workers could afford to buy. The result was increased competition between the industrialized nations for empires, markets, and spheres of influence.

Overt government suppression of dissenting groups by state and federal court action ultimately checked the Council's support. By spring of 1918, almost one-third of the Council's leadership had been sentenced to federal prison. Meanwhile, with Wilson's approval, Postmaster General Albert S. Burleson barred from the mails all socialist antiwar publications, thereby cutting the intellectual lifeline of organized socialism in the United States and the largest single source of wartime opposition. The People's Council had been silenced.

African Americans added their own perspective to antiwar dissent. W.E.B. Du Bois, one of the leading black intellectuals of the twentieth century, argued early on that racism and colonialism were basic sources of war. In his essay, "Credo," first published in *The Independent* on October 6, 1904, and widely distributed throughout the world, Du Bois openly criticized militarism and war and called for global justice, equality, and world peace. In a *New York Times* editorial on December 12, 1909, and in another editorial entitled "Peace" appearing in the May 1913 issue of *The Crisis*, Du Bois maintained that the van of human progress must ride on the hopes for female emancipation, universal peace, political democracy, human brotherhood, and, most importantly, the socialization of wealth. However, once world war commenced, pressures for conformity and government efforts to unite the nation under the banner of patriotic loyalty proved too much even for Du Bois.

Eventually, many African Americans followed Du Bois's lead after he was pressured by President Wilson, supporting the war and putting black rights second to demonstrating their loyalty (a position for which they were not rewarded). But there was black opposition to the war. A good example is the monthly publication of *The Messenger*, a socialist periodical founded by Chandler Owen and A. Philip Randolph of the Brotherhood of Sleeping Car Porters, which questioned how the country could fight for democratic freedoms overseas while failing to bestow those rights on everyone at home (**Document 12**). *The Messenger* urged blacks not to fight, enlist, or be drafted into the army. Many African Americans believed that the war was started because nations like England, France, and Germany were fighting over the riches they could obtain from their colonial possessions and to see who would rule over the darker peoples of Africa and Asia. For Randolph the war was also about cheap labor. A socialist and pacifist, Randolph insisted that war was one way in which white capitalists could continue to oppress minorities and keep them from achieving economic equality.

The patriotic hysteria of World War I and its aftermath is unparalleled in American history, and many members of the various peace societies jumped enthusiastically on the caissons. Many others, however, remained firm in their convictions and suffered from both informal and governmental repression. Significantly, the greatest opposition to World War I was not a pacifist movement but a radical one. It taught pacifists to pay more attention to the long-neglected economic causes of war and diverted them from their prewar purity to a closer relationship with radical groups. The American Civil Liberties Union—founded in reaction to the wartime mockery of civil liberties—defended both religious and radical pacifists. New organizations replaced the American Peace Society, which now became a mere shell of its former self. The Fellowship of Reconciliation, War Resisters League, and Women's International League for Peace and Freedom maintained close relations with radical organizations and incorporated radical thought into their programs.

The wartime xenophobia, accurately noted by Randolph Bourne, destroyed the underpinnings of the "practical" peace movement. During World War I, the suppression of freedom enjoyed the almost unanimous support of the patriotic populace and the various agencies of the government—national, state, and local. Before the war was over, almost every major Socialist Party official had been indicted for antiwar activity. Enraged mobs had also cracked down on radical dissent everywhere, violently attempting to silence and destroy such groups as the IWW.

Perhaps most importantly, the inability of the organized peace movement to prevent mass killing and bloodshed on the field of battle strengthened its resolve and redefined its mission. Supporters of peace would regroup and reassess their strategies for building a more humane society. A new and stronger peace movement would emerge in the aftermath of the most devastating war in history to that time, a "modern" movement committed to domestic reform at home and eradication of war worldwide.

Document 1:   *The Business Man and International Law* (1911)

The May 1911 meeting of the Lake Mohonk Conference on International Arbitration featured a number of prominent educators, members of the clergy, and businesspeople. This "Business Men's Bulletin No. 10" emphasized the interest of business leaders in supplanting the system of war through international law and a world court. It was signed by eight prominent business leaders from New York, Philadelphia, Chicago, and Boston. The bulletin was taken from an article written by Harry E. Hunt, Esq., of Detroit.

There is at least one thing upon which business men agree. Commercial endeavor is best served when law is certain. This principle is universally recognized and of easy and usual application in domestic trade law. Its force is many times overlooked, however, in the broader fields of business activity even though there is infinitely greater reason for its recognition.

Whether or not one's business is large or small, domestic or foreign, it is affected by the uncertainty of international law. It works out this way. We manufacture and raise more goods and produce in eight months than we consume at home in twelve. The four months' surplus must be either exported or the home capacity for consumption greatly increased. Merchants who have secured foreign markets not only open the avenues to their own output, but by lessening the competition at home, materially assist the man whose business is local. Merchants who supply the home market are interested in an uninterrupted continuance of foreign exports, because any disturbance of foreign trade throws back upon this country goods which must be sold in direct competition with theirs. Therefore, whatever disturbs or embarrasses free commerce, such as war, internal revolution, fear of war or an uncertain international law is a detriment to all commercial activity. The wise businessman has taken the cue; he is considering the tomorrows of trade as well as the todays.

This tendency is best illustrated by comparing the texts of the two Hague Conferences. Read them. The first (1899) was dominated by the monarch and the moralist. Humane conventions predominated. But throughout the Second (1907) may be traced the influence of the business man. In defining and enlarging the rights of neutral nations and their commerce and shipping, it achieved a work second to none in the field of national endeavor. There is not a business man on the corners who does not profit by some one of its provisions.

No matter how steady the hand, how cool the nerve, how well known the flag, commercial predominance that depends upon battleships, coaling stations and state secrets is at best a thing temporary, containing within itself the germs of its own possible destruction. Gunboat government tends to lawless law. Is it any wonder that our private international law which feebly attempts to harmonize the rules of nations upon such topics as contracts and their interpretation, agency, judgments, bankruptcy, patents, etc., is languishing?

Now that business men realize that the people of other lands are prospective if not actual customers, now that they are thinking in terms of hemispheres, now that they see that successful domestic business leans upon a constant export trade, it is for them to place international relations upon a safe foundation—one that will make possible a certain, universal law. This means that they must discredit the war game no matter who stands ready and willing to play it. War and commercial certainty, like disgruntled litigants, are not on speaking terms.

There are plenty of existing agencies about which to rally in support of international arbitration, treaties of arbitration, international courts, conferences and other forces making for a better and more certain law of nations. The main thing is active cooperation for the desired end.

Source: "The Business Man and International Law." Bulletin No. 10. Lake Mohonk Conference on International Arbitration, May 24–26, 1911. New Paltz, NY: Lake Mohonk Conference, 1911, pp. 185–189.

QUESTIONS

1. According to the document, why should businessmen be concerned about peace?
2. Why is international law the best means to avoid war?
3. What is the role of government in ensuring peaceful trade between nations?

Document 2: Lucia Ames Mead
International Police (1903)

Lucia Ames Mead and her husband Edwin were active in the American Peace Society and leaders in the World Peace Foundation. One of the founders of the Woman's Peace Party in 1915, she served as its national secretary. Her views here represent the "practical" approach to peacemaking that was popular in the pre-World War I years. This piece was first published in the journal *Outlook* and was an outgrowth of her views expressed in May of that year at the Lake Mohonk meeting.

What would an international police do? It would bring stubborn nations to the World's Court with the same efficiency as the city police separate two men glaring at each other with murderous knives unsheathed, and drag them to the Police Court. Of what would the International Police be composed? Of a small body of armed men and battleships paid and organized by practically all the nations of the world and controlling them through a World Legislature which would make laws to be carried out by the Hague court. We have the Hague court. Next winter Congress will be asked to propose to the nations to establish an International Congress to meet at regular intervals to discuss international problems. This will not be a World Legislature, as its delegates will have, as at the Hague Conference, no power to do more than to refer questions to their nations for ratification.... It may be decades before it develops into a genuine Legislature with power. But a World Legislature is as definitely bound to come as the Isthmian [Panama] canal or the Cape to Cairo railroad. Not until it is established, and perhaps several decades after that, can we talk practically about forming an International Police; we must first, of course, all pledge ourselves to carry international differences to court. But though the period of complete national disarmament may be relegated to another century, it is of immense importance for the world to know that it is approximately near, that we need not wait until sin and quarrels have been banished from the earth before we find a rational way of treating them.

The police force will remain to bring men to court. The militia will remain to compel riotous mobs and lynchers to leave their quarrels and their vengeance to the courts. The international police will supplant the national, paid bodies of executioners who, under our present anarchic system of international relations, execute in absence of law, according to national whim or passion or prejudice. The reign of law has come in families, in cities, in the States, in the nations. It is coming between the nations. There is no new principle to be invented, simply the extension of an old and tried principle.

_____

Source: Lucia Ames Mead, "International Police," *Outlook* 74 (July 18, 1903): 705–706.

QUESTIONS

1. According to the document, what would the role of an international police force entail?
2. Why might Mead have believed a World Legislature was bound to come?
3. Based on Mead's views, how does an activist of peace justify the formation of an international police force backed by the use of arms?

Document 3:   Andrew Carnegie
A League of Peace (1905)

Born in Scotland but acquiring his wealth in America, Andrew Carnegie became one of the richest men of his time. His large fortune came mainly from the Carnegie Steel Corporation, later United States Steel. A firm believer in international harmony, Carnegie decided to give away a portion of his fortune to promote educational awareness of the importance of peace. In some respects, his initiative led to discussions that would later take shape in the form of the League of Nations.

*I*t may surprise you to learn that from the date of the Jay Treaty, one hundred and eleven years ago, no less than five hundred and seventy one international disputes have been settled by arbitration. Not in any case has an award been questioned or disregarded, except I believe in one case, where the arbiters misunderstood their powers. If in every ten of these differences so quietly adjusted without a wound, there lurked one war, it follows that peaceful settlement has prevented fifty-seven wars—one every two years. More than this, had the fifty-seven wars, assumed as prevented by arbitration, developed, they would have sown the seeds of many future wars....

Much has been written upon the fearful cost of war in our day, the ever-increasing blood tax of nations, which threatens soon to approach the point of exhaustion in several European lands....

The military and naval expenditure of Britain is fully half of her total expenditure; that of the other great Powers, though less, is rapidly increasing.

All the great national debts...are the legacies of war.

This drain, with the economic loss of life added, is forcing itself upon the nations concerned as never before. It threatens soon to become dangerous unless the rapid increase of recent years be stopped; but it is to be feared that not till after the financial catastrophe occurs will nations devote themselves seriously to apply the cure.

The futility of war as a means of producing peace between nations has often been dwelt upon. It is really the most futile of all remedies, because it embitters contestants and sows the seeds of future struggles.

Generations are sometimes required to eradicate the hostility engendered by one conflict.... [In] the recent terrible war just concluded [the Russo–Japanese War of 1904–1905]...neither contestant obtained what he fought for.... Such considerations find no place, however, in the fiery furnace of popular clamor; as little do those of cost or loss of life. Only if the moral wrong, the sin in itself, of man-slaying is brought home to the conscience of the masses may we hope speedily to banish war. There will, we fear, always be demagogies in our day to inflame their brutal passions and urge men to fight, as a point of honor and patriotism, scouting arbitration as a cowardly refuge. All thoughts of cost or loss of human life vanish when the brute in man, thus aroused, gains sway.

It is the crime of destroying human life by war and the duty to offer or accept peaceful arbitration as a substitute which needs to be established, and which, as we think, those of the Church, the Universities, and of the Professions are called upon to strongly emphasize.

...Five nations cooperated in quelling the recent Chinese disorders and rescuing their representatives in Peking. It is perfectly clear that these five nations could banish war. Suppose even three of them formed a League of Peace inviting all other nations to join and agreed that since war in any part of the civilized world affects all nations, and often seriously, no nation shall go to war, but shall refer international disputes to the Hague Conference or other arbitral body for peaceful settlement, the League agreeing to declare non-intercourse with any nation refusing compliance. Imagine a nation cut off today from the world. The League also might reserve to itself the right, where non-intercourse is likely to fail or has failed to prevent war, to use the necessary force to maintain peace, each member of the League agreeing to provide the needed forces, or money in lieu thereof, in proportion to her population or wealth. . . . Further provisions, and perhaps some adaptations, would be found requisite, but the main idea is here.

Source: John Whiteclay Chambers II, ed. *The Eagle and the Dove: The American Peace Movement and United States Foreign Policy, 1900–1922.* Syracuse, NY: Syracuse University Press, 1991, pp. 10–13.

QUESTIONS

1. According to Andrew Carnegie, what consequences befall a nation that does not utilize arbitration?
2. Why doesn't war lead to lasting peace in Carnegie's view?
3. What role(s) would the League of Peace play in preventing war?

Document 4: William James
The Moral Equivalent of War (1910)

William James was the author of numerous books and articles, including *Principles of Psychology* and *Varieties of Religious Experience.* Believing that martial virtues could be channeled in more constructive ways, the philosopher and psychologist called for an army that would perform civic works rather than fight in wars. This essay is a classic in the history of nonviolence.

*A*ll these beliefs of mine put me squarely into the antimilitarist party. But I do not believe that peace either ought to be or will be permanent on this globe, unless the states pacifically organized preserve some of the old elements of army discipline. A permanently successful peace economy cannot be a simple pleasure economy. In the more or less socialistic future toward which mankind seems to be drifting we must still subject ourselves collectively to those severities which answer to our real position upon this only partly hospitable globe. We must make new energies and…continue the manliness to which the military mind so faithfully clings. Martial virtues must be the enduring cement; intrepidity, contempt of softness, surrender of private interest, obedience to command, must still remain the rock upon which states are built—unless, indeed, we wish for dangerous reactions against commonwealths fit only for contempt and liable to invite attack whenever a center of crystallization for military-minded enterprise gets formed anywhere in their neighborhood.

The war party is assuredly right in affirming and reaffirming that the martial virtues, although originally gained by the race through war, are absolute and permanent human goods. Patriotic pride and ambition in their military form are, after all, only specifications of a more general competitive passion. They, are its first form, but that is no reason for supposing them to be its last form. Men now are proud of belonging to a conquering nation, and without a murmur they lay down their persons and their wealth, if by so doing they may fend off subjection. But who can be sure that other aspects of one's country may not, with time and education and suggestion enough, come to be regarded with similarly effective feelings of pride and shame? Why should men not someday feel that it is worth a blood tax to belong to a collectivity superior in any ideal respect? Why should they not blush with indignant shame if the community that owns them is vile in any way whatsoever? Individuals, daily more numerous, now feel this civic passion. It is only a question of blowing on the spark till the whole population gets incandescent, and on the ruins of the old morals of military honor, a stable system of morals of civic honor builds itself up. What the whole community comes to believe in grasps the individual as in a vise. The war function has grasped us so far; but constructive interests may someday seem no less imperative, and impose on the individual a hardly lighter burden.

Let me illustrate my idea more concretely. There is nothing to make one indignant in the mere fact that life is hard, that men should toil and suffer pain. The planetary conditions once for all are such, and we can stand it. But that so many men, by mere accidents of birth and opportunity, should have a life of nothing else but toil and pain and hardness and inferiority imposed upon them, should have no vacation, while others natively no more deserving never get any taste of this campaigning life at all—this is capable of arousing indignation in reflective minds. It may end by seeming shameful to all of us that some of us have nothing but campaigning, and others nothing but unmanly ease. If now—and this is my idea—there were, instead of military conscription a conscription of the whole youthful population to form for a certain number of years a part of the army enlisted against nature, the injustice would tend to be evened out, and numerous other goods to the commonwealth would follow. The military ideals of hardihood and discipline would be wrought into the growing fiber of the people; no one would remain blind as the luxurious classes now are blind, to man's relations to the globe he lives on, and to the permanently sour and hard foundations of his higher life. To coal and iron mines, to freight trains, to fishing fleets in December, to dish washing, clotheswashing and window-washing, to road-building and tunnel-making, to foundries and stokeholes, and to the frames of skyscrapers, would our gilded youths be drafted off, according to their choice, to get the childishness knocked out of them, and to come back into society with healthier sympathies and soberer ideas. They would have paid their blood tax, done their own part in the immemorial human warfare against nature; they would tread the earth more proudly, the women would value them more highly, they would be better fathers and teachers of the following generation.

Such conscription, with the state of public opinion that would have required it, and the many moral fruits it would bear, would preserve in the midst of a pacific civilization the manly virtues which the military party is so afraid of seeing disappear in peace. We should get toughness without callousness, authority with as little criminal cruelty as possible, and painful work done cheerily because the duty is temporary, and threatens not, as now, to degrade the whole remainder of one's life. I spoke of the "moral equivalent" of war. So far, war has been the only force that can discipline a whole community, and until an equivalent discipline is organized, I believe that war must have its way. But I have no serious doubt that the ordinary prides and shames of social man, once developed to a certain intensity, are capable of organizing such a moral equivalent as I have sketched, or some other just as effective for preserving manliness of type. It is but a question of time, of skilful propagandism, and of opinion-making men seizing historic opportunities.

The martial type of character can be bred without war. Strenuous honor and disinterestedness abound elsewhere. Priests and medical men are in a fashion educated to it, and we should all feel some degree of it imperative if we are conscious of our work as an obligatory service to the state. We should be owned, as soldiers are by the army, and our pride would rise accordingly. We could be poor, then, without humiliation, as army officers now are. The only thing needed henceforth is to inflame the civic temper as past history has inflamed the military temper.

Source: William James. "Moral Equivalent of War." First published in *McClure's Magazine* (August 1910).

QUESTIONS

1. What is James's philosophy in regard to war?
2. According to James, how could society put the concept of conscription to better use?
3. What are the "manly virtues" James sees as natural and worth developing?

Document 5:   James Oppenheim
Bread and Roses (1912)

Attempts to organize workers among the many ethnic groups in the United States met with stiff resistance by employers and state militias. Women workers were not exempt from oppressive working conditions and low wages. Inspired by the 1912 textile workers strike in Lawrence, Massachusetts, this song—based on a poem by James Oppenheim—speaks to the struggle for justice by and for women.

As we come marching, marching,
In the beauty of the day
A million darkened kitchens, a thousand mill-lofts gray
Are touched by all the radiance
That a sudden sun discloses
For the people hear us singing
Bread and Roses, Bread and Roses
As we come marching, marching, we battle too for men
For they are women's children
And we mother them again

Our lives shall not be sweated

From birth until life closes

Hearts starve as well as bodies, give us bread but give us roses

As we come marching, marching,

Unnumbered women dead

Go crying through our singing

Their ancient call for bread

Small art, or love, or beauty their drudging spirit knew

Yet it is bread we fight for but we fight for roses too

As we come marching, marching,

We bring the greater days

For the rising of the women

Means the rising of the race

No more the drudge and idler,

ten that toil where one reposes

But the sharing of life's glories, bread and roses,

Bread and roses

Source: "Bread and Roses" lyrics by James Oppenheim, 1912. Tune adapted by Mimi Farina, 1976, *Here's to the Women and the Liberated Woman's Songbook*, http://CreativeFolk.com (accessed February 4, 2009).

QUESTIONS

1. What do the "roses" symbolize?
2. How does this song convey the empowerment of women?
3. How does "the rising of the women" mean the rising of all humanity?

Document 6:   "Peace Program of the Socialist Party" (1915)

The Socialist Party ran Eugene Debs for president five times between 1900 and 1920. Debs's homegrown brand of socialism relied on organizing unions and electing socialists to public office in order to challenge existing power relations. The party issued its peace program after World War I broke out in Europe. It is an important declaration emphasizing the economic roots of war.

*T*he immediate causes of the war are obvious. Previous wars and terms of settlement which created lasting hatreds and bred thoughts of revenge; imperialism and commercial rivalries; the Triple Alliance and the Triple Entente dividing all Europe into two hostile camps; secret intrigue of diplomats and lack of democracy; vast systems of military and naval equipment; fear and suspicion bred and spread by a vicious jingo press in all nations; powerful armament interests that reap rich harvests out of havoc and death, all these have played their sinister parts. But back of these factors lie the deeper and more fundamental causes, causes rooted in the very system of capitalist production.

Every capitalist nation on earth exploits its people. The wages received by the workers are insufficient to enable them to purchase all they need for the proper sustenance of their lives. A surplus of commodities accumulates. The capitalists cannot consume all. It must be exported to foreign countries.

...Hence arise the strategy, the intrigues of secret diplomacy, till all the world is involved in a deadly struggle for the capture and control of the world market. Thus capitalism, inevitably leading to commercial rivalry and imperialism and functioning through the modern state with its vast armaments, secret diplomacies and undemocratic governments, logically leads to war.

For more than half a century the Socialist movement has warned the world of this impending tragedy. With every power at their command the Socialists of all nations have worked to prevent it. But the warning has gone unheeded and the Socialist propaganda against imperialism, militarism and war has been ignored by the ruling powers and the majority of the people of all nations.

To the Socialist and labor forces in all the world and to all who cherish the ideals of justice, we make our appeal, believing that out of the ashes of this mighty conflagration will yet arise the deeper internationalism and the great democracy and peace.

As measures calculated to bring about these results we urge:

I. TERMS OF PEACE AT THE CLOSE OF THE PRESENT WAR MUST BE BASED ON THE FOLLOWING PROVISIONS:
   1. No indemnities.
   2. No transfer of territory except upon the consent and by vote of the people within the territory.

3. All countries under foreign rule be given political independence if demanded by the inhabitants of such countries.

II. INTERNATIONAL FEDERATION—THE UNITED STATES OF THE WORLD:

1. An international congress with legislative and administrative powers over international affairs and with permanent committees in place of present secret diplomacy.
2. Special Commissions to consider international disputes as they may arise. The decisions of such commissions to be enforced without resort to arms.
3. International ownership and control of strategic waterways such as the Dardanelles, the Straits of Gibraltar and the Suez, Panama and Kiel Canals.
4. Neutralization of the seas.

III. DISARMAMENT.

1. Universal disarmament as speedily as possible.
2. Abolition of manufacture of arms and munitions of war for private profit, and prohibition of exportation of arms....
3. No increase in existing armaments under any circumstances.
4. No appropriations for military or naval purposes.

IV. EXTENSION OF DEMOCRACY.

1. Political democracy.
   (a) Abolition of secret diplomacy and democratic control of foreign policies.
   (b) Universal suffrage, including woman suffrage.
2. Industrial democracy.
   Radical social changes in all countries to eliminate economic causes for war, such as will be calculated to gradually take the industrial and commercial processes of the nations out of the hands of the irresponsible capitalist class and place them in the hands of the people, to operate them collectively for the satisfaction of human wants and not for private profits, in cooperation and harmony and not through competition and war.

V. IMMEDIATE ACTION.

Immediate and energetic efforts shall be made through the organizations of the Socialist parties of all nations to secure universal cooperation of all Socialist and labor organizations and all true friends of peace to obtain the endorsement of this program.

_____

Source: John Whiteclay Chambers II, ed. *The Eagle and the Dove: The American Peace Movement and United States Foreign Policy, 1900–1922.* Syracuse, NY: Syracuse University Press, 1991, pp. 62–64.

QUESTIONS

1. According to the Socialists, what factors laid the foundation for World War I and what could have prevented it?
2. What effect does capitalism have on a nation?
3. What policies do the Socialists believe will prevent war in the future?

Document 7: Jane Addams
Patriotism and Pacifists in War Time (1917)

Jane Addams devoted her life to the cause of peace and social justice. One of the pioneers in the settlement house movement, she later devoted all her energies to the cause of world peace. She was one of the founders of the Woman's Peace Party and later the Women's International League for Peace and Freedom. In 1931 she was awarded the Nobel Peace Prize, the first American woman to receive the coveted prize. This essay takes direct aim at those who accuse pacifists of being unpatriotic and cowardly.

*I*n the stir of the heroic moment when a nation enters war, men's minds are driven back to the earliest obligations of patriotism, and almost without volition the emotions move along the worn grooves of blind admiration for the soldier and of unspeakable contempt for him who, in the hour of danger, declares that fighting is unnecessary. We pacifists are not surprised, therefore, when apparently striking across and reversing this popular conception of patriotism, that we should not only be considered incapable of facing reality, but that we should be called traitors and cowards. It makes it all the more incumbent upon us, however, to demonstrate, if we can, that in our former advocacy we urged a reasonable and vital alternative to war, and that our position now does not necessarily imply lack of patriotism or cowardice.

First: The similarity of sound between the words "passive" and "pacifism" is often misleading.... [W]e pacifists, so far from passively wishing nothing to be done, contend on the contrary that this world crisis should be utilized for the creation of an international government able to make the necessary political and economic changes when they are due; we feel that it is unspeakably stupid that the nations should have failed to create an international organization through which each one, without danger to itself, might recognize and even encourage the impulse toward growth in other nations.

Pacifists believe that in the Europe of 1914, certain tendencies were steadily pushing towards large changes which in the end made war, because the system of peace had no way of effecting those changes without war, no adequate international organization which could cope with the situation. The conception of peace founded upon the balance of power or the undisturbed status quo, was so negative that frustrated national impulses and suppressed vital forces led to war, because no method of orderly expression had been devised.

In reply to the old charge of lack of patriotism, we claim that we are patriotic from the historic viewpoint as well as by other standards. American pacifists believe—if I may go back to those days before the war, which already seem so far away—that the United States was especially qualified by her own particular experience to take the leadership in a peaceful organization of the world....

With such a national history back of us, as pacifists we are thrown into despair over our inability to make our position clear when we are accused of wishing to isolate the United States and to keep our country out of world politics. We are, of course, urging a policy exactly the reverse....

We had also hoped much from the varied population of the United States, for whether we will or not, our very composition would make it easier for us than for any other nation to establish an international organization founded upon understanding and good will, did we but possess the requisite courage and intelligence to utilize it.

Some of us once dreamed that the cosmopolitan inhabitants of this great nation might at last become united in a vast common endeavor for social ends. We hoped that this fusing might be accomplished without the sense of opposition to a common enemy which is an old method of welding people together, better fitted for military than for social use. If this for the moment is impossible, let us at least place the spirit of cooperation above that of bitterness and remember the wide distinction between social control and military coercion.

When as pacifists we urge a courageous venture into international ethics, which will require a fine valor as well as a high intelligence, we experience a sense of anti-climax when we are told that because we do not want war, we are so cowardly as to care for "safety first," that we place human life, physical life, above the great ideals of national righteousness....

With visions of international justice filling our minds, pacifists are always a little startled when those who insist that justice can only be established by war, accuse us of caring for peace irrespective of justice. Many of the pacifists in their individual and corporate capacity have long striven for social and political justice with a fervor perhaps equal to that employed by the advocates of force, and we realize that a sense of justice has become the keynote to the best political and social activity in this generation.

We believe that the ardor and self sacrifice so characteristic of youth could be enlisted for the vitally energetic role which we hope our beloved country will inaugurate in the international life of the world.

With such a creed, can the pacifists of today be accused of selfishness when they urge upon the United States not isolation, not indifference to moral issues and to the fate of liberty and democracy, but a strenuous endeavor to lead all nations of the earth into an organized international life worthy of civilized men?

Source: John Whiteclay Chambers II, ed. *The Eagle and the Dove: The American Peace Movement and United States Foreign Policy, 1900–1922.* Syracuse, NY: Syracuse University Press, 1991, pp. 119–121.

QUESTIONS

1. How does Addams respond to charges that pacifists are traitors and cowards?
2. Why might people have accused pacifists of isolationism? What is Addams's response?
3. In Addams's view, what sorts of institutions and ideas would help develop and maintain world peace?

Document 8: John Haynes Holmes
War and the Social Movement (1914)

John Haynes Holmes was a Harvard-trained Unitarian minister and radical pacifist who was influenced by the writings of the Social Gospel clergymen. Devoted to peace and social justice, he helped found the National Association for the Advancement of Colored People, the American Union against Militarism, and the American Civil Liberties Union. This essay first appeared in the September issue of *The Survey*, a magazine devoted to social work and social reform.

---

*I*n the storm and stress of the stupendous conflict now raging in Europe, it is inevitable that our attention should be absorbed by the more obvious horrors of the situation. Captured cities, burning harvest fields, desolate homes, bleeding men, weeping women and children— these are the things which are holding our interests to the exclusion of everything else. Yet there must be quiet moments, now and then, when we see more clearly and think more deeply than is possible in the hours of reading newspapers and watching bulletin boards.

Then it is that we begin to understand that there is a calamity in this warfare which is more permanently terrible than any of the surface incidents of the struggle. I refer to the awful fact that suddenly, as in the wink of an eye, three hundred years of progress is cast into the melting pot. Civilization is all at once gone, and barbarism comes....

...And who, we may add here, cares a fig about the social movement?...

For who is talking in England today about national insurance, woman suffrage, or the breaking of the land monopoly? Who is interested in the enactment of the plural voting bill?...Where is the campaign for franchise reform in Germany? Who cares about cooperation in Belgium, or syndicalism in France, or socialism anywhere? Is there an international labor movement any longer; and if there can be said to be such a movement, what does it amount to?

...We are three thousand miles away from the smoke and flame of combat, and have not a single regiment or battleship involved. And yet—who in these United States is thinking at this moment of recreation centers, improved housing, or the minimum wage? Who is going to fight the battle for widows' pensions, push the campaign against child labor, or study exhaustively the problem of unemployment?...

What are the suffragists going to do to stir a ripple of interest in their cause? . . .

Nor can we hope for any revival of the social movement with the conclusion of the war. If, as now seems probable, the nations fight to the point of exhaustion, the question facing the world at the conclusion of peace will not be that of social progress at all, but simply and solely that of social survival.

Source: John Whiteclay Chambers II, ed. *The Eagle and the Dove: The American Peace Movement and United States Foreign Policy, 1900–1922.* Syracuse, NY: Syracuse University Press, 1991, pp. 39–40.

QUESTIONS

1. How did Holmes describe the realities of the war in Europe?
2. What did Holmes fear most about the domestic consequences of waging war?
3. What did he perceive would be the biggest challenge to progress once the fighting stopped?

Document 9: Randolph Bourne
The State (1919)

A writer and bohemian intellectual in Greenwich Village in lower Manhattan, Bourne saved his greatest effort for attacking the intellectuals who supported Woodrow Wilson's call to arms in 1917. Bourne castigated the way in which intellectuals such as Dewey chose expediency over thoughtful criticism, hoping they would learn a lesson for the next time such a situation arose.

*T*o most Americans of the classes which consider themselves significant the war brought a sense of the sanctity of the State, which, if they had had time to think about it, would have seemed a sudden and surprising alteration in their habits of thought. In times of peace, we usually ignore the State in favor of partisan political controversies, or personal struggles for office, or the pursuit of party policies. It is the Government rather than the State with which the politically minded are concerned. The State is reduced to a shadowy emblem which comes to consciousness only on occasions of patriotic holiday.

With the shock of war, however, the State comes into its own again. The Government, with no mandate from the people, without consultation of the people, conducts all the negotiations... which slowly bring it into collision with some other Government, and gently and irresistibly slides the country into war. For the benefit of proud and haughty citizens, it is fortified with a list of the intolerable insults which have been hurled toward us by the other nations; for the benefit of the liberal and beneficent, it has a convincing set of moral purposes which our going to war will achieve; for the ambitious and aggressive classes, it can gently whisper of a bigger role in the destiny of the world. The result is that, even in those countries where the business of declaring war is theoretically in the hands of representatives of the people, no legislature has ever been known to decline the request of an Executive, which has conducted all foreign affairs in utter privacy and irresponsibility, that it order the nation into battle....

The patriot loses all sense of the distinction between State, nation, and government. In our quieter moments, the Nation or Country forms the basic idea of society. We think vaguely of a loose population spreading over a certain geographical portion of the earth's surface. Our idea of Country concerns itself with the non-political aspects of a people, its ways of living, its personal traits, its literature and art, its characteristic attitudes toward life....The Country, as an inescapable group into which we are born, and which makes us its particular kind of a citizen of the world, seems to be a fundamental fact of our consciousness, an irreducible minimum of social feeling....

The State is the country acting as a political unit, it is the group acting as a repository of force, determiner of law, arbiter of justice. International politics is a "power politics" because it is a relation of States and that is what States infallibly and calamitously are, huge aggregations of human and industrial force that may be hurled against each other in war. When a country acts as a whole in relation to another country, or in imposing laws on its own inhabitants, or in coercing or punishing individuals or minorities, it is acting as a State....

Government, on the other hand,... is a framework of the administration of laws, and the carrying out of the public force. Government is the idea of the State put into practical operation in the hands of definite, concrete, fallible men....Government is the only form in which we can envisage the State, but it is by no means identical with it. That the State is a mystical conception is something that must never be forgotten. Its glamour and its significance linger behind the framework of Government and direct its activities.

Wartime brings the ideal of the State out into very clear relief, and reveals attitudes and tendencies that were hidden.... For war is essentially the health of the State. The ideal of the State is that within its territory its power and influence should be universal.... War sends the current of purpose and activity flowing down to the lowest level of the herd, and to its most remote branches,... and the State becomes what in peacetimes it has vainly struggled to become—the inexorable arbiter and determinant of men's business and attitudes and opinions.... [Modern, mass war] cannot exist without a military establishment, and a military establishment cannot exist without a State organization.... For it meets the demands of no other institution, it follows the desires of no religious, industrial, political group. If the demand for military organization and a military establishment seems to come not from the officers of the State but from the public, it is only that it comes from the State-obsessed portion of the public, those groups which feel most keenly the State ideal....

All of which goes to show that the State represents all the autocratic, arbitrary, coercive, belligerent forces within a social group, it is a sort of complex of everything most distasteful to the modern free creative spirit, the feeling for life, liberty, and the pursuit of happiness. War is the health of the State. Only when the State is at war does the modern society function with that unity of sentiment, simple uncritical patriotic devotion, cooperation of services, which have always been the ideal of the State lover....

Source: Charles Chatfield and Ruzanna Illukhina, eds. *Peace/Mir: An Anthology of Historic Alternatives to War.* Syracuse, NY: Syracuse University Press, 1994, pp. 184–186.

QUESTIONS

1. From your reading of the document, explain in detail what Bourne means when he says, "War is essentially the health of the State."
2. When war is declared, Bourne believes, "The patriot loses all sense of the distinction between the State, nation, and government." Summarize what Bourne believes each one to be and explain how they interact with each other in shaping the political consciousness of the people.

3. The Progressive Era of the late nineteenth and early twentieth centuries was an era of reform marked by optimism about human progress, potential, and peace. From your understanding of this era, explain why Bourne calls the State, "A sort of complex of everything most distasteful to the modern free spirit, the feeling for life, liberty, and the pursuit of happiness."

Document 10: "Statement of Conscientious Objection" (1917–1918)

Of the approximately 4,000 conscientious objectors in World War I, some 1,300 eventually entered noncombatant military service in the Medical Corps, the Quartermaster Corps, and the Engineer Service. About 1,200 were given furloughs to do farm work, while 100 were assigned to Quaker war relief in France. Five hundred COs were court-martialed and convicted. In 1933, President Roosevelt pardoned all those still in prison.

The Statements of conscientious objectors that follow illustrate the variety of their motives. Political objector Carl Haessler became a college professor; Roger Baldwin later became the first president of the American Civil Liberties Union.

[Carl Haessler]

I, Carl Haessler, Recruit, Machine Gun Company, 46th Infantry, respectfully submit the following statement in extenuation in connection with my proposed plea of guilty to the charge of violation of the 64th Article of War, the offense having been committed June 22, 1918, in Camp Sheridan, Ala.

The offense was not committed from private, secret, personal, impulsive, religious, pacifist or pro-German grounds. An admixture of quasi-personal motives is admitted, but they were in no sense the guiding or controlling factors. I have evidence for each of these assertions, should it be required.

The willful disobedience of my Captain's and of my Lieutenant-Colonel's orders to report in military uniform arose from a conviction which I hesitate to express before my country's military officers but which I nevertheless am at present unable to shake off, namely, that

America's participation in the World War was unnecessary, of doubtful benefit (if any) to the country and to humanity, and accomplished largely, though not exclusively, through the pressure of the Allied and American commercial imperialists.

Holding this conviction, I conceived my part as a citizen to be opposition to the war before it was declared, active efforts for a peace without victory after the declaration, and a determination so far as possible to do nothing in aid of the war while its character seemed to remain what I thought it was. I hoped in this way to help bring the war to an earlier close and to help make similar future wars less probable in this country.

I further believe that I shall be rendering the country a service by helping to set an example for other citizens to follow in the matter of fearlessly acting on unpopular convictions instead of forgetting them in time of stress. The crumbling of American radicalism under pressure in 1917 has only been equaled by that of the majority of German socialist leaders in August, 1914.

Looking at my case from the point of view of the administration and of this court, I readily admit the necessity of exemplary punishment. I regret that I have been forced to make myself a nuisance and I grant that this war could not be carried on if objections like mine were recognized by those conducting the war. My respect for the administration has been greatly increased by the courteous and forbearing treatment accorded me since having been drafted, but my view of international politics and diplomacy, acquired during my three years of graduate study in England, has not altered since June, 1917, when I formally declared that I could not accept service if drafted. Although officers have on three occasions offered me noncombatant service if I would put on the uniform, I have regretfully refused each time on the ground that "bomb-proof" service on my part would give the lie to my sincerity (which was freely granted by Judge Julian Mack when he and his colleagues examined me at Camp Gordon). If I am to render any war services, I shall not ask for special privileges.

I wish to conclude that long statement by reiterating that I am not a pacifist or pro-German, not a religious or private objector, but regard myself as a patriotic political objector, acting largely from public and social grounds.

I regret that, while my present view of this war continues, I cannot freely render any service in aid of the war. I shall not complain about the punishment that this court may see fit to mete out to me....

[Roger N. Baldwin]

*T*he compelling motive for refusing to comply with the draft act is my uncompromising opposition to the principle of conscription of life by the state for any purpose whatever, in time of war or peace. I not only refuse to obey the present conscription law, but I would in future refuse to obey any similar statute which attempts to direct my choice of service and ideals. I regard the principle of conscription of life as a flat contradiction of all our cherished ideals of individual freedom, democratic liberty, and Christian teaching.

I am more opposed to the present act, because it is for the purpose of conducting war. I am opposed to this and all other wars. I do not believe in the use of physical force as a method of achieving any end, however good. . . .

I am not complaining for myself or others. I am merely advising the court that I understand full well the penalty of my heresy, and am prepared to pay it. The conflict with conscription is irreconcilable. Even the liberalism of the President and Secretary of War in dealing with objectors leads those of us who are "absolutists" to a punishment longer and severer than that of desperate criminals.

But I believe that most of us are prepared even to die for our faith, just as our brothers in France are dying for theirs. To them we are comrades in spirit—we understand one another's motives, though our methods are wide apart. We both share deeply the common experience of living up to the truth as we see it, whatever the price.

Though at the moment I am of a tiny minority, I feel myself just one protest in a great revolt surging up from among the people— the struggle of the masses against the rule of the world by a few— profoundly intensified by the war. It is a struggle against the political state itself, against exploitation, militarism, imperialism, authority in all forms. . . .

Having arrived at the state of mind in which those views mean the dearest things in life to me, I cannot consistently, with self-respect, do other than I have, namely, to deliberately violate an act which seems to me to be a denial of everything, which ideally and in practice I hold sacred.

Source: Staughton Lynd, ed. *Nonviolence in America: A Documentary History.* Indianapolis, IN: Bobbs-Merrill Co., 1966, pp. 173–177.

QUESTIONS

1. Summarize and analyze Carl Haessler's argument that "America's participation in the World War was unnecessary, of doubtful benefit (if any) to the country and to humanity."
2. By his stance against America's involvement in the World War, Haessler believes that he is "rendering the country a service." Analyze and explain his perspective by drawing upon the goals of the conscientious objector.
3. Analyze Roger Baldwin's statement that he "regard(s) the principle of conscription of life as a flat contradiction of all our cherished ideals. . . ." Do you agree or disagree with him?

Document 11:   Eugene Debs
Address to the Jury (1918)

Eugene Debs's "Address to the Jury" represents a remarkable defense of the right of free speech and the American radical tradition. Debs had witnessed the bloodshed resulting from President Grover Cleveland's order to dispatch federal troops during the Pullman Strike. During World War I he was an outspoken critic of the war and the draft. In an antiwar speech in Canton, Ohio, Debs called for workers not to enlist in the armed forces, and, if drafted, to foment insubordination. Convicted and sentenced to ten years in the federal prison in Atlanta for violating the 1917 Espionage Act, Debs had his sentence commuted by President Harding in 1921.

May it please the court, and gentlemen of the jury:

. . . A century and a half ago when the American colonists were still foreign subjects; when there were a few men who had faith in the common people and their destiny, and believed that they would rule themselves without a king; in that day to question the divine right of the king to rule was treason. If you will read Bancroft or any other American historian, you will find that a great majority of the colonists were loyal to the king and actually believed that he had a divine right to rule over them. . . . But there were a few men in that day who said, "We don't need a king; we can govern ourselves." And they began an agitation that has immortalized them in history.

Washington, Jefferson, Franklin, Paine and their peers were the rebels of their day. When they began to chafe under the rule of a foreign king and to sow the seed of resistance among the colonists they were opposed by the people and denounced by the press.... But they had the moral courage to be true to their convictions, to stand erect and defy all the forces of reaction and detraction; and that is why their names shine in history, and why the great respectable majority of their day sleep in forgotten graves....

From the beginning of the war to this day I have never by word or act been guilty of the charges embraced in this indictment. If I have criticized, if I have condemned, it is because I believed it to be may duty, and that it was my right to do so under the laws of the land. I have had ample precedents for my attitude. This country has been engaged in a number of wars and every one of them has been condemned by some of the people, among them some of the most eminent men of their time. The war of the American Revolution was violently opposed. The Tory press representing the "upper classes" denounced its leaders as criminals and outlaws.

The War of 1812 was opposed and condemned by some of the most influential citizens; the Mexican war was vehemently opposed and bitterly denounced, even after the war had been declared and was in progress, by Abraham Lincoln, Charles Sumner, Daniel Webster, Henry Clay and many other well-known and influential citizens. These men denounced the President, they condemned his administration while the war was being waged, and they charged in substance that the war was a crime against humanity. They were not indicted; they were not charged with treason nor tried for crime. They are honored today by all of their countrymen.

The Civil War between the states met with violent resistance and passionate condemnation. In the year 1864 the Democratic Party met in national convention at Chicago and passed a resolution condemning the war as a failure. What would you say if the Socialist Party were to meet in convention today and condemn the present war as a failure? You charge us with being disloyalists and traitors. Were the Democrats of 1864 disloyalists and traitors because they condemned the war as a failure?

And if so, why were they not indicted and prosecuted accordingly? I believe in the Constitution. Isn't it strange that we Socialists stand almost alone today in upholding and defending the Constitution of the United States? The revolutionary fathers who had been oppressed under king rule understood that free speech, a free press and the right of free assemblage by the people were fundamental principles in democratic government....

That is the right I exercised at Canton on the sixteenth day of last June; and for the exercise of that right, I now have to answer to this indictment. I believe in the right of free speech, in war as well as in peace. I would not, under any circumstances suppress free speech. It is far more dangerous to attempt to gag the people than to allow them to speak freely what is in their hearts....

Gentlemen, I am the smallest part of this trial. I have lived long enough to realize my own personal insignificance in relation to a great issue that involves the welfare of the whole people. What you may choose to do to me will be of small consequence after all. I am not on trial here. There is an infinitely greater issue that is being tried today in this court, though you may not be conscious of it. American institutions are on trial here before a court of American citizens. The future will render the final verdict.

And now, your honor, permit me to return my thanks for your patient consideration. And to you, gentlemen of the jury, for the kindness with you have listened to me.

I am prepared for your verdict.

Source: Timothy Patrick McCarthy and John McMillan, eds. *The Radical Reader: A Documentary History of the American Radical Tradition.* New York: The New Press, 2003, pp. 310–313.

QUESTIONS

1. How did Debs use historical examples in defense of his position opposing World War I?
2. What did he mean by saying "American institutions are on trial here"?
3. Do you find his passionate defense of free speech compelling? Why or why not?

Document 12: A. Philip Randolph
Editorial, *Pro-Germanism Among Negroes* (1918)

A. Philip Randolph was one of the most influential African American activists of the twentieth century. A socialist and labor organizer who believed in the principle of nonviolence, he was a major force behind the March on Washington. Opposed to World War I, Randolph and Chandler Owen published their own socialist journal, *The Messenger*, a periodical mixing political commentary on the war and trade unionism with sketches of leading radicals of the time. One of its first editorials stated: "Patriotism has no appeal to us; justice has. Party has no weight with us; principle has. Loyalty is meaningless; it depends on what one is loyal to. . . ."

At a recent convention of the National Association for the Advancement of Colored People (NAACP), a member of the Administration's Department of Intelligence was present. When Mr. Julian Carter of Harrisburg was complaining of the racial prejudice which American white troops had carried into France, the administration representative rose and warned the audience that the Negroes were under suspicion of having been affected by German propaganda.

In keeping with the ultra-patriotism of the old-line, old-type Negro leaders the NAACP failed to grasp its opportunity. It might have informed the Administration representatives that the discontent among Negroes was not produced by propaganda, nor can it be removed by propaganda. The causes are deep and dark—though obvious to all who care to use their mental eyes. Peonage, disfranchisement, Jim-Crowism, segregation, rank civil discrimination, injustice of legislatures, courts and administrators—these are the propaganda of discontent among Negroes.

The only legitimate connection between this unrest and Germanism is the extensive government advertisement that we are fighting "to make the world safe for democracy," to carry democracy to Germany; that we are conscripting the Negro into the military and industrial establishments to achieve this end for white democracy four thousand miles away, while the Negro at home, through bearing the burden in every way, is denied economic, political, educational and civil democracy.

Source: The Messenger 2 (July 1918): 13.

QUESTIONS

1. Why was Randolph dismayed by the "old-line, old-type" of Negro leaders in the NAACP?
2. What were the causes of "Negro discontent" that he alludes to?
3. According to Randolph, what must the government do in order to convince African Americans to embrace patriotism and the war?

5

Radical Pacifism and Economic and Racial Justice

Disillusionment with World War I left a determination in millions of Americans never to fight or support war again; no one was willing to stand up now and joyously sing songs like "Rally Round the Flag" or attend romantic plays like "The Drummer Boy of Shiloh." The Unknown Soldier— the American doughboy whose very identity remained buried beneath the rubble of the war's destruction—symbolized this was a fight to forget. At no time in U.S. history was the hold of pacifism, or disdain for war, as strong or compelling as it was between World War I and World War II.

No one captured this sentiment more than educator John Dewey. Battered and bruised by Randolph Bourne for surrendering his critical faculties and supporting World War I, Dewey became one of the leading figures in the 1920s calling for the abolishment of the war system. Since the U.S. Senate refused to ratify the Treaty of Versailles, thus negating participation in the newly created League of Nations, many peace advocates looked for other alternatives. After returning from a lecture tour in the Far East

For the People, pages 127–166
Copyright © 2009 by Information Age Publishing

in 1919–1920, Dewey actively supported peace campaigns such as the out-lawry of war in order to overcome his former students' criticisms that his support for the war was technique-conscious and morally blind. He began calling upon national leaders to find an appropriate way to substitute the rule of law for the use of violence. His support for Chicago lawyer Salmon O. Levinson's Outlawry of War Campaign, in particular, was a carefully cal-culated attempt to replace the attachment to patriotic militarism with a realistic reasoned approach to nations settling their differences through agreement on international principles based on the rule of law (**Docu-ment 1**). Dewey's view represented the thinking of many intellectuals and progressives who were disappointed with the bickering and petty national-istic jealousies demonstrated during peace treaty negotiations at Versailles but did not abandon their own idealistic hopes that the United States could lead the way in securing a permanent world order.

Dewey's sentiments were shared by a vast majority of the American pub-lic. World War I was never idealized by the American people as earlier wars had been; the magnitude and severity of death and destruction had much to do with that. Revisionist historians strengthened the commonly felt at-titude that the war had been a complete mistake. In 1926, Harry Elmer Barnes, professor of Sociology at Smith College, published his *Genesis on the World War*, an attack on the widely accepted idea of German responsibility for the conflict. Two years later, Sidney B. Fay's two-volume *Origins of the World War* left little doubt that the official Allied propaganda did not square at some points with a critical analysis of archival and other material. The fact that scholars, including those who had supported war in the name of progressive social reform, were now questioning it gave greater credence to those who had openly challenged Wilson's reasons for going to war.

Virtually all American literary men and women who wrote about the war expressed disappointment or downright disillusionment, including Willa Cather in *One of Ours*, John Dos Passos in *Three Soldiers*, Lawrence Stallings and Sherwood Anderson in *What Price Glory*, and Ernest Heming-way in *A Farewell to Arms*. The prevailing antipathy toward any idealizing of the war also found expression in the popularity of former German soldier Erich Remarque's *All Quiet on the Western Front*, which produced enormous sales in the United States.

World War I also marked the birth of the "modern" American peace movement; a movement so noted by the late historian Charles DeBenedetti as being defined by its commitment to domestic reform as well as world peace. After 1915, peace and antiwar advocates approached the problem from two different angles: internationalism and pacifism. Internationalists, on the one hand, were gradualist reformers who believed in the benefits of the capitalist system. Pacifists, on the other hand, proved more receptive to the nature of capitalism's failings and more radical in their prescriptions for its reconstruction. While applauding the importance of internationalism they also approached the peace problem from a domestic perspective. Before world peace was achievable, it was imperative to address the social and economic problems at home. Pacifists understood peace as the condition that followed the destruction of the war system through international measures as well as the abolishment of pernicious social institutions breeding economic inequality and social injustice.

It would be the pacifists who shaped the "modern" peace movement, and both radical secular and Christian pacifists began forging their own form of political protest. They and the organizations they helped form were receptive to social and economic change through radical nonresistance. The organizations they established were influenced by both internationalism and social justice pacifism. The most noted of these peace groups were the following: Women's International League for Peace and Freedom (WILPF); American Friends Service Committee (AFSC); War Resisters League (WRL); and the religious-pacifist American Fellowship of Reconciliation (FOR). With the exception of the American Friends Service Committee, founded by the Quakers during the war without any political agenda, these new organizations developed a radically conscious position linking peace with domestic social reform. The pacifist position would remain intact; what was new would be their deploying the doctrine of nonresistance in conjunction with visible and manifest forms of public protest, which became known as "direct action" during the post-World War II period.

An examination of one particular group, the War Resisters League, illustrates the peace movement's changing philosophy. In 1924, peace activists Tracy Mygatt, Frances Witherspoon, and Jessie Wallace Hughan combined a cross section of peace seekers and antiwar workers into the American branch of the War Resister's League, whose motto, "Wars Will Cease When Men Refuse to Fight," expressed its emphasis during its early history. This diverse group of philosophical anarchists and pacifists planned to stop the next war through a massive general strike. With a total membership of about 19,000 in 1924, they held firmly to their conviction that war was "a crime against humanity."

The principal leader of the group was the socialist-pacifist Jessie Wallace Hughan. Her goal was to unite political, humanitarian, and philosophical objectors to war. Hughan, who obtained her Ph.D. in economics from Columbia University prior to World War I, was drawn into socialist circles while researching the problems that faced an increasingly industrial and urban America. During World War I, she established an organization for war opponents who had no traditional religious basis for their pacifist beliefs. Along with her close friends, Witherspoon and Mygatt, Hughan, a high school English teacher from Brooklyn, formed the Anti-Establishment League in 1915. Operating out of her own apartment, she managed to enroll 3,500 men who willingly signed a declaration against military enlistment. The pledge read: "I, being over eighteen years of age, hereby pledge myself against enlistment as a volunteer for any military or naval service in international war, either offensive or defensive, and against giving my approval to such enlistment on the part of others." When America entered the war, the organization folded. Attacked for opposing the war on socialist grounds, Hughan was allowed to keep her teaching job because charges of disloyalty had been leveled prior to the actual declaration of war. During the Red Scare, though, the Lusk Committee of the New York State Legislature denied her the Certificate of Character and Loyalty because she deliberately added the following words to the state's teacher loyalty oath: "this obedience being qualified always by dictates of conscience." The U.S. Senate Judiciary Committee added her name to its list of dangerous radicals along with Jane Addams, Lillian D. Wald, and Oswald Garrison Villard.

In the early 1920s, Hughan received the approval of the FOR and women's peace groups to create the War Resisters League. The absolute or radical pacifists who joined enabled the WRL to transform the meaning of pacifism into more than just repudiation of war. WRL enrolled anarchists, socialists, radicals, and even capitalists who were serious about peace, while it worked in conjunction with FOR, AFSC, WILPF, and other peace organizations. WRL became part of a nonviolent social movement—a secular pacifist one. The organization popularized the modern peace movement's goal of resisting the evils of war by demanding a just social and economic order at home (**Document 2**). During the WRL's early years, Hughan delivered numerous speeches and wrote pamphlets and tracts on the use of active nonviolence. She organized various public protests against war and militarism, including some New York "NO MORE WAR" parades. Much of the organization's support came from pacifist members of the Socialist Party when it became apparent that the FOR could not relate to nonreligious conscientious objectors. Anyone was eligible to become a member of the WRL if he or she signed a pledge renouncing participation in war. The WRL did most of its interwar work in the education field as well as providing legal support to conscientious objectors

The newly formed peace organizations of the modern movement, as illustrated by the WRL, faced major contradictions in American culture:

a growing desire to prevent another "global catastrophe" emerged during a time of economic growth, which made Americans more protective of their gains and stimulated the powerful appeal of nationalism at the expense of internationalism. For peace workers, the job was difficult. How could they convince fellow Americans that their nation's economic prosperity could be served best by sacrificing some autonomy for the sake of international harmony?

In answer to this question a number of Protestant ministers, particularly members of the FOR, began reflecting on the issues promoted by the pre-World War I Social Gospelers, which included regulation of big business, assisting immigrants in their transition to American life, and weeding out urban corruption and slums. Many were also enthusiastic about working closely with the Friends Service Committee given their growing commitment to Christian nonviolence. Led by John Haynes Holmes, Kirby Page, Reinhold Niebuhr, Harry Emerson Fosdick, Charles Clayton Morrison, Sherwood Eddy, and other clerics, Protestant leaders throughout the country alerted their parishioners to the necessity for international harmony. Many were desirous of forsaking the patriotic proclamations that had rolled off their tongues during the last war. Noted clerics were now willing to admit that the churches possessed a special obligation to overcome the war menace. Moving beyond traditional dictates of moral exhortation, a new breed of antiwar clergymen started producing critical analyses of the structural basis of war and injustice in modern society.

Furthermore, those like Fosdick, who had enthusiastically "presented arms" in 1917, took a solemn vow from the pulpit that they would never again come to the support of war. Morrison, irascible editor of *The Christian Century*, also became one of the most outspoken critics of postwar American foreign policy. Disturbed by the injustices of the Versailles Treaty, he opposed the League of Nations, calling it an instrument of European reactionaries bent on frustrating America's world peace mission. In Morrison's opinion, America had to play an active, independent role in rescuing Europe through moral vigor and the proven power of law.

In general, Protestant churches, remorseful about excessive militarism exhibited during the war, followed Fosdick and Morrison in accepting a commitment to Christian pacifism. Christian peace groups, such as the Church Peace Union and World Alliance for International Fellowship, flourished in such an atmosphere, especially in the seminaries. Countless Protestant ministers had sworn that they would never again support a war. Many wondered if even police forces could be justified and, among radicals, the question of justifying violence in the class struggle became divisive for some members of the clergy, as will be noted later in the case of Niebuhr.

Nonetheless, so committed were the churches to world peace that by 1929 the Federal Council of Churches greeted the United States Senate's consent to the Kellogg–Briand Peace Pact with jubilation: "Let Church bells be rung, songs sung, prayers of thanksgiving be offered, and petitions for help inform God that our nation may ever follow the spirit and meaning of the Pact." Thus, the recurring campaigns among Protestant peace agencies and clergy for disarmament, the World Court, peace education, social justice, and outlawry of war created a spirit of immediacy and hope that had not been felt since before the guns of August dashed dreams of international harmony.

Bolstered by religious leaders' abhorrence of force and violence, Devere Allen became a one-person publicity machine for religious peace groups like the FOR in his dogged determination to convince rational people to accept his view that war resistance is war prevention (**Document 3**). A student at Oberlin College during the war, Allen caught the eye of pacifists and was appointed executive secretary of The Young Democracy and editor of its journal. In 1921, he became managing editor of *The World Tomorrow* and worked with Protestant leaders in the FOR such as Page, Sayre, and Niebuhr in making the religious-pacifist organization's journal the leading communicator for the liberal social gospel and radical theological criticisms of war and social injustice in America.

A socialist and internationalist, Allen promoted a reform-minded philosophy of nonviolent action and encouraged the development of a transnational peace movement through modern means of communication. His views would germinate during the 1920s and finally gain widespread publicity in the next decade. His popular historical survey *The Fight for Peace* (1930) reached a large audience. In addition, receiving a subvention from the American Friends Service Committee, Allen established the *No Frontier News* service (later renamed the *Worldover Press*) in 1933. It had two basic goals. First, it provided peace groups with information related to new peace efforts abroad and an intelligent analysis of world events. Second, it reached people outside peace groups by providing information to a host of media outlets such as religious papers, labor journals, rural weeklies, and city dailies. It even initiated a two-way flow of information by serving periodicals in Europe and Latin America.

Allen firmly believed that it was essential to develop a capacity for independent judgment and action; the peace movement and the public alike needed information that often was not carried by the major wire/news services. Similarly, in a world where news was defined largely by its relationship to governments, peace groups needed independent information about one another. By 1935, Allen's project was serving papers with a total circulation of close to nine million readers.

During the interwar years the clergy's and Allen's support for peace and nonviolence was also advanced by Gandhi disciple Richard Gregg (**Document 4**). A Harvard-trained lawyer, Gregg wrote an engaging book, *The Power of Nonviolence,* at the height of the Great Depression. It became the virtual manual of action for nonviolent activists over the next generation. Gregg's purpose, based on his own encounters with the labor and anticolonial movements, was to reinvigorate nonviolence as an instrument for social reconstruction and to develop a strategic politics bringing power to oppressed social groups. Such techniques were especially valuable to progressive labor organizers during the 1930s and religious activists seeking to assist the unemployed. In his book, Gregg advocated coercive but nonviolent techniques in domestic and international relations—fasts, mass protests, sit-downs—aimed at reaching a compromise amenable to both sides. He traced the practice of nonviolence in the history of Western civilization—pointing to such incidents as the Magyar struggle against Hapsburg autocracy in the 1860s—to support his contention that nonviolence was something more than a "peculiarly Hindu practice." His proposal for a new mode of conflict resolution was applied to all aspects of disagreement in order that "speaking truth to power" would resolve conflicts in the name of social and economic justice.

Not everyone who initially supported pacifism and the radical religious critique of war in the 1920s and early 1930s accepted Gregg's position due to the impact of economic catastrophe. Perhaps no one individual more accurately captured the pacifist dilemma regarding nonviolence than the distinguished Protestant theologian Reinhold Niebuhr. By the early 1930s, faced with high unemployment, worker discontent, and the appearance of military dictatorships in Europe and the Far East, Niebuhr left the FOR, grudgingly accepting force as an instrument of necessity given the circumstances of the Depression and the rise of fascism (**Document 5**). Over the course of his religious life, Niebuhr crafted an ethics of Christian realism that ultimately clarified the ethical basis of pacifism within a social context while giving new meaning and support to the just war theory. Publishing *Moral Man and Immoral Society* in 1932, he began arguing that social and political choices require a realistic assessment of their consequences as well as taking into account the role of power in human affairs. In terms of society, justice can only be obtained through an equitable distribution of power. Although comfortable with the social consciousness of reform pacifists like

Sayre and Page, Niebuhr gradually challenged the unquestioning commitment to nonviolence in the face of economic calamity and the failures of the Versailles Treaty.

As he kept questioning his position, he finally determined that nonviolence was justifiable as a social strategy in relative political terms, but not on absolute religious principles. In other words, there were times when the use of violence was acceptable for improving social conditions. Pacifism was a personal philosophy of nonviolence, not a public policy guidebook. Although his ideas on social action strategy anticipated Gregg's nonviolent resistance theory, Niebuhr's paradoxical views on the social ethics of pacifism brought to the forefront the dilemma facing absolute war resisters and antiwar peace advocates. By the mid-1930s he openly criticized the absolute pacifist position, eventually arguing that it was no longer relevant to the existing situation.

Unlike Niebuhr, there were other clerics who refused to abandon their pacifist principles in the name of peace and justice. Most notable was Kirby Page, who insisted that war is sin and nothing more (**Document 6**). He worked closely with the AFSC in encouraging the creation of educational programs for world peace, such as peace caravans. Composed of college students who traveled from town to town throughout the nation between 1926 and 1941, the caravans distributed peace literature while addressing people in clubs and churches wherever an audience could be found. Throughout these years the program reached thousands of people in many remote parts of the country.

Page's plea for social reform through peaceful means also assumed greater import in the face of the twin blockbusters of economic disaster and impending international conflict. He stood behind the establishment of summer work camps to assist the poor and unemployed during the hardest years of the Great Depression. Pacifism, he insisted, applies not only in the case of international war, but also in new ways of bringing about essential changes in the social order through creative rather than destructive methods. To abolish the sin of war involved much more than disarmament and peace treaties. It entailed economic justice for all.

Page's call to create work camps assisting the needy was heeded by many high school- and college-age men and women. The AFSC set up camps in various areas of the country, providing large numbers of poor and unemployed people with food and shelter. During the winter of 1931–32, for instance, the AFSC fed 42,000 children in the bituminous coal areas.

Young people also worked in groups at physical tasks that were wide-ranging: a group of high school seniors helped to construct a tourist camp in the TVA region; fifty college students and others built a dam for a fish-growing pond in the Tennessee Valley area; forty people assisted in building roads and chicken houses and installing a water system in a homestead community in Fayette County, Pennsylvania; one work camp did a house-renovating job in Philadelphia; another work camp did some housing construction and built a bridge on the Delta Cooperative Farm in Mississippi; and a group of volunteers repaired buildings and did farm work on an Indian reservation near Quaker Bridge, New York. In each case, an adult educational program was implemented to bring students into touch with the local problems of conflict or of experimentation in the community where they were working, together with some study of the technique of social change without the use of violence. The work camps were an important example of peace activists' commitment to the idea of peace as reform and a testimony to Page's own interpretation of pacifism. Whereas Niebuhr intellectualized pacifism's ineffectualness, Page found new avenues to make it justified.

Student groups during the interwar period were also particularly active when it came to promoting political awareness of peace and justice issues. Moved by fresh signs of increasing international conflict and inspired by left-wing activism on many college campuses, student activists started their own crusade for lasting peace. The Student League for Industrial Democracy and the National Student League organized a "Student Strike Against War." The event occurred on April 13, 1934, precisely at eleven o'clock—the time of the entrance of the United States into World War I. Twenty-five thousand students participated in the strike throughout the nation and affirmed their hatred of war by taking the British student Oxford Pledge (February 1933), which declared that "this House refuses to fight for King and Country in any war." On April 22, 1936, the largest campus protests took place in which close to 500,000 students participated in the "Strike Against War."

Student activism in the 1930s was not only antiwar but also socially concerned. One such group representing this dual view was the American Youth Congress. Local youth organizations melded into a national federation and lobbied to promote the goals of progressive reform. It expanded the idea of peace and connected it to matters of justice. It vigorously lobbied the national government for more federal spending on education, a meaningful jobs program, and an end to racial discrimination (**Document 7**). The AYC was not a strictly pacifist organization, though it shared pacifists' goals of social reform.

Specifically, members of the American Youth Congress supported policymakers' desire for neutrality during these uncertain times, particularly the mid-1930s. Their actions encouraged longtime peace activists from both the internationalist and pacifist camps to work in harmony in order to keep the United States out of another likely war. The Youth Congress' peace activism proved effective in galvanizing an unlikely, but short-lived, alliance between internationalists and pacifists who shared some common goals.

Equally important, growing concern regarding the impact of America's industrial system on workers also led peace seekers to unite their cause with the liberal wing of the labor movement. Using simplified and dramatized socialist observations, these peace workers criticized America's capitalistic system as a threat to peace and a major factor in industrial oppression.

Such views were developed and taught at Brookwood Labor College in Katonah, New York, which had been established in 1921. Nestled in a pastoral setting, Brookwood was labor's most noticeable peace representation during the interwar period. Led by respected pacifist clergyman A.J. Muste, Brookwood was America's first and most famous residential labor school. Its primary goal was to train workers in the crusade for unionization. One of the most striking characteristics of Brookwood was its attempt to link war with industrial oppression as a means of elevating the social consciousness of the worker. Primarily through lectures, class discussions, and plays, Brookwood created an intellectual environment thoroughly sympathetic to world peace. Norman Thomas, Scott Nearing (author of *The Great Madness* and noted antiwar critic), and John Nevin Sayre were frequent visitors at Brookwood. The college received a large endowment from liberal bohemian and antiwar philanthropist Charles Garland.

Throughout the college's existence, 1921–1937, students and faculty carried on a theatrical program designed to dramatize their concern for world peace. This concern was inspired, in part, by socialist argument linking war to capitalist oppression. It was one of the more unique aspects of the interwar workers' education program in the United States, as well as that of the peace movement. Performing in New York, St. Paul, Detroit, Baltimore, Toledo, Boston, Philadelphia, and thirty other major cities, the Brookwood players satirized the folly of war in front of enthusiastic labor audiences. The Brookwood Players put on some telling performances like "Coal Digger Mule Goes to War," which depicted the hypocrisy and glorification of war, and "Uncle Sam Wants You," warning workers against supporting war with promises of more pay and a secure job in the face of a turbulent economy. One of the more popular antiwar plays was "Guncotton," which described a young munitions factory worker's conflicting allegiance to his job while fretting over the horrible instruments of death he was helping to build. "God and Country" was another one that appealed to worker audiences. This play was particularly striking in that it illustrated the fate of four soldiers (a cockney cab driver, a German woodcarver, a French small farmer, and an American mechanic) who are killed in combat and then talk about their fate in the afterworld . At the conclusion of every performance, the audience was aroused and asked to sing the "D.A.R. Song" with the players. Verse 5 went as follows:

> My sons were moved to Wilson's Plea
> To end all strife they bore guns.
> They fought to save democracy
> (They saved the Fords and Morgans.)
> You say their ardors banished war
> Dictators barred forevermore:
> That now not want or woe is seen?
> That was nineteen seventeen!

Brookwood's concern for labor organizing was also dramatically illustrated during the unionization drives in the auto industry of the mid-1930s. Efforts by the Congress of Industrial Organizations to unionize auto workers took an important turn in 1936–37 at the Fisher Body Plants of General Motors in Flint, Michigan. Without any warning the assembly line's production came to a complete standstill. Quickly, the strike spread to auto plants in Detroit, Cleveland, Toledo, and other parts of the country. Some 112,000 of General Motor's 150,000 workforce became immobilized.

The strike at Flint was totally new to plant managers and employers. It took the form of a "sit-down," a tactic that had been taught at Brookwood (**Document 8**). Led by United Auto Worker organizers and former Brookwood students Roy Reuther and Merlin Bishop, the laborers at the Fisher Body Plant refused to leave the plant; they simply sat at their workbenches. Plant managers were dumbfounded and were caught totally off guard.

The sit-down was not an act of violence but one of passive resistance. The strike dragged on for weeks during one of the coldest recorded winters for that area, with crucial support work coming from women outside the plant. Finally, on February 4, 1937, with the sit-downers barricaded in the factories and protecting themselves against the expected tear gas with skimpy cheesecloth masks, the impasse between General Motors and the United Automobile Workers was broken. GM management decided to recognize the UAW as the bargaining agent for its members, to drop injunction proceedings against the strikers, to refrain from discriminating in any way against union members, and to take up such grievances as the speed-up and other matters. Although the UAW failed to achieve a minimum wage and thirty-hour work week, it succeeded in capturing another anti-union stronghold. Its success was attributable to the discipline exhibited during the sit-down and the avoidance of bloodshed.

Building a new social order required an intense commitment to racial and economic justice and nowhere was this more apparent than in the South. There, many African American coal miners experienced brutal discrimination. Unequal treatment and unequal pay was the standard; Angelo Herndon was one worker who experienced this firsthand. Angered at his treatment as well as the system of segregation that restricted African American lives, he found a safe haven when he joined the Communist Party in order to challenge these conditions. The party had taken the lead in the fight for racial justice after nine black male youths were accused of raping two white girls in Scottsboro, Alabama, in 1931. The black youths were convicted on slim evidence by all-white juries, and members of the Communist Party continued the battle for their release. Admiring their efforts, Herndon joined the party and began organizing unemployed blacks in Birmingham, Alabama; he also assisted in the creation of the Unemployed Councils and played a prominent role in organizing protests composed of black and white workers who had lost their jobs.

As a result of his organizing activities, Herndon was eventually arrested in Atlanta in 1933, under an old Civil War statute of "inciting to insurrection." He was found guilty by an all-white jury and sentenced to eighteen to twenty years in prison. His case would eventually reach the nation's highest court, which ruled that his conviction was unconstitutional (**Document 9**). Many peace activists were drawn to the Herndon case and quickly recognized the connection between economic depression and racial injustice in the south.

Despite a war that was supposedly fought to "make the world safe for democracy," racial discrimination and segregation continued to haunt African Americans. Black veterans found it especially hard to comprehend that the rights for which they were sent to Europe to fight and die were still denied to them at home. Some of the most prominent African American thinkers and activists such as Richard Wright, Herndon, Paul Robeson, and W.E.B. Du Bois supported radical organizations to combat racial injustice in the 1930s. So did poet Langston Hughes, a founder of the Harlem Renaissance who was well known in literary circles. His writings opened new vistas to the suppression African Americans had been subjected to and called attention to the powerful contributions they made to American society. In a 1938 poem, he wrote about how his native land had let him down, asking when America would live up to its promise as the land of the free (**Document 10**).

Compounding the challenges posed by racial injustice and economic depression was the rise of Japanese militarism in the Far East and the rapid spread of fascism in Italy and Nazism in Germany. Alarmed by the political instability and rising militarism in Europe and Asia, beginning with the Japanese invasion of Manchuria in 1931, the American people were even more convinced that isolation from war was the best policy for government leaders to follow. The antiwar feelings in the early 1930s strengthened isolationism more than peace activism; still peace workers and other citizens worried about conflict in other parts of the world were willing to try anything in order to check the growing tide of war.

One of the more novel attempts to promote peace consciousness during these perilous times was not undertaken by pacifists or the peace movement itself. Rather, it evolved from the mind of a bubble gum entrepreneur, Warren Bowman. In 1937, while listening to a radio broadcast about the Japanese invasion of the Chinese mainland, Bowman called upon his advertising executive George Moll to develop a series of collector cards depicting the brutality of war and use them to sell his gum. While realizing that children would be attracted to the cards depicting various battle scenes, he instructed Moll and his editors to write meaningful stories on the back of each card, which would highlight the importance of peace rather than the sensationalism of war (**Document 11**).

What soon followed was a card series describing battle scenes and attacks on civilian populations. Each piece of gum, which sold for a penny, contained a card. The series, which produced 288 cards in the end, grossed over $100 million. Although Bowman became rich, he insisted that his primary purpose was to teach peace by exposing the tragedies of war—each GUM, Inc. card had printed at the bottom of the back, "To know the **HORRORS OF WAR** is to want **PEACE**." World Peaceways gave its full endorsement and even President Franklin D. Roosevelt attempted to use the cards as a way to explain the terrors of war to the American public in an effort to justify his policies of neutrality.

Those policies, combined with the worsening situation in Europe, brought to the forefront the divisions that would ultimately wreck the peace movement in the second half of the 1930s. Convinced that there were no serious moral differences among the European powers, pacifists urged Washington to carry out FDR's neutrality legislation and to revise the Versailles Treaty to placate German and Italian demands. Internationalists were not as hopeful and pressed for more presidential discretionary authority in case the international situation worsened. They were convinced that Mussolini and Hitler would eventually wage war to destroy the Versailles system. Leading internationalists called upon American officials to cooperate more fully with League powers in maintaining the current European order. The peace coalitions formed in the mid-to-late 1930s among internationalists and pacifists struggled to make the goal of neutrality a workable reality.

The tenuousness of the peace coalitions reflected how ineffective they became after 1935. Peace historians such as Charles DeBenedetti, Charles Chatfield, and Lawrence Wittner have described how the organized peace movement underwent a disastrous split in 1935 when the obvious collapse of the League of Nations and heightened European militarism created fears of another great war. The National Council for the Prevention of War, the Women's International League for Peace and Freedom, and staunchly pacifist groups—realizing their inability to prevent war in Europe—focused their attention on isolating America from that war. Conservative elements, however—including the Carnegie Endowment for International Peace, the Church Peace Union, the World Alliance for International Friendship through the Churches, the Catholic Association for International Peace, and the League of Nations Association—gradually shifted to doctrines of collective security. In the heated neutrality debates, the former groups supported the maintenance of mandatory neutrality, while the latter worked for the modification of the neutrality provisions and, eventually, for their repeal.

Neither wing of the antiwar movement, pacifist-neutralists nor internationalists, formed a unified political whole: each represented a loose, shifting coalition. Even though each advocated some of the same positions, they remained two distinct and frequently conflicting bodies of thought and action. At the very core was the troubling issue of whether Americans' commitment was to a wider world community or a narrow nationalism. The practical and philosophical questions of a world court, the outlawry of war, economic sanctions, and militarism were all dwarfed by this single overshadowing dilemma. In time of peace, the question seemed to fade in significance; but each time the threat of war loomed large and menacing, it arose again to test the courage and principles of those who sought a world without war.

It was left to a tiny group of pacifists, then, to keep the commitment to nonviolence alive. Though events would prove their efforts futile, their consciences remained clear. Those who steadfastly opposed the internationalist–interventionist line of reasoning developed carefully planned strategies and techniques, which would eventually have great impact on the protest movements of the 1960s. This would prove to be their lasting testimony to the nonviolent crusade for peace and justice.

Document 1: John Dewey
Shall the United States Join the World Court
(1923)

In a debate with Professor Manley O. Hudson of Harvard University at the Unitarian Laymen's League in Boston on May 21, 1923, and subsequently published in _The Christian Century_, Dewey expressed his feelings about the tragedies of modern warfare and proposed that the war system be replaced with a pledge to renounce the use of force as an instrument of war on the part of all signatory nations. This campaign resulted in the signing of the 1928 Kellogg–Briand Pact, also known as the Pact of Paris, hailed at the time as a significant achievement for the forces of peace.

---

*O*ur American idealism is not dead, it is not even sleeping; but it is confused, distracted, perplexed.... It has retired, discouraged into itself. It has found itself blocked in the manifestation of its will to enter into co-operative relations with European nations; that will has been blocked by the hatreds and intrigues of the political order of Europe, embodied in its diplomacies, its foreign offices and its conferences of ambassadors. The disorder of European international relations, including treaties and international law, centers about the war system.

We have word ... that the warmongers are still active in Europe; that the standing armies and navies of Europe are larger than they were before the war; that the budgets devoted to war purposes in Europe, the money raised by taxation of the people for the support of armies and navies, is greater today than it was before the late war, in spite of the overwhelming triumph of the allies, the broken power of the prostrate enemies, and the absence of anybody in sight against whom this increase of military and naval power is to be directed. Naturally, under such circumstances American idealism has been discouraged and is waiting for something that will unite its desire to assist in a real reign of international amity and peace. It is waiting for the discovery of a channel through which it can operate, a channel that does not conduct to the political system of Europe which is at bottom bound up at every point with the war system—a system of deceit and intrigue, predation and violence. Such a proposition has at last been put before the American people. Its short name is the Outlawry of War.

This name denotes more than a sentiment of moral justice. It denotes a general plan consisting of a few simple, understandable principles. War is not merely thought of and denounced as criminal; it is to be made a pubic crime by international law. It is not outlawed by rhetorical resolutions passed by either peace societies or parliaments.... I will not go out of my way to apply it to the so-called permanent court of international justice. A judicial substitute for wars as a method of settling disputes is created in the form of a supreme court of the nations of the world, the court sitting and deciding cases under and by an international law that has made war a crime and the instigators or breeders of war as much criminals as any other kind of murderers that now infest the earth....

...In disputes among nations the way of violence is...established. The word "established" is used advisedly. The evils of particular wars tend to blind us to a particular fact, namely, that the world lives today under a war system; a system entrenched in politics, in diplomacy, in existing international law and in every court that sits under existing international law.

The proposition, then, is not the moral proposition to abolish wars. It is the much more fundamental proposition to abolish the war system as an authorized and legally sanctioned institution. The first idea is either utopian at present or merely sentiment. This other proposition, to abolish the war system as an authorized, established institution sanctioned by law, contemplated by law, is practical. To grant the difference between these two propositions, one simply to do away with wars and the other to eliminate the war system as the reigning system under international politics, diplomacy and relations are conducted—to understand the difference between these two propositions is fundamental. Recourse to violence is not only *a* legitimate method for settling international disputes at present, under certain circumstances it is the only legitimate method, the ultimate reason of state....

I have referred several times to the fact that this outlawry of war is a new mode of approach, an attack from a different angle. And in conclusion I wish to refer to it again. We are asked not merely, what is the ultimate method of procedure, but how are we to proceed? Well, this new method of approach applies here, too. Other schemes for peace, excepting the purely educational and moral ones, have relied upon the initiative of rulers, politicians or statesmen, as has been the case, for example, in the constitution of the league of nations. Here at last is a movement for peace which starts from the people themselves, which expresses their will, and demands that the legislators and politicians and the diplomats give effect to the popular will for peace. It has the advantages of the popular educational movement, but unlike the other educational movement for peace it has a definite, simple, practical legislative goal.... Just think what a difference it makes whether you begin with the people and end with the politicians, or begin with the politicians and end by putting something over on the people....

Source: The Christian Century XL (October 1923): 1329–1334.

QUESTIONS

1. Why did Dewey consider American ideals as being confused and distracted? What did Dewey consider the redeeming virtue of the outlawry of war plan?
2. How did he seek to distinguish the outlawry of war plan from the existing permanent court of international justice? Why was he suspicious of "Old World" politics?
3. How was Dewey able to distinguish the moral proposition from the practical proposition in this debate? What did he consider the most important element for this plan to succeed? How did this plan reflect the views of interwar peace activists?

Document 2: "The War Resisters' International: Statement of Principles" (1924)

The War Resisters' International (WRI) was an extension of the American War Resisters' League. Founded after World War I by Jessie Wallace Hughan and other pacifists, WRI was open to all objectors to war, regardless of religious beliefs or politics. It was opposed to conscription and dedicated to the principle of conscientious objection. It was also radical in its proposals for peace and justice based on socialist ideology.

The War Resisters' International (1924)

Declaration

"War is a crime against humanity. We therefore are determined not to support any kind of war and to strive for the removal of all the causes of war."

Statement of Principles

WAR IS A CRIME AGAINST HUMANITY.

It is a crime against life, and uses human personalities for political and economic ends.

WE, THEREFORE,

actuated by an intense love for mankind,

ARE DETERMINED NOT TO SUPPORT

either directly by service of any kind in the army, navy, or air forces, or indirectly by making or consciously handling munitions or other war material, subscribing to war loans or using our labour for the purpose of setting others free for war service,

ANY KIND OF WAR,

aggressive or defensive, remembering that modern wars are invariably alleged by Governments to be defensive.

Wars would seem to fall under three heads:—

Wars to defend the State to which we nominally belong and wherein our home is situated. To refuse to take up arms for this end is difficult:

Because the State will use all its coercive powers to make us do so.

Because our inborn love for home has been deliberately identified with love of the State in which it is situated.

Wars to preserve the existing order of society with its security for the privileged few. That we would never take up arms for this purpose goes without saying.

Wars on behalf of the oppressed proletariat, whether for its liberation or defense. To refuse to take up arms for this purpose is most difficult:

Because the proletarian regime, and, even more, the enraged masses, in time of revolution would regard as a traitor anyone who refused to support the New Order by force.

Because our instinctive love for the suffering and the oppressed would tempt us to use violence on their behalf.

However, we are convinced that violence cannot really *preserve order,* *defend* our home, or *liberate* the proletariat. In fact, experience has shown that in all wars, order, security, and liberty disappear, and that, so far from benefiting by them, the proletariat always suffers most.

We hold, however, that consistent pacifists have no right to take up a merely negative position, but *must recognize*

AND STRIVE FOR THE REMOVAL OF ALL THE CAUSES OF WAR.

We recognize as causes of war not only the instinct of egoism and greed, which is found in every human heart, but also all agencies which create hatred and antagonism between groups of people. Among such, we would regard the following as the more important of today:—

Differences between *races,* leading by artificial aggravation to envy and hatred.

Differences between *religions,* leading to mutual intolerance and contempt.

Differences between the *classes,* the possessing and the non-possessing, leading to civil war, which will continue so long as the present system of production exists, and private profit rather than social need is the outstanding motive of society.

Differences between *nations,* due largely to the present system of production, leading to world wars and such economic chaos as we see today, which eventualities, we are convinced, could be prevented by the adoption of a system of world economy which had for its end the well-being of the entire human race.

Finally, we see an important cause of war in the prevalent misconception of the State. The State exists for man, not man for the State. The recognition of the sanctity of human personality must become the basic principle of human society.... We feel, therefore, that consistent pacifists have no right to take up a merely negative position, but must devote themselves to abolishing classes, barriers between the peoples, and to creating a world-wide brotherhood founded on mutual service.

Source: Charles Chatfield, ed. *International War Resistance through World War II.* New York: Garland Publishing, Inc., 1971, pp. 57–58.

QUESTIONS

1. The "Just War" theory or tradition has a long history in Western thought and could be considered a "relative ethic." The Statement of Principles, on the other hand, seems to adopt an "absolute ethic" against all wars. Compare and contrast these two "ethics" and briefly summarize how both could be applied to World War I.

2. The Statement of Principles lists three heads under which wars seem to fall. What argument does the WRI make against each of these types of wars?
3. The Statement of Principles recognizes five important causes of war that must be removed from civilization to prevent future wars. List the causes and briefly describe a war that was motivated by each.

Document 3:   Devere Allen
War Resistance as War Prevention (1925)

Devere Allen was an editor, journalist, and historian of American pacifism. Here he discusses the significance of resistance to war, explaining the social, economic, and political dimensions behind pacifism as a viable instrument for domestic reform. Note his reference to William James's idea of a moral equivalent of war.

*P*acifism, essentially, is a method of social change, of social development. Its dynamic power is goodwill. War is of course pacifism's greatest contradiction....

When 11,000 British pacifists and 4,000 in the United States who refused to fight regardless of consequences in the last war joined with many in other warring countries, a movement was started which since the war has developed differently from earlier pacifism both in quantity and quality. A great impetus was given to conscientious objection but "conscientious objection" also began to yield to "war resistance," and the change of terms is not without significance. The old flame of conscience and idealism still flared brightly and gave light, but like an acetylene torch it was used to cut through the iron mail of militarism....

Among hundreds of thousands...the spirit of sturdy war resistance has grown into deep conviction. Increasingly war resisters cease to think and talk of their viewpoint as personal "testimony" merely, and examine into the practical effect of mass resistance on war-breeding governments.

They have become acutely aware of recent developments in modern warfare and in modern civilization. Every day it becomes more clearly apparent that a modern war cannot be waged successfully if it is opposed at home by any appreciable minority not susceptible to threat or intimidation. Complicated as are the forces of manufacturing, transportation and communication, and the distribution of products nowadays, a condition approximating complete national unity is essential to war. Hence the increasing use by war governments of propaganda coupled with ruthless suppression of dissent. . . .

What will happen to the state if minority groups thus seek to impose their will and prevent a war deemed necessary? . . . Chiefly, it boils down to this. A war is seldom desired by a majority in any country; most if not all wars are produced by the stupid blundering or the dangerous diplomacy of small groups of officials acting in the interests of other small groups, usually economic. Not yet has democracy in its true sense functioned, for war-making governments do not take their people into their confidence. A group of resisters exercising obstructive power is the lingering popular conscience which has at length been shouted down or terrified into silence. Society cannot afford to suppress its innovators, even if there is risk involved in tolerance; for by the prophecy of those willing to pay a price for their convictions states make their most profound social gains. . . . Almost all advances the human race has thus far made have been due to the defiant rebellion of minorities. A minority is not always right; yet whatever is right has to come through a minority. The whole evolution of morality, socially considered, has proceeded in such a fashion. . . .

Is war resistance anything but negative? One may as well declare health negative, "negative" as a physician pronounces the result of a test when he can find no pathological condition. Negative? Consider some effects of war resistance.

It strikes directly at man-power, the indispensable elements of warfare in all ages. Not yet do Robots stalk over no-man's land under the flare of radio-directed star shells; and when that day arrives, if ever, a human brain will be back of every last mechanical device. Military experts quarrel over cavalry; naval experts debate the place of battleships; but all agree that flesh and bone are the *sine qua non* of war.

It cuts to the root of a fatal popular state of mind, the reliance on war as a last resort. Let people believe in war as a final reluctant weapon, and they are ready for any propaganda which assures them that everything else has failed. A conviction firmly held by a considerable minority that nothing other than peaceful means of settlement will be tolerated can go far to stimulate the inventive genius of diplomats.

It can aid in the conquest of international fears. If great demonstrations of military preparedness (such as the now defunct Mobilization Day) can instill fear into the minds of other peoples, certainly a demonstration of pacifist conviction can do something to alleviate fear and afford a sounder basis for the growth of goodwill. The presence of that 130,000 in England, small in influence as they still may be, is a reassuring evidence to every other country that no British government can start a war without encountering stubborn opposition from British subjects. The fact that Britain's labor movement stopped a threatened war on Russia in 1920 and has recently adopted a strong war resistance resolution certainly lessens fear to some extent of a future war launched by a shameless ministry. Britain has been selected as an illustration because she is a great power and because in England war resistance has reached its most vigorous peak; but what is true of England would be equally true of any other power.

It can push governments toward peace. The history of war is an evolution which has sloughed off many a once appealing *casus belli* for which governments could no longer obtain popular support. Religious wars, for example, have become all but non-existent, partly for economic reasons, to be sure, but also because the old dreads have been somewhat reduced. War resistance removes every *casus belli* from tolerance and lends a new insistence to demands for peaceful settlement.

It supplies a moral and dramatic equivalent for war. Struggle, color, sacrifice, danger, heroism—all these elements must present in any cause that is to command the allegiance of youth at its finest. There is in war resistance no emotion of the killer, but it demands men and women, not cowards, and at no time is a war resister free from danger. Like the fireman at his post, the war resister stands poised for action and, most probably, for costly action. In countries where there is no peace-time conscription it often takes a war to expose a war resister to perils more serious than economic insecurity and the contumely of patrioteers. But in many countries young men by scores are today serving out sentences of brutal severity. Seventy-two members of the Nazarene religion, for example, are starting ten-year sentences in Jugoslavia, after already spending five years in prison awaiting a disposal of their case. . . .

Source: Charles Chatfield, ed. *Devere Allen and A Radical Approach to War.* New York: Garland Publishing, Inc., 1971, pp. 62–71.

QUESTIONS

1. What is the difference between conscientious objection and war resistance, according to Allen?

2. "Not yet has democracy in its true sense functioned, for war-making governments do not take their people into their confidence." Analyze this statement and formulate a detailed response in regard to America's involvement and entrance into World War I.
3. Allen lists five effects of war resistance. What major contribution has each one had historically in preventing war? Give an example for each.

Document 4:   Richard Gregg
The Power of Nonviolence (1934)

Richard Gregg was a Harvard-trained lawyer who traveled to India in the 1920s, where he met Gandhi and became a devoted disciple. He then studied in earnest Gandhian principles of nonviolence. His best-known work, published in 1934, *The Power of Nonviolence*, became the bible of American pacifists in the late 1930s as the threat of another war loomed on the horizon.

[Nonviolent resistance] does not avoid hardships, suffering, wounds or even death. In using it men and women may still risk their lives and fortunes and sacrifice all. Nevertheless, the possibilities of casualties and death are greatly reduced under it, and they are all suffered voluntarily and not imposed by the nonviolent resisters.

It is more efficient than war because it cost[s] far less in money as well as in lives and suffering. Also usually it permits a large part of the agricultural and industrial work of the people to go on, and hence the life of the country can be maintained during the struggle.

It is again more efficient than war because "the legitimate object of war is a more perfect peace." If the peace after the war is to be better than that which preceded it, the psychological processes of the conflict must be such as will create a more perfect peace.... Mutual violence inevitably breeds hatred, revenge and bitterness—a poor foundation for a more perfect peace. The method of nonviolent resistance, where there really is resistance, so as to bring all the issues out into the open, and a really new settlement worked out as nearly as possible in accord with the full truth of the issues at stake—this method does not leave a sense of frustration and will bring a more perfect peace.

Considering the completeness of its effects, nonviolent resistance is quick and probably quicker than war by violence. It is a weapon that can be used equally well by small or large nations, small or large groups, by the economically weak and by the apparently strong, and even by individuals. It compels both sides and neutrals to seek the truth, whereas war blinds both sides and neutrals to the truth.

... Nonviolent resistance certainly produces less ill effect, if any, than does violent war, and this decrease of ill effects applies to the users of nonviolence, to the opposing side, and to society and the world at large.

May we not then fairly describe nonviolent resistance as an effective substitute for war?

It is realistic in that it does not eliminate or attempt to eliminate possibilities of conflict and differences of interest, and includes *all* factors in the situation both material and imponderable, physical and psychological.

It does not require any nation to surrender any part of its real sovereignty or right of decision, as a real league of nations might. It does not surrender the right of self-defense, although it radically alters the nature of defense. It requires no expensive weapons or armament, no ... grounds for secrecy. It does not demoralize those who take part in it, but leaves them finer men and women than when the struggle began.

Moreover, the method does not require the machinery of a government or a large wealthy organization. It may be practiced and skill may be acquired in it in every situation of life, at home and abroad, by men and women of any and all races, nations, tribes, groups, classes, or castes, young and old, rich and poor.

Source: Charles Chatfield and Ruzanna Illukhina, eds. *Peace/Mir: An Anthology of Historic Alternatives to War.* Syracuse, NY: Syracuse University Press, 1994, pp. 248–249.

QUESTIONS

1. From your reading of the document, describe Gregg's understanding of "a more perfect peace" in the context of violence (war) versus nonviolence resistance.

2. Gregg states that nonviolent resistance "compels both sides and neutrals to seek the truth, whereas war blinds both sides and neutrals to the truth." Analyze this statement in light of World War I, the Versailles Treaty, and the state of Germany at the time

of Gregg's writing. Does Gregg make his case? Use historical facts and information to support your answer.

3. From Gregg's assessment of the nonviolent resistance method, explain and support how it could be a perfect weapon in bringing about reform.

Document 5:   Reinhold Niebuhr
                Why I Leave the F.O.R. (1934)

One of the foremost Protestant theologians of the first half of the twentieth century, Niebuhr was a visible critic of war in the 1920s and early 1930s. He was an influential figure in the Fellowship of Reconciliation until the Great Depression caused him to reconsider his belief in absolute pacifism. Niebuhr's classic work, _Moral Man and Immoral Society_ (1932), provides an early glimpse of his rethinking about Christian liberalism and the Social Gospel. In this essay, which appeared in the January 1934 issue of _The Christian Century_, he maps out his reasons for leaving the peace organization due to internal ideological debates involving the working-class struggle.

---

*H*istorically the Fellowship of the Reconciliation is an organization of pacifists, born during the war and holding to the Quaker position on war beyond the confines of the Quaker fellowship. . . . As long as they could believe that the injustice of Capitalism could be abolished by moral suasion there seemed to be no particular conflict between the pacifists and their socialism. They held to the generally accepted position of Christian socialists who believed that the peculiar contribution of religion to the social struggle must be an insistence upon nonviolent or even non-coercive methods of social change. In the recent poll of the membership it was revealed that 21 percent of the membership still believed that the Fellowship should endeavor through "method of love" to bring about a new order "without identifying itself with either the underprivileged or the privileged class." . . .

In the case of the social struggle that is being waged between the privileged and the disinherited classes in every Western nation, some of us, at least, know that there are possibilities that modern civilization will drift into barbarism with the disintegration of the capitalistic system. We believe that not only fascism but communism has the perils of barbarism in it. The peril of the latter arises not so much from its preaching of violence as from its preaching of hatred. Hatred is very blinding; and those who are blind cannot be good enough statesman to become the instrument of a new unity amid the complexities of the Western civilization. We would certainly have as much sense of responsibility toward the avoidance of barbaric civil strife as any other intelligent and responsible person. . . .

We realize that the problem of social justice is pragmatic and even a technical one. Modern capitalism breeds injustice because of the disproportions of economic power that it tolerates and upon which it is based. We expect no basic economic justice without destruction of the present disproportion of power and we do not expect the latter without a social struggle. Once we have accepted the fact of the reality of the social struggle we do not feel we can stop where the middle portion of the Fellowship has stopped. We are unable to stop there because we can find no stable absolute in the shifting situation of the social struggle where everything must be finally decided on pragmatic terms.

If we should agree with some portion of this middle section that we use nonviolent coercion in behalf of the disinherited but will discourage any coercion that may issue violence; we feel that we would give an undue moral advantage to that portion of the community which is always using nonviolent coercion against the disinherited. This is precisely what the liberal church is constantly tempted to do. It is furthermore usually oblivious to the fact that nonviolence may be converted violence. Children do starve and old people freeze to death in the poverty of our cities, a poverty for which everyone who has more than the bare necessities of life must feel some responsibility.

We cannot agree with another group of these qualified pacifists who would participate in an armed social conflict but who would not personally participate in its violence, contenting themselves with noncombatant services, because we have come to believe that such an attitude represents an abortive effort to maintain personal purity while holding an organic relation to a social movement that is bound to result in some degree of violence in the day of crisis.

. . . As a Marxian and as a Christian it reveals to me the futility of finding a moral absolute in the relativities of politics. If anyone should suggest that those of us who have thus renounced the pacifist position ought not any longer to regard ourselves as Christian, I would answer that it is only Christianity that suffers from modern liberal illusions, that has ever believed that the law of love could be made an absolute guide of conduct in social morality and politics. As a Marxian and as a

Christian I recognize the tragic character of man's social life, and the inevitability of conflict in it arising from the inability of man ever to bring his egoism completely under the dominion of conscience.

As a Marxian I will try to guide that conflict to a goal that guarantees a basic economic justice and creates a society that makes modern technical civilization sufferable. As a Christian I will know that even the justice of a socialist commonwealth will reveal the imperfections of natural man and will not destroy the contest of wills and interests which will express itself in every society. As a Christian I will achieve at least enough contrition before the absolute demands that God makes upon me and that I never completely fulfill to be able to deal with those who oppose me with a measure of forgiveness. Christianity means more than any moral attitude that can express itself in social politics. But it must at least mean that the social struggle is fought without hatred. Non-hatred is a much more important sin and symbol of Christian faith than nonviolence....

...In so far as we are radical Christians we must find a more solid ground for the combination of radicalism and Christianity than the creed of pacifism supplied. But we will always maintain our respect for the purity of purpose that animates the men who conceived the Fellowship of Reconciliation and will carry it on in spite of discouragement in these critical days. Perhaps the day will come when we will be grateful for their counsels. Recognizing, as liberal Christianity does not, that the world of politics is full of demonic forces, we have chosen on the whole to support the devil of vengeance against the devil of hypocrisy. In the day in which we live, a dying social system commits the hypocrisy of hiding its injustices behind the form of justice, and the victims of injustice express their politics in terms of resentment against this injustice.... We cannot follow them because we believe that consistency would demand flight to the monastery if all the devils of man's collective life were to be avoided. But our traffic with devils may lead to corruption, and the day may come when we will be grateful for those who try to restrain all demons rather than choose between them.

Source: Peter Mayer, ed. *The Pacifist Conscience.* Chicago: Henry Regenery Co., 1967, pp. 250–255.

QUESTIONS

1. What is the main theme or idea of this article? Why is Niebuhr leaving the FOR?

2. What is Niebuhr's view of the world, and why does he see it this way?

3. Was Niebuhr abandoning his opposition to war? How did he explain the failings of the Fellowship with respect to the class struggle?

Document 6:   Kirby Page
War is Sin (1935)

Kirby Page, a socialist, pacifist, and ordained minister, edited the periodical *The World Tomorrow*. A social evangelist, independent author, speaker, and organizer, Page connected his religious beliefs to social justice and international peace. This piece is one of the strongest defenses of Christian pacifism between the world wars.

"*War* is sin." This conviction has been expressed in scores of resolutions passed by religious assemblies and broadcast in various proclamations signed by eminent leaders of religious institutions.... The commission on world peace of the general conference of the Methodist Episcopal church, for example, says: "Our fundamental conviction is that war is sin ... because it involves (a) the slaughter of human beings, (b) violation of personality, (c) lying propaganda, (d) deliberate breeding of the spirit of hate, (e) vast destruction of property, (f) it puts in the place of moral law the doctrine of military necessity, (g) it distorts the religion of Jesus into the religion of a war god."

The Lambeth conference of the Anglican communion in 1930 declared: "We affirm that war as a method of settling international disputes is incompatible with the teaching and example of our Lord Jesus Christ." The commission on international justice and goodwill of the Federal Council of the Churches of Christ in America issued a manifesto from which these words are taken: "The war-system of the nations is the outstanding evil of the present-day civilization. It is the most ominous anti-Christian phase of modern life."

That these emphatic pronouncements are warranted is apparent from an examination of the nature of modern war. Much confusion may easily be avoided by remembering that *war is a method*. It is not an end, nor is it a spirit. War has ends in view and is waged in a certain spirit, but war is not noble objectives and it is not the spirit of courage and sacrifice. War is method, the method of military necessity....

Therefore—what?...

The agencies of religious education should teach that since war is sin, no Christian may legitimately engage in it....

If war is sin, no candidate for ordination to the ministry of the Christian church who professes a willingness to sanction war or to participate in it should be accepted as a minister of the Prince of Peace....

If war is sin, official chaplains of religion should be withdrawn from this sinful business, and arrangements made for serving soldiers and sailors in non-official and non-sinful ways....

If war is sin, young Christians should be taught that they must not take military training in high school or college....

If war is sin, the churches must advocate total disarmament and must cease to place any reliance whatever in armed preparedness against other nations....

If war is sin, the churches should demand a friendly and cooperative foreign policy on the part of their government....

If war is sin, the churches must seek to create public opinion in behalf of international agencies of justice....

If war is sin, the churches should seek to transform the economic and political systems out of which war emerges....

If war is sin, and if the churches act as if war is sin, a revolution in thought will be accomplished by a revolution in policy with regard to economic and political systems....

Source: Charles Chatfield and Ruzanna Illuchina, eds. *Peace/Mir: An Anthology of Historic Alternatives to War.* Syracuse, NY: Syracuse University Press, 1994, pp. 234–235.

QUESTIONS

1. Kirby Page lists seven fundamental convictions put forth by the Methodist Episcopal Church as to why war is sin. Name each conviction, and, by drawing on your knowledge of the early 20th century, give and summarize a historical fact for each one to substantiate the Methodist position.

2. "The war-system of the nations is the outstanding evil of the present-day civilization." You are challenged to debate this suppo-

sition. Choose a side and state your position by drawing on early 20th-century historical facts and information to back up your choice.

3. Page states, "War is a method." Explain what he means by this statement by drawing on your knowledge of the social, political, and economic causes of both world wars.

Document 7: American Youth Congress
The Declaration of the Rights of American Youth (July 4, 1936)

Founded in 1934, the American Youth Congress championed the cause of job programs for low-income students and unemployed youth. The group sponsored its own aid bill, the American Youth Act. Though the bill never made it through Congress, the Roosevelt Administration repeatedly enlisted the group's support for the National Youth Administration's aid programs. The movement's leaders encouraged domestic reform, free speech on college campuses, support for the CIO's industrial organizing drives, establishment of campus cooperatives, and campaigns against racial discrimination in higher education.

*O*n the Fourth of July one hundred and sixty years ago our forefathers declared their independence from despotic rule in order to realize their inalienable rights to life, liberty, and the pursuit of happiness.—Today our lives are threatened by war; our liberties threatened by reactionary legislation; and our right to happiness remains illusory in a world of insecurity.—Therefore, on this Fourth day of July, 1936, we, the young People of America, in Congress assembled, announce our own declaration—A Declaration of the Rights of American Youth.

We declare that our generation is rightfully entitled to a useful, creative, and happy life, the guarantees of which are: full educational opportunities, steady employment at adequate wages, security in time of need, civil rights, religious freedom, and peace.

We have a right to life! Yet we are threatened by wars that are even now being prepared by those who profit by destruction, wars from which we can reap nothing but misery, mutilation and death. We oppose this war and its trappings of militarized youth and mounting armaments. We do not want to die! We assert our right to peace and our determination to maintain peace.

We have a right to liberty! In song and legend America has been exalted as a land of the free, a haven for the oppressed. Yet on every hand we see this freedom limited or destroyed. Progressive forces are persecuted. Minority nationalities are exposed to arbitrary deportation. The negro people are subjected to constant abuse, discrimination and lynch laws. Workers who strike for a living wage are met with increasing violence.—These we affirm to be the omens of that modern tyranny, fascism. More brutal, more vicious and reactionary than even that against which our forefathers rebelled in 1776.—We are determined to realize in actuality the ideals of a free America. We demand not only the maintenance but the extension of our elementary rights of free speech, press and assemblage. We oppose company unions and affirm the right of workers to join labor unions of their own choosing in order to advance their economic interests. We consider full academic freedom essential to progress and enlightenment. We strongly oppose fascism, with its accompanying demagogy, as a complete negation of our right to liberty.

We have a right to happiness! Our country with its natural resources and mighty industries can more than provide a life of security and comfort for all. But today we are not provided with this security, are not permitted to enjoy its comforts. We want to work, to produce, to build, but millions of us are forced to be idle.... We urge a system of unemployment and social insurance as an immediate improvement in the condition of unemployed youth and we affirm our right to be employed on all relief projects at equal wages for equal work.... We stand unalterably opposed to any program which destroys crops and livestock while millions remain unfed and undernourished.... Our right to work includes the right of proper preparation for work. Education must be available to everyone without discrimination, poor as well as rich, Negroes as well as white.... We declare that the workers of hand and brain, the producers of our wealth, the builders of our country are the decisive force with which all true friends of peace, freedom and progress must ally themselves. We recognize that we young people do not constitute a separate social group, but that our problems and aspirations are intimately bound up with those of all the people.... We look at this country of ours. We love it dearly; we are its flesh and marrow. We have roamed its roads; we have camped in its mountains and forests; we have smelled its rich earth; we have tended its fields and dug its earthly treasures. We have toiled in it. Because we know it so well, we know that it could be a haven of peace, security and abundance for all.

Therefore, we the young people of America, reaffirm our right to life, liberty and the pursuit of happiness. With confidence we look forward to a better life, a larger liberty and freedom. To those ends we dedicate our lives, our intelligence and our unified strength.

Source: "American Youth Congress Declaration of the Rights of American Youth," http://newdeal.feri.org/students/ayc.htm (accessed March 15, 2007)

QUESTIONS

1. How does the AYC frame its arguments for the rights of American youth? Why does it present itself in the language that it does?
2. How can you tell this was written during the Great Depression? Does it still apply in any way?
3. What are the AYC's arguments against war and fascism?

Document 8:   Joel Seidman
Sit-Down (1937)

Joel Seidman was a labor educator and labor economist who followed the organizing drives of the CIO during the Great Depression. He wrote numerous works on the principles of unionization and lectured at Brookwood Labor College. His description of the sit-down strikes, which reached their peak in 1936–37, is drawn from a report of the League for Industrial Democracy. He discusses the effectiveness of nonresistance or nonviolence as a new tactic in the labor struggles.

*W*hen they tie the can to a union man,
Sit Down! Sit Down!
When they gave him the sack, they'll take him back,
Sit Down! Sit Down!

Chorus
Sit down, just take a seat
Sit down, and rest your feet

Sit down, you've got'em beat.
Sit down! Sit down!

A new strike technique has swept the country, arousing enthusiasm among workers, and bewilderment among employers. In industry after industry, in state after state, the workers remained at their post but refused to work. No longer is it possible to introduce strikebreakers, for the workers are in possession. Nor are the workers readily dispersed, for they can barricade themselves in a strong defensive position. If strikebreakers or police storm the factory gate, they are clearly responsible in the eyes of the public for whatever violence may occur. The employer can not too easily afford to alienate public opinion, not risk damage to his machinery. And so the workers remain in possession of the plant, in much more comfort and security than on the picket line. . . .

Early Uses of Sit-Down in America

It is impossible to determine accurately when and where the sit-down strike was first used. It seems such a logical tactic for workers to employ that there are probably many unrecorded instances, each one short in duration, going back almost as far as modern industrial civilization. The wonder is that its use did not become widespread much earlier.

In at least two American industries it has been long common for workers to stop work without leaving their place of employment. In the anthracite coal fields the breaker boys, whose task it was to remove impurities from the coal, early formed the practice of stopping work without leaving their places when they were dissatisfied. Similarly miners have stopped loading coal when they are not adequately supplied with timber for safety protection.

In the women garment industry, as far back as 1910, workers have ceased operations without leaving the shop. Partly this has been done when a contract forbade strikes, the workers arguing that a mere stoppage was not a violation. These stoppages, as they were called, attracted little attention because they were usually settled within a few hours, and lacked the drama and publicity value of a picket line. Seldom, if ever, did the workers remain at their places overnight, though stoppages often continued for several days. In the Schenectady, NY, plant of General Electric Company, similarly, a sit-down strike occurred as early as 1906. In 1933, 2,500 employees of the Hormel packing company in Austin, Minnesota, sat down for three days and won their strike against speed-up, for shorter hours and better wages. Many other instances doubtless occurred in other industries. During the depression the unemployed in New Jersey and elsewhere, took possession of legislative chambers, in an effort to dramatize their plight and force more adequate relief policies.

Seamen used the sit-down strike on the Pacific coast early in 1936. Seamen on the Panama Pacific liner *California* had signed on the Atlantic coast rates. In an effort to obtain the higher Pacific coast rates, they struck for three days while the ship was at the San Pedro, California docks. The men remained onboard, but refused to work. Had they struck while the ship was at sea, they would have been subject to the charge of mutiny. As it was, they narrowly escaped arrest on that charge. The line refused to re-employ the strikers when the ship reached New York, and a long strike against the International Mercantile Marine Company was the result.

Source: Staughton Lynd, ed. *Nonviolence in America: A Documentary History.* Indianapolis, IN: Bobbs-Merrill Co., 1966, pp. 241–270.

QUESTIONS

1. What is a sit-down and why would it occur?
2. Using your knowledge of history and this passage, describe how this method was used before and after the 1930s.
3. Why would this technique appeal to pacifists?

Document 9: Angelo Herndon
You Cannot Kill the Working Class (1937)

Herndon's words tell of the injustices African American workers faced in the South and the laws that were used to silence unions and political organizations that favored the working class. While the Communist Party took up the cause of racial justice in the South, anyone remotely associated with the party was quick to find themselves under suspicion. Being black and a member of the Communist Party was more than was needed for Herndon to be convicted by an all-white jury on a bogus charge. In 1937, the U.S. Supreme Court invalidated the Georgia statute under which Herndon was found guilty and he was released from prison.

$\mathcal{W}$e lived in the company town. It was pretty bad. The houses were just shacks and unpaved streets. We seldom had anything to eat that was right. We had to buy everything from the company store, or we'd have lost our jobs.... We got advances in the form of clackers, which could be used only in the company store. Their prices were very high. I remember paying 30 cents a pound for pork-chops in the company store and then noticing that the butcher in town was selling them for 20 cents. The company store prices were just robbery without a pistol.

The safety conditions in the mine were rotten.... There were some bad accidents while I was there. I took all the skin off my right hand pushing a car up into the facing. The cars didn't have enough grease and there were no cross-ties just behind me to brace my feet against. That was a bit of the company's economy. The car slipped, the truck turned over, and the next thing I knew I had lost all the skin and a lot of the flesh off my right hand. The scars are there to this day.

This DeBardeleben mine in Lexington was where the Jim-Crow system first hit me. The Negroes and whites seldom came in contact with each other.... The Negroes worked on the North side of the mine and the whites on the South.

The Negroes never got a look-in on most of the better-paying jobs. They couldn't be section foremen, or electricians, or surveyors, or head bank boss, or checkweighman, or steel sharpeners, or engineers. They could only load the coal, run the motors, be mule-boys, pick the coal, muck the rock. In other words, they were only allowed to do the muscle work.

Besides that, the negro miners got the worst places to work. We worked in the low coal, only 3 or 4 feet high. We had to wear knee pads, and work stretched flat on our bellies most of the time....

One day in June, 1930, walking home from work, I came across some handbills put out by the Unemployment Council in Birmingham...I joined the Unemployment Council, and some weeks later the Communist Party. I read all the literature of the movement that I could get my hands on....

We organized a number of block committees of the Unemployment Councils and got rent and relief for a large number of families. We agitated endlessly for unemployment insurance.

In the middle of June, 1932, the state closed down all the relief stations. A drive was organized to send all the jobless to the farms.

We gave out leaflets calling for a mass demonstration at the courthouse to demand that the relief be continued. About 1000 workers came, 600 of them white. We told the commissioners we didn't intend to starve. We reminded them that $800,000 had been collected in the Community Chest drive. The commissioners said there wasn't a cent to be had.

On the night of July 11, I went to the Post Office to get my mail. I felt myself grabbed from behind and turned over to see a police officer.

I was placed in a cell, and was shown a large electric chair, and told to spill everything I knew about the movement. I refused to talk, and was held incommunicado for eleven days. Finally I smuggled out a letter through another prisoner, and the International Labor Defense got on the job.

Assistant Solicitor John Hudson rigged up the charge against me. It was the charge of "inciting to insurrection." It was based on an old statute passed in 1861, when the Negro people were still chattel slaves, and the white masters needed a law to crush slave insurrection and kill those found giving aid to the slaves. . . .

The trial was set for Januaury 16, 1933. The state of Georgia displayed the literature that had been taken from my room, and read passages of it to the jury. They questioned me in great detail. Did I believe that the bosses and government ought to pay insurance to unemployed workers? That Negroes should have complete equality with white people? Did I believe in the demand for the self-determination of the Black Belt—that the Negro people should be allowed to rule the Black Belt territory, kicking out the white landlords and government officials? Did I feel that the working-class could run the mills and mines and government? That it wasn't necessary to have bosses at all? . . .

The state held that my membership in the Communist Party, my possession of Communist literature, was enough to send me to the electric chair. They said to the jury: "Stamp this damnable thing out now with a conviction that will automatically carry with it a penalty of electrocution."

And the hand-picked lily-white jury responded:

"We the jury, find the defendant guilty as charged, but recommend that mercy be shown and fix his sentence at from 18 to 20 years. . . ."

. . . I spoke to the court and said:

"They can hold this Angelo Herndon and hundreds of others, but it will never stop these demonstrations on the part of Negro and white workers who demand a decent place to live in and proper food for their kids to eat.... If you really want to do anything about the case, you must go out and indict the social system. But this you will not do, for your role is to defend the system under which the toiling masses are robbed and oppressed."...

Source: Timothy McCarthy and John McMillan, eds. *The Radical Reader.* New York: The New Press, 2003, pp. 344–348.

QUESTIONS

1. What was a company town? What were conditions like for African American miners in the South?
2. In what way did the Unemployed Councils and the Communist Party attempt to assist Southern workers during the Great Depression?
3. How did Georgia state authorities attempt to silence working-class organizers and what fears did they rely on to support their actions?

Document 10:   Langston Hughes
Let America Be America Again (1938)

Langston Hughes (1902–1967) is one of America's most famous African American poets. He was also a novelist, playwright, and esteemed essayist on matters of race. He rose to fame as a poet during the 1920s and 1930s as the Harlem Renaissance offered its own version of black identity and literary achievement to the arts. In this poem Hughes calls on America to live up to its professed ideals of liberty and equality.

*L*et America be America again.
Let it be the dream it used to be.
Let it be the pioneer on the plain
Seeking a home where he himself is free
(America never was America to me.)
Let America be the dream the dreamers dreamed—
Let it be that great strong land of love
Where never kings connive nor tyrants scheme

That any man be crushed by one above.
(It never was America to me.)
O, let my land be a land where Liberty
Is crowned with no false patriotic wreath,
But opportunity is real, and life is free,
Equality is in the air we breathe.
(There's never been equality for me,
Nor freedom in this "homeland of the free.")
Say, who are you that mumbles in the dark?
And who are you that draws your veil across the stars?
I am the poor white, fooled and pushed apart,
I am the Negro bearing slavery's scars.
I am the red man driven from the land,
I am the immigrant clutching the hope I seek—
And finding only the same old stupid plan
Of dog eat dog, of mighty crush the weak....
Yet I'm the one who dreamt our basic dream
In the Old World while still a serf of kings,
Who dreamt a dream so strong, so brave, so true,
That even yet its mighty daring sings
In every brick and stone, in every furrow turned
That's made America the land it has become.
O, I'm the man who sailed those early seas
In search of what I meant to be my home—
For I'm the one who left dark Ireland's shore,
And Poland's plain, and England's grassy lea,
And torn from Black Africa's strand I came
To build a "homeland of the free...."
O' let America be America again—
The land that never has been yet—
And yet must be—the land where every man is free.
The land that's mine—the poor man's, Indians, Negro's, ME—
Who made America,
Whose sweat and blood, whose faith and pain,
Whose hand at the foundry, whose plow in the rain,
Must bring back our mighty dream again....

Source: Langston Hughes, "Let America Be America Again," http://
    southerncrossreview,org/29/hughes (accessed Feburary 2, 2009).

QUESTIONS

1. What does Hughes mean by his statement, "America never was America to me"?
2. What examples does Hughes provide in his poem to justify his critique of America? Who is being oppressed in his view?
3. Is he optimistic about the future?

Document 11: "Horrors of War" Card Series (1938)

Warren Bowman, owner of Gum, Inc., was disturbed by the atrocities he heard about when Japan invaded the Chinese mainland. He decided to produce a series of collector cards describing the realities of modern warfare, including the Spanish Civil War and the Italian invasion of Ethiopia. Inscribed on the bottom of each cardback were the following words: "To know the **HORRORS OF WAR** is to want **PEACE**." The one-cent cards with a piece of bubble gum became a bestseller and additional cards were made focusing on the growing threat of Nazi aggression in Europe. Below are two illustrated cards. Excerpts from the cardbacks are provided for clarity.

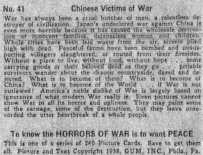

Figure 5.1 "Chinese Victims of War": "War has always been a cruel butcher of men, a relentless destroyer of civilization. Japan's undeclared war against China is even more horrible because it has caused the wholesale destruction of innocent families.... What is to become of the World . . . if War is not outlawed!" *Source:* "Horrors of War Bubblegum Cards," http://www.dekescollection.net (accessed September 10, 2008).

QUESTIONS

1. What might make these "Chinese Victims" have to move through the mountains?
2. How might this card promote peace?

Figure 5.2 "Death Among the Water Lilies": "The picture shows one of the artistic little ponds—once the decoration of a local mandarin's garden—now a pathetic scene of desolation unnoticed by the triumphant but callous procession of Chinese troops." *Source*: "Horrors of War Bubblegum Cards," http://www.dekescollection.net (accessed September 10, 2008).

QUESTIONS

1. How has this picturesque scene been changed by the war?
2. Why did the creators choose this as a scene to promote peace?

6

Nonviolent Direct Action for Equality and Disarmament

The Japanese attack on Pearl Harbor in December 1941 divided the peace movement into two groups. Religious sectarians and pacifists protested the war by refusing induction into the armed forces, volunteering for noncombatant service in the Civilian Public Service Camps or accepting a federal prison term, aiding conscientious objectors, arguing against the military strategy of saturation bombing, and calling for the Allies to pursue a negotiated settlement. Internationalists did not protest the war but supported the Allied war aims as the basis for establishing a new, more workable international organization that would be acceptable to the American public.

The discontinuity in aims and strategies between pacifists and internationalists earmarked the ineffectiveness of the movement during World War II. Both elements desperately wanted peace, but the prescriptions they offered to treat the illness of war were entirely different. The pacifist prescription was noncooperation, while the internationalist remedy was using force to end the conflict.

For the People, pages 167–207
Copyright © 2009 by Information Age Publishing
All rights of reproduction in any form reserved.

With the approach of war, pacifists retreated to a defensive position, reasserting the essential religious quality of pacifism and clinging to a personal resistance to all forms of warfare. This shift in emphasis left them without the functional, secular theory of nonviolence they had been developing in the 1930s that could more easily sustain the principle of conscientious objection on nonreligious grounds.

In general, the protest against war and militarism in 1941 was much weaker than in 1917. Hitler and Mussolini were real threats and the Japanese did strike first. However, that did not hinder the efforts of strongly committed pacifists groups such as the War Resisters League to promote alternatives to war and violence (**Document 1**). Despite constant and unrelenting harassment by the Federal Bureau of Investigation on the grounds of evasion of the Registration Act (Selective Service Act, 1940), the WRL's pamphlets, speeches, and counseling services were not aimed at blatantly obstructing the draft during the war years. They were principally interested in informing pacifists and other individuals of available choices. Believing in the First Amendment's guarantee of freedom of speech, the League's pamphlets criticized the imprisonment of Japanese Americans for so-called security reasons and insisted that all nations should share responsibility for the causes that led to war. One of its leaders, Evan Thomas, correctly, but impetuously, accused the allies of secret preparations for war. Whatever the case, the WRL, like its ally the FOR, continued the struggle on behalf of peace and respect for individual conscience.

By 1937, more than 12,000 Americans had already signed the WRL pledge "War is a crime against humanity. I, therefore, am determined not to support any kind of war, international or civil, and to strive for the removal of all causes of war." During the war, WRL had a core of 2,300 active members who were united in their humanitarian, political, and philosophical objections to war. These hard-core radical pacifists, who adhered strictly to the teachings of Richard Gregg, would prove to be the backbone of a more militant civil disobedience movement during the early Cold War years.

Pacifists tested their nonviolent civil disobedience as conscientious objectors. During World War II, almost 43,000 Americans were conscientious objectors: close to 25,000 received noncombatant status, and of these 11,950 did alternative service work in Civilian Public Camps, and 12,662 draft violators were imprisoned or forced to enter the armed forces. More than 6,000 were sent to prison for failing to meet the requirements for conscientious objector status under the narrow provision of the Selective Service Law. Many were objectors not only to war but also to conscription as well. Refusing to register for the draft, they charged—like the WWI COs—that conscription was incompatible with human freedom.

In October 1940, eight students at Union Theological Seminary in New York City who had been living in voluntary poverty in Harlem while pursuing their studies initiated a legal confrontation when they refused to register for the draft. The court testimony, given the following year, of Donald Benedict, Joseph J. Bevilacqua, Meredith Dallas, David Dellinger, George M. Houser, William H. Lovell, Howard E. Spragg, and Richard J. Wichlei reaffirmed their belief that conscription was part of an evil system (**Document 2**). Their dissent was in keeping with the fundamental American belief in individual conscience. For these objectors, it was extremely important to fight against the "totalitarian" nature of conscription. Their stand was not simply a negative reaction to an unpleasant situation; rather, it was an attempt to establish a movement trained in the techniques of nonviolent opposition to the encroachments of militarism and fascism. It was, in their opinion, the only possible way to stall the war machine at home.

As the war proceeded, their ranks were swelled by many within the CPS camps. Initially, the major pacifist groups, WRL and FOR, had cooperated in the establishment of an alternative service program for objectors. (In 1940, the Historic Peace Churches created a National Service Board for Religious Objectors under the chairmanship of French Quaker Paul Comly; the Board assumed financial responsibility as well as supervision and control of the camps.) In fact, when Congress was about to vote on the Selective Service Act in 1940, polls indicated that a third of all Americans called for either forcing COs to fight in combat units or be imprisoned. Congress went along with the plan conceived by the various religious groups. The peace groups were convinced that it was the best alternative that could be salvaged under the circumstances and that CPS camps would render a humanitarian service in a world at war. Yet, military control, inconsequential work projects, and a sense of futility led many in the camps to believe that they had betrayed their basic principles.

The daily life of the CO was strictly regimented. All assigned work was to be carried out promptly and efficiently. The CO was responsible for taking care of all government property in his possession. His living quarters, including his person, clothing, and equipment, had to be neat and clean. Lastly, his personal behavior had to be beyond reproach and bring no discredit to himself or to the CPS program. Whenever so ordered he could be moved to another camp.

In addition to such tasks as reforestation and conservation programs, CPS men were involved in a series of dangerous and painful experiments.

There were typhus tests in which the "volunteers" had to wear lice-infested clothing for 3 weeks while continuing their usual work day, were placed in semi-starvation diets, and made to participate in atypical pneumonia experiments that involved drinking throat washings from infected soldiers. Thirty men in CPS camps died, more than 1,500 were discharged for physical disabilities, and yet the men and their families were not granted pay, dependency allotments, or workmen's compensation. These individuals had their consciences severely tested.

One of the more positive aspects of the CO experience was the battle against racial segregation. Jim Peck, sentenced to 28 months in jail for opposing the war, was a leader in the 135-day strike against segregation in the mess hall at the federal prison in Danbury, Connecticut. David Dellinger refused to register for the draft and was sent to Lewisburg Penitentiary in Pennsylvania for two years; he took part in a 60-day fast to protest the prison's racial segregation. Bayard Rustin drove his jailers crazy by constantly protesting segregation and the other arbitrary rules imposed by authorities. Such nonviolent protests by radical pacifists against racial discrimination and segregation would prove to have long-lasting implications.

The connections between pacifism and civil rights were forged outside prison walls as well, notably in Chicago in 1942, where the local Committee of Racial Equality organized sit-ins by small interracial groups at Stoner's, a white tablecloth restaurant in the heart of the Loop. So successful was the Committee in cracking the color line along Chicago's Loop that a national conference of persons and groups interested in this technique was called the following year. The result was the establishment of CORE (Congress of Racial Equality), a federation of local interracial groups that used the tactic of nonviolent direct action to challenge segregation. CORE's national coordinators, George Houser and Bayard Rustin, worked out of the Fellowship of Reconciliation office in New York City.

Rustin was among those CORE leaders who pioneered in efforts to apply Gandhian methods in opposition to racial injustice (**Document 3**). During its formative years, local CORE groups picketed restaurants, amusement parks, swimming pools, barbershops, hotels, bowling alleys, playgrounds, and theaters. All the groups were small, comprising fewer than fifty persons, and sometimes as few as a dozen. But while progress was slow, it was steady. Through its summer workshops and direct actions, CORE successfully trained hundreds of organizers in the use of nonviolent techniques. By 1948, it had succeeded in integrating theaters in Denver, restaurants in Detroit, a public bath in Los Angeles, and Palisades Amusement Park in New Jersey. CORE took the issue of racial injustice to the national level after the U.S. Supreme

Court's 1946 decision outlawing segregation in interstate travel. In the spring of 1947, CORE and FOR co-sponsored the first freedom ride, known as the Journey of Reconciliation. An interracial group of protestors that included George Houser, Bayard Rustin, and Jim Peck, among others, hopped aboard Greyhound and Trailways buses. Testing the Court's decision, the freedom riders rode through the upper South where they encountered little harassment, but some arrests. Rustin, Igal Rodenko, and Joe Felment were arrested and given thirty-day sentences on segregated North Carolina chain-gangs for sitting together in the front of a Greyhound bus. This Journey of Reconciliation garnered national publicity for CORE, serving as an example of nonviolent direct action in the struggle for equal rights.

While the emerging civil rights campaign was spurred on by the rhetoric of World War II, the end of the war did not bring a lasting peace. Instead, it brought forth a national-security state of enormous proportions as well as a permanent war economy. The heightening tensions between the United States and the Soviet Union, formally called the Cold War, led to the following government actions: the establishment of the National Security Council, Central Intelligence Agency, and National Security Resources Board; extension of the Selective Service Act; and billions of dollars appropriated for military measures. The peacemakers' attempts to establish a cooperative peace beyond the reach of Great Power dominance became ever more complicated.

The new militarism was most apparent in the large percentage of the national budget devoted to war preparations and in the close connection between the armed forces and American industry. As noted by Hanson Baldwin's "When the Big Guns Speak," in order to support the largest peacetime military establishment in American history, approximately one-third of the total federal budget, or almost $12 billion, was appropriated in 1947 for the army and navy. In addition, a number of the top military men were assigned key posts in various federal agencies. This had frightening implications for a democratic society, as government became more secretive. Even if the new war economy could be maintained without seriously impairing American ideals, it created other problems. The inflationary economics of preparedness disregarded individual consumers, except as their interests served those of the state. As the government developed closer ties with private business and industry, it was involved also in practices incompatible with free and responsible self-government. American politics was subject to a new kind of institutionalized graft dependent on securing governmental contracts. Although the standards of individual government employees were often high, the maze of government–business relations fostered the rise of a new profession of high-powered lobbyists bent on securing federal spoils for their wealthy clients.

At the same time as an emergent military–industrial complex took shape, pacifists who opposed the newly formed United Nations' collective security policies remained the only segment of the antiwar movement to survive the 1950s without being bruised by the Cold War politics of peace. Between 1945 and 1948, Gandhian activists such as David Dellinger and Jim Peck kept alive the vision of spiritual nonviolence. These radical pacifists encouraged an "inner revolution" within peace-minded individuals that would form the basis of a popular movement against war and institutionalized violence. They helped form Peacemakers and the Committee for Nonviolent Action, two organizations adhering to the creed of individual resistance as a form of social protest.

Radical pacifists recently released from prison or CPS camps initiated a series of demonstrations calling for amnesty for COs, opposition to atomic testing, elimination of permanent conscription, an end to racial discrimination, and cessation of the growing militarization of society. In Peck's case, as in many others, events in the 1930s radicalized his social consciousness. Dropping out of Harvard after his freshman year, Peck's career would be marked by putting his life on the line in support of trade unionism, civil rights, and world peace. He joined WRL in 1940, and after his release from prison, he edited publications of CORE and WRL. In February 1947, he was one of a group of men who burned their draft cards in front of the White House. During the 1950s Peck was instrumental in organizing numerous demonstrations against civil defense drills.

Like Peck, Dellinger emerged from prison to become involved in active nonviolent protests against war and nuclear testing. Born in Wakefield, Massachusetts, he attended Yale and Union Theological Seminary. Before the war, he helped set up a communal colony in Newark, New Jersey; he also worked as a community organizer in the slums of Harlem and Newark. After his release from prison, Dellinger helped organize other radical pacifists in order to establish a strong nonviolent movement for economic and political change. He also helped edit radical periodicals such as *Direct Action* and *Alternative* while participating in peace groups such as WRL, Peacemakers, and the Committee for Nonviolent Action.

Peck and Dellinger, along with other radical pacifists, were important for translating Gandhian tactics to the American Left. Direct actionists relied on a decentralized system based on consensus decision making. But, above all, they readily used the tactic of nonviolent individual resistance characterized by their willingness to put their bodies on the line. In many ways, their actions and forms of protest were remarkably similar to those of individuals in the antebellum period. Some traditional pacifists, however, wavered regarding this type of radical action for fear of losing their mantle of respectability in the public's eye. Throughout the post–World War II period and during the Vietnam War, tension between radical pacifists and moderate pacifists was readily apparent.

Protests by radical pacifists were often symbolic in form and substance. One of the first such actions of the postwar era was a demonstration in Times Square in New York in the summer of 1946. The occasion was the first Bikini atomic bomb test explosion, in which goats were used to test the effects of the blast. Peck and other demonstrators rented a stuffed goat, placed it on wheels, and led it down 42nd Street with a sign that read, "Today Me, Tomorrow You." Pacifists also carried out amnesty protests at the White House on Christmas Day in 1946 and 1947. Demonstrators wore black and white–striped prison suits to call attention to their message. On February 12, 1947, the first draft card burnings took place, one in front of the White House, the other at the Labor Temple in New York City. One of the more innovative forms of symbolic protest was radical pacifists goose-stepping in rented Uncle Sam costumes in front of the White House wearing placards that read, "The Draft Means a Goose-Stepping Uncle Sam." As in most of these early demonstrations, the numbers of protestors were small, usually no more than thirty; however, their message was loud and clear.

Interested in further developing direct action tactics, more than one hundred war resisters formed the Committee for Nonviolent Revolution in February 1946. The name was intended to convey the message that fundamental and dramatic change can occur without resorting to violence as the instrument for transformation. This loosely organized group urged a democratic, decentralized socialist society. It held a few minor demonstrations urging closure of the Big Flats CPS camp in New York State and protested attempts by the world's leading military powers to restructure the United Nations, the world's new peacekeeping organization, to their own liking. The Committee never achieved its stated goals, yet it did help raise awareness of important issues through its use of direct action techniques. Its views would eventually reach a wider audience in the late 1950s when the fear of nuclear weapons provided radical pacifism a more fair hearing.

The conscience of radical pacifism was best personified by the FOR's long-time secretary, A.J. Muste. Distraught over the Hiroshima and Nagasaki bombings, Muste led pacifists in a variety of activities in the postwar era. One of the most daring protests was income tax resistance. The idea had already been carried out during World War II based on a popular essay by Richard Gregg. In early 1945, the WRL disseminated a sticker to be attached to tax payments: "This tax goes chiefly for war purposes; as a pacifist,

I pay it only under protest." During World War II, a law requiring employers to withhold taxes from their employees caused particular difficulties for pacifists. Some, working for pacifist groups, asked their employers to refuse cooperation with this law since it made tax refusal practically impossible. Groups with tax-exempt status—nonprofit organizations—were often reluctant to jeopardize this situation by disobeying the law. As a result, some pacifists resigned rather than permit the money to go to the military.

Such concerns led Muste and others to form the Peacemakers in 1948, whose main thrust was in the area of war tax resistance. At a national conference held in Chicago, Marion Coddington, Ernest Bromley, Caroline Urie, Walter Gormly, Valerie Riggs, and Ralph Templin were designated as a committee to promote tax refusal. For many years, they provided research, literature, action suggestions, and publicity for those in the tax-resistance movement. During the 15 years after 1948, hundreds of people followed Muste's call to refuse paying income taxes. The government prosecuted and imprisoned only six: James Otsuka, Indiana; Maurice McCrackin, Ohio; Eroseanna Robinson, Illinois; Walter Gormly, Iowa; Arthur Evans, Colorado; and Neil Howorth, Connecticut. These imprisonments and the seizure of a few cars and houses by the Internal Revenue Service highlighted the penalties imposed on tax resisters.

Although the Korean War was unpopular—in the end costing the U.S. approximately $100 billion, some 37,000 soldiers killed and 103,000 wounded—public protest against it was minimal. This was largely due to the anti-Communist Red Scare, which marked dissenters as "un-American." As a result of the red scare, in which "peace" itself became a scary word often associated with Communism, traditional protest groups, including the left and the pacifist wing of the peace movement, became hopelessly divided.

Intense government pressure was placed on war dissenters, although it did not stop the noted African American intellectual W.E.B. Du Bois from speaking his mind. Faced with a peace movement divided by competing factions and government harassment, Du Bois insisted the U.S. could coexist peacefully with the Soviet Union. It was time for the American government, he urged, to seek means of cooperation with Communist powers such as Russia and China. (**Document 4**). As head of the Peace Information Center, Du Bois was indicted by the Justice Department for circulating the Stockholm Peace Petition, a worldwide signature campaign aimed at outlawing the atomic bomb. Du Bois had supported U.S. participation in both world wars, but by the Cold War era he had concluded that U.S. imperial ambitions were the greatest threat to world peace.

There was also no equivocation in the views of Charlotta Bass, the 1952 Vice Presidential candidate of the Progressive Party. A proud African American woman, Bass was a Los Angeles newspaper owner and member of the Republican Party for close to forty years. As a community activist she had succeeded in getting local businesses to hire African American workers. Disillusioned by the way black veterans were treated in America after fighting for democracy overseas, she moved to the left in her political leanings. She supported Henry Wallace and the Progressive Party in 1948, and four years later was the first African American woman to be nominated by a political party for the nation's second highest office. Forced by government harassment to cease publication of her newspaper, the *California Eagle*, at the height of the Korean War she called for peace and justice in her remarks at the 1952 Progressive Party convention in Chicago (**Document 5**). She was unrelenting in her work against war and racial injustice, and was still organizing—this time against the Vietnam War—in her retirement home in the 1960s. Her words at the Progressive party convention were a stark reminder of how much further America had to travel to become a just and peaceful society.

Although the Korean War was indeed unpopular, Cold War fears and the specter of McCarthyism, bolstered by a garrison state mentality, proved too overwhelming for opponents of this war. Unlike later years, moreover, there was no organized draft resistance movement and draft evasion and desertion were no higher than during World War II. The only ones who remained true to form in their steadfast opposition to the war were dedicated neo-isolationists, Communists, and committed pacifists like Muste and the organizations he represented. For Muste it was a matter of "holy disobedience" and choosing love over military arms (**Document 6**). Yet even liberal intellectuals and those in the academy desirous of criticizing the war were muzzled by the rising tide of McCarthyism.

One exception was the iconoclastic journalist I.F. Stone. While attending the University of Pennsylvania in the 1920s he wrote stories for the *Philadelphia Inquirer*. Greatly influenced by the socialist views of novelist Jack London, Stone became a member of the Socialist Party of America and actively campaigned for Norman Thomas in the 1928 presidential election. Devoted to independent radical journalism, Stone was active in the Popular Front in opposition to Adolf Hitler. Shortly before the outbreak of World War II, Stone became associate editor of *The Nation* and subsequently moved on to the *Daily Compass* until it went out of business in 1952. During the Korean War he wrote a highly controversial book, *Hidden History of the Korean War* (1952), charging that South Korea initiated hostilities with North Korea by constant and unprovoked border attacks and that South Korean president Syngman Rhee and the United States welcomed the conflict. In 1953, Stone started his own political newspaper, *I.F. Stone's Weekly*. Refusing to be intimidated by threats of censorship, Stone unabashedly attacked McCarthyism, expressed fears about hydrogen warfare, and promoted racial equality (**Document 7**).

The peace movement reached rock bottom during this period in spite of the unceasing efforts of people like Muste and Stone. Its leaders were confused; the coalitions it had generated quickly split apart. As a result, many diehard peace seekers began to concentrate not on war itself, but on social justice; at least they could work on eradicating some of the economic and social causes leading to war. Bolstered by the Freedom Ride of 1947, passage of civil rights legislation during the Truman years, and, most importantly, the 1954 Supreme Court decision, *Brown v. Board of Education*, pacifists in particular found renewed hope in their efforts to reform American society. The civil rights issue would become a central focus for them as they attempted to link together the twin issues of peace and justice.

One of the most well-known nonviolent acts in the American civil rights struggle, the Montgomery bus boycott, took place in 1955–56. The mass boycott lasted an entire year as 42,000 black people in Montgomery, Alabama, simply ceased riding the city's buses rather than be humiliated any longer by segregated seating. The effort had been initiated by Rosa Parks, an African American woman who had been trained in nonviolent strategies at the Highlander Folk School in Tennessee. The successful boycott catapulted to fame a 26-year-old Baptist minister, originally from Atlanta, Martin Luther King, Jr. Until his assassination in 1968, King was the outstanding leader of the nonviolent civil rights movement.

Money and advisers from CORE and FOR poured into the Montgomery Improvement Association, the local organization formed to sustain the boycott. Radical pacifists helped train local people in the techniques of nonviolent resistance to abuse. At the same time, King studied the writings of Gandhi and Tolstoy and underwent a complete conversion to nonviolent resistance, fusing his Christianity with peaceful mass protests. Reflecting later on the boycott, King said: "Christ furnished the spirit and motivation, while Gandhi furnished the method." In that statement, King connected the peace and civil rights movements for the next decade (**Document 8**). Ultimately, he merged the concerns of middle-class northern whites and liberals throughout America with the needs of forgotten southern blacks. He also channeled suppressed black outrage into a massive, nonviolent movement that demonstrated the relevance of Gandhian techniques in the crusade for social justice.

Promoting nonviolence resistance, King joined clergymen Fred Shuttle-worth and Ralph Abernathy in forming the Southern Christian Leadership Conference (SCLC) in January 1957. SCLC sought to mobilize southern blacks for the overthrow of institutionalized racial segregation in order to "save the soul of America." King worked closely with northern white paci-fists associated with CORE and FOR to prove that mass nonviolent resis-tance was the most effective approach to the problem of social injustice in America.

Some Americans thought the Montgomery bus boycott might set off similar mass protests, but a noticeable chain reaction did not begin until four years later. On February 1, 1960, a sit-in by four black college students at a Woolworth's lunch counter in Greensboro, North Carolina, started a wave of sit-ins. Within a month, these had spread to twenty-five cities in five states. Within the first year of the sit-ins, 134 southern communities had desegregated their lunch counters. The sit-ins also inspired student activists like Julian Bond, under the tutelage of SCLC organizer Ella Baker, to establish the Student Nonviolent Coordinating Committee in May 1960 (**Document 9**). With black and white students working together to abolish segregation through nonviolence, SNCC was designed as an organizing in-strument for a nationwide campaign against racial discrimination. During the early 1960s, SNCC volunteers organized sit-ins throughout the South and joined other civil rights organizations in sponsoring voter register cam-paigns. During the 1964 presidential election, its members helped organize the Mississippi Freedom Democratic Party, whose challenge to the all-white Mississippi delegation eventually led to increased minority participation within the Democratic Party. In its early years, SNCC was, by far, the most radical and influential civil rights organization, especially as far as young people were concerned. Before infighting and government harassment led to its eventual demise in the late 1960s, SNCC staff members impressed people with their willingness to sacrifice, working for a few dollars a week under dangerous circumstances. Led by the likes of John Lewis, a former divinity school student who later became a U.S. Congressman, and Bob Moses, who left Harvard Graduate School to join the movement, and with a small membership, minimum budget, decentralized structure, and willing-ness to put their bodies on the line, SNCC's efforts captured a great deal of public sympathy for the cause.

In addition to sit-ins, boycotts, and voter registration drives, another successful tactic to abolish social injustice was the freedom rides. Such ac-tion had been tested in 1947 by members of CORE and FOR following the 1946 U.S. Supreme Court decision in *Morgan v. Virginia*, which banned segregated seating on interstate busing. The 1947 Freedom Riders challenged the policy in the northern-most southern states.

In the summer of 1961, however, blacks and whites from different parts of the country converged to challenge travel segregation all over the South. Their strategy was to travel in integrated groups across state lines and to ignore distinctions between "white" and "colored" waiting rooms and facilities at bus terminals. The planned ride was scheduled to begin on May 4 in Washington, D.C., and end in New Orleans on May 17, the anniversary of the 1954 school desegregation decision. Riders were met by violence along the way—with some beaten so brutally they could not continue the ride—but eventually one group made it to Jackson, Mississippi. Here they were immediately arrested and jailed for "disturbing the peace." However, in September the Interstate Commerce Commission, after some 360 people had been arrested, issued new regulations prohibiting segregation on interstate carriers.

The massive, nonviolent crusade against segregation in both the North and South climaxed on August 28, 1963, when a quarter of a million people participated in the March on Washington for Jobs and Freedom in Washington, D.C. There, King delivered one of the most famous speeches in twentieth-century U.S. history. The next year Congress passed an important civil rights act, followed by the Voting Rights Act of 1965, breaking the back of legalized segregation.

The civil rights movement of this era represented a turning toward more fundamental social change—inevitable when masses of people, not just "solitary intellectuals" who trumpet individual conscience as the best roadmap, become involved in action. Though not every civil rights activist accepted nonviolence as a way of life, as a tactic it was vital because in all instances the protestors were outnumbered and outgunned, and their refusal to retaliate when attacked won them necessary and devoted sympathizers.

In terms of pacifists' political strategy, civil rights nonviolent action ultimately became nonviolent revolution, encompassing a variety of issues. Before the Vietnam War took center stage among nonviolent resisters, civil disobedience was widely practiced by pacifists to express their displeasure with the nuclear arms race, specifically with mandatory air raid drills. Dissent against civil defense drills began in earnest and with fervor on a warm day in 1954. On June 14, air raid sirens wailed throughout the United States, signaling millions of Americans to take "shelter"—a mass burial—from a mock nuclear attack. This was the first nationwide civil defense drill, which were to continue for eight years. The most common air raid drill, "duck and cover," was directed at schools. Students dropped to the floor or crawled under their desks at the teacher's command and took what a professor of education called "the atomic head clutch position": backs to the windows, faces tucked between their knees, hands clasped on the back of their necks, ears covered with their arms to silence the accompanying noise, and eyes shut tight. Duck and cover was supposed to protect children from the bomb flash, flying glass, and falling timbers that would accompany an enemy attack. The National Education Association warned teachers to have their students take the "atomic clutch" position immediately if a sudden dazzling light appeared outside the school to indicate the bomb's arrival.

To peaceseekers, this approach belied reality, falsely suggesting that people could hide from an atomic bomb. After a modest start in 1954, when a few WRL members distributed leaflets opposing the drills, the WRL and other peace groups organized a more substantial nonviolent disobedience action in 1955. Twenty-eight people (including A.J. Muste and Dorothy Day, a founder of the Catholic Worker Movement) sat in City Hall Park in New York during the drill holding signs "End War—The Only Defense Against Atomic Weapons." All were arrested, tried, and convicted. A defense committee was organized to carry out an appeal in the courts. The legal defense was that the arrests were a denial of the defendants' rights of free speech and assembly, right to petition, and rights of conscience under the provisions of both the state and federal constitutions. Though the appeal was in the courts for about four years and was lost, civil disobedience protests and arrests continued in New York and elsewhere—usually involving small numbers of participants. By 1960, however, the protesters numbered in the hundreds and, in 1961, the demonstrations were larger and more widespread than ever. That year in City Hall Park, more than a thousand people refused to take shelter. This demonstration marked the last of compulsory public air raid drills.

The air raid drills lost public credibility as nuclear weapons grew larger and the time for defense preparation grew shorter. But pacifists had yet to answer the more profound question of how to influence government policies to make the bomb's use less likely. In the late 1950s, a new group of "nuclear pacifists" emerged to address this issue.

The same year that the Soviet Union launched the *Sputnik* rocket, 1957, nuclear and radical pacifists formed two interdependent organizations. The nuclear pacifists set up the National Committee for a Sane Nuclear Policy (SANE) and the radical pacifists founded the Committee for Nonviolent Action (CNVA).

Concerned over the atmospheric testing of hydrogen bombs, Larry Scott, American Friends Service Committee Peace Education Director in Chicago, organized an April meeting in Philadelphia to plan a strategy for stopping

H-bomb tests. He gathered the support of A.J. Muste, Bayard Rustin, and Robert Gilmore, AFSC New York secretary. From that meeting emerged a three-pronged movement: an ad-hoc liberal, nuclear pacifist organization referring to itself as SANE; an ad-hoc radical pacifist, direct action-oriented group to be known as CNVA; and the older peace organizations, like FOR, WILPF, and AFSC, which would concentrate on the nuclear testing issue while giving support and encouragement to ad-hoc committees. Scott and Muste, both of whom relished activism, organized CNVA. Robert Gilmore, Norman Cousins, and secretary emeritus of the AFSC, Clarence Pickett, formed SANE.

By the summer of 1958, after a fall 1957 SANE advertisement in the *New York Times* garnered overwhelming response to its plea for "an immediate suspension of atomic testing," SANE had about 130 chapters consisting of 5,000 Americans. A number of prominent people filled its ranks, including some old-line United World Federalists: Oscar Hammerstein, the music composer; Walter Reuther, head of the United Auto Workers; and Donald Keys, SANE's first full-time executive director.

When the United States and the Soviet Union voluntarily (though temporarily) suspended nuclear tests in 1958, SANE broadened its goal to include a general disarmament treaty. During the 1958–59 Geneva talks on disarmament between President Dwight Eisenhower and Soviet Premier Nikita Khrushchev, SANE gathered thousands of signatures urging a test ban. It initiated peace demonstrations modeled after Britain's Aldermaston March—an annual march from London to Aldermaston, the main nuclear bomb factory in Britain—and worked in support of a Senate resolution endorsing efforts to secure a test-ban treaty.

But at the height of SANE's success, anti-Communist attacks on the organization drastically curtailed its effectiveness. The Senate Internal Security Committee, headed by Thomas Dodd (D-Connecticut) accused SANE of harboring avowed Communists. SANE's board of directors responded by trying to purge the organization of anyone it deemed suspicious. The divisions that followed—Muste, for instance, thought SANE had passed up a golden opportunity to challenge congressional committees that sought to intimidate peace organizations—hurt SANE's credibility. This factor, along with the 1961 creation of the semi-autonomous Arms Control and Disarmament Agency, and the American–Soviet accord on a nuclear test-ban treaty two years later, led to a decreased focus on the issue of nuclear weapons.

In contrast to SANE, whose approach was largely educational, CNVA was a loosely organized group of radical pacifists committed to nonviolent direct action. Although CNVA's original goal was opposition to nuclear testing, underlying its support for nonviolent direct action was a commitment to broad social change. Before the Vietnam War led the peace movement as a whole to develop techniques of nonviolent direct action, CNVA's separate efforts had been widely regarded. Through peace walks, vigils, voyages by peace ships into nuclear test sites in the South Pacific, and other forms of civil disobedience, CNVA activists were able to express their own personal commitment to peace and change as well as educate the general public about the important of peace issues.

Its first significant act took place on August 6, 1957, twelve years after the Hiroshima bombing. Eleven radical pacifists, including Larry Scott, were arrested at an Atomic Energy Commission bomb test project in Nevada for deliberately trespassing onto government property. Their Prayer and Conscience Vigil was the first anti-nuclear protest conducted at an actual site of nuclear explosions.

The next year, CNVA undertook a far more ambitious project, the protest voyage of the *Golden Rule*. This ketch, with four Quakers aboard, attempted to sail into the restricted area of the Pacific where the Atomic Energy Commission was conducting hydrogen bomb tests. The boat's captain, former World War II naval commander Albert Bigelow, felt compelled to act. His wartime experiences and conversion to Quakerism convinced him to find ways to make "our witness and protest heard" (**Document 10**). Although the *Golden Rule* was stopped in Hawaii and its crew sentenced to sixty days in jail, the *Phoenix*, with the family of Earle Reynolds and a Japanese mate aboard, picked up and carried on the protest. Reynolds was not arrested until well inside the forbidden zone and his trial, with the help of CNVA, gained worldwide attention. These actions made the public increasingly aware of the dangers of radioactivity resulting from nuclear tests.

As Gandhian nonviolence in the form of direct action became more popular in the United States, the CNVA gained more momentum. To protest atmospheric nuclear testing, CNVA conducted a month-long vigil in front of the White House. In Cheyenne, Wyoming, concerned pacifists took part in nonviolent intervention in the path of construction equipment where missile bases were being built. Two similar projects were undertaken at the Cape Canaveral Missile Base. Traditional approaches designed to inform and persuade were replaced by more militant actions. CNVA began to confront and coerce by staging sit-ins in front of military bases and blocking cars and trucks from entering. Upon arrest, they did not resist; they surrendered peacefully. These tactics were designed to maximize public awareness of the dangers of nuclear testing and proliferation.

In the summer of 1959, an offshoot of CNVA, Omaha Action (Nonviolence against Nuclear Missile Policy) staged a series of demonstrations against

Intercontinental Ballistic Missile bases in Nebraska. Starting with official meetings in Lincoln and Omaha, the project continued during the summer with vigils, leafleting, and direct action involving civil disobedience; these actions resulted in a number of protestors being arrested, including A.J. Muste and Brad Lyttle, a young scholar and disciple of Gandhian nonviolent action. Uplifting to these demonstrators was 73-year-old Muste climbing the fence and penetrating the Omaha base while awaiting arrest.

In Connecticut, the New England branch of CNVA undertook an ongoing program of education and training for direct action in connection with the building of Polaris submarines, which carried nuclear missiles. CNVA also organized the San Francisco to Moscow Walk for Peace. This culminated in October 1961 with a demonstration in Red Square protesting the militarism of both East and West. It was the first group to successfully carry such a message to both superpowers.

Clearly, during World War II and the early years of the Cold War, the crusade for peace underwent some dramatic changes. Traditional liberal pacifists survived and expanded their humanitarian impulse in the area of social service programs. The war, however, put them on the defensive. Their political energy was sapped by public support for the war. Their effectiveness within the peace movement became less and less as pacifists that were more radical sharpened their forms of protest while serving in CPS camps or in prison. In the aftermath of war, radical pacifism would find expression in civil rights campaigns and in acts of civil disobedience. But the 1950s were far from kind to peace activists, as the Cold War and accompanying Red Scare nearly shattered the movement.

Nevertheless, liberal pacifists, and those with more radical intentions, kept alive the spirit of nonviolent civil disobedience in their continued and determined civil rights protests during the latter part of the 1950s. At the same time, they continued to dramatize their opposition to the threat of nuclear war. Direct-action techniques symbolized their strategies and protests. Their efforts would spark a new, more militant wave of antiwar protests in the 1960s, as American troops were sent to Southeast Asia in the name of stopping Communism.

Document 1: Jessie Wallace Hughan
If We Should be Invaded (1940)

Hughan's effort here is akin to Mark Twain, Ernest Howard Crosby, and William Graham Summer, who developed their own fictional accounts of what might happen if the shoe was on the other foot. Examining the observations of the brilliant British mathematician, philosopher, and educator Bertrand Russell, Wallace presents a case for nonviolent defense against violent attack.

$\mathscr{B}$ehind all our thoughts of the international confusion of today, behind all our devices to rid the world of the insanity of armament and war, there lurks a spectrum, the menacing shape of Fear. Sooner or later, it makes its presence felt, and the discussion shifts from considerations of idealism and chivalry, of Christianity, ethics and democracy, to the stark question, **"What If We Should Be Invaded?"**

A Battle Without Arms

Let us now envisage the situation presented by the fantastic hypothesis of a possible invasion. An ultimatum has been issued and refused, the world has its ear to the radio and our government and people, morally and physically, prepared, have braced themselves for conflict. As defense involves not only of those of military age, but every man, woman, and child in the community, care has been taken to evacuate from threatened localities as far as possible all persons likely to be incapacitated through fear or physical weakness. Provision has been made for emergency supplies and communication. Civil officials, including directors of public utilities as well as government, have accepted the full responsibilities and dangers of leadership; succession to each important office has been provided for in the event of death or imprisonment, and citizens are well acquainted with the order in which those names upon the long list of honor will take place of those who have fallen. . . .

The citizens in general follow the same rigid program of passive resistance as public employees. No one insults the interlopers, but no one sells to them or works for them. The usurping commander issues orders, which are firmly ignored, but strict obedience is given to these legitimate officers who remain in authority. Civilian occupations go on as usual till the enemy touches them. In that case, work stops by magic and that particular unit of industry remains frozen till further notice.

Everywhere the invaders meet the same conditions—no battles, no opposing armies, no dangers, and no chances for heroism. On the other hand, no surrenders to figure in the dispatches, no peasants offering food, no sullenly obedient populace, no technicians, or workers to man the utilities. The soldiers have nothing to do but to serve themselves by routine labor, varied by assaults upon unarmed citizens and ignominious robbing of shops and hen-roosts. Such was the conclusion in 1916 of such a brilliant reasoner as Bertrand Russell, and, even, in the last terrifying twenty years, nothing has occurred to destroy its validity.

Not only has his plan never received even a nominal trial, but events have shown very clearly the futility of defense by force of arms when modern militarism chooses to invade a weak or undeveloped neighbor. . . .

Summary: What Do We Propose?

What would a pacifist United States do if invaded? It would not give its women and children to slaughter in a futile gesture of armed defense as the weak nations, Ethiopia, Spain and China have done. It would not select its finest boys and send them overseas to murder or be murdered as the strong nations have done to preserve their great possessions. It would not prepare for a hypothetical invasion by continuing in the panic-stricken armament race of the Powers, arming in so-called defense against one another until the signal strikes for the last great suicide.

The past two years have seen not only the weak, but the strong nations give up thousands of their women and children to death in a romantic gesture doomed to futility. Britain, perhaps the strongest and most civilized of all, is sacrificing its children body and soul, (delinquency among younger adolescents has increased in Britain, 62% since the war began), but it still refuses to lose face or foot of its imperial possessions by proposing to the Axis powers conditions for a just and honorable peace.

What would it do to act upon the knowledge now common to all, that war rather than any foreign state is the supreme enemy of our own country and of mankind, and to organize its people for a bitter end fight against war through the diametrically opposite method of nonviolent non-cooperation.

First, it would rid itself of the few incentives it still holds forth to international robbery.

Second, it would put in practice, with the aid of organized international machinery, such enlightened foreign policies as to bind all other nations to itself with ties of friendship and mutual interest.

Third, by the frank gesture of complete and open disarmament it would destroy all fear and distrust of itself in the minds of its neighbors.

Fourth, it would bring home to its people through practical experience the value of liberty and democracy as to lead the average citizen to choose hardship, imprisonment and even death rather than submit to dictatorship, foreign or domestic.

Fifth, it would prepare a deliberate system of nonviolent defense along the line already suggested, with the purpose of preventing any potential aggressor, however ruthless, from achieving the objectives for which invasion might be undertaken.

Granted, nonviolent defense is no patent medicine to cure painlessly in a day the result of a lifetime folly.

Granted, if any potential enemy is given a pretext for invasion, any type of defense will involve heavy cost and suffering.

Granted, neither pacifist nor militarist has any magic to insure success.

Yet we know this, that the very initiation of this policy by a nation such as ours would immediately wipe out, as far as we are concerned, the chief incentives for invasion with which a modern aggressor can appeal to his people—fear and economic necessity. We know, moreover, that the hypothesis we have frankly faced, of the unprovoked invasion of a disarmed industrial nation by a modern power, is one for which no precedents exists, and which has required the highest flight of fancy even to imagine. Most important of all, we know that competition in armaments, inseparable from military measures of defense, is the direct road to another world war and that such a war will bring the attempted invasion of the United States from the realm of fantasy to that of actuality.

On the one hand is the well-nigh certain prospect of the destruction, not only of the ideals for which our country stands, but of all that we hold valuable in Western civilization. This fate is rushing upon us with every advance toward the worship of military defense, which is another name for Fascism.

On the other hand is the hope of ridding ourselves and the rest of the world by one bold stroke from the nightmare fear, which weighs us down, and of liberating the forces for good will, democracy and expert intelligence to bring "freedom, peace and plenty" to mankind.

Is there some other country stronger and more courageous than America to take the risk of stepping forward as the champion of humanity?

Or must we wait till safety is guaranteed?

_____

Source: Charles Chatfield, ed. _International War Resistance through World War II._ New York: Garland Publishing, Inc., 1971, pp. 619–642.

QUESTIONS

1. What is the main idea or theme of the document?
2. What is the reasoning behind the method of nonviolent noncooperation?
3. Out of the five steps to the nonviolent method that Hughan lays
   out, which step do you think would be the most effective and why?

Document 2: *Why We Refuse to Register* (1941)

Unlike the legislation of World War I, the Burke-Wadsworth Bill of 1940
provided an alternative to military service for conscientious objectors in
the form of Civilian Public Service camps. Some objectors, however, felt
that planting trees or fighting fires under government auspices was an inadequate testimony. In October 1940 eight students at the Union Theological
Seminary in New York City refused to register for the draft. This document
is the statement to the court by some members of this group.

---

*I*t is impossible for us to think of the conscription law without at
the same time thinking of the whole war system, because it is clear to
us that conscription is definitely a part of the institution of war. . . .

To us, the war system is an evil part of our social order, and we
declare that we cannot cooperate with it in any way. War is an evil
because it is a violation of the Way of Love as seen in God through
Christ. It is a concentration, and accentuation of all the evils of our
society. War consists of mass murder, deliberate starvation, vandalism,
and similar evils. Physical destruction and moral disintegration are
the inevitable result. The war method perpetuates and compounds
the evils it purports to overcome. It is impossible, as history reveals, to
overcome evil with evil. The last World War is a notorious case of failure of the war system, and there is no evidence to believe that this war
will be any different. It is our positive proclamation as the followers
of Jesus Christ that we must overcome evil with good. We seek in our
daily living to reconcile that separation of man from man and man
from God, which produces war.

We have also been led to our conclusion on the conscription law
in the light of its totalitarian nature. It is a totalitarian move when
our government insists that the manpower for a nation take a year

of military training. It is a totalitarian move for the President of the nation to be able to conscript industry to produce certain materials, which are deemed necessary for national defense without considering the actual physical needs of the people. We believe, therefore, that by opposing the Selective Service law, we will be striking at the heart of totalitarianism as well as war.

We feel a deep bond of unity with those who decide to register as conscientious objectors, but our own decision must be different for the following reason:

If we register under the act, even as conscientious objectors, we are becoming part of the act. The fact that we as conscientious objectors may gain personal exemption from the most crassly un-Christian requirements of the act does not compensate for the fact that we are complying with it and accepting its protection. If a policeman (or a group of vigilantes) stops on the street, our possession of the government's card shows that we are "all right"—we have complied with the act for the militarization of America. If that does not hurt our Christian consciences, what will? If we try to rationalize on the theory that we must go along with the act in order to fight the fascism and militarism of which it is a part, it seems to us that we are doing that very thing which all pacifist Christians abhor: we are consciously employing bad means on the theory that to do so will contribute to a good end. . . .

In similar vein, it is urged that great concessions have been won for religious pacifists and that we endanger these by our refusal to accept them. Fascism, as it gradually supplanted democracy in Germany, was aided by the decision of Christians and leftists to accept a partial fascism rather than to endanger those democratic concessions which still remained. It is not alone for our own exemption from fighting that we work—it is for freedom of the American people from fascism and militarism.

Partial exemption of the conscientious objectors has come about partly through the work of influential pacifists and partly through the open mindedness of certain non-pacifists. But it has also been granted because of the fear of the government that, without such a provision, public opposition to war would be too great to handle. In particular, it seems to us that one of the reasons the government has granted exemption to ministers and theological students is to gain a religious sanction for its diabolical war. Where actual support could not be gained, it hoped to soothe their consciences so that they could provide no real opposition.

We do not contend that the American people maliciously choose the vicious instrument of war. In a very perplexing situation, they lack the imagination, the religious faith, and the precedents to respond in a different manner. This makes it all the more urgent to build in this country and throughout the world a group trained in the techniques of nonviolent opposition to the encroachments of militarism and fascism. Until we build such a movement, it will be impossible to stall the war machine at home. When we do build such a movement, we will have forged the only weapon which can ever give effective answer to foreign invasion. Thus in learning to fight American Hitlerism we will show an increasing group of war disillusioned Americans how to resist foreign Hitlers as well.

For these reasons we hereby register our refusal to comply in any way with the Selective Training and Service Act. We do not expect to stem the war forces today; but we are helping to build the movement that will conquer in the future.

Source: Staughton Lynd, ed. *Nonviolence in America: A Documentary History.* Indianapolis, IN: Bobbs-Merrill Co., 1966, pp. 296–298.

QUESTIONS

1. Why did these people refuse to register? Do you agree or disagree with their reasoning? Why or why not?
2. What do they mean by "the war system"?
3. Why do they accuse the U.S. of fascism and totalitarianism?

Document 3: Bayard Rustin
Nonviolence vs. Jim Crow (1942)

Bayard Rustin was the principal architect for the August 1963 March on Washington for Jobs and Freedom. A pacifist and civil rights organizer, Rustin did much of the behind-the-scenes work and never truly received the credit he deserved. During World War II he spent three years in the federal penitentiary in Ashland, Kentucky, for his refusal to perform alternative service as a registered conscientious objector. In later years, he helped transmit Gandhian tactics to the civil rights movement. This essay describes his courageous stand against segregation on a bus ride from Louisville to Nashville in 1942.

$\mathscr{R}$ECENTLY I WAS PLANNING to go from Louisville to Nashville by bus. I bought my ticket, boarded the bus, and, instead of going to the back, sat down in the second seat. The driver saw me, got up, and came toward me.

"Hey, you. You're supposed to sit in the back seat."

"Why?"

"Because that's the law. Niggers ride in back."

I said, "My friend, I believe that is an unjust law. If I were to sit in back I would be condoning it."

Angry, but not knowing what to do, he got out and went into the station. He soon came out again, got into his seat, and started off.

This routine was gone through at each stop, but each time nothing came of it. Finally the driver in desperation, must have phoned ahead, for about thirteen miles north of Nashville I heard sirens approaching. The bus came to an abrupt stop, and a police car and two motorcycles drew up with a flourish. Four policeman got into the bus, consulted shortly with the driver, and came to me.

"Get up, you ------- nigger!"

"Why?" I asked.

"Get up, you black ------- !"

"I believe that I have a right to sit here," I said quietly. . . . "It is my sincere conviction that the power of love in the world is the greatest power existing. If you have a greater power, my friend, you may move me."

How much they understood of what I was trying to tell them I do not know. By this time they were impatient and angry. As I would not move, they began to beat me about the head and shoulders and shortly I found myself knocked to the floor. Then they dragged me out of the bus and continued to beat me. . . .

I was put into the back seat of the police car, between two policemen. Two others sat in front. On the thirteen-mile ride to town they called me every conceivable name and said anything they could to incite me to violence. I found that I was shaking with nervous strain, and to give myself some solace, I took out a piece of paper and pencil, and began to write from memory a chapter from St. Paul's letters.

When I had written a few sentences, the man on my right said, "What're you writing?" and snapped the paper from my hand. He read it, then crumpled it into a ball and pushed it in my face. The man on the other side gave me a kick. . . .

When we reached Nashville, a number of policemen were lined up on both sides of the hallway, which I had to pass on my way to the captain's office. They tossed me from one to another like a volleyball. By the time I reached the office, the lining of my best coat was torn, and I was conspicuously rumpled. I straightened myself as best I could and went in. They had my bag, and went through my papers, finding much of interest, especially in the *Christian Century* and *Fellowship*.

Finally the captain said, "Come here, nigger."

I walked directly to him. "What can I do for you?" I asked.

"Nigger," he said menacingly, "you're supposed to be scared when you come in here!"

"I am fortified by truth, justice and Christ," I said. "There's no need for me to fear. . . ."

The assistant district attorney [Mr. Ben West] questioned me about my life, the *Christian Century*, pacifism, for about half an hour. Then he asked the police to tell their side of what had happened. They did, slighting the truth a good deal in spots and including several lies for seasoning. Mr. West then asked my side.

"Gladly," I said, "and I want you," turning to the young policeman who sat in the front seat, "to listen to what I say and stop me if I deviate from the truth in the least."

Holding his eyes with mine, I told the story exactly as it happened, stopping often to say, "right?" or "Isn't that what happened?" to the young policeman. During the whole time he never interrupted me, and when I was through I said, "Did I tell the truth just as it happened?'" and he said, "Well. . ."

Then Mr. West dismissed me, and I was sent to wait along in the dark room. After an hour, Mr. West came in and said very kindly, "You may go, Mister Rustin."

I left the courthouse believing all the more strongly in the nonviolent approach. . . .

Source: Courtesy of the Estate of Bayard Rustin and http://www.explorehistory.com/pdocument.php (accessed February 13, 2009)

QUESTIONS

1. Why was Rustin arrested just outside of Nashville and not earlier on his bus trip?
2. What tactic did Rustin employ, which only angered the policeman more? What did the police do to try to provoke Rustin to respond to their actions?
3. How did this event reinforce Rustin's belief in the power of nonviolence as a viable instrument in the civil rights crusade?

Document 4: W.E.B. Du Bois
Work for Peace (1950)

W.E.B. Du Bois, born in Great Barrington, Massachusetts, was the first African American Ph.D. from Harvard University. Trained as a sociologist Du Bois rose to fame with the publication of *Souls of Black Folk*. As a founder of the NAACP and editor of its journal, *Crisis*, he was instrumental in promoting racial equality. But his concerns were global, and as the Cold War set in he became more outspoken on peace issues.

My connection with the peace movement had been long. Even in my college days I had vowed never to take up arms. I wrote in *The Crisis* in 1913 concerning the meeting of peace societies at St. Louis: "Peace today, if it means anything, means the stopping of the slaughter of the weaker by the stronger in the name of Christianity and culture. The modern lust for land and slaves in Africa, Asia, and the South Seas is the greatest and almost the only cause of war between the so-called civilized peoples. For such 'colonial' aggression and 'imperial' expansion, England, France, Germany, Russia, and Austria are straining every nerve to arm themselves; against such policies Japan and China are arming desperately. And yet the American peace movement thinks it bad policy to take up this problem of machine guns, natives, and rubber, and wants 'constructive' work in 'arbitration treaties and international law.' For our part we think that a little less dignity and dollars and a little more humanity would make the peace movement in America a great democratic philanthropy instead of an aristocratic refuge." ...

[At the world peace conference in Paris in 1949] ... At this Conference I emphasized colonialism and said: "Let us not be misled. The real cause of the differences, which threaten world war, is not the spread of socialism or even of the complete socialism which communism envisages. Socialism is spreading all over the world and even in the United States. ... Against this spread of socialism, one modern institution is working desperately and that is colonialism, and colonialism has been and is and ever will be one of the chief causes of war. ... Leading this new colonial imperialism comes my own native land, built by my father's toil and blood, the United States. The United States is a great nation; rich by grace of God and prosperous by the hard work of its humblest citizens. ... Drunk with power we are leading the world to hell in a new colonialism with the same old human slavery which once ruined us; and to a Third World War which will ruin the world." ...

[Moscow all-Soviet peace conference, August 1949] ... In the United States today the object is to center and increase the power of those who control organized wealth and they seek to prove to Americans that no other system is so successful in human progress. But instead of leaving proof of this to the free investigation of science, the reports of a free press, and the discussion of the public platform, today in the United States, organized wealth owns the press and chief news gathering organs and is exercising increased control over the schools and making public discussion and even free thinking difficult and often impossible.

The cure for this and the way to change the socially planned United States into a welfare state is for the American people to take control over the nation in industry as well as government. ... But knowledge of this ... does not reach the mass of people. They are being carried away by almost hysterical propaganda that the freedoms, which they have, and such individual initiative as remains are being threatened and that a third world war is the only remedy. ...

[July 14, 1950, response to U.S. Secretary of State Dean Acheson's attack on the Peace Information Center] The main burden of your opposition to this Appeal [Stockholm Resolution] and to our efforts lies in the charge that we are part of a spurious peace offensive of the Soviet Union. Is it our strategy that when the Soviet Union asks for peace, we insist on war? Must any proposals for averting atomic catastrophe be sanctified by Soviet Opposition? ... Does it not occur to you, Sir, that there are honest Americans who, regardless of their differences on other questions, hate and fear war and are determined to do something to avert it? ...

We have got to live in the world with Russia and China. If we worked together with the Soviet Union against the menace of Hitler, can we not work with them again at a time when only faith can save us from utter atomic disaster? Certainly hundreds of millions of colonial peoples in Asia, Africa, Latin America and elsewhere, conscious of our support of Chiang Kai-shek, Bao Dai and the colonial system, and mindful of the oppressive discrimination against the Negro people in the United States, would feel that our intentions also must be accepted on faith.

Today in this country it is becoming standard reaction to call anything "Communist" and therefore subversive and unpatriotic, which anybody for any reason dislikes. We feel strongly that this tactic has already gone too far; that it is not sufficient today to trace a proposal to a Communist source in order to dismiss it with contempt.

We are a group of Americans, who upon reading this Peace Appeal, regard it as a true, fair statement of what we ourselves and many countless other Americans believed. Regardless of our other beliefs and affiliations, we united in this organization for the one and only purpose of informing the American people on the issues of peace.

Source: W.E.B. Du Bois, *The Autobiography of W.E.B. Du Bois: A Soliloquy on Viewing My Life from the Last Decade of Its First Century.* New York: International Publishers Co., Inc., 1968), pp. 343–360. Also cited in http://www2.pfeiffer.edu (accessed April 4, 2007).

QUESTIONS

1. Which causes of war concerned Du Bois the most?
2. Why does Du Bois criticize those who pursue "constructive" work in "arbitration and international law"?
3. How did Du Bois try to connect American democracy to totalitarianism? What tactic did the American government employ to silence people like Du Bois?

Document 5: Charlotta Bass
Acceptance Speech for Vice Presidential Candidate of the Progressive Party (1952)

Charlotta Bass was a community organizer and newspaper publisher in Los Angeles. A long-time Republican, she turned to the Progressive Party in 1948 because it championed racial equality and peace. She was accused of being a Communist because of the views she expressed on these issues. Below is an excerpt from the speech she gave accepting the nomination to run for vice president on the Progressive Party ticket.

I stand before you with great pride.

This is a historical moment in American political life.

Historic for myself, for my people, for all women.

For the first time in the history of this nation a political party has chosen a Negro woman for the second highest office in the land. . . .

I shall tell you how I come to stand here. I am a Negro woman. My people came before the Mayflower. I am more concerned with what is happening to my people in my country than in pouring out money to rebuild a decadent Europe for a new war. We have lived through two wars and seen their promises turn to bitter ashes. Two Negroes were the first Americans to be decorated for bravery in France during World War I, that war that was fought to make the world safe for democracy. But when it ended, we discovered we were making Africa safe for exploitation by the very European powers whose freedom and soil we had defended. And that war was barely over when a Negro soldier, returning to his home in Georgia, was lynched almost before he could take off his uniform. That war was scarcely over before my people were stoned and shot and beaten in a dozen northern cities. The guns were hardly silenced before a reign of terror was unloosed against every minority that fought for a better life.

And then we fought another war. You know Dorie Miller, the spud peeler who came out of his galley to fight while white officers slept at Pearl Harbor. And I think of Robert Brooks, another "first Negro," and of my own nephew. We fought a war to end fascism whose germ is German race superiority and the oppression of other peoples. A Negro soldier returned from that war—he was not even allowed to take off his uniform before he was lynched for daring to exercise his constitutional right to vote in a Democratic primary. . . .

Yes, it is my government that supports the segregation by violence practiced by a Malan in South Africa, sends guns to maintain a bloody French rule in Indo-china, gives money to help the Dutch repress Indonesia, props up Churchill's rule in the Middle East and over the colored peoples of Africa and Malaya. . . .

Shall my people support a new war to create new oppressions? We want peace and we shall have freedom. We support the movement for freedom of all peoples everywhere—in Africa, in Asia, in the Middle East, and above all, here in our own country. . . . We will not be stopped by the reign of terror let loose against all who speak for peace and freedom and a share of the world's goods, a reign of terror the like of which this nation has never seen. . . .

. . . For there is an evil that stalks in our land, evil that strikes at my people, that would enslave all people, that would send up the world in flames, rob us of our earnings to waste on arms, destroy our living standards, corrupt our youth, silence and enslave us with Smith Acts, McCarran Acts, passed by concentration camp congressmen. . . .

This is what we fight against. We fight to live. We want the $65 billion that goes for death to go to build a new life. Those billions could lift the wages of my people, give them jobs, give education and training and new hope to our youth, free our sharecroppers, build new hospitals and medical centers. The $8 billion being spent to rearm Europe and crush Asia could rehouse all my people living in the ghettos of Chicago and New York and every large city in the nation....

And I am impelled to accept this call, for it is the call of my people and call to my people. Frederick Douglass would rejoice, for he fought not only slavery but the oppression of women. Above all, Douglass would counsel us not to falter, to "continue the struggle while a bondsman in his chains remain to weep."...

I make this pledge to my people, the dead and the living—to all Americans, black and white. I will not retire nor will I retreat, not one inch, so long as God gives me vision to see what is happening and strength to fight for the things I know are right.

Source: http://www.socallib.org/bass/pdfs/vp1.pdg (accessed September 10, 2008)

QUESTIONS

1. How does Bass characterize American foreign policy? Does it promote democracy or hinder it?
2. How were African Americans treated in the United States after World War II, according to Bass?
3. How does Bass drive home her point about spending for reconstruction of postwar Europe and what needs to be done at home? What reconstruction plan is she referring to?

Document 6:   A. J. Muste
Of Holy Disobedience (1952)

One of twentieth-century America's most famous pacifist-activists, Abraham Johannes Muste was an ordained minister and leading member of the Fellowship of Reconciliation. Drawn to the labor struggles of the 1920s and 1930s, Muste became Dean of Brookwood Labor College, the country's most famous residential workers' education experiment. After a brief flirtation with Trotskyism in the mid-1930s, he returned to his pacifist beliefs.

Until his death in 1967, Muste was a leader in direct action movements, acts of civil disobedience, and criticism of war.

*M*ost believers in democracy and all pacifists begin, of course, with an area of agreement as to the moral necessity, the validity and the possible social value of No-saying or Holy Disobedience. Pacifists and/or conscientious objectors all draw the line at engaging in military combat and most of us indeed at any kind of service in the armed forces. But immediately thereupon questions arise as to whether we should not emphasize "positive and constructive service" rather than the "negative" of refusal to fight or to register; or questions about the relative importance of "resistance" and "reconciliation," and so on. It is to this discussion that I wish to attempt a contribution. It may be that it will be most useful both to young men of draft age and to other readers if we concentrate largely on the quite concrete problem of whether the former should register, conform to other requirements of the Selective Service Act which apply to conscientious objectors and accept or submit to the alternative service required of them under the law as amended in June, 1951; or whether they shall refuse to register, or if they do register or are "automatically" registered by the authorities, shall refuse to conform at the next stage; and in any event refuse to render any alternative service under conscription. We deal, in other words, with the question whether young men who are eligible for it shall accept the IV-E classification or take the more "absolutist," non-registrant position. (For present purposes, consideration of the I-A-O position, the designation used for draftees who are willing to accept service in the armed forces provided this is non-combatant in character, may be omitted. The IV-E classification is the designation used for persons who are on grounds of religious training and belief opposed to participation in any war. Those who are given this classification are required to render alternative service, outside the armed forces and under civilian auspices, and designed to serve "the health, safety and interest of the United States.")

Two preliminary observations are probably necessary in order to avoid misunderstanding. In the first place, in every social movement there are varied trends or emphases, and methods of working. Those who hold to one approach are likely to be very critical of those who take another. Disagreements among those within the same movement may be more intense or even bitter than with those on the outside. I suppose it can hardly be denied that every movement has in it individuals whose contribution is negative, and that such individuals do not all come from within one wing of the movement. Objective evaluation also leads to the view that the cause is forwarded by various methods and through the agency of diverse individuals and groups. But this does not mean that discussion within the movement of trends and methods of work is not useful and essential. Even if it were true that each of several strategies was *equally* valid and useful, it would still be necessary that each be clearly and vigorously presented and implemented in order that the movement might develop its maximum impact.

Secondly, in what I shall have to say I am not passing moral judgment on individual draftees. But from the fact that a pacifist minister should not pass moral condemnation on the young man in his congregation who in obedience to his conscience enlists or submits to conscription, we do not deduce that this minister should abandon his pacifism or cease to witness to it. Similarly, the fact that in the pacifist movement we support various types of COs in following the lead of conscience does not rule out discussion as to the validity and usefulness of various strategies. It is one thing for a young and immature draftee to follow a course which amounts to "making the best of a bad business" and for others to give him sympathetic understanding and help. It is a very different thing for pacifist organizations or churches to advocate such a course or to rationalize it into something other than it really is.

As some of the readers of this statement are likely to be aware, the writer has advocated the non-registrant position. The majority in the pacifist movement probably believe that it is preferable for COs to accept or submit to the alternative civilian service, which was required under the World War II Selective Service Act and is now again required under "peacetime conscription."

The varied considerations and arguments which currently enter into the discussion of this choice confronting the youth of the draft age tend, as I see it, to fall into three categories, though there is a good deal of overlapping. One set of considerations may be said to center largely around the idea of Christian or human "vocation"; a second set has to do with the problem of "the immature 18-year old"; the third with the relation of the pacifist and citizens generally to military conscription and the modern Power-State.

The argument for accepting alternative service, under the first category, has been stated somewhat as follows:

> God calls us to love and serve our fellowmen. This is for Christians and other pacifists a matter of vocation. If, then, the government

in war time, or under peace time conscription, requires some service of mercy or construction from us, which is not obviously and directly a part of war-making, we will raise no objection to undertaking such work. We may even seek, and shall certainly be grateful for the opportunity to demonstrate our desire to be good citizens and helpful members of society, and to show a reconciling spirit. This question of the meaning and implications of Christian or human vocation in the context of military conscription clearly needs careful analysis.

Source: Staughton Lynd, ed. *Nonviolence in America: A Documentary History.* (Indianapolis, IN: Bobbs-Merrill Co., 1966, pp. 310–339.

QUESTIONS

1. What does Muste mean by "holy disobedience"?
2. As described in this document, explain the circumstances surrounding a draftee who would be required to provide "alternative service" under the requirements of the Selected Service Act amended in June 1951. Why was it necessary for the government to allow alternative service for conscripts?
3. What position does Muste advocate here with regard to pacifist ministers, churches, or organizations supporting alternative service?

Document 7:   I. F. Stone
Anticommunism (1954)

Independent journalist I.F. Stone started his own newspaper in 1953 at the height of the McCarthy era. Stone challenged the nation's anti-Communist paranoia that was spread by Senator Joe McCarthy, the Wisconsin Republican, whose fear-mongering Stone despised. Stone was especially concerned about how much damage McCarthy had done to democracy and free speech in the United States. In this column, Stone asks his readers to look at the bigger picture and what is really at stake for Americans.

*I*f Communists are some supernatural breed of men, led by diabolic master minds in that distant Kremlin, engaged in a Satanic conspiracy to take over the world and enslave all mankind—and this is the thesis endlessly propounded by American liberals and conservatives alike, echoed night and day by every radio station and in every newspaper, the thesis no American dare any longer challenge without himself becoming suspect—then how to fight McCarthy?

If the public mind is to be conditioned for war, if it is being taught to take for granted the destruction of millions of human beings, few of them tainted with this dreadful ideological virus, all of them indeed presumably pleading for us to liberate them, how can we argue that it matters if a few possibly innocent men lose jobs or reputations because of McCarthy? Is not this additional cost too slight, are not the stakes too great? How contend for constitutional niceties while acquiescing in the spread of poisonous attitudes and panicky emotions?

Writ in the skies of the H-bomb era is the warning that mutual destruction is the alternative to coexistence. Until there is a national leadership willing to take a pragmatic view of revolution, a charitable and Christian view of the misery that goes with the great rebirths of mankind, a self-respecting view of the example a free America can set and the constructive leadership an unafraid America can give, we cannot fight the drift to fascism at home and war abroad. We cannot inculcate unreasoning hate and not ultimately be destroyed by it ourselves. We who prate constantly of "atheistic communism" forget that this is what all the great teachers of mankind have taught. There is retribution that lies in wait for the arrogant and self-righteous. Where is the man big enough to reach the American people with this message before it is too late?

Source: Karl Weber, ed. *I. F. Stone, The Best of I. F. Stone.* New York: Public Affairs, 2006, p. 29.

QUESTIONS

1. According to Stone, what was the best way to fight McCarthy?
2. Who or what is the real enemy in Stone's estimation? Is his concern about "the drift to fascism at home and war abroad" similar to that of others in this era?
3. In Stone's view, what is the best course of action for Americans to take in order to ensure a peaceful world? Explain what he means by "a pragmatic view of revolution."

Document 8: Martin Luther King, Jr.
Pilgrimage to Nonviolence (1958)

The preeminent leader of the modern civil rights movement, King received his Doctorate in Divinity from Boston University. A pacifist, he modeled his actions after Thoreau and Gandhi, and wrote his own tract on nonviolence, "Letter from a Birmingham Jail." Awarded the Nobel Peace Prize for his efforts, King argued that the "triple evils" that had to be fought were racism, poverty, and militarism.

*O*ften the question has arisen concerning my own intellectual pilgrimage to nonviolence. In order to get at this question it is necessary to go back to my early teens in Atlanta. I had grown up abhorring not only segregation but also the oppressive and barbarous acts that grew out of it. I had passed spots where Negroes had been savagely lynched, and had watched the Ku Klux Klan on its rides at night. I had seen police brutality with my own eyes, and watched Negroes receive the most tragic injustice in the courts. All of these things had done something to my growing personality. I had come perilously close to resenting all white people.

I had also learned that the inseparable twin of racial injustice was economic injustice. Although I came from a home of economic security and relative comfort, I could never get out of my mind the economic insecurity of many of my playmates and the tragic poverty of those living around me. During my late teens I worked two summers, against my father's wishes—he never wanted my brother and me to work around white people because of the oppressive conditions—in a plant that hired both Negroes and whites. Here I saw economic injustice first-hand, and realized that the poor white was exploited just as much as the Negro. Through these early experiences I grew up deeply conscious of the varieties of injustice in our society.

So when I went to Atlanta's Morehouse College as a freshman in 1944 my concern for racial and economic justice was already substantial. During my student days at Morehouse I read Thoreau's *Essay on Civil Disobedience* for the first time. Fascinated by the idea of refusing to cooperate with an evil system, I was so deeply moved that I reread the work several times. This was my first intellectual contact with the theory of nonviolent resistance.

Not until I entered Crozer Theological Seminary in 1948, however, did I begin a serious intellectual quest for a method to eliminate social evil. Although my major interest was in the fields of theology and philosophy, I spent a great deal of time reading the works of the great social philosophers. I came early to Walter Rauschenbusch's *Christianity and the Social Crisis*, which left an indelible imprint on my thinking by giving me a theological basis for the social concern, which had already grown up in me as a result of my early experiences. Of course there were points at which I differed with Rauschenbusch. I felt that he had fallen victim to the nineteenth-century "cult of inevitable progress" which led him to a superficial optimism concerning man's nature. Moreover, he came perilously close to identifying the Kingdom of God with a particular social and economic system—a tendency that should never befall the Church. But in spite of these shortcomings Rauschenbusch had done a great service for the Christian Church by insisting that the gospel deals with the whole man, not only his soul but his body; not only his spiritual well-being but his material well-being. It has been my conviction ever since reading Rauschenbusch that any religion, which professes to be concerned about the souls of men and is not concerned about the social and economic conditions that scar the soul, is a spiritually moribund religion only waiting for the day to be buried. It well has been said: "A religion that ends with the individual, ends."...

During the Christmas holidays of 1949 I decided to spend my spare time reading Karl Marx to try to understand the appeal of communism for many people. For the first time I carefully scrutinized *Das Kapital* and *The Communist Manifesto*. I also read some interpretive works on the thinking of Marx and Lenin. In reading such Communist writings I drew certain conclusions that have remained with me as convictions to this day. First I rejected their materialistic interpretation of history. Communism, avowedly secularistic and materialistic, has no place for God. This I could never accept, for as a Christian I believe that there is a creative personal power in this universe who is the ground and essence of all reality—a power that cannot be explained in materialistic terms. History is ultimately guided by spirit, not matter. Second, I strongly disagreed with communism's ethical relativism. Since for the Communist there is no divine government, no absolute moral order, there are no fixed, immutable principles; consequently almost anything—force, violence, murder, lying—is a justifiable means to the "millennial" end. This type of relativism was abhorrent to me. Constructive ends can never give absolute moral justification to destructive means, because in the final analysis the end is preexistent in the mean. Third, I opposed communism's political totalitarianism. In communism the individual ends up in subjection to the state. True, the Marxist would argue that the state is an "interim" reality, which is to be eliminated when the classless society emerges; but the state is the end while it lasts, and man only a means to that end. And if any man's so-called rights or liberties stand in the way of that end, they are simply swept aside. His liberties of expression, his freedom to vote, his freedom to listen to what news he likes or to choose his books are all restricted. Man becomes hardly more, in communism, than a depersonalized cog in the turning wheel of the state. . . .

But in spite of the shortcomings of his analysis, Marx had raised some basic questions. I was deeply concerned from my early teen days about the gulf between superfluous wealth and abject poverty, and my reading of Marx made me ever more conscious of this gulf. Although modern American capitalism had greatly reduced the gap through social reforms, there was still need for a better distribution of wealth. Moreover, Marx had revealed the danger of the profit motive as the sole basis of an economic system: capitalism is always in danger of inspiring men to be more concerned about making a living than making a life. We are prone to judge success by the index of our salaries or the size of our automobiles, rather than by the quality of our service and relationship to humanity—thus capitalism can lead to a practical materialism that is as pernicious as the materialism taught by communism. . . .

My reading of Marx also convinced me that truth is found neither in Marxism nor in traditional capitalism. Each represents a partial truth. Historically capitalism failed to see the truth in collective enterprise and Marxism failed to see the truth in individual enterprise. Nineteenth-century capitalism failed to see that life is social and Marxism failed and still fails to see that life is individual and personal. The Kingdom of God is neither the thesis of individual enterprise nor the antithesis of collective enterprise, but a synthesis, which reconciles the truths of both. . . .

Source: Staughton Lynd, ed. *Nonviolence in America: A Documentary History.* Indianapolis, IN: Bobbs-Merrill Co., 1966, pp. 379–383.

QUESTIONS

1. How did Walter Rauschenbusch and Karl Marx influence King's thinking?
2. Why did King believe nonviolence was the most appropriate strategy for achieving equality in American society?
3. How did King's Christian beliefs make him critical of Communism?

Document 9: Student Nonviolent Coordinating Committee Founding Statement (1960)

The Student Nonviolent Coordinating Committee was formed when more than 120 student protest leaders attended a conference at Shaw University in Raleigh, North Carolina, in April 1960. Originally conceived as a coordinating body for independent local protest groups, SNCC became a group of full-time organizers who aimed to put an end to segregation in the South. Its founding statement was inspired by Gandhian supporter and expelled Vanderbilt divinity student James Lawson. The statement fully expressed the nonviolent foundation of student-led direct action movements, for which SNCC was the most important model.

We affirm the philosophical or religious ideal of nonviolence as the foundation of our purpose, the presupposition of our belief, and the manner of our action.

Nonviolence, as it grows from the Judeo-Christian tradition, seeks a social order of justice permeated by love. Integration of human endeavor represents the crucial first step towards such a society.

Through nonviolence, courage displaces fear. Love transcends hate. Acceptance dissipates prejudice; hope ends despair. Faith reconciles doubt. Peace dominates war. Mutual regard cancels enmity. Justice for all overthrows injustice. The redemptive community supersedes immoral social systems.

By appealing to conscience and standing on the moral nature of human existence, nonviolence nurtures the atmosphere in which reconciliation and justice become actual possibilities.

Although each local group in this movement must diligently work out the clear meaning of this statement of purpose, each act or phase of our corporate effort must reflect a genuine spirit of love and good-will.

Source: "Student Nonviolent Coordinating Committee Founding Statement," http://www.2.iath.virginia.edu/sixties/HTML_docs/Resources/ Primary/Manifestos/SNCC (accessed February 2, 2009)

QUESTIONS

1. Why did this civil rights organization affirm the philosophical or religious ideal of nonviolence in the face of stiff physical resistance?

2. What is the meaning of "the redemptive community supersedes immoral social systems"?

3. How did SNCC's founding statement represent the ideals of the modern American peace movement?

Document 10: Albert Bigelow
Why I am Sailing into the Pacific Bomb-Test Area (1958)

Albert Bigelow, a member of the Society of Friends, adopted the new tactic of direct action that came to symbolize the efforts of radical pacifists during the early Cold War period. Bigelow would later become involved in a Quaker action group opposing the war in Vietnam and the alternative community action group known as the Movement for a New Society. Here is his story of how he and his "peacemates" attempted to challenge the military's testing of atomic weapons in the South Pacific.

My friend Bill Huntington and I are planning to sail a small vessel westward into the Pacific H-bomb test area. By April we expect to reach nuclear testing grounds at Eniwetok. We will remain there as long as the tests of H-bombs continue. With us will be two other volunteers.

Why? Because it is the way I can say to my government, to the British government, and to the Kremlin: "Stop! Stop this madness before it is too late. For God's sake, turn back!"

How have I come to this conviction? Why do I feel under compulsion, under moral orders, as it were, to do this?

The answer to such questions, at least in part, has to do with my experience as a Naval officer during World War II. The day after Pearl Harbor was attacked, I was at the Navy recruiting offices. I had a lot of experience in navigating vessels. Life in the Navy would be a glamorous change from the dull mechanism of daily civilian living. My experience assured me of success. All this adventure ahead and the prospect of becoming a hero into the bargain....

The Turkey Shoot

From March to October of 1943 I was in command of a submarine chaser in the Solomon Islands, during the fighting. It was during this period that more than 100 Japanese planes were shot down in one day. This was called "the Turkey Shoot." The insensitivity which decent men must develop in such situations is appalling. I remember that the corpse of a Japanese airman who had been shot down was floating bolt upright in one of the coves, a position resulting from the structure of the Japanese life belts, which were different from our Mae Wests. Each day as we passed the cove we saw this figure, his face growing blacker under the terrific sun. We laughingly called him Smiling Jack. As a matter of fact, I think I gave him that name myself and felt rather proud of my wit.

Later in World War II, I was Captain of the destroyer escort *Dale W. Peterson*—DE 337—and I was on her bridge as we came into Pearl Harbor from San Francisco when the first news arrived of the explosion of an atomic bomb over Hiroshima. Although I had no way of understanding what an atom bomb was I was absolutely awestruck, as I suppose all men were for a moment. Intuitively it was then that I realized for the first time that morally war is impossible.

I don't suppose I had the same absolute realization with my whole being, so to speak, of the immorality and "impossibility" of nuclear war until the morning of August 7, 1957. On that day, I sat with a score of friends, before dawn, in the Nevada desert just outside the entrance to the Camp Mercury testing grounds. The day before, eleven of us, in protest against the summer-long tests, had tried to enter the restricted area. We had been arrested as we stepped one after another over the boundary line, and had been carried off to a ghost town which stands at the entrance to Death Valley. There we had been given a speedy trial under the charge of trespassing under the Nevada laws. Sentencing had been suspended for a year, and later in the afternoon we had returned to Camp Mercury to continue Prayer and Conscience Vigil along with others who had remained there during our civil disobedience action.

In the early morning of August 7 an experimental bomb was exploded. We sat with our backs to the explosion site. But when the flash came I felt again the utterly impossible horror of this whole business, the same complete realization that nuclear war must go, that I had felt twelve years before on the bridge of U.S.S. *Dale W. Peterson*, off Pearl Harbor.

I think also that deep down somewhere in me, and in all men at all times, there is a realization that the pattern of violence meeting violence makes no sense, and that war violates something central in the human heart—"that of God," as we Quakers sometimes say. . . .

Tell it to the Policeman

I was asked by the New England office of the American Friends Service Committee to take to the White House 17,411 signatures to a petition to cancel the Pacific tests. Ten thousand signatures had previously been sent in. I realize that even a President in good health cannot see personally everyone who has a message for him. Yet the right of petition exists—in theory—and is held to be a key factor in democratic process....

Twenty-seven thousand is quite a few people to have signed a somewhat unusual petition....I am known to Maxwell Rabb with whom I worked in Republican politics in Massachusetts. I was a precinct captain for Eisenhower in the 1952 primaries. Yet a couple of days work on the part of the staff of the Friends Committee on National Legislation failed to secure even an assurance that some time on Tuesday, December 31, the day I would be in Washington, Max Rabb would see me to receive the petitions. On that day I made five calls and talked with his secretary. Each time I was assured that she would call me back within ten minutes. Each time the return call failed to come and I tried again. The last time, early in the afternoon, I held on to the telephone for ten minutes, only to be told finally that the office was about to close for the day.

Each time I telephoned, including the last, I was told I could, of course, leave the petitions with the policeman at the gate. This I refused to do. It seems terrible to me that Americans can no longer speak to or be seen by their government. Has it become their master, not their servant? Can it not listen to their humble and reasonable pleas?...At any rate, the experience has strengthened in me the conviction that we must, at whatever cost, find ways to make our witness and protest heard.

I Am Going Because ...

I am going because, as Shakespeare said, "Action is eloquence." Without some such direct action, ordinary citizens lack the power any longer to be seen or heard by their government.

I am going because it is time to *do something* about peace, not just *talk* about peace.

I am going because, like all men, in my heart I know that *all* nuclear explosions are monstrous, evil, unworthy of human beings.

I am going because war is no longer a feudal jousting match; it is an unthinkable catastrophe for all men.

I am going because it is now the little children, and, most of all, the as yet unborn who are the front line troops. It is my duty to stand between them and this horrible danger.

I am going because it is cowardly and degrading for me to stand by any longer, to consent, and thus to collaborate in atrocities.

I am going because I cannot say that the end justifies the means. A Quaker, William Penn, said, "A good end cannot sanctify evil means; nor must we ever do evil that good may come of it." A Communist, Milovan Djilas, says, "As soon as means which would ensure an end are shown to be evil, the end will show itself as unrealizable."

I am going because, as Gandhi said, "God sits in the man opposite me; therefore to injure him is to injure God himself."

I am going to witness to the deep inward truth we all know, "Force can subdue, but love gains."

I am going because however mistaken, unrighteous, and unrepentant governments may seem, I still believe all men are really good at heart, and that my act will speak to them.

I am going in the hope of helping change the hearts and minds of men in government. If necessary I am willing to give my life to help change a policy of fear, force and destruction to one of trust, kindness, and help.

I am going in order to say, "Quit this waste, this arms race. Turn instead to a disarmament race. Stop competing for evil, compete for good."

I am going because I have to—if I am to call myself a human being....

Source: Staughton Lynd, ed. *Nonviolence in America: A Documentary History.* Indianapolis, IN: Bobbs—Merrill Co., 1966, pp. 340–346.

QUESTIONS

1. Explain Albert Bigelow's views toward war during his time spent in the Solomon Islands when he participated in the event known as the "Turkey Shoot." How did the atomic bomb affect his position on war?

2. What is it that Bigelow is dissenting against and how would you describe his method of protest?

3. In this document, Bigelow mentions how he was asked to bring 17,411 signatures to the White House in order to petition against the Pacific tests. Why did Bigelow reject the idea of leaving these signed petitions with the policeman at the gate and how did this refusal appear to strengthen his convictions?

7

Protesting Imperialism, Promoting Democracy

While the 1950s offered a glimmer of hope that flickered on and off, the next decade produced the most active and sustained antiwar protests in American history. In 1960, John F. Kennedy was elected president, and one of his major concerns was Cuba, where Fidel Castro had led a successful revolution a year earlier. In response to Cuba's nationalization of industries, including those belonging to American companies, the U.S. drastically reduced its imports of Cuban sugar and within a few years instituted a blockade of the island.

In an effort to present Cuba's side of the story and offset U.S. government attempts to isolate and undermine Castro's government, a sympathetic group came together in New York City in early April 1960. It took the name Fair Play for Cuba Committee (FPCC). Led by Waldo Frank and Carleton Beals, the group's purpose was to generate grassroots support for the Cuban Revolution and challenge U.S. government policy. A number of FPCC groups were set up in the United States and Canada. Among its mem-

---

For the People, pages 209–259

209

bers and sponsors were a number of prominent intellectuals: writers James Baldwin, Norman Mailer, Truman Capote, Allen Ginsberg, and Julian Mayfield; academics William Appleman Williams and John Henrik Clarke; philosopher Jean Paul Sartre; and labor journalist Sidney Lens.

FPCC initiated its defense of Cuba with a full-page ad in the *New York Times* on April 6, 1960 (**Document 1**). Evoking memories of the Monroe Doctrine, the "Big Stick" policy, and "Dollar Diplomacy," the Committee challenged press accounts of Communist atrocities and the idea that the Castro government posed a danger to the United States. Many in the committee believed that the revolution was justified and that American business interests were responsible for much of the poverty that had existed before Castro came to power. In large measure, the committee insisted that the U.S. government was using the Cuban Revolution as an excuse to heighten Cold War fears and thereby garner more support in its conflict with the Soviet Union. In 1961, the committee opposed the Bay of Pigs invasion and criticized the U.S. embargo against Cuba. Though the FPCC did not succeed in changing U.S. government policies toward the Third World, those policies—such as the Bay of Pigs invasion that was meant to spark an overthrow of Castro—and FPCC's charges of American imperialism helped spark the political awareness of many disaffected college students. These students saw U.S. Cold War policies and continued racial discrimination as hypocritical to the values on which they had been raised. Concerned about the state of American democracy and the seeming apathy of their own generation, students, civil rights workers, and action-minded intellectuals organized as a "New Left." Speaking out on a range of issues, from the support of American businesses for apartheid South Africa to the nuclear arms race to racial discrimination and poverty at home, they sought to gain more of a voice in politics through the means of direct action. Many of them had socialist leanings, but they differed from their 1930s predecessors (the Old Left) in their emphasis on democracy and decentralization. There was to be no "party line" imposed from above.

The most prominent New Left organization was Students for a Democratic Society, which traced its beginnings to a convention held in June 1962 at Port Huron, Michigan. There, about 200 activists put forth the *Port Huron Statement*, which made an explicit connection between ending the Cold War and advancing domestic reform (**Document 2**). These activists looked first to college campuses, where knowledge was produced, in their call for social reconstruction and political awareness.

Two issues especially troubled this generation. First was the stark reality of American citizens as victims of an unfair social and economic system, symbolized by the struggle against racial bigotry. Many college student activists recognized the debilitating effects of racial discrimination in America. After all, they had grown up in the wake of the murder of Emmett Till, the resistance to *Brown v. Board*, and the images of African Americans challenging segregation in Montgomery and Little Rock. The growing awareness of structural violence in the urban ghetto—where one's life chances were severely restricted if one happened to be born black—owed much to African American novelist James Baldwin. In a moving letter to his nephew, Baldwin eloquently suggested that the solution to racism was love of humanity. The issue for him was not how the oppressed might learn to adapt to America; rather, it was time for people to work together to make things right (**Document 3**).

Second, the Cold War, symbolized by the Bomb, brought insecurity and a desperate desire for change before it was too late. New Left activists wanted reform from the bottom up, and one important part of the equation for reform was a reorganization of the nation's priorities. How much more money could be devoted to health care, improving the inner cities, creating jobs for the poor, and building better schools if it were not being put into the Pentagon's pockets? Would there be future generations given the awesome power of the Bomb? Their challenge to the military machine was expressed well in the popular song "Masters of War" by Bob Dylan (**Document 4**). In Thoreau-like terms these college-age students asserted their individualism in the name of collective responsibility.

No longer was it acceptable to just sit back and accept things as they were. Only a New Left of young people, committed to political action, could succeed in creating a more responsive democracy. On the national level, SDS had a highly decentralized structure barely kept together by a tiny, highly mobile, and poorly paid staff located in Chicago. Distrusting bureaucratic structures, the organization insisted that each local chapter work out its own programs. After SDS sponsored the first big demonstration against the Vietnam War in April 1965, hundreds of chapters sprang up around the country. Each one was autonomous and addressed a range of issues, from local concerns as mundane as male visiting hours in women's dormitories to national elections and international issues. SDS members approached peace and social justice issues with high moral conviction and emotional commitment.

SDS became a vehicle for students to critique the society their parents' generation had built, which in their view placed too much emphasis on material gain at the expense of more meaningful pursuits. Their actions also marked the era of "obstructive demonstration" and a new, more confrontational approach to trying to stop the war machine and military involvement in Vietnam. Employing the SDS's call for radical action, for example, students would lie down in front of troop trains in order to block their progress. In its origins, however, SDS was mainly concerned with expanding democracy in order to end racism and poverty in America.

SDS was not the only organization that grew along with increasing U.S. troop commitments to Vietnam. Failing to learn from the French colonial failure, the United States agreed to support the repressive regime of South Vietnamese president Ngo Dinh Diem in August 1963. For several months, peace groups in America called for a ceasefire in the war between the Republic of Vietnam, led by Diem, and the Communist-backed National Liberation Front. During the winter of 1964–65, after the Lyndon Johnson administration committed combat troops to Vietnam, the antiwar movement began to increase in size and activity. The larger movement included anti-imperialists who believed that the real enemy was America's corporate ruling class, radical pacifists who saw war as the real enemy, and mainline peace liberals who emphasized the traditional means of political pressure to compel U.S. policymakers to negotiate an end to the war.

Despite its disparate composition, the most significant characteristic of the antiwar movement was its ability to coalesce and form new coalitions, which enabled the movement to sustain its momentum. The range of those involved broke across ideological lines that had divided Americans for decades, and the broad agreement and determined opposition to the war could be seen in public statements from 1965 on (**Document 5**). In the vast line of protest marches, one could find priests, nuns, socialists, anarchists, members of the SDS, campus peace groups, veterans, even staunch Republicans. Coalitions formed among those who resented the immorality and brutality of the war and those who questioned its premise while linking the war to domestic poverty and racial injustice.

One of the earliest indications that American citizens, especially intellectuals, were uncertain about the course of action the Johnson Administration had undertaken in Southeast Asia was the growing popularity of "teach-ins" that swept through the nation's colleges and universities in 1965. Having supported Johnson in 1964 as the "peace candidate," many faculty members and students felt betrayed as he sent thousands of troops to Vietnam. The idea behind the teach-ins was to use the academic community's expertise to examine U.S. policy and get to the bottom of the administration's rationale for war. On March 24, 1965, an all-night teach-in at the University of Michigan attracted 3,000 participants. This event touched off a series of teach-ins at hundreds of campuses across the United States during the remainder of the year. While the one at Michigan was clearly intended as a protest against the war, in many other places they were debates between the antiwar and pro-government points of view. Speaking at the University of Oregon, Senator Wayne Morse—one of only two senators who had voted against the Gulf of Tonkin resolution, which authorized Johnson to order military action—predicted: "Twelve months from tonight, there will be hundreds of thousands of American boys fighting in Southeast Asia—and tens of thousands of them will be coming home in coffins." At the University of Michigan, Arthur Waskow of the Institute of Policy Studies, condemning militarism and conscription, cited Jefferson on slavery: "I tremble for my country when I reflect that God is just."

Such protests helped inspire Senator J. William Fulbright, head of the Senate Foreign Relations Committee, to hold hearings on the war to determine its true nature. The nationally televised hearings, like the teach-ins, helped counter the propaganda coming from the Johnson Administration and illustrated to the public that patriotic officials could also be opponents of war. The hearings, in turn, further spurred on the antiwar movement and coalition-building.

A good example of the coalition-building that characterized the movement was a demonstration held in New York in February 1966. The Fifth Avenue Peace Parade Committee, organized by Muste, and the National Coordinating Committee to End the War in Vietnam (NCCEWV) brought out 5,000 pickets to oppose the presentation of a Freedom House Award to Lyndon Johnson. For Muste and his followers the war was an immoral act that had to end immediately (**Document 6**). The following month, between 20,000 and 25,000 marchers participated in another international protest action under the auspices of the National Committee. Led by a sizeable contingent of disillusioned American war veterans and African Americans against the war, parade participants were a racially and politically mixed lot that highlighted the diversity of the opposition to the war. At a rally in Central Park, Muste, Vietnam veteran Donald Duncan, and writer Norman Mailer spoke out against the war in the face of hecklers and egg-throwers.

A month later, under CNVA sponsorship, A.J. Muste, veteran activist Barbara Deming, Brad Lyttle, Karl Meyer, outspoken antiwar scientist William Davidson, and peace movement novice Sherry Thurber flew to Saigon to show the South Vietnamese that some Americans opposed the war. Also involved in promoting this citizen peace delegation were members of Women Strike for Peace (WSP). This organization was formed in 1961 by mothers who were concerned about the effects of nuclear weapons testing on children. When the Vietnam War began, WSP turned its attention to trying to end it. The organization's views were expressed by Ethel Barol Taylor, one of its original members who later traveled to Hanoi with two other women in search of reconciliation (**Document 7**).

By 1967, antiwar sentiment in America was at fever pitch. A series of events magnified the intensity with which organizations and individuals were protesting the war. First, A.J. Muste, German pastor Martin Niemoller (age 75), Anglican Bishop Ambrose Reeves (age 67), and American Rabbi Abraham Feinberg (age 67 and serving a congregation in Toronto) spent ten days in North Vietnam (January 9–19). In outright contradiction to statements from Washington denying American air attacks in the area around Hanoi, Muste wrote from that city to the CNVA that no more than three or four blocks from his hotel in the center of town there were civilian neighborhoods reduced to rubble. Based on what they were seeing, Muste directed Americans back home to convey a message to Washington to cease the relentless B-52 bombings, which had done little to further the peace talks. Second, on the heels of Muste's trip to Hanoi a group of trade unionists organized the National Labor Leadership Assembly for Peace, hoping to convince workers in defense plants of the war's immorality. Third, in the summer, heavyweight boxing champion Muhammad Ali was sentenced to five years in jail and a $10,000 fine for refusing induction on the grounds that his Black Muslim beliefs precluded him from fighting in a white man's war. Fourth, army surgeon Captain Howard Levy made public his refusal to train combat first-aid teams for action in Vietnam. Finally, respected Harvard economist John Kenneth Galbraith published a pamphlet arguing that the United States was in a war it could not win and should not wish to win.

One of the most significant developments in 1967 was Martin Luther King's speaking out against the war, which he did most famously and unequivocally in a speech at Riverside Church in April. In "A Time to Break Silence," he charged the United States government with being "the greatest purveyor of violence in the world today" (**Document 8**). King had been cautioned by his colleagues in the Southern Christian Leadership Conference that coming out against the war would hurt the cause of civil rights. He answered them in his speech by pointing out the many ways in which these issues were linked. By that time, he was too disturbed by the brutal images of the war, by the resources being devoted to it, and the disproportionally high percentage of African American casualties to keep silent anymore. Asserting that the war was draining much-needed resources from domestic programs, King's statements against the war helped rally more African American activists to the antiwar cause while boosting the moral stance of the movement and encouraging the public to question the credibility of the Johnson Administration.

By this time, the rate of conscientious objection was four times as large as during World War II, while levels of draft evasion, violations, and exile to Canada or into the domestic underground reached record heights. Though many young men volunteered for military service or accepted the draft willingly, unprecedented personal antiwar decisions became more and more commonplace.

Alice Lynd compiled an anthology in which the inner feelings of antiwar activists were explored. In *We Won't Go*, Lynd discussed the reasons for young American men fleeing to Canada and included their own personal statements for maximum effect. For example, to David Taube, an Army reservist, the thought of killing "innocent Vietnamese" was a reality with which he could not live. "Since living with myself is important to me . . . I was about to go to jail. Although this wouldn't be as good as active rebellion for the antiwar cause, it would have at least made the U.S. feed and clothe me for five years. . . . Canada seemed to be nicer than a jail . . ."

Dissent became so common that by 1968 many Americans began wondering whether the nation had reached its breaking point. Between April and September of that year, the U.S. witnessed the assassinations of Martin Luther King, Jr. and Robert F. Kennedy, violence on college campuses, more and more public burning of draft cards, and demonstrations aimed at disrupting the Democratic National Convention in Chicago in order to call attention to the war. According to the National Commission on the Causes and Prevention of Violence, set up to investigate the events of "Chicago '68," the violence there constituted a "police riot" against demonstrators and members of the press. Complicating the increasing polarization of the society was the resentment of "the Establishment" toward the counterculture; while some hippies avoided politics altogether, others actively promoted their values of antimaterialism, love, and peace, offending even their allies in the antiwar movement with their casual style of dress and unwillingness to conform to prevailing modes of respectability. Such differences combined with the turmoil of the late 1960s to create the strange phenomenon wherein most Americans opposed the war but also opposed the protest movement.

The year 1968 also saw the public debut of the feminist movement with its protest against the Miss America pageant. Challenging the pageant's objectification of women's bodies as symbolic of the oppression of women more generally, they announced their own "liberation" movement by filling a "freedom trashcan" with objects that restricted them (bras, girdles, etc.). The women's liberation movement challenged deeply held beliefs about the proper roles for women, so while it grew rapidly because many women agreed with its premises, it also unleashed a backlash that would last for decades. Women's rights activists—male and female—had already addressed head-on the more public issues such as equal pay for equal work and opening up women's employment opportunities beyond the standard teacher–nurse–secretary–flight attendant options. The goals of equal rights had been set forth in the statement of purpose put forth by the National Organization for Women in 1966 (**Document 9**). What was different from 1968 on was that more radical feminists also challenged the division of labor by gender in the home, raising issues from housework to sexuality. The women's liberation movement also highlighted the ultra-democratic nature of 1960s protest in that it spread not through building organizations but through a process called "consciousness raising." Small groups of women met in consciousness-raising groups to talk about their experience as women and what they could do to liberate themselves from oppressive situations. The hallmark of the women's movement was the idea that "the personal is political," meaning that the way one lived one's daily life had political significance. This idea was taken to heart by movements for peace and justice in subsequent years.

Whether it was women challenging traditional roles, visible countercultural activists rejecting basic values of the society, students taking over buildings on campuses to protest university policies, black power advocates no longer mincing words about their goal of ending racism and police brutality, or antiwar protesters burning draft cards or marching in the streets, to many Americans the foundation of their society was being shaken. Even the Catholic Church became divided in this era.

As part of the escalating protests against the war, Catholic peace activists began to destroy draft board files. In October 1967, four of them poured blood on draft files at a Selective Service office in Baltimore and were quickly dubbed the "Baltimore Four." Catholic priests and brothers Daniel and Philip Berrigan, along with seven other activists, achieved front-page coverage when, on May 17, 1968, they entered Local Board #33 in Catonsville, Maryland, and burned hundreds of Selective Service Records with napalm outside in the parking lot (**Document 10**). The nine activists had notified local law enforcement authorities prior to their act and were promptly arrested. During their trial they became known as the "Catonsville Nine."

These antiwar activists carried direct action to a new level of protest. Their so-called ultraresistance was based on fearless individual action, not organized mass pressure. Functioning as religious rituals and relying on religious symbols such as blood and fire, the ultraresisters defied the law and the federal government. Alerting the media to come along on their planned protests, the Catholic left sparked a long series of draft board raids that did not terminate until 1972. From coast to coast, similar raids occurred in Boston, New York, Milwaukee, Chicago, Los Angeles, Evanston, Illinois, and San Jose, California. In addition, such action prompted attention to corporate involvement in the war. Corporation office and factory raids followed much the same style as action against draft boards. In Washington, D.C., a group of nine Catholics raided the offices of Dow Chemical Company and exposed official documents tying Dow directly to the manufacture of napalm used in the war. Some months later, another group, calling itself "The Beaver 55," scrambled computer tapes at Dow's Midland, Michigan, research center.

The inspiration for these raids had come from the establishment of the Catholic Peace Fellowship in the summer of 1964. Formed in the spirit of Vatican II, which "turned the Church to the world," CPF became the only Catholic peace group that was institutionally connected to non-Catholics—namely, the primarily Protestant, ecumenical Fellowship of Reconciliation. CPF emphasized the pacifist traditions of the Catholic Church, participated in direct, nonviolent antiwar protests, organized study conferences, and counseled conscientious objectors. Additionally, in the summer of 1965, much to the chagrin of the hawkish Francis Cardinal Spellman of New York, Daniel Berrigan helped create the interdenominational Clergy and Laity Concerned about Vietnam.

Throughout these years, the Catholic left, inspired by the Berrigans' actions, resorted to other targets. The Media, Pennsylvania, office of the FBI was raided by an anonymous group. Their expropriation of certain documents proved that the FBI was conducting covert and illegal surveillance of groups and individuals working for social change. One group dismantled bomb casings at a York, Pennsylvania, manufacturer, and one at Hickam Air Force Base in Hawaii poured blood on secret documents concerning electronic warfare.

Generally, these hit-and-run raids were experiments with various types of resistance that held the line at destroying property rather than people. While the issue of property destruction did raise many eyebrows within pacifist circles, the question of property rights versus human rights was brought to the attention of millions of Americans in a very significant way. To those who carried them out, the draft board/corporation actions were important contributions to the strategy of war resistance at a time when many people felt powerless to stop the war machine.

Another constituency of the antiwar movement that contributed new tactics and ideas were Vietnam veterans and GIs. A handful of vets had marched together in antiwar parades in 1967, but they became a strong voice of protest within a few years, giving the movement some much-needed credibility since they had experienced the war firsthand. In addition to resistance at the front and antiwar activity in GI coffeehouses and newspapers, veterans brought the war home to the American public. One particular action raised popular awareness of the brutality of the war and its effects on both Vietnamese and American soldiers—it was called the Winter Soldier Investigation. Described by John Kerry in testimony before the Fulbright Committee in 1971 (**Document 11**), the investigation consisted of days of testimony by veterans about the war crimes they had committed in Southeast Asia. This was testimony from the horse's mouth, thus much harder to ignore than protests by college students, pacifists, and hippies. It came in the wake of publicity about the My Lai massacre—an incident from a few years earlier in which a company of U.S. infantrymen destroyed a hamlet and slaughtered the inhabitants, men, women, and children—alerting people to the fact that this had not been an isolated incident. It also followed on the heels of the release of the Pentagon Papers, which revealed that the government had been dishonest about the war from the very beginning. Nixon's credibility was already shaken; having promised not to widen the war, he had sent troops into Cambodia in April 1970, sparking a series of angry protests across the nation, especially on college campuses. One of these ended in tragedy when Ohio National Guardsmen fired on a group of students, killing four of them. The war had, indeed, come home.

By the late 1960s, in the context of urban riots, war in Southeast Asia, and an emerging feminist movement, veteran peace activists were more than ever determined to find ways to address the moral, political, and structural violence plaguing American society. One of these activists was Barbara Deming, who wrote a famous essay on the power of nonviolence from the perspective of an experienced civil rights worker, pacifist, and feminist. A descendant on her mother's side of the "learned blacksmith" Elihu Burritt, Deming was educated in Quaker schools and later attended Bennington College in Vermont. In 1959, after traveling in India, she avidly read Gandhi's work and started to identify herself as a pacifist. But it was her trip to Cuba in 1960 where she met Castro—an opponent of imperialism who many young people considered a liberator—that convinced her to devote her full energies to world peace and social justice. She was also influenced by members of the Peacemakers and CVNA.

In 1963–64, she was part of the Quebec–Washington–Guantanamo Walk for Peace. Arrested in Albany, Georgia, for attempting to walk through town with an interracial group, she spent a month in jail. Her experience led to the publication of *Prison Notes* in 1966, considered a classic about southern justice and imprisonment. She later spent eleven days in North Vietnam with three other women where she witnessed the devastating effects of U.S. bombing raids. In her best-known essay, "Revolution and Equilibrium," she explores the essence and power of nonviolence. Only through self-assertion and respect for others, she maintained, will those institutions breeding violence be forever eliminated (**Document 12**).

Civil rights activism, opposition to the war, creation of alternative communities, and efforts to reverse structural and patriarchal violence were major components of 1960s protest, recognized by scholars and popular media alike. Less acknowledged was the ongoing struggle for economic justice and the specific connections between organizing workers and promoting peace. From the Knights of Labor to Cesar Chavez's United Farm Workers, union organizers and the peace movement had shared goals, focused on enabling every individual to live in dignity. Martin Luther King's growing interest in the issue of poverty, for instance, had much to do with the resources he saw being squandered by the war in Vietnam.

Even as the economy grew in the 1960s, many working people continued to labor under harsh conditions with no hope of advancement. In California, where large landowners controlled most of the agricultural land, migrant workers performed back-breaking labor for low wages, with little job security and no access to government programs such as Social Security. (Migrant labor was exempt from New Deal measures that gave other workers such protections.) Throughout the years, migrant workers had made numerous efforts to organize, but in every instance their efforts were violently beaten down. The owners consistently sought cheap labor that was drawn from the poorest populations, including Filipinos, Chinese, Japanese, Mexicans, and Chicanos. By the early 1960s, coinciding with civil rights and the antiwar movements, efforts were again underway to organize migrant laborers. On September 8, 1965, Filipinos who were members of the Agricultural Workers Organizing Committee of the American Federation of Labor–Congress of Industrial Organizations (AFL-CIO) conducted a strike in the grape fields of Delano, California. The following week they were joined by Mexican American laborers of the National Farm Workers Association. It signaled the first successful strike by farm workers for union recognition in U.S. history.

The person most responsible was Cesar Chavez, leader of the NFWA, which joined hands with the AWOC in mounting a 300-mile march from Delano to the state capital of Sacramento, publicizing their strike against the fruit growers. The walk ended on Easter Sunday 1966, with the announcement of the very first farm worker contract. The large wine grape grower, Schenley Industries, entered into the contract. On August 22, 1966, the two union groups merged to form the United Farm Workers' Organizing Committee. Chavez was selected as director (**Document 13**).

Chavez brought to the farm labor organizing struggles a personal commitment to nonviolence, which helped migrant workers gain attention and respect for their cause. With Chavez in the lead, the protests took the form of pickets, sit-ins, and processions, marked by strong religious overtones. Catholic masses were often conducted to boost the morale of strikers. Many clergy also joined the movement. Perhaps the new union's most effective tactic was the grape boycott. In February 1968, in an effort to draw national attention to the boycott and strike, Chavez began a twenty-five-day fast. The International Grape Boycott organized that year also resulted in organizers canvassing more than 100 cities in the United States and Canada. The loss of sales from the boycott, combined with strong public pressure and clergy backing, forced the twenty-six Delano growers to sign the first wide scale union contracts in California on July 26, 1970.

Throughout the 1970s and 1980s, Chavez used his personal commitment to nonviolence to publicize and promote the cause of the migrant farm workers. Relying on boycotts and nonviolent strikes the UFW singled out the lettuce growers in Salinas in the early 1970s, reached an agreement with Coca-Cola's Minute Maid subsidiary in Florida covering mostly African American orange pickers in 1972, and in June 1975, marking the first time in American history, the California legislature granted the right of agricultural workers to vote for the union they wanted to join. The efforts of Chavez and the UFW bore testimony to the effectiveness of nonviolence in the struggle for economic and social justice in America.

The protest movements of the 1960s left an important legacy. With SNCC as a model, in particular, they brought the use of nonviolent tactics on behalf of peace and justice to many places on behalf of a variety of causes. The UFW improved the lives and working conditions of migrant laborers, while the civil rights and black power movements erased the legal basis of segregation, encouraged black participation in politics, and changed the way Americans saw their own history. Of course these struggles are not over, but the changes they brought about are evident in everyday life. By the same token, it is unclear how much credit the antiwar movement deserves for bringing an end to the Vietnam War. But it clearly achieved some things: It clarified the political and moral issues involved in the conflict; it set limits on the war policy by mobilizing significant opposition; and it added to the war's social cost due to the large-scale controversy it caused.

Equally significant, the anti–Vietnam War movement altered the historic foundation of the peace movement in a number of ways, democratizing the movement itself as it sought to bring greater democracy to society as a whole. Actions against the war provided flexibility to local branches and individuals through a wide range of options. Innovative forms of dissent and protest were carried out, from acts of civil disobedience to street theater. Mass demonstrations were controlled through discipline by paying careful attention to the media. Antiwar activists also practiced party politics at both the electoral and congressional levels. One of the most significant contributions the movement made was challenging the Cold War policy of containment and calling into question the meaning of "national security." In the eyes of peace and justice movements, national security had as much to do with promoting social welfare in the form of jobs, education, health care, and protecting democratic values such as free speech as it did with preventing Communism by waging war in faraway countries. Lastly, by adopting a decentralized model of organizing, antiwar activists created forms of networking to replace the command/top-down style exhibited by previous protest movements. Thus, not only did the activists of this period have a profound impact on U.S. foreign policy, but also by the policies and strategies they chose to carry out, they dramatically changed the course and outlook of the peace movement itself.

Document 1: Newspaper Ad
What is Really Happening in Cuba? (1960)

The Fair Play for Cuba Committee ran this full-page ad in the *New York Times,* April 6, 1960. In an effort to counter a number of false and misleading reports by the U.S. press, the FPCC listed its own findings and challenged the news media to a fair and impartial recounting of the facts. The ad was signed by a distinguished group of intellectuals who hoped to raise awareness about U.S. policies in the Third World.

"We Only Report The Facts," U.S. Newsmen Are Accustomed to Say, Is this True? Compare the Following "Facts."

COMMUNISM: "A pro-Communist state has been established in Cuba with the clear objective of bargaining with Soviet Russia for the munitions of war . . ."—Sokolsky in the *New York Journal American.* True or false?

False. Not a shred of evidence has been produced to support such allegations as the one above, charges consistently used to create a smoke screen behind which the social objectives of the Cuban revolution can be attacked and sabotaged. Cuba's recent trade pact with the Soviet Union represents an effort to find new markets for Cuban sugar, and to obtain, not arms, but agricultural implements and industrial machinery for which credit has been denied in the United States. Many other American republics trade with the Soviets—as does the United States itself....

CONFISCATION: In Cuba, Castro is stealing American property with impunity."—*U.S. News & World Report*

False. Although the word "confiscation" has often been used by the press in a context which would suggest illegal seizure, nothing has been stolen from any American—or any Cuban. The Agrarian Reform Law, designed to diversify Cuban agriculture and to give 100,000 landless peasants a stake in their own rich agricultural country, conforms in all respects with international law and the practice of all civilized countries... this compares favorably with, for example, the U.S. land reform program imposed on Japan by General MacArthur after World War II....

CHAOS: "All that now remains is for Castro to give the word, and the Terror, the ruthless hunting down and shooting of Fidel's opponents, will begin."—*Newsweek*

False. Despite the above prediction, Nov. 3, 1959, and the incessant references to "terror," "chaos," and "dictatorship" in the U.S. press, the great work of revolutionary reform and reconstruction now in progress in Cuba is going forward in an atmosphere of extraordinary optimism and energy, as any tourist can testify. The island is being governed by a provisional government under the Constitution of 1940, which is notable in the Hemisphere for its liberality. Cubans—and visitors to the island—remain freer in many respects than do U.S. citizens. For example, no police permit is required for a pubic meeting or demonstration, as in New York City.... Despite an attempted invasion from Santo Domingo, a widespread counter-revolutionary conspiracy, and numerous small acts of sabotage and terrorism on the part of former Batista henchmen, the government has refrained from invoking the death sentence against convicted counter-revolutionaries. *Newsweek* notwithstanding, not one of them has been shot.

"WHAT HAVE WE DONE..." asks a new and hopeful generation of Cubans, viewed with hostility in Washington and Wall Street, accused of "impudence" for seeking their independence, threatened with economic and diplomatic "isolation" in the Hemisphere.

Perhaps their crime is their youth.... Perhaps they have aspired toward too much, too soon. (Three thousand low-cost housing units built in the first year of revolution, more than 7,000 classrooms, hundreds of miles of new roads, 500 flourishing agricultural co-operatives, thousands of jobs created in new industries established through the voluntary contributions of a million Cuban workers.) Perhaps the explanation is simply that there are in the United States, powerful interests bent on frustrating the primary purpose of the Revolution: to give Cuba back to the Cubans.... [T]hey are in the American tradition. Certainly, they deserve a hearing. This much the American tradition owes them. This much we, as Americans, owe them.

Would you like to know more of the truth about revolutionary Cuba as it is today?

Source: John Henrik Clarke Papers, Schomburg Center for Research in Black Culture, New York Public Library.

QUESTIONS

1. Why did so many prominent Americans support Castro's revolution?
2. How did the U.S. press try to stir up Cold War fears and why?
3. What facts did the committee present to offset the news depictions of the revolution in Cuba? What "American tradition" did the committee attempt to link to the Cuban Revolution?

Document 2: *The Port Huron Statement* (1962)

The major document of the early New Left emerged from a retreat attended by a number of student activists in Port Huron, Michigan. The primary author was Tom Hayden, who later served in the California State Assembly and the State Senate. The statement was inspired by the growing civil rights struggles as well as the influential writings of Columbia University sociologist C. Wright Mills. It became the intellectual basis for Students for a Democratic Society. The document introduced the concept of "participatory democracy" and supported the labor, peace, and civil rights movements of that period.

Port Huron Statement

Introduction: Agenda for a Generation

We are people of this generation, bred in at least modest comfort, housed now in universities, looking uncomfortably to the world we inherit.

When we were kids the United States was the wealthiest and strongest country in the world; the only one with the atom bomb, the least scarred by modern war, an initiator of the United Nations that we thought would distribute Western influence throughout the world. Freedom and equality for each individual, government of, by, and for the people—these American values we found good, principles by which we could live as men. Many of us began maturing in complacency.

As we grew, however, our comfort was penetrated by events too troubling to dismiss. First, the permeating and victimizing fact of human degradation, symbolized by the Southern struggle against racial bigotry, compelled most of us from silence to activism. Second, the enclosing fact of the Cold War, symbolized by the presence of the Bomb, brought awareness that we ourselves, and our friends, and millions of abstract "others" we knew more directly because of our common peril, might die at any time. We might deliberately ignore, or avoid, or fail to feel all other human problems, but not these two, for these were too immediate and crushing in their impact, too challenging in the demand that we as individuals take the responsibility for encounter and resolution.

While these and other problems either directly oppressed us or rankled our consciences and became our own subjective concerns, we began to see complicated and disturbing paradoxes in our surrounding America. The declaration "all men are created equal..." rang hollow before the facts of Negro life in the South and the big cities of the North. The proclaimed peaceful intentions of the United States contradicted its economic and military investments in the Cold War status quo.

We witnessed, and continue to witness, other paradoxes. With nuclear energy whole cities can easily be powered, yet the dominant nation-states seem more likely to unleash destruction greater than that incurred in all wars of human history. Although our own technology is destroying old and creating new forms of social organization, men still tolerate meaningless work and idleness. While two-thirds of mankind suffers under nourishment, our own upper classes revel amidst superfluous abundance. Although world population is expected to double in forty years, the nations still tolerate anarchy as a major principle of international conduct and uncontrolled exploitation governs the sapping of the earth's physical resources. Although mankind desperately needs revolutionary leadership, America rests in national stalemate, its goals ambiguous and tradition-bound instead of informed and clear, its democratic system apathetic and manipulated rather than "of, by, and for the people."

We regard *men* as infinitely precious and possessed of unfulfilled capacities for reason, freedom, and love.

Men have unrealized potential for self-cultivation, self-direction, self-understanding, and creativity. It is this potential that we regard as crucial and to which we appeal, not to the human potentiality for violence, unreason, and submission to authority.

We would replace power rooted in possession, privilege, or circumstance by power and uniqueness rooted in love, reflectiveness, reason, and creativity. As a social system we seek the establishment of a democracy of individual participation, governed by two central aims: that the individual share in those social decisions determining the quality and direction of his life; that society be organized to encourage independence in men and provide the media for their common participation.

In social change or interchange, we find violence to be abhorrent because it requires generally the transformation of the target, be it a human being or a community of people, into a depersonalized object of hate. It is imperative that the means of violence be abolished and the institutions—local, national, international—that encourage nonviolence as a condition of conflict be developed.

The Students

In the last few years, thousands of American students demonstrated that they at least felt the urgency of the times. They moved actively and directly against racial injustices, the threat of war, violations of individual rights of conscience, and, less frequently, against economic manipulation. They succeeded in restoring a small measure of controversy to the campuses after the stillness of the McCarthy period. They succeeded, too, in gaining some concessions from the people and institutions they opposed, especially in the fight against racial bigotry.

The significance of these scattered movements lies not in their success or failure in gaining objectives—at least, not yet. Nor does the significance lie in the intellectual "competence" or "maturity" of the students involved—as some pedantic elders allege. The significance is in the fact that students are breaking the crust of apathy and overcoming the inner alienation that remain the defining characteristics of American college life.

Tragically, the university could serve as a significant source of social criticism and an initiator of new modes and molders of attitudes. But the actual intellectual effect of the college experience is hardly distinguishable from that of any other communications channel—say, a television set—passing on the stock truths of the day. Students leave college somewhat more "tolerant" than when they arrived, but basically unchallenged in their values and political orientations.

Any new left in America must be, in large measure, a left with real intellectual skills, committed to deliberativeness, honesty, reflection as working tools. The university permits the political life to be an adjunct to the academic one, and action to be informed by reason.

A new left must be distributed in significant social roles throughout the country. The universities are distributed in such a manner.

A new left must consist of younger people who matured in the postwar world, and partially be directed to the recruitment of younger people. The university is an obvious beginning point.

A new left must include liberals and socialists, the former for their relevance, the latter for their sense of thoroughgoing reforms in the system. The university is a more sensible place than a political party for these two traditions to begin to discuss their differences and look for political synthesis.

A new left must start controversy across the land, if national policies and national apathy are to be reversed. The ideal university is a community of controversy, within itself and in its effects on communities beyond.

A new left must transform modern complexity into issues that can be understood and felt close up by every human being. It must give form to the feelings of helplessness and indifference, so that people may see the political, social, and economic sources of their private troubles, and organize to change society. In a time of supposed prosperity, moral complacency, and political manipulation, a new left cannot rely on only aching stomachs to be the engine force of social reform. The case for change, for alternatives that will involve uncomfortable personal efforts, must be argued as never before. The university is a relevant place for all of these activities.

As students for a democratic society, we are committed to stimulating this kind of social movement, this kind of vision and program in campus and community across the country. If we appear to seek the unattainable, as it has been said, then let it be known that we do so to avoid the unimaginable.

_____

Source: Port Huron Statement, http://www.2.iath.virginia.edu/sixties/HTML _docs/Resources/Primary/Manifestos/Port Huron Statement (accessed May 16, 2009)

QUESTIONS

1. What did SDS mean by "participatory democracy"? What in their view was wrong with American democracy as it was?
2. Why did SDS consider students and universities as important agents of social change?
3. What was the view of violence and nonviolence put forth in this document?

_____

Document 3:   James Baldwin
My Dungeon Shook (1963)

James Baldwin is one of the most acclaimed African American writers of twentieth-century America. Born into a poor family in Harlem and serving as a Pentecostal preacher in his Baptist church as a young teenager, Baldwin began writing during the early Cold War years. Disillusioned with America and its racist attitudes, Baldwin relocated to Paris for several years. When he returned to the United States, his criticisms of race relations were trenchant and compelling. This excerpt is from his 1963 book, *The Fire Next Time.*

My Dungeon Shook: Letter to My Nephew
on the One Hundredth Anniversary of the Emanicipation

James Baldwin

Dear James:

I have begun this letter five times and torn it up five times. I keep seeing your face, which is also the face of your father and my brother. Like him, you are tough, dark, vulnerable, moody—with a very definite tendency to sound truculent because you want no one to think you are soft. You may be like your grandfather in this, I don't know, but certainly both you and your father resemble him very much physically. Well, he is dead, he never saw you, and he had a terrible life; he was defeated long before he died because, at the bottom of his heart, *he really believed what white people said about him.* This is one of the reasons that he became so holy. I am sure that your father has told you something about all that. Neither you nor your father exhibit any tendency towards holiness; you really are of another era, part of what happened when the Negro left the land and came into what the late E. Franklin Frazier called "the cities of destruction." You can only be destroyed by believing that you really are what the while world calls a *nigger.* I tell you this because I love you, and please don't you forget it.

I have known both of you all your lives, have carried your Daddy in my arms and on my shoulders, kissed and spanked him and watched him learn to walk. I don't know if you've known anybody from that far back; if you've loved anybody that long, first as an infant, then as a child, then as a man, you gain a strange perspective on time and human pain and effort. Other people cannot see what I see whenever I look into your father's face, for behind your father's face as it is today are all those other faces which were his. Let him laugh and I see a cellar your father does not remember and a house he does not remember and I hear in his present laughter his laughter as a child. Let him curse and I remember him falling down the cellar steps, and howling, and I remember, with pain, his tears, which my hand or your grandmother's so easily wiped away. But no one's hands can wipe away those tears he shed invisibly today, which one hears in his laughter and in his speech and in his songs. I know what the world has done to my brother and how narrowly he has survived it. And I know, which is much worse, and this is the crime of which I accuse my country and my countrymen, and for which neither I nor time nor history will ever forgive them, that they have destroyed and are destroying hundreds of thousands of lives and do not know it and do not want to know it. One can be, indeed one must strive to become, tough and philosophical concerning destruction and death, for this is what most of mankind has been best at since we have heard of man. (But remember: most of mankind is not all of mankind.) But it is not permissible that the authors of devastation should also be innocent. It is the innocence which constitutes the crime.

Now, my dear namesake, these innocent and well-meaning people, your countrymen, have caused you to be born under conditions not very fare removed from those described for us by Charles Dickens in the London of more than a hundred years ago. (I hear the chorus of the innocents screaming, "No! This is not true! How *bitter* you are!"—but I am writing this letter to *you* to try to tell you something about how to handle *them*, for most of them do not yet really know that you exist. I *know* the conditions under which you were born, for I was there. Your countrymen were *not* there, and haven't made it yet. Your grandmother was also there, and no one has ever accused her of being *bitter*. I suggest that the innocents check with her. She isn't hard to find. Your countrymen don't know that *she* exists, either, though she has been working for them all their lives.)

Well, you were born, here you came, something like fifteen years ago; and though your father and mother and grandmother, looking about the streets through which they were carrying you, staring at the walls into which they brought you, had every reason to be heavy-hearted, yet they were not. For here you were, Big James, named for me—you were a big baby, I was not—here you were: to be loved. To be loved, baby, hard, at once, and forever, to strengthen you against the loveless world. Remember that: I know how black it looks today, for you. It looked bad that day, too, yes, we were trembling. We have not stopped trembling yet, but if we had not loved each other none of us would have survived. And now you must survive because we love you, and for the sake of your children and your children's children.

This innocent country set you down in a ghetto in which, in fact, it intended that you should perish. Let me spell out precisely what I mean by that, for the heart of the matter is here, and the root of my dispute with my country. You were born where you were born, and faced the future that you faced because you were black and *for no other reason*. The limits of your ambition were, thus, expected to be set forever. You were born into a society which spelled out with brutal clarity, and in as many ways as possible, that you were a worthless human being. You were not expected to aspire to excellence: you were expected to make peace with mediocrity. Wherever you have turned, James, in your short time on this earth, you have been told where you could go and what you could do (and *how* you could do it) and where you could do it and whom you could marry. I know your countrymen do not agree with me about this, and I hear them saying, "You exaggerate." They do not know Harlem, and I do. So do you. Take no one's word for anything, including mine—but trust your experience. Know whence you came. If you know whence you came, there is really no limit to where you can go. The details and symbols of your life have been deliberately constructed to make you believe what white people say about you. Please try to remember that what that believe, as well as what they do and cause you to endure, does not testify to your inferiority but to their inhumanity and fear. Please try to be clear, dear James, through the storm which rages about your youthful head today, about the reality which lies behind the words *acceptance* and *integration*. There is no reason for you to try to become like white people and there is no basis whatever for their impertinent assumption that *they* must accept *you*. The really terrible thing, old buddy, is that *you* must accept *them*. And I mean that very seriously. You must accept them and accept them with love. For these innocent people have no other hope. They are, in effect, still trapped in a history which they do not understand; and until they understand it, they cannot be released from it. They have had to believe for so many years, and for innumerable reasons, that black men are inferior to white men. Many of them, indeed, know better, but, as you will discover, people find it very difficult to act on what they know. To act is to be committed, and to be committed is to be in danger. In this case, the danger, in the minds of most white Americans, is the loss of identity. Try to imagine how you would feel if you woke up one morning to find the sun shining and all the stars aflame. You would be frightened because it is out of the order of nature. Any upheaval in the universe is terrifying because it so profoundly attacks one's sense of one's own reality. Well, the black man has functioned in the white man's world as a fixed star, as an immovable pillar: and as he moves out of his place, heaven and earth are shaken to their foundations. You, don't be afraid. I said that it was intended that you should perish in the ghetto, perish by never being allowed to go behind the white man's definitions, by never being allowed to spell your proper name. You have, and many of us have, defeated this intention; and by a terrible law, a terrible paradox, those innocents who believed that your imprisonment made them safe are losing their grasp of reality. But these men are your brothers—your lost, younger brothers. And if the word *integration* means anything, this is what it means: that we, with love, shall force our brothers to see themselves as they are, to cease fleeing from reality and begin to change it. For this is your home, my friend, do not be driven from it; great men have done great things here, and will again, and we can make America what America must become. It will be hard, James, but you come from sturdy, peasant stock, men who picked cotton and dammed rivers and built railroads, and in the teeth of the most terrifying odds, achieved an unassailable and monumental dignity. You come from a long line of poets, some of the greatest poets since Homer. One of them said, *The very time I thought I was lost, My dungeon shook and my chains fell off.*

You know, and I know, that the country is celebrating one hundred years of freedom one hundred years too soon. We cannot be free until they are free. God bless you, James, and Godspeed.

Your uncle,

James

Source: James Baldwin, *The Fire Next Time.* New York: Random House, 1963, pp. 2–6.

QUESTIONS

1. What does Baldwin mean when he says "it is the innocence that constitutes the crime"?
2. What is the difference between *acceptance* and *integration*, according to Baldwin? Why does he tell his nephew he must accept white people with love?
3. Who is trapped in a history they do not understand? In Baldwin's opinion, who really needs to be set free?

Document 4: Bob Dylan
Masters of War (1963)

Bob Dylan was born Robert Zimmerman in 1941 and grew up in Hibbing, Minnesota. He found his voice in the folk scene in Greenwich Village in New York in the late 1950s and early 1960s. Strongly influenced by protest singer and songwriter Woody Guthrie, Dylan expressed in music many of the concerns of the New Left. The threat of nuclear war inspired him to compose this song prior to American military involvement in Vietnam.

Masters of War

*C*ome you masters of war
You that build all the guns
You that build the death planes
You that build the big bombs
You that hide behind walls
You that hide behind desks
I just want you to know
I can see through your masks

You that never done nothin'
But build to destroy
You play with my world
Like it's your little toy
You put a gun in my hand
And you hide from my eyes
And you turn and run farther
When the fast bullets fly

Like Judas of old
You lie and deceive
A world war can be won
You want me to believe
But I see through your eyes
And I see through your brain
Like I see through the water
That runs down my drain

You fasten the triggers
For the others to fire
Then you set back and watch
When the death count gets higher
You hide in your mansion
As young people's blood
Flows out of their bodies
And is buried in the mud

You've thrown the worst fear
That can ever be hurled
Fear to bring children
Into the world

For threatening my baby
Unborn and unnamed
You ain't worth the blood
That runs in your veins

How much do I know
To talk out of turn
You might say that I'm young
You might say I'm unlearned
But there's one thing I know
Though I'm younger than you
Even Jesus would never
Forgive what you do

Let me ask you one question
Is your money that good
Will it buy you forgiveness
Do you think that it could
I think you will find
When your death takes its toll
All the money you made
Will never buy back your soul

Source: http://bobdylan.com (accessed February 14, 2009)

QUESTIONS

1. Who are the "masters of war"?
2. What values does this song promote?
3. Why might young people in particular have found this song appealing?

Document 5: *Declaration of Conscience against the War in Vietnam* (1965)

In 1960, 121 French intellectuals, including Jean-Paul Sartre, Simone de Beauvoir, and Andre Breton, signed a manifesto supporting civil disobedience against the French government's policy of violently suppressing the independence movement in its colony, Algeria. In early 1965, an even larger group of Americans put forth a similar declaration in regard to U.S.

policies in Vietnam. By that summer some six thousand people had signed it, including such veterans of the nonviolent movement as David Dellinger, A.J. Muste, John Lewis, Bayard Rustin, and a number of other intellectuals, among them Nobel Prize winner Linus Pauling.

Because the use of the military resources of the United States in Vietnam and elsewhere suppresses the aspirations of the people for political independence and economic freedom;

Because inhuman torture and senseless killing are being carried out by forces armed, uniformed, trained and financed by the United States;

Because we believe all peoples of the Earth, including both Americans and non-Americans, have an inalienable right to life, liberty, and the peaceful pursuit of happiness in their own way; and

Because we think that positive steps must be taken to put an end to the threat of nuclear catastrophe and death by chemical or biological warfare, whether these result from accident or escalation—

We hereby declare our conscientious refusal to cooperate with the United States government in the prosecution of the war in Vietnam.

We encourage those who can conscientiously do so to refuse to serve in the armed forces and to ask for discharge if they are already in.

Those of us who are subject to the draft ourselves declare our own intentions to refuse to serve.

We urge others to refuse and refuse ourselves to take part in the manufacture or transportation of military equipment, or to work in the fields of military research and weapons development.

We shall encourage the development of other nonviolent acts, including acts, which involve civil disobedience, in order to stop the flow of American soldiers and munitions to Vietnam.

Note: Signing or distributing this Declaration of Conscience might be construed as a violation of the Universal Military Training and Service Act, which prohibits advising persons facing the draft to refuse service. Penalties of up to 5 years imprisonment, and/or a fine of $5,000 are provided. While prosecutions under this provision of the law almost never occur, persons signing or distributing this declaration should face the possibility of serious consequences.

Source: Staughton Lynd, ed. *Nonviolence in America: A Documentary History.* Indianapolis, IN: Bobbs-Merrill Co, 1966, pp. 376–378.

QUESTIONS

1. What is your response to the reasons the signatories gave for refusing to cooperate with U.S. prosecution of the war?
2. What was the risk of signing this Declaration? Why did so many sign anyway?
3. What do you think is the impact of declarations such as this one?

Document 6:   A. J. Muste
The Movement to Stop the War in Vietnam (1966)

By the end of 1965, the prospect of further escalation of the Vietnam war, including the fear that it might take on global proportions, led respected pacifist A.J. Muste to write his own observations on why the war should be stopped immediately. In response to a statement that appeared in the November 25, 1965, issue of *The New York Review of Books* entitled "The Vietnam Protest," Muste set forth his own views about the war and the protest movement in the January 1966 issue of *Liberation* magazine.

The signers of the statement declare their belief "that the present United States policy in Vietnam is morally and politically disastrous." Very welcome, also, in view of the contrary opinion frequently expressed, is their categorical rejection of the argument that recent demonstrations against the war may persuade the Chinese and the Vietnamese Communists to prolong the war because they might be misled into supposing that the American people do not support the government's policy: "It is the kind of demagogic appeal characteristically advanced by governments embarked upon adventures in which they do not have full confidence."

It is when the signers undertake to set forth their own proposal and the arguments in support of it and to criticize aspects of the developing protest movement that questions arise. . . .

The kind of difficulty with which we are faced, in my opinion, is illustrated by the fact that the signers immediately criticize as "vague and unfocused" the slogan employed in the October 16 New York parade: "Stop the War in Vietnam Now." It provided "no guidelines for action." (Spokesmen for various points of view were represented on the platform on that occasion and organizations were free to distribute leaflets of their own, which were quite specific.) The program of a protest movement must, then, after all, be somewhat focused, and it has to take considerable account of the historic background and political context, as indeed the signers do in their opening section. The problem then arises of how the movement is to be focused.

To tackle a delicate question: the purpose of the movement is to end a cruel and futile war, "not to give explicit or covert political support for the Viet Cong." Many Americans will hold that for the United States to declare, as the signers propose, its readiness to negotiate with the National Liberation Front, the political arm of the Viet Cong, does give explicit, *de facto* political support to the Viet Cong. The Saigon regime, which recently has explicitly rejected negotiation with "the enemy," will certainly also regard this as giving the latter political "encouragement" if not support. . . .

The United States is deriving little, if any, honor from its role in Vietnam now. It is not altogether fantastic to suppose that for the United States to recognize that the day of Western military intervention in Asia is at an end and that to act on that assumption would accrue to its honor, would save lives there and in other parts of the world, and would be a much more efficacious way to stop "Communist or Chinese" expansion than the course we are now pursuing. I am not for a moment suggesting that it is a simple matter to carry out the approach I am advocating. . . . I am suggesting that it is politically and morally a sounder one, that we may be forced to take it in any case and that it will be to our honor and a boon to mankind if we choose to take it. . . .

For example, if there were enough young men who, on essentially religious or moral grounds, could not stomach participation in any war or in a particular war, if the number of such individuals went beyond a certain point—taking into account the inevitable side effects of such escalation among youth—it would become impossible for a government to wage war, especially if the dissenters included—as would almost certainly be the case in such climate—some scientists and engineers in key positions. Such individual conscientious objection would constitute a political action of profound impact. The government would undoubtedly regard it as political and subversive if it went beyond a certain point. . . .

Furthermore, I deny the right of a government, certainly in a military context, to conscript a man for so-called civilian service. The place where he is may be the place where he ought to be, the work he is doing may be what he ought to be doing. It is presumption and an invasion of human dignity for a government, because it happens to be waging war or preparing for it, to order him against his will to drop what he has been doing and do something else which it deems useful and fitting. Some of the proposals which have been made in statements issued for consideration by Students for a Democratic Society have, in my opinion, disregarded this important consideration. Moreover, they have not always made clear that they are not proposing "alternative service," in the context of the Selective Service Act, which seems to me only to make it easier for the government to administer the draft and carry on the war. . . .

It is to be expected that in the midst of this upsurge of antiwar sentiment and of a war such as the one in Vietnam, proposals for an "end-the-war movement" should emerge and efforts to build such a movement—*the* movement which would do the job—should be undertaken. It also is inevitable that the question of whether the "end-the-war movement" might not be made the starting point for a new political alignment, a new "revolutionary" line-up, and what have you, should be broached, and that various groups should think they have *the* answer to that broader question and proceed to act upon it. All this is obviously too vast a matter to be discussed in detail here.

I am not at the moment sanguine that *the* "movement" is about to come into existence. But I am convinced that movement, revolt, cannot be suppressed and that this in itself is a "revolutionary" development. If the revolt is to express itself in various ways, and not in a single "movement," then it is my hope that the adherents of each tendency or program will work very hard at their job as they see it and, while not abandoning political dialogue, will not dissipate energy in personal or organizational attacks on each other. This issue will in any event be decided largely by forces and developments over which none of us exercises a substantial measure of control.

Source: Nat Hentoff, ed. _The Essays of A.J. Muste._ New York: Simon & Schuster, 1967, pp. 503–513.

QUESTIONS

1. Muste noted that the signers of the statement "The Vietnam Protest" declared their belief that the policy of the United States in Vietnam was "morally and politically disastrous." Do you see criticism of the Bush Administration's military actions in Afghanistan and Iraq as being similar?

2. What does Muste have to say about alternative service and why does he question the SDS position on the matter?

3. At the conclusion of this article, Muste says he hopes those within the movement who have differences will not abandon political dialogue. What does he mean when he says "This issue will . . . be decided largely by forces and developments over which none of us exercises a substantial measure of control."

Document 7: Oral History Interview with Ethel Barol Taylor Discussing Women Strike for Peace

Ethel Barol Taylor, who became very active in Women Strike for Peace (WSP), was born in Philadelphia in 1916. Moved by concern for her daughter, who was a small child when the first atomic bomb was dropped on Hiroshima, she began her own crusade along with other housewives to oppose nuclear testing and promote world peace. During the Vietnam War she gained national attention when she and two other women from WSP traveled to Hanoi, the capital of North Vietnam. Below is an oral history recollection of her days in WSP during the 1960s.

I was catapulted into the peace movement with the dropping of the bomb on Hiroshima. I was pretty apolitical up to that point. I used to get up in the morning and start polishing the furniture until I was polishing the polish. I thought, "There must be more to life than this." . . .

A columnist once wrote a piece about me, and she called it "Rebel in White Gloves" because in the early days of Women Strike for Peace, women in the demonstrations, who were generally middle-class women, wore white gloves and hats. We used to do things like sit down and not move in the middle of the street, or whatever, but we would have our hats and white gloves on. I always thought that was a real protection until once we had an action, and hundreds of people went to Washington as a symbolic takeover of Congress. We walked and we came to a narrow street. The police said, "Cross this street and you get arrested." Well, I realized then that, what could they do? They're not going to electrocute me. They're not going to shoot me. It was much easier to cross that street than not to cross that street, so I crossed that street. Then we sat on the ground and waited to be arrested. We sat down, but we decided we weren't going to be yanked by our armpits, we were going to walk like ladies to the police van. We did. We got to the jail, and they opened the back door of the van. I looked out, and there was a five-foot drop to the ground. I waited for the policeman to help me down. The policeman came around and said, "Jump, sister." So I jumped into an entirely new world....

My anger is directed towards leaders who threaten the lives of children now and those yet unborn with their inhumane policy of nuclear weapons. We started because of children, because the scientists and doctors said that the strontium 90 and iodine 131 from the atomic tests would poison our children's milk and cause cancer.... We were concerned about an epidemic, like polio before vaccines, except that polio is viral and these were man-made epidemics. Those who were children then now have children themselves.

In 1962 some WSP members were brought before the House Un-American Activities Committee [HUAC]. In order to show solidarity, many of us wrote to the chair of the committee asking for an opportunity to testify.... It was pure theatre.... When some of us walked in, the guards were standing out in the hall outside the hearing room minding baby carriages and babies. We all carried red roses, and each time a woman would step down from testifying, we would present her with a bouquet, and we would applaud....

During the Vietnam War three of us went to Hanoi to discuss the transmission of mail and packages between the prisoners of war and their families. It was the most exciting event in my life because up until that point very few letters were getting through. The Vietnamese didn't consider our soldiers prisoners of war under the Geneva Convention, since the war had never been declared. They considered them war criminals.... The Vietnamese said they would not deal with the subject of prisoners with the government, but only with the peace movement.

A couple who lived in my neighborhood had a son who was shot down in 1964, and my trip was in 1969. They didn't know if he was alive or dead. When they heard I was going they asked me to try to find out about him, and they gave me a letter for him. They were active in the National Organization of Families of POWs. They notified their group that I was going to Vietnam, and I was flooded with letters for delivery from all over the country.... We brought these letters with us. While I was in Vietnam I asked the Vietnamese women about the status of my neighbor's son. One of the women left the room and later came back with a letter from him.... I sent them [his family] a cable,

"John is alive and well and I have a letter for you." Get this—it was Christmas. I came home with over thirty letters. My husband and I sat down and we called families all over the country to tell them their son or husband was alive and that I was sending them his letter.

When I got back I was nearly deluged by the press. I was having a press conference in my living room when the phone rang. My husband...said, "It's a colonel from the Pentagon." I spoke to him. He said, "Mrs. Taylor, I want to tell you that you and the two other women have done a most marvelous job that no one else could do."...A couple of weeks later the FBI warned the families not to accept any mail from our committee; they accused us of being a Communist group. Would you believe that one family wouldn't accept mail that we brought from their son?...

Women have proven that they can be a tremendous power in their neighborhoods. Participatory democracy is alive and growing—mothers and fathers get together and block a street until the city provides a stop sign to save the lives of their children. We've got to make the antiwar issue that kind of issue so that people will get together, not only because the arms race is a threat to their children, but because of the tremendous displacement of funds for bombs instead of funds for people....

Source: Judith Porter Adams, ed. *Peacework: Oral Histories of Women Peace Activists.* Boston: Twayne Publishers, 1991, pp. 15–21.

QUESTIONS

1. What were some of the things that distinguished Women Strike for Peace from other protest groups?
2. What brought Taylor to the organization, and what sense of empowerment did she gain by participating in WSP?
3. How did the government attempt to discredit WSP's actions in the early 1960s and during the Vietnam War?

Document 8:   Martin Luther King, Jr.
Beyond Vietnam: a Time to Break Silence (1967)

Nearly three thousand people crowded into the famed Riverside Church on Manhattan's Upper West Side to hear the Reverend Martin Luther King, Jr., deliver this speech on April 4, 1967. It met with strong reactions on all sides. The antiwar movement was heartened by King's public support, but he was attacked by newspaper columnists, government officials, and even some of his colleagues in the civil rights movement. Consider, as you read it, why King believed it was time to speak out strongly against the war.

I come to this magnificent house of worship tonight because my conscience leaves me no other choice. I join with you in this meeting because I am in deepest agreement with the aims and work of the organization which has brought us together: Clergy and Laymen concerned about Vietnam. The recent statements of your executive committee are the sentiments of my own heart and I found myself in full accord when I read its opening lines: "A time comes when silence is betrayal." That time has come for us in relation to Vietnam. . . .

Since I am a preacher by trade, I suppose it is not surprising that I have seven major reasons for bringing Vietnam into the field of my moral vision. There is at the outset a very obvious and almost facile connection between the war in Vietnam and the struggle I, and others, have been waging in America. A few years ago there was a shining moment in that struggle. It seemed as if there was a real promise of hope for the poor—both black and white—through the poverty program. There were experiments, hopes, new beginnings. Then came the buildup in Vietnam and I watched the program broken and eviscerated as if it were some idle political plaything of a society gone mad on war, and I knew that America would never invest the necessary funds or energies in rehabilitation of its poor so long as adventures like Vietnam continued to draw men and skills and money like some demonic destructive suction tube. So I was increasingly compelled to see the war as an enemy of the poor and to attack it as such.

Perhaps the more tragic recognition of reality took place when it became clear to me that the war was doing far more than devastating the hopes of the poor at home. It was sending their sons and their brothers and their husbands to fight and to die in extraordinarily high proportions relative to the rest of the population. We were taking the black young men who had been crippled by our society and sending them eight thousand miles away to guarantee liberties in Southeast Asia which they had not found in southwest Georgia and East Harlem. So we have been repeatedly faced with the cruel irony of watching Negro and white boys on TV screens as they kill and die together for a nation that has been unable to seat them together in the same schools. . . .

My third reason moves to an even deeper level of awareness.... As I have walked among the desperate, rejected and angry young men I have told them that Molotov cocktails and rifles would not solve their problems. I have tried to offer them my deepest compassion while maintaining my conviction that social change comes most meaningfully through nonviolent action.... They asked if our own nation wasn't using massive doses of violence to solve its problems, to bring about changes it wanted. Their questions hit home, and I knew that I could never again rise my voice against the violence of the oppressed in the ghettos without having first spoken clearly to the greatest purveyor of violence in the world today—my own government....

For those who ask the question, "Aren't you a civil rights leader?" and thereby mean to exclude me from the movement for peace, I have this further answer.... [I]t should be incandescently clear that no one who has any concern for the integrity and life of America today can ignore the present war. If America's soul should become totally poisoned, part of the autopsy must read Vietnam. It can never be saved so long as it destroys the deepest hopes of men the world over. So it is that those of us who are yet determined that America will be led down the path of protest and dissent, working for the health of our land....

And as I ponder the madness of Vietnam and search within myself for ways to understand and respond to compassion my mind goes constantly to the people of that peninsula. I speak now not of the soldiers of each side, not of the junta in Saigon, but simply of the people who have been living under the curse of war for almost three decades now....

We have destroyed their two most cherished institutions: the family and the village. We have destroyed their land and their crops. We have cooperated in the crushing of the nation's only non-Communist revolutionary political force—the unified Buddhist church. We have supported the enemies of the peasants of Saigon. We have corrupted their women and children and killed their men. What liberators? ...

...I am as deeply concerned about our troops there as anything else. For it occurs to me that what we are submitting them to in Vietnam is not simply the brutalizing process that goes on in any war where armies face each other and seek to destroy. We are adding cynicism to the process of death, for they must know after a short period there that none of the things we claim to be fighting for are really involved. Before long they must know that their government has sent them into a struggle among Vietnamese, and the more sophisticated surely realize that we are on the side of the wealthy and the secure while we create hell for the poor.

Somehow this madness must cease. We must stop now. I speak as a child of God and brother to the suffering poor of Vietnam. I speak for those whose land is being laid waste, whose homes are being destroyed, whose culture is being subverted. I speak for the poor of America who are paying the double price of smashed hopes at home and death and corruption in Vietnam. I speak as a citizen of the world, for the world as it stands aghast at the path we have taken. I speak as an American to the leaders of my own nation. The great initiative in this war is ours. The initiative to stop must be ours. . . .

Source: http://www.hartford-hwp.com/archives (accessed April 4, 2007)

QUESTIONS

1. What were the principal reasons Dr. King gave for publicly proclaiming his opposition to the war in Vietnam?
2. How did the war highlight issues of race?
3. How did Dr. King equate the oppressed peasants of Vietnam to minorities at home? How did he seek to buttress his criticisms of the war while attempting not to alienate those actually fighting in it?

Document 9: National Organization for Women *Statement of Purpose* (1966)

Written by Betty Friedan, author of *The Feminine Mystique* (1963), a book that helped spark the women's liberation movement, this statement set forth the views of the newly formed National Organization for Women (NOW). Younger, more radical feminists soon challenged NOW to take up a host of other issues such as lesbian and gay rights, racism, and welfare rights. Compare this document with the declaration that came out of the Seneca Falls meeting in 1848.

We, men and women who hereby constitute ourselves as the National Organization for Women, believe that the time has come for a new movement toward true equality for all women in America, and toward a fully equal partnership of the sexes, as part of the world-wide revolution of human rights now taking place within and beyond our national borders.

The purpose of NOW is to take action to bring women into full participation in the mainstream of American society now, exercising all the privileges and responsibilities thereof in truly equal partnership with men.

We believe the time has come to move beyond the abstract argument, discussion and symposia over the status and special nature of women which has raged in America in recent years; the time has come to confront, with concrete action, the conditions that now prevent women from enjoying the equality of opportunity and freedom of choice which is their right, as individual Americans, and as human beings.

NOW is dedicated to the proposition that women, first and foremost, are human beings, who, like all other people in our society, must have the chance to develop their fullest human potential. We believe that women can achieve such equality only by accepting to the full the challenges and responsibilities they share with all other people in our society, as part of the decision-making mainstream of American political, economic and social life.

We organize to initiate or support action, nationally, or in any part of this nation, by individuals or organizations, to break through the silken curtain of prejudice and discrimination against women in government, industry, the professions, the churches, the political parties, the judiciary, the labor unions, in education, science, medicine, law, religion and every other field of importance in American society.

Despite all the talk about the status of American women in recent years, the actual position of women in the United States has declined, and is declining, to an alarming degree throughout the 1950's and 60's. Although 46.4% of all American women between the ages of 18 and 65 now work outside the home, the overwhelming majority—75%—are in routine clerical, sales, or factory jobs, or they are household workers, cleaning women, hospital attendants. About two-thirds of Negro women workers are in the lowest paid service occupations. Working women are becoming increasingly—not less—concentrated on the bottom of the job ladder. As a consequence full-time women workers today earn on the average only 60% of what men earn, and that wage gap has been increasing over the past twenty-five years in every major industry group. In 1964, of all women with a yearly income, 89% earned under $5,000 a year; half of all full-time year round women workers earned less than $3,690; only 1.4% of full-time year round women workers had an annual income of $10,000 or more.

Further, with higher education increasingly essential in today's society, too few women are entering and finishing college or going on to graduate or professional school. Today, women earn only one in three of the B.A.'s and M.A.'s granted, and one in ten of the Ph.D.'s.

In all the professions considered of importance to society, and in the executive ranks of industry and government, women are losing ground. Where they are present it is only a token handful. Women comprise less than 1% of federal judges; less than 4% of all lawyers; 7% of doctors. Yet women represent 51% of the U.S. population. And, increasingly, men are replacing women in the top positions in secondary and elementary schools, in social work, and in libraries—once thought to be women's fields.

Official pronouncements of the advance in the status of women hide not only the reality of this dangerous decline, but the fact that nothing is being done to stop it. The excellent reports of the President's Commission on the Status of Women and of the State Commissions have not been fully implemented. Such Commissions have power only to advise. They have no power to enforce their recommendation; nor have they the freedom to organize American women and men to press for action on them. The reports of these commissions have, however, created a basis upon which it is now possible to build. Discrimination in employment on the basis of sex is now prohibited by federal law, in Title VII of the Civil Rights Act of 1964. But although nearly one-third of the cases brought before the Equal Employment Opportunity Commission during the first year dealt with sex discrimination and the proportion is increasing dramatically, the Commission has not made clear its intention to enforce the law with the same seriousness on behalf of women as of other victims of discrimination. Many of these cases were Negro women, who are the victims of double discrimination of race and sex. Until now, too few women's organizations and official spokesmen have been willing to speak out against these dangers facing women. Too many women have been restrained by the fear of being called "feminist." There is no civil rights movement to speak for women, as there has been for Negroes and other victims of discrimination. The National Organization for Women must therefore begin to speak.

WE BELIEVE that the power of American law, and the protection guaranteed by the U.S. Constitution to the civil rights of all individuals, must be effectively applied and enforced to isolate and remove patterns of sex discrimination, to ensure equality of opportunity in employment and education, and equality of civil and political rights and responsibilities on behalf of women, as well as for Negroes and other deprived groups.

We realize that women's problems are linked to many broader questions of social justice; their solution will require concerted action by many groups. Therefore, convinced that human rights for all are indivisible, we expect to give active support to the common cause of equal rights for all those who suffer discrimination and deprivation, and we call upon other organizations committed to such goals to support our efforts toward equality for women.

WE DO NOT ACCEPT the token appointment of a few women to high-level positions in government and industry as a substitute for serious continuing effort to recruit and advance women according to their individual abilities. To this end, we urge American government and industry to mobilize the same resources of ingenuity and command with which they have solved problems of far greater difficulty than those now impeding the progress of women.

WE BELIEVE that this nation has a capacity at least as great as other nations, to innovate new social institutions which will enable women to enjoy the true equality of opportunity and responsibility in society, without conflict with their responsibilities as mothers and homemakers. In such innovations, America does not lead the Western world, but lags by decades behind many European countries. We do not accept the traditional assumption that a woman has to choose between marriage and motherhood, on the one hand, and serious participation in industry or the professions on the other. We question the present expectation that all normal women will retire from job or profession for 10 or 15 years, to devote their full time to raising children, only to reenter the job market at a relatively minor level. This, in itself, is a deterrent to the aspirations of women, to their acceptance into management or professional training courses, and to the very possibility of equality of opportunity or real choice, for all but a few women. Above all, we reject the assumption that these problems are the unique responsibility of each individual woman, rather than a basic social dilemma which society must solve. True equality of opportunity and freedom of choice for women requires such practical, and possible innovations as a nationwide network of child-care centers, which will make it unnecessary for women to retire completely from society until their children are grown, and national programs to provide retraining for women who have chosen to care for their children full-time.

WE BELIEVE that it is as essential for every girl to be educated to her full potential of human ability as it is for every boy—with the knowledge that such education is the key to effective participation in today's economy and that, for a girl as for a boy, education can only be serious where there is expectation that it will be used in society. We believe that American educators are capable of devising means of imparting such expectations to girl students. Moreover, we consider the decline in the proportion of women receiving higher and professional education to be evidence of discrimination. This discrimination may take the form of quotas against the admission of women to colleges, and professional schools; lack of encouragement by parents, counselors and educators; denial of loans or fellowships; or the traditional or arbitrary procedures in graduate and professional training geared in terms of men, which inadvertently discriminate against women. We believe that the same serious attention must be given to high school dropouts who are girls as to boys.

WE REJECT the current assumptions that a man must carry the sole burden of supporting himself, his wife, and family, and that a woman is automatically entitled to lifelong support by a man upon her marriage, or that marriage, home and family are primarily woman's world and responsibility—hers, to dominate—his to support. We believe that a true partnership between the sexes demands a different concept of marriage, an equitable sharing of the responsibilities of home and children and of the economic burdens of their support. We believe that proper recognition should be given to the economic and social value of homemaking and child-care. To these ends, we will seek to open a reexamination of laws and mores governing marriage and divorce, for we believe that the current state of "half-equity" between the sexes discriminates against both men and women, and is the cause of much unnecessary hostility between the sexes.

WE BELIEVE that women must now exercise their political rights and responsibilities as American citizens. They must refuse to be segregated on the basis of sex into separate-and-not-equal ladies' auxiliaries in the political parties, and they must demand representation according to their numbers in the regularly constituted party committees—at local, state, and national levels—and in the informal power structure, participating fully in the selection of candidates and political decision-making, and running for office themselves.

IN THE INTERESTS OF THE HUMAN DIGNITY OF WOMEN, we will protest, and endeavor to change, the false image of women now prevalent in the mass media, and in the texts, ceremonies, laws, and practices of our major social institutions. Such images perpetuate contempt for women by society and by women for themselves. We are similarly opposed to all policies and practices—in church, state, college, factory, or office—which, in the guise of protectiveness, not only deny opportunities but also foster in women self-denigration, dependence, and evasion of responsibility, undermine their confidence in their own abilities and foster contempt for women.

NOW WILL HOLD ITSELF INDEPENDENT OF ANY POLITICAL PARTY in order to mobilize the political power of all women and men intent on our goals. We will strive to ensure that no party, candidate, president, senator, governor, congressman, or any public official who betrays or ignores the principle of full equality between the sexes is elected or appointed to office. If it is necessary to mobilize the votes of men and women who believe in our cause, in order to win for women the final right to be fully free and equal human beings, we so commit ourselves.

WE BELIEVE THAT women will do most to create a new image of women by acting now, and by speaking out in behalf of their own equality, freedom, and human dignity—not in pleas for special privilege, nor in enmity toward men, who are also victims of the current, half-equality between the sexes—but in an active, self-respecting partnership with men. By so doing, women will develop confidence in their own ability to determine actively, in partnership with men, the conditions of their life, their choices, their future and their society.

Source: http://www.now.org/history/purpos66.html (accessed May 13, 2009)

QUESTIONS

1. What were the goals of NOW in its origins?
2. How did NOW frame its rationale for women's equality? What particular rights did it assert?
3. Did it surprise you to know that men were members of NOW? What does the document itself say about men and the struggle for equality?

Document 10: *Statement of the Catonsville Nine* (1968)

On May 17, 1968, Catholic priests Daniel and Philip Berrigan, along with Brother David Darst, John Hogan, Thomas Lewis, Marjorie Bradford Melville,

Thomas Melville, George Mische, and Mary Moylan, broke into the Selective Service Board #33 in Catonsville, Maryland. Inside they seized draft files, took them outside, and burned them with napalm based on a recipe they took from the Army's Special Forces Handbook. Three-hundred and seventy-eight files were destroyed. Below is an excerpt from the press statement they read during their arrests.

As American citizens, we have worked with the poor in the ghetto and abroad. In the course of our Christian ministry, we have watched our country produce more victims than an army of us could console or restore. Two of us face immediate sentencing for similar acts against Selective Service. All of us identify with the victims of American oppression all over the world. We submit voluntarily to their involuntary fate.

We use napalm on these draft records because napalm has burned people to death in Vietnam, Guatemala, and Peru; and because it may be used in America's ghettos. We destroy these draft records not only because they exploit young men, but because these records represent misplaced power, concentrated in the ruling class of America....

Above all, our protest attempts to illustrate why our country is torn at home and harassed abroad by enemies of its own creation. For a long time the United States has been an empire, and today it is history's richest nation. Representing 6 per cent of the world's people, our country controls half of the world's productive capacity and two-thirds of its finance....

The military participates with economic and political sectors to form a triumvirate of power which sets and enforces policy. With an annual budget of more than 80 billion dollars, our military now controls over half of all Federal property (53 per cent, or 183 billion dollars) while U.S. nuclear and conventional weaponry exceeds that of the whole remaining world....

We believe that some property has no right to exist. Hitler's gas ovens, Stalin's concentration camps, atomic-bacteriological-chemical weaponry, files of conscription, and slum properties have no right to exist. When people starve for bread, and lack decent housing, it is usually because the rich debase themselves with abuse of property, causing extravagance on their part and oppression and misery in others....

... Let our President and the pillars of society speak of "law and justice" and back up their words with deeds. Then there will be "order."

We have pleaded, spoken, marched, and nursed the victims of their injustice. Now this injustice must be faced, and this we intend to do, with whatever strength of mind, body, and grace that God will give us. May He have mercy on our nation.

Source: Philip Berrigan, *A Punishment for Peace.* New York: Macmillan & Co., 1969.

QUESTIONS

1. Explain what these activists meant by "some property has no right to exist"? What historical analogies did they draw upon to justify their actions?
2. How did the conflict in Southeast Asia, in their view, represent an imperialistic venture? What other countries were victims of American economic and military conquest?
3. How did they place their struggle for justice in the context of "law and order"?

Document 11: Statement of John Kerry, Vietnam Veterans Against the War (1971)

John Kerry testified before the Senate Foreign Relations Committee as part of its hearings on proposals related to ending the war in Southeast Asia. A powerful myth has persisted that the antiwar movement was extremely hostile to those who fought in the war. Kerry's testimony highlights the fact that many Vietnam vets saw themselves as allies of the antiwar movement and worked with it to publicize the realities of the war and increase pressure to end it. Here Kerry describes one of the creative tactics of VVAW, the "Winter Soldier Investigation," held in Detroit a few months before this statement was made.

*T*hank you very much, Senator Fulbright, Senator Javits, Senator Symington, Senator Pell. I would like to say for the record, and also for the men behind me who are also wearing the uniforms and their medals, that my sitting here is really symbolic. I am not here as John Kerry. I am here as one member of the group of 1,000, which is a small representation of a very much larger group of veterans in this country, and were it possible for all of them to sit at this table they would be here and have the same kind of testimony . . .

Winter Soldier Investigation

I would like to talk, representing all those veterans, and say that several months ago in Detroit, we had an investigation at which over 150 honorably discharged and many very highly decorated veterans testified to war crimes committed in Southeast Asia, not isolated incidents but crimes committed on a day-to-day basis with the full awareness of officers at all levels of command.

It is impossible to describe to you exactly what did happen in Detroit, the emotions in the room, the feelings of the men who were reliving their experiences in Vietnam, but they did. They relived the absolute horror of what this country, in a sense, made them do.

They told the stories at times they had personally raped, cut off ears, cut off heads, taped wires from portable telephones to human genitals and turned up the power, cut off limbs, blown up bodies, randomly shot at civilians, razed villages in fashion reminiscent of Genghis Khan, shot cattle and dogs for fun, poisoned food stocks, and generally ravaged the countryside of South Vietnam in addition to the normal ravage of war, and the normal and very particular ravaging which is done by the applied bombing power of this country.

We call this investigation the "Winter Soldier Investigation." The term "Winter Soldier" is a play on words of Thomas Paine in 1776 when he spoke of the Sunshine Patriot and summertime soldiers who deserted at Valley Forge because the going was rough.

We who have come here to Washington have come here because we feel we have to be winter soldiers now. We could come back to this country; we could be quiet; we could hold our silence; we could not tell what went on in Vietnam, but we feel because of what threatens this country, the fact that the crimes threaten it, not reds, and not redcoats but the crimes which we are committing that threaten it, that we have to speak out.

Feelings of Men Coming Back from Vietnam

I would like to talk to you a little bit about what the result is of the feelings these men carry with them after coming back from Vietnam. The country doesn't know it yet, but it has created a monster, a monster in the form of millions of men who have been taught to deal and to trade in violence, and who are given the chance to die for the biggest nothing in history; men who have returned with a sense of anger and a sense of betrayal which no one has yet grasped.

As a veteran and one who feels this anger, I would like to talk about it. We are angry because we feel we have been used in the worst fashion by the administration of this country.

In 1970 at West Point, Vice President Agnew said "some glamorize the criminal misfits of society while our best men die in Asian rice paddies to preserve the freedom which most of those misfits abuse," and this was used as a rallying point for our effort in Vietnam.

But for us, as boys in Asia whom the country was supposed to support, his statement is a terrible distortion from which we can only draw a very deep sense of revulsion. Hence the anger of some of the men who are here in Washington today. It is a distortion because we in no way consider ourselves the best men of this country, because those he calls misfits were standing up for us in a way that nobody else in this country dared to, because so many of us who have died would have returned to this country to join the misfits in their efforts to ask for an immediate withdrawal from South Vietnam, because so many of those best men have returned as quadraplegics and amputees, and they lie forgotten in Veterans' Administration hospitals in this country which fly the flag which so many have chosen as their own personal symbol. And we cannot consider ourselves America's best men when we are ashamed of and hated what we were called on to do in Southeast Asia.

In our opinion, and from our experience, there is nothing in South Vietnam, nothing which could happen that realistically threatens the United States of America. And to attempt to justify the loss of one American life in Vietnam, Cambodia, or Laos by linking such loss to the preservation of freedom, which those misfits supposedly abuse is to us the height of criminal hypocrisy, and it is that kind of hypocrisy which we feel has torn this country apart.

We are probably much more angry than that and I don't want to go into the foreign policy aspects because I am outclassed here. I know that all of you talk about every possible alternative of getting out of Vietnam. We understand that. We know you have considered the seriousness of the aspects to the utmost level and I am not going to try to dwell on that, but I want to relate to you the feeling that many of the men who have returned to this country express because we are probably angriest about all that we were told about Vietnam and about the mystical war against communism.

What Was Found and Learned in Vietnam

We found that not only was it a civil war, an effort by a people who had for years been seeking their liberation from any colonial influence whatsoever, but also we found that the Vietnamese whom we had enthusiastically molded after our own image were hard put to take up the fight against the threat we were supposedly saving them from.

We found most people didn't even know the difference between communism and democracy. They only wanted to work in rice paddies without helicopters strafing them and bombs with napalm burning their villages and tearing their country apart. They wanted everything to do with the war, particularly with this foreign presence of the United States of America, to leave them alone in peace, and they practiced the art of survival by siding with whichever military force was present at a particular time, be it Vietcong, North Vietnamese, or American.

We found also that all too often American men were dying in those rice paddies for want of support from their allies. We saw first hand how money from American taxes was used for a corrupt dictatorial regime. We saw that many people in this country had a one-sided idea of who was kept free by our flag, as blacks provided the highest percentage of casualties. We saw Vietnam ravaged equally by American bombs as well as by search and destroy missions, as well as by Vietcong terrorism, and yet we listened while this country tried to blame all of the havoc on the Vietcong.

We rationalized destroying villages in order to save them. We saw America lose her sense of morality as she accepted very coolly a My Lai and refused to give up the image of American soldiers who hand out chocolate bars and chewing gum.

We learned the meaning of free fire zones, shooting anything that moves, and we watched while America placed a cheapness on the lives of orientals.

We watched the U.S. falsification of body counts, in fact the glorification of body counts. We listened while month after month we were told the back of the enemy was about to break. We fought using weapons against "oriental human beings," with quotation marks around that. We fought using weapons against those people which I do not believe this country would dream of using were we fighting in the European theater, or let us say a non-third-world people theater, and so we watched while men charged up hills because a general said that hill has to be taken, and after losing one platoon or two platoons they marched away to leave the high ground for the reoccupation by the North Vietnamese because we watched pride allow the most unimportant of battles to be blown into extravaganzas, because we couldn't lose, and we couldn't retreat, and because it didn't matter how many American bodies were lost to prove that point. And so there were Hamburger Hills and Khe Sanhs and Hill 881's and Fire Base 6's and so many others . . .

Each day to facilitate the process by which the United States washes her hands of Vietnam someone has to give up his life so that the United States doesn't have to admit something that the entire world already knows, so that we can't say that we have made a mistake. Someone has to die so that President Nixon won't be, and these are his words, "the first President to lose a war."

We are asking Americans to think about that because how do you ask a man to be the last man to die in Vietnam? How do you ask a man to be the last man to die for a mistake?

Source: http://www.wintersoldier.com/index.php?topic=Testimony (accessed May 13, 2009)

QUESTIONS

1. According to Kerry, what was revealed by the Winter Soldier Investigation?
2. Why were the veterans who came to Washington so angry?
3. How does Kerry tie the Vietnam War to questions of racism?

Document 12:   Barbara Deming
Revolution and Equilibrium (1968)

Barbara Deming was a civil rights activist, pacifist, and feminist. Educated in Quaker schools, she devoted her early career to writing essays, poems, and short stories. Shortly before her death she was one of fifty-four women arrested at the Seneca Women's Peace Encampment in western New York in July 1983. This essay was first published in *Liberation* magazine in 1968 and eloquently discusses what she learned from her journey in the nonviolent protest movements of the 1960s.

Nonviolent Battle

*A*ctually, something seems wrong to many people, I think, when—in nonviolent struggle—they receive any casualties at all. They feel that if they are not hurting anybody, then they shouldn't get hurt themselves. (They shouldn't. But it is not only in nonviolent battle that the innocent suffer.) It is an intriguing psychological fact that when the ghetto uprising provoked the government into bringing out troops and tanks—and killing many black people, most of them onlookers—observers like [Alexander] Kopkind decided that the action had been remarkably effective, citing as proof precisely the violence of the government's response. But when James Meredith [slain civil rights leader from Mississippi] was shot, just for example, any number of observers editorialized: "See, nonviolence doesn't work." Those who have this reaction overlook the fact that nonviolent battle is still battle, and in battle of whatever kind, people do get hurt. If personal safety had been Meredith's main concern, he could, as the saying goes, have stayed at home. . . .

To recognize that men have greater, not less control in the situation when they have committed themselves to nonviolence requires a drastic readjustment of vision. And this means taking both a long-range view of the field and a very much cooler, more objective one. Nonviolence can inhibit the ability of the antagonist to hit back. (If the genius of guerrilla warfare is to make it impossible for the other side really to exploit its superior brute force, nonviolence can be said to carry this even further.)

And there is another sense in which it gives one greater leverage—enabling one both to put pressure upon the antagonist and to modulate his response to that pressure. In violent battle the effort is to demoralize the enemy, to so frighten him that he will surrender. The risk is that desperation and resentment will make him go on resisting when it is no longer even in his own interest. He has been driven beyond reason. In nonviolent struggle the effort is of quite a different nature. One doesn't try to frighten the other. One tries to undo him—tries, in the current idiom, to "blow his mind"—only in the sense that one tries to shake him out of former attitudes and force him to appraise the situation now in a way that takes into consideration your needs as well as his. . . . In this sense a liberation movement that is nonviolent sets the oppressor free as well as the oppressed.

The Genius of Nonviolence

The most common charge leveled against nonviolence is that it counts upon touching the heart of an adversary—who is more than likely to be stony of heart. His heart, his conscience need not be touched. His mind has been. The point is that you prevent him from reacting out of fear—in mindless reflex action. You also prevent him from being able to justify to others certain kinds of actions that he would like to take against you – and may for a while attempt to take.

Here one can speak of still another sense in which nonviolence gives one greater control. If the antagonist is unjustifiably harsh in his countermeasures, and continues to be, one will slowly win away from him allies and supporters—some of them having consciences more active than his perhaps; or perhaps all of them simply caring about presenting a certain image, caring for one reason or another about public relations. An adversary might seem to be immovable. One could nevertheless move him finally by taking away from him the props of his power—those men upon whose support he depends. The special genius of nonviolence is that it can draw to our side not only natural allies—who are enabled gradually to recognize that they are allies because in confrontation with us their minds are not blurred by fear but challenged. . . . Even beyond this, it can move to act on our behalf elements in society who have no such natural inclination.

When the Quebec to Guantanamo walkers were fasting in jail in Albany, Georgia, the men who finally put most pressure upon authorities to release them and let them walk through town were clergymen not at all sympathetic either to the walkers as individuals or to the message on their signs and leaflet. Nonviolent tactics can move into action on our behalf men not naturally inclined to act for us; whereas violent tactics draw into actions that do harm us men for whom it is not at all natural to act against us. A painful example of this was Martin Luther King's act of declaring that the authorities were right in calling out troops to deal with the ghetto uprisings. . . . Violence makes men "dizzy"; it disturbs the vision, makes them see only their own immediate losses and fear of losses. Any widespread resort to violence in this country by those seeking change could produce such vertigo among the population at large that the authorities would be sure to be given more and more liberty to take repressive measures—in the name of "Order."

Man versus Function

If we insist on treating them not as part of a machine but as men, we gain a much greater control.

. . . It is necessary to remember . . . that "the enemy is not a few men but a whole system," to remember that when the men with whom we struggle confront us it is as functional elements in this system that they do so, behaving in a certain sense automatically. It is necessary to know this well. But it is precisely if we refuse to treat them as nothing more than this—if we insist on treating them not as parts of a machine but as men, capable of thought and of change—that we gain very much greater control in the situation. . . .

A Balance of Instincts

This life-serving balance—equilibrium between self-assertion and respect for others—has evolved among animals on the physiological plane. In human beings it can be gained only on the plane of consciousness. And the plea this essay makes is precisely that we make the disciplined effort to gain it—all those of us who hope really to change men's lives. . . . My plea is that the key to a revolution that would "go forward all the time . . . in the company of Man, in the company of all men," lies in discovering within ourselves this poise. But it calls equally for the strengthening of two impulses—calls both for assertion (for speaking, for acting out "aggressively" the truth, as we see it, of what our rights are) and for restraint towards others (for the acting out of love for them, which is to say of respect for their human rights). May those who say that they believe in nonviolence learn to challenge more boldly those institutions of violence that constrict and cripple our humanity.

Source: Barbara Deming, "Revolution and Equilibrium." New York: A.J. Memorial Institute Pamphlet No. 2 (reprint 1968), pp. 1–32.

QUESTIONS

1. What are the long-term objectives of a nonviolent movement, according to Deming? How might the negative reactions of an adversary benefit the cause?
2. How can one gain greater control over an adversary by using nonviolent tactics? Why does Deming say it is not necessary to reach an adversary's heart?
3. Given the realities of life in a patriarchal society, how might humans attain the equilibrium Deming calls for? What are the essential ingredients for overcoming the penchant to resort to forceful measures?

Document 13: Cesar Chavez
Letter from Delano (1969)

Cesar Chavez was born in Arizona in 1927. In the early 1960s, Chavez took up the struggle to organize farm workers into trade unions. Deeply committed to nonviolence, he employed strikes, boycotts, picketing, and fasts in his campaigns against the large farm owners of California. By the early 1980s it was estimated that membership in the United Farm Workers was almost 90,000.

Good Friday 1969
E.L. Barr, Jr., President
California Grape and Fruit Tree League
717 Market St.
San Francisco, California

Dear Mr. Barr:

I am sad to hear about your accusations in the press that our union movement and table grape boycott have been successful because we have used violence and terror tactics. If what you say is true, I have been a failure and should withdraw from the struggle; but you are left with the awesome moral responsibility, before God and Man, to come forward with whatever information you have so that corrective action can begin at once. If for any reason you fail to come forth to substantiate your charges, then you must be held responsible for committing violence against us, albeit of the tongue. I am convinced that you as a human being did not mean what you said but rather acted hastily under pressure from the public relations firm that has been hired to try to counteract the tremendous moral force of our movement. . . .

Today on Good Friday 1969, we remember the life and the sacrifice of Martin Luther King, Jr., who gave himself totally to the nonviolent struggle for peace and justice. In his *Letter From a Birmingham Jail* Dr. King describes better than I could our hopes for the strike and boycott: "Injustice must be exposed, with all the tensions its exposure creates, to the light of human conscience and the air of national opinion before it be cured." For our part I admit that we have seized upon every tactic and strategy consistent with the morality of our cause to expose that injustice and thus to heighten the sensitivity of the American conscience so that farm workers will have, without bloodshed, their own union and the dignity of bargaining with their agribusiness employers. . . . Unwittingly perhaps, you may unleash that other force which our union by discipline and deed, censure and education has sought to avoid, that panacea shortcut: that senseless violence which honors no color, class, or neighborhood. . . .

Once again, I appeal to you as the representative of your industry and as a man. I ask you to recognize and bargain with our union before the economic pressure of the boycott and strike takes an irrevocable toll; but, if not, I ask you to at least sit down with us to discuss the safeguards necessary to keep our historical struggle free of violence. I make this appeal because as one of the leaders of our nonviolent movement, I know and accept my responsibility for preventing, if possible, the destruction of human life and property. . . .

This letter does not express all that is in my heart, Mr. Barr. But if it says nothing else it says that we do not hate you or rejoice to see your industry destroyed; we hate the agribusiness system that seeks to keep us enslaved and we shall overcome and change it not by retaliation or bloodshed but by a determined nonviolent struggle carried on by those masses of farm workers who intend to be free and human.

Sincerely yours,

Cesar Chavez
United Farm Workers Organizing Committee
A.F.L.-C.I.O.
Delano, California

Source: Angie O'Gorman, ed. *The Universe Bends Towards Justice.* Philadelphia: New Society Publishers, 1990.

QUESTIONS

1. How does Chavez try to win over his adversary, or at least allow him to save face?
2. How did he liken the struggle of the migrant farm workers to the civil rights struggles of his era?
3. How did Chavez use the "power of nonviolence" to rally support for his cause?

8

A Broad Agenda

Continuing Struggles for Peace and Justice

The free speech, civil rights, and justice movements of the 1960s included a renewed effort to call attention to the position of Native Americans in U.S. society. By the late 1960s, Indians from all tribes and nations organized in a concerted effort to raise awareness of Native American culture and the history of their oppression at the hands of white America. Ironically, as the courts began to support the rights of African Americans in the early 1950s, the Eisenhower Administration and Congress imposed some restrictive measures on Native Americans. The federal government gradually began to eliminate many Indian reservations and social services. Native American nations were also forced to surrender properties shared by the respective tribes into private holdings to be run by individuals or corporations. While the goal was to expand the rights of individual Native Americans, the result was increased government regulation of their economic affairs and personal lives.

Ultimately, between 1954 and 1960, sixty-one tribes lost their federal benefits and many of the reservations were absorbed by the states, thereby

For the People, pages 261–306

forcing the tribes to pay state taxes and obey state regulations. To pay for state taxes tribes had to sell land and mineral rights to outside interests. Native American poverty began to rise and within a few years, an increasing number of Indians left the reservations. By the end of the 1960s, nearly half the Native American population had relocated to urban areas where they encountered the same economic limitations and discrimination as other peoples of color experienced.

One of these urban areas was San Francisco. By the mid-1960s, an estimated 40,000 Indian people from 100 tribal groups had relocated to the city. In 1968, the American Indian Movement (AIM), led by Russell Means, was established for calling attention to their long history of oppression in the United States. With the creation of AIM and emboldened by the antiwar and civil rights movements, Native Americans from all tribes in the Bay Area decided to carry out their own nonviolent protest. On the morning of November 20, 1969, seventy-nine American Indians sailed to Alcatraz and occupied the abandoned federal penitentiary there. Despite an attempted Coast Guard blockade, the protestors made their way onto the island and began a 19-month occupation, which captured the attention of the nation and the world. In so doing, they issued their own proclamation and treaty demands, which emphasized past injustices and their commitment to a peaceful resolution of their grievances (**Document 1**).

Peaceful and creative means of protest have been a major feature of the peace movement since the 1970s. One of the more dramatic developments in the post–Vietnam War era was the attempt of citizen activists to control and halt the construction of new nuclear power plants. These protests, one outgrowth of the environmental activism taking shape during that time, relied on nonviolent direct action and presented a new style of politics shaped by concerns for an ecologically balanced and more egalitarian way of life. In practicing mass civil disobedience in opposition to the development of nuclear power plants, these action groups expanded their efforts to the arms race of the early 1980s.

But before the arms race of the Reagan years occupied their time and attention, these new-style political activists focused all of their attention on dismantling and halting construction of nuclear power plants. Not only was it extremely expensive to build these plants, but environmental and safety issues were inadequately addressed. Critics charged that the promise of cheaper electricity could not compensate for the dangers associated with radiation and toxic wastes spewing from nuclear power plants into the rivers and lakes of America. Apart from environmental concerns, activists also questioned the hazards involved to uranium miners and plant workers.

What would happen to nearby communities, moreover, should a nuclear power plant suffer a meltdown? What provisions would be made to protect the residents, and what costs would be involved in cleaning up the surrounding area should such a catastrophe occur? Such concerns resulted in a grassroots citizens movement that protested the construction of such power plants.

The movement started in 1976 when some forty protestors in New England, led mainly by Sam Lovejoy, sought to halt the proposed construction of a nuclear power plant at Seabrook, New Hampshire. They called themselves the Clamshell Alliance in deference to the clams living in sand and mud flats along the seacoast that would be destroyed by nuclear wastewater. Some six hundred activists gathered at the construction site on August 1, 1976. Employing nonviolent civil disobedience, eighteen members walked along the railroad tracks to the site and were arrested. During the last week of August, the number of protestors arrested for trespassing grew to 178, while 1,200 rallied to their support.

During the winter months, the Clamshell Alliance grew to a coalition consisting of some thirty-five New England action groups. The Alliance established a small-group structure in which each group had a spokesperson who served on a "spokes-council." There, by consensus, all decisions were made. On April 30, 1977, for a period lasting twenty-four hours, two hundred "Clams" occupied the parking lot of the construction site. On May 1 the police moved in and arrested almost 1,500 protestors who refused to post bail, forcing the State of New Hampshire to incarcerate them in National Guard armories (**Document 2**). It was a costly and embarrassing move on the part of state authorities. They were forced to release the activists without collecting any bail. This particular strategy, called "Bail Solidarity," became a new and effective strategy within the nonviolent direct action movement. On June 24–25, 1978, the protests, having gained national attention, grew even larger. Some 6,000 "Clams" camped at the Seabrook site, accompanied by 14,000 members of the general public. To that point in time it was the largest antinuclear power rally in American history. Speakers at this rally included Dr. Benjamin Spock, actor and comedian Dick Gregory, and representatives from NOW, while Pete Seeger and Arlo Guthrie provided music. One of the more novel acts of protest was an offshore "boat picket" blocking the plant's drilling platform.

The Clamshell Alliance sparked other direct action groups across the nation. In addition to consensus decision making and bail solidarity, the protests at Seabrook added other innovative elements of protest such as affinity groups (ten to twenty people familiar with each other and trained to

conduct nonviolent protests together) and mandatory nonviolence training for acts of civil disobedience. Copying the "Clams" politics of protest became the order of the day for direct action against nuclear power plants.

Another spectacular demonstration was organized by the Abalone Alliance in California. In August 1977, 47 people were arrested as 1,500 demonstrators organized a nonviolent occupation of the Diablo Canyon plant.
The following year, over 6,000 people mobilized at the site while 490 oc-
cupiers entered the plant and were arrested. Throughout the late 1970s
the antinuclear campaign, committed to nonviolent direct action, demonstrated the same vigor as the antiwar demonstrations a decade earlier.

Further support for the antinuclear movement was one result of the
accident at the Three Mile Island nuclear power plant on March 28, 1979,
in which there was a near meltdown of the core. The movement was already
quite active, but this incident outside Harrisburg, Pennsylvania, touched
off another large wave of protests and demonstrations. Some 125,000 "no
nukes" protestors made their feelings known in Washington, D.C., in May
of that year. On Long Island in June, 600 protestors were arrested at the
Shoreham power plant construction site. In September close to 200,000
people rallied in New York City to oppose the nuclear power plant program
in the United States.

Stepped-up demonstrations continued into the 1980s. In September
1981, for instance, the Abalone Alliance conducted a two-week "human
blockade" to prevent the startup of the Diablo plant. More than 10,000
demonstrators showed up; some 1,900 occupied the plant and were arrested in the largest anti-nuclear civil disobedience action ever conducted.
Those arrested used ladders to climb over the fence from many different
directions and hiked over rugged terrain to the plant. Other protestors,
aided by the environmentalist action group Greenpeace, approached the
plant by sea. The degree and extent of the mass civil disobedience protests
at Diablo Canyon ultimately came to represent the high point in the "plant
occupation" movement.

The growing support for antinuclear action seriously crippled the
nuclear power plant industry. Although some plants went online, including Diablo Canyon, no new construction plants were ordered after the late
1970s. Peace activists can point to this particular movement as one example
of the success of nonviolent direct action.

One important byproduct of the "no nukes" movement was the establishment of the Livermore Action Group (LAG), which was spawned as a
result of the September 1981 Diablo Canyon plant blockade. Some of the
protestors at Diablo were part of a Berkeley-based affinity group. After serv-

ing their jail sentences, they connected with an ongoing campaign headed by the Labs Conversion Project. The Livermore Lab was an important weapons design think tank for the military, and many of its scientists had been working on the MX missile project. Dubbed the "peacekeeper" by the government, the MX was a new intercontinental ballistic missile that could hold as many as ten independently targeted reentry vehicles. Its capabilities, along with plans to move it around the country on railroad tracks, caused many people to see it as a destabilizing force rather than a "peacekeeper."

LAG began in earnest on June 21, 1982. More than 40,000 people demonstrated outside the lab. Many of the protestors, trained in the tactics of nonviolent civil disobedience, sat down in the road to block cars and buses from entering the lab. These were mainly "respectable" citizens: grandmothers, social workers, doctors, students, and ministers. During the two-day demonstration, more than 1,400 people were arrested. In June 1983, another blockade was carried out in which about 1,000 protestors were arrested for acts of civil disobedience. The LAG was a prime example of how direct action groups sought to link the issues of nuclear power and nuclear weapons and redefine the idea of national security.

In this period, peace and justice activists connected nuclear power plant protests to the much larger issue of the arms race, which involved the ever-present threat of global annihilation. They wanted to expose the myth that genocidal weapons offered greater national security. In reality, humankind had never been less secure. In the mid-1970s, the *Bulletin of Atomic Scientists* changed the famous symbol on its cover. The drawing was a "doomsday clock," which displayed the time symbolizing the nearness of a possible nuclear holocaust. The time was changed to *nine minutes to midnight* in response to the new escalations of the arms race, in particular the development of multiple independently targetable reentry vehicles, which would carry more nuclear warheads than ever before. In 1984 the clock was set at *three minutes to midnight*, the closest it had been since the early 1950s, as U.S.–Soviet relations reached their worst point in decades and the U.S. sought to develop space-based missiles.

By the 1980s, many people, both within and outside the peace movement representing a variety of perspectives and values, were thinking about the bomb again. The haunting nuclear specter was a recurring theme in many books, articles, and TV specials. These included the following: Jonathan Schell, *The Fate of the Earth*; Larry Collins and Dominique LaPierre, *The Fifth Horseman*; Nigel Calder, *Nuclear Nightmares*; Louis Rene Beres, *Apocalypse*; Eisei Ishikawa and David L. Swain (eds.), *Hiroshima and Nagasaki*; E.P. Thompson, *Beyond The Cold War*; Bernard J. O'Keefe, *Nuclear Hostages*; Fred

Kaplan, *The Wizards of Armageddon; Harvard Magazine*'s "The First Nuclear War"; *The American Journal of Public Health*'s "Addressing Apocalypse Now"; and television specials "First Strike," "Nuclear Nightmares," and "The Islamic Bomb." An off-Broadway play, "Dead End Kids," was an impressionistic and satirical production that climaxed with someone brandishing a dead chicken while "an unperturbed announcer" reads a National Academy of Sciences report titled "Effect of Radioactive Fallout on Livestock in the Event of a Nuclear War." Popular media, musicians, and educators were among those raising greater awareness of the issue and in the process providing legitimacy to the peace movement.

As part of the broader context of social reform movements, antinuclear activism had its roots in local communities throughout the nation. From 1979 to 1981, there were more than two hundred church-based community conferences discussing the nuclear arms race. The wellspring for this action came from religious leaders and church groups whose membership possessed a deep and abiding respect for human life and social justice. The movement for halting the construction of nuclear power plants and nuclear weapons proliferation can only be understood in terms of the activists' individual views about citizenship and how they chose to rebuild local communities based on peace and justice. The new direction of the 1980s peace movement took its lead from activists who internalized their approach to political change—one guided by religious and moral values.

Complementing community-based activism was the attention that the medical profession, generally an inactive constituency, began devoting to what doctors were calling "the final epidemic." The theme of three conferences held in 1980 was "The Medical Consequences of Nuclear Weapons and Nuclear War," all heavily attended by health care professionals and medical students. Organized by Physicians for Social Responsibility, a group of doctors concerned about nuclear war, the conferences were held in Cambridge (Massachusetts), New York, and San Francisco and drew more than 2,000 people. They were sponsored by prominent medical institutions in each region including Harvard Medical School, Columbia University College of Physicians and Surgeons, the School of Public Health at Berkeley, and Stanford University Medical School.

Behind the physicians' concern was the stark realization that conventional projections of death and destruction were likely to be vastly exceeded in the event of an actual nuclear attack (**Document 3**). Jennifer Leaning, a member of Physicians for Social Responsibility, observed that in all likelihood there would be tens of millions of deaths in the ensuing months or years as well as long-term ecological damage. Administration and Pentagon officials who argued that a nuclear war was winnable created the worst possible kind of sin: false hope. In Leaning's opinion, a survivalist movement was unrealistic. Planning for civil defense measures instead of pursuing a comprehensive disarmament agreement to prevent nuclear war was sheer folly. It was, at best, highly unrealistic, and, at worst, extremely dangerous.

Following the lead of Physicians for Social Responsibility were members from the teaching ranks: Educators for Social Responsibility was established in 1981. Operating mainly from Columbia University Teachers College—with Betty Reardon, Doug Sloan, and Willard Jacobson leading the way—this organization sought to get the teaching profession more involved in raising awareness of the dangers posed by nuclear weapons and presenting peace as a positive force rather than simply a reaction to the possibility of global annihilation. In attempting to reveal and tap the energies and impulses that make possible the full human capacity for a meaningful existence, Educators for Social Responsibility suggested that problems of war and peace should be studied in connection with other related issues. Among those issues were economic development, economic aspects of the arms race, social justice, human rights, ecological balance, and conceptions of a just world order. The interrelations among military spending, economic development, and human rights, the organization maintained, are fundamental and demand analysis and understanding.

Highlighting these organizational activities was the push for a "nuclear freeze." This campaign, initiated in 1980 by Randall Forsberg of the Institute for Defense and Disarmament Studies, was bilateral in intent. It called on the U.S. and the Soviet Union to "adopt a mutual freeze on the testing, production, and deployment of nuclear weapons and of missiles, and new aircraft designed primarily to deliver nuclear weapons." The freeze proposal was intended as a first step in a complicated process to remake world politics.

The freeze also struck at the heart of the military buildup initiated by Jimmy Carter and continued by Ronald Reagan. President Jimmy Carter's Presidential Directive 59 endorsed plans for a first-strike nuclear option and the massive diversion of federal funds to the military, especially for research and development of nuclear weapons. Carter was defeated in his bid for reelection in 1980 by Ronald Reagan, who then presided over the largest peacetime military buildup in American history.

Organizations and local communities quickly responded to the proposal for a nuclear freeze, whose importance was underscored by a NATO plan to deploy intermediate-range nuclear missiles in five European countries. The growth of antinuclear movements in Western Europe helped provoke a sharp response in the United States. In 1981 massive protests against the deployment of Euromissiles took place in Paris, Rome, London, Amsterdam, Brussels, and Bonn. Inspired by these protests and by activists such as British historian E.P. Thompson, American pacifists initiated a series of direct-action campaigns aimed at defense plants, submarine bases, missile sites, and the Pentagon.

Other developments contributed significantly to the growing protests in the United States. Concerns about the Senate's failure to ratify the 1979 SALT II treaty limiting strategic offensive nuclear weapons were compounded by President Reagan's talk about fighting and surviving a nuclear war and his administration's enormous increases to the Pentagon budget. Responding to the fear engendered by such policies, a group calling itself Ground Zero—the flash point where a nuclear bomb detonates—organized a week of antinuclear protests in April 1982. These demonstrations were supported by such groups as the American Association for the Advancement of Science, the National Education Association, the United States Catholic Conferences, the United Steel Workers of America, the United Automobile Workers, and the United Food and Commercial Workers.

Two months later, in June, the broad support for disarmament and the abolition of nuclear weapons was dramatically illustrated at a rally outside the United Nations building in New York City. Close to a million people participated, making it the largest political demonstration in the history of the United States. In November 1982, the proposal for a nuclear freeze appeared on state and local ballots across the nation, constituting the largest referendum on any issue in American history. Supported by at least 70 percent of the public, the freeze was approved by 275 city governments, 12 state legislatures, and by voters in nine of the ten states where it appeared on the ballot. Democratic party leaders pledged their support for the freeze proposal, which became part of the party's campaign platform in 1984. By that time, the House of Representatives had already approved a resolution endorsing the freeze. Despite strong, widespread support, the freeze movement was unable to achieve its ultimate goal. Its coalition was tenuous from the start; groups with a long history of institutional ties to the establishment preferred to use political influence on behalf of "arms control" rather than mass demonstrations for disarmament. Pacifists and other direct-action groups had many competing claims for their attention due to President Reagan's confrontational Cold War policies; thus, while continuing the freeze campaign, they also became involved in other activities such as trying to end U.S. ties with apartheid South Africa and prevent a military incursion into Nicaragua. For his own part, President Reagan skillfully maneuvered his 1984 campaign so that his reelection was not a referendum on either the freeze or the United States' own national security program. In 1984, Reagan proclaimed a new commitment to arms control negotiations and offered to restore summit meetings with the Soviet Union while he continued to promote the Strategic Defense Initiative, the space-based missile system that became known as "Star Wars."

The antinuclear arms movement brought about a change in attitude, both at home and abroad. What emerged, as chronicled in Larry Wittner's trilogy *The Struggle Against the Bomb*, was a strong global antinuclear protest movement, resulting in further arms control and reduction agreements. The movement in the 1980s became the largest grassroots citizens' movement in modern history. One of its accomplishments was the creation of a compelling vision shared by the worldwide community. The movement's focus was not only on educating elites, but also on informing all citizens. As a powerful social movement, the antinuclear campaign forced political leaders to consider undertaking newer and bolder steps to reduce armaments of mass destruction.

In addition to concerns about the environment and the nuclear arms race, the peace movement took action on a number of other issues in this period. Activists such as California Congressman Ron Dellums led continued efforts to end the discriminatory and segregationist policies of the South African government. The role of the AFSC in this struggle is particularly instructive, though it was certainly not the only peace group focusing its energies on ending apartheid. The AFSC's long involvement in peace and justice issues intensified in the 1970s and 1980s based on the popularity of "liberation pacifism" (a term coined by peace historian Dave Hostetter) in the name of social justice. Its involvement, nonetheless, goes back further.

Efforts to address specifically the devastating effects of apartheid had begun in the late 1950s. While students were already protesting against U.S. investments in apartheid South Africa, with Chase Manhattan Bank as a specific target, the AFSC was providing money, material, and expertise for housing and agricultural development in southern Africa. These investments of relief aid continued during the next decade along with initiating a dialogue with Chase Manhattan Bank in 1965, where AFSC accounts were held. Initially, AFSC attempted to use friendly persuasion with Chase Bank president David Rockefeller to see if the financial institution would change its investment policies with the South African government. When, after a few years, it became apparent that Chase would not revise its policies, AFSC told Rockefeller to close its account. A nonviolent strategy of divestment had been initiated.

From the 1960s through the 1980s, the AFSC carried out a multi-pronged program aimed at creating links with exiled freedom and liberation movements, developing education programs in the United States to assist other anti-apartheid programs, and bringing its own distinguished history of relief work to the forefront on matters involving South Africa. By 1974, the AFSC leadership set up a Southern Africa Representative Board and hired Bill Sutherland to head this program. An African American pacifist, Sutherland had spent several years in prison as a World War II conscientious objector, then left the U.S. during the McCarthy era to work in Africa for the nonviolent liberation of all peoples. His experience there spanned many decades and he participated in a number of struggles, including the 1952 Defiance Campaign, a nonviolent strike led by the African National Congress and Nelson Mandela, and the 1959 protest against the French atomic bomb tests in the Sahara desert.

In 1976, the AFSC initiated the South Africa Program of the Peace Education Division. Working through AFSC offices in the United States, Sutherland's anti-apartheid efforts were aided in part by staff members Lyle Tatum, a former member of SNCC; Michael Simmons; Jim Bristol; and Peter Molotsi, an exiled South African. In an effort to promote the goal of divestment, the AFSC established a South Africa Summer project in 1978. In some ten cities around the United States, approximately forty South Africa Summer volunteers, mainly college and high school students, worked to end loans from United States banks to South Africa and circulated petitions calling for a ban on the sale of Krugerrand gold coins. To drive home its commitment the AFSC announced that it had divested itself of $1.3 million worth of stock in American corporations doing business in South Africa. Spurred by this action some business firms tried to reassure AFSC leaders that it was working toward equitable wages and banning segregated places of work.

AFSC's divestment actions picked up steam by the 1980s as a larger, more insistent movement formed around the issue. In conjunction with Bishop Desmond Tutu, 1984 Nobel Peace Prize winner who was sponsored by the committee, AFSC worked diligently to promote the goal of divestment while also working with other religious and peace and solidarity groups. Producing important publications such as *Automating Apartheid*, exposing how United States computer companies sent hardware and software to security forces in South Africa, and *Challenge and Hope*, a summary of the history of injustices resulting from apartheid, many more Americans became aware of the importance of bringing down apartheid and questioning the Cold War rationale of the Reagan administration for continued investments in South Africa (**Document 4**). It became only a matter of time when the American government as well as leading corporations that invested millions of dollars in South Africa were forced to reconsider their position and publicly admit that apartheid had to go. The efforts of the AFSC, students on college campuses, Congressional representatives, and many others—most importantly the African National Congress—to bring down apartheid finally succeeded in the early 1990s. In the wake of U.S. imposition of economic sanctions on South Africa and the end of the Cold War, South Africa held its first election as a multiracial democracy.

Nonviolent protests to raise awareness also characterized the work of gay rights activists. Attempts to combat deeply held prejudice and discrimination received an added boost in the 1970s when the American Psychiatric Association declassified homosexuality as a mental disorder and encouraged the extension of civil rights to gays. As greater openness about sexuality grew, gays and lesbians advanced their interests by publishing their own newspapers and magazines while also lobbying city, state, and federal officials seeking equal access in the areas of jobs, housing, and government programs.

Intolerance and fear of homosexuality persisted, however. After Miami's city council banned discrimination against homosexuals, singer Anita Bryant started the Save Our Children movement, which successfully repealed the law by a 2–1 margin in 1977. In November 1978, San Francisco mayor George Moscone and city councilman Harvey Milk, an openly gay leader, were gunned down after they led a protest march condemning Miami's repeal of the law. Their assassin, Dan White, who voted against San Francisco's gay rights law, was convicted of voluntary manslaughter rather than murder after he claimed that an excessive consumption of Twinkies left him temporarily insane.

Compounding matters was the growing epidemic of HIV/AIDS, which hit the gay community especially hard. Angered by the government's apparent indifference to this serious issue, members of New York's gay community and AIDS activists formed ACT-UP (AIDS Coalition to Unleash Power) in 1987. Developing a confrontational nonviolent campaign, ACT-UP focused on a number of issues underlying the AIDS crisis. Among them were inadequate government research funds for prevention, inattentive AIDS service organizations, extremely high drug prices, and media coverage that was very biased.

Employing innovative nonviolent strategies, ACT-UP members used phone and fax zaps, die-ins, office takeovers, expressive artwork, videos, and agitational propaganda designed to spark political responses. Perhaps its most widely acknowledged nonviolent method was staging large demonstrations and recording speeches at these rallies for broadcast on the Internet and elsewhere. One of the most compelling testimonies is that of Vito

Russo who, three years before he died, called upon all concerned citizens and the media to forsake prejudices and fight the common enemy that was killing innocent people (**Document 5**).

The battle against AIDS and HIV in the United Sates coincided with the militarization of U.S. policies in Central America. Peace and justice activists were quick to challenge President Reagan's Latin American policies and support the "liberation pacifism" that was spreading in Latin America. One bold attempt to assist victims of bloodshed was the interfaith movement—Witness for Peace—formed in 1983. It was created in response to guerrillas, armed and trained by U.S. forces, who had been attacking civilian farms and individuals in Nicaragua. The country had been under the leadership of socialist Daniel Ortega since a popular revolution overthrew the dictator Anastasio Somoza in 1979. The Reagan Administration supported the "contras"—the U.S.-financed guerrillas (many of them former members of the National Guard under Somoza) who hoped to bring down the government. Beginning in October 1983, Witness for Peace strategically placed volunteers trained in the tactic of nonviolence and peaceful civil disobedience in the besieged town of Jalapa, which was surrounded by contra forces. The contras did not want to risk losing their financial backing by killing American citizens. By December, teams of twenty to eighty volunteers came to Jalapa and other threatened communities for two-week stays. While there, members of Witness for Peace would meet with the victims of the war and with civic, religious, and political leaders. They helped rebuild damaged schools and clinics and planted crops in what were once fertile fields—now deliberately laid barren by the torches of the contras. They also returned home with documented stories of rape and murder committed by the contras. Thus, Witness for Peace served as an unarmed peace monitoring force in southern Nicaragua's demilitarized zone (**Document 6**).

Throughout much of the 1980s Witness for Peace activists were busy protesting, lobbying, working the news media, engaging in civil disobedience, and other grassroots efforts to stop the internal war that eventually claimed more than 30,000 Nicaraguan lives. In 1984, in one of its most important confrontations, a peace delegation riding aboard a small shrimp boat motored its way in front of a U.S. destroyer off the coast of Corinto. The efforts of WFP to investigate and record the contra atrocities directly challenged the misinformation put out by the U.S. government regarding its involvement in Nicaragua. The thousands who traveled to Nicaragua as part of the short-term delegations were strongly motivated by a desire to challenge U.S. foreign policy in Latin America. These noncombatant pacifist observers eventually helped bring about an end to military aid to the contras; along with other Latin American solidarity groups, they were important in shaping views of the conflict among the public and members of Congress. At the start of the 1990s, peace, not violence, would prevail.

As the Cold War finally came to an end, it seemed all sorts of opportunities for peace were on the horizon: an end to apartheid, a less militarized U.S. policy in Latin America, a "peace dividend" wherein revenue would be freed up for social needs such as education and health care, and progress toward peace in the Middle East. Just as many such possibilities were at hand, Iraqi dictator Saddam Hussein invaded the small oil-rich country of Kuwait. In reaction, the United States called upon the members of the UN to join in an effort to remove Hussein's forces from Kuwait. Months before war began in January 1991, an antiwar movement organized. On October 20, 1990, some 15,000 protestors marched in New York and 15 other cities across the country. This time peace activists were more determined than ever to prevent war before it started. Between October 1990 and January 1991 a number of protests took place; in San Francisco, for instance, a TV station was interrupted and the Golden Gate Bridge was blockaded on several occasions. Prior to the commencement of the fighting, opinion polls suggested that at least half of the U.S. population opposed military intervention. Yet no serious attempts to negotiate a withdrawal of Iraqi forces from Kuwait took place.

When the war was launched on January 16, 1991, over 3,000 Bostonians immediately turned out to protest the war. Members of the Initiative for Peace led a rally that began with speeches at the government center and continued at Boston Common. Speakers at this antiwar rally invoked the lessons of the Vietnam War and characterized the war in the Persian Gulf as a conflict over oil. On January 26, a week after 15,000 turned out in force for a demonstration in Washington, D.C., more than 70,000 protestors returned. Estimates of the crowd varied from 70,000 to as high as 250,000. This turnout prompted *Newsweek* to state the following: "and there was, finally, undeniably, the presence of more than 150,000 Americans on the Mall last Saturday, little more than a week into a war whose worst horrors surely lie ahead of us. The peace movement, like the troops themselves, has barely begun to fight."

Yet no sooner had the troops begun to fight and the antiwar movement to mobilize than the war ended after a month. A massive air attack demoralized the Iraqi forces and its Republican Guard retreated to Baghdad when faced with a superior American military force. Some U.S. forces involved in the conflict, however, questioned the need for this massive military response (**Document 7**). Throughout the 1990s and until the 2003 Iraq War, UN sanctions against Hussein's government resulted in the deaths of some 500,000

Iraqi children due to malnutrition and infections. Defying U.S. law, peace activists, principally from FOR, AFSC, and Voices in the Wilderness, brought badly needed medical supplies into Iraq. In retaliation, heavy fines and, in some cases, imprisonment was imposed on these activists and peace groups.

By the fall of 2002, George W. Bush's Administration had decided it was time to use military force against Iraq. President Bush implied that Saddam Hussein was linked to the 9/11 attacks by al-Qaeda on the World Trade Center and the Pentagon, a link that did not exist. The explicit justification for the first strike was that Hussein possessed weapons of mass destruction. Evidence later revealed that such was not the case, thus strengthening opposition to the war.

At first, many Americans backed Bush's military intervention into Iraq, especially when Saddam Hussein's regime fell and President Bush proclaimed "mission accomplished." As the war dragged on, however, more and more people began to question whether it was worth it. A large portion of the American public found it hard to come to grips with the idea of a preemptive war. The so-called "war by choice" policy of the Bush Administration—a deliberate decision to wage war without provocation or outright attack on American forces or interests in the region—troubled many people at home and abroad who saw in such unilateral policies a blatant disregard for world opinion, the United Nations (which did not authorize the war), and the horrible consequences of war. Lingering doubts were raised at the time of the invasion that America's ability to foster democracy in the Middle East was seriously undermined by the Iraq War and that it would lead to a wave of anti-American sentiment, especially in the Islamic world (**Document 8**). Peace activists began undertaking their own policies of "situational anti-unilateralism."

Long before the invasion began, peace groups quickly mobilized. As early as October 3, 2002, an antiwar group, Americans Against War with Iraq (AAWWI), ran a full-page ad in the *New York Times* with blaring headlines, "Bush's Weapons of Mass Distraction: War With Iraq." The subtitle read: "Is the Bush administration pushing this war because . . . war will take our minds off our failing economy, our broken education system, the environmental meltdown, the healthcare emergency, the raids on social security, the corporate scandals, the new $157 billion deficit? And we won't notice the loss of our civil liberties." Surrounding the ad were hundreds and hundreds of names endorsing it as well as encouraging Americans to call upon their senators and representatives in Congress to vote against an invasion of Iraq.

By October antiwar coalitions were putting pressure on government officials to stop talk of an invasion. On October 6, 2002, thousands rallied at Central Park's East Meadow in New York City. Speaker after speaker denounced the impending invasion. The event was organized by the antiwar group, NOT IN OUR NAME. Throughout the crowds were signs and T-shirts reading, "It Takes Courage NOT TO MAKE WAR" and "Imagine," a reference to the popular song by John Lennon that some radio stations had banned after 9/11. On October 26, 2002, a massive antiwar rally, with International ANSWER acting as the clearinghouse, was held in Washington, D.C. In December, ninety-nine people were arrested in front of the U.S. mission to the UN. Dramatic acts of civil disobedience took place. Among those arrested were Daniel Ellsberg of the Pentagon Papers case and Ben Cohen, co-founder of Ben and Jerry's Ice Cream.

In the United States and around the world, antiwar sentiment continued to be expressed in 2003. A January 17 ad by Americans Against War with Iraq that appeared in the *Los Angeles Times* asked, "Who's Against a U.S. War on Iraq?" and then answered: 2 out of 3 Americans, 7 out of 8 Brits, 1 out of 1 Popes. Indeed, the war was condemned by religious leaders around the world. Sixteen protestors were arrested across from the White House while others, invoking the spirit of Martin Luther King, Jr., in observance of his birthday, shouted a familiar refrain from the Vietnam period, "Give Peace a Chance." On February 15, 2003, a crowd estimated at between 100,000 to 250,000 marched through the streets of New York, making it the largest political demonstration the city had seen since the anti-nuclear weapons movement two decades earlier. Around the world, the campaign against the invasion of Iraq was the largest, most intensive mobilization of antiwar sentiment in history. It was not just in New York that large numbers of people came out to protest on February 15. In the largest single day of antiwar protest ever, an estimated 10 million people demonstrated, including more than a million in London, and just as many in Rome and Barcelona. (In England, Italy, and Spain, the majority of the population said "no" to war as their political leaders were saying "yes" to the U.S. government.) Hundreds of thousands turned out in Madrid, Berlin, Sydney, and dozens of other cities. The global outcry was in part a reflection of how Internet organizing was able to generate massive opposition to the war policies of the Bush Administration.

On March 9, 2003, remarkably similar to WSP's actions in the 1960s, some 3,000 pink-clad activists, women who were organized by the feminist antiwar group Code Pink for Peace, marched around the White House. On March 15, the last massive demonstrations before the war began witnessed tens of thousands of protestors participating in antiwar rallies from Portland, Oregon, to Los Angeles to Washington, D.C., in a final attempt to head off war.

The numbers of arrests and the magnitude of the protests increased exponentially once the attack took place. Groups such as United for Peace and Justice continued to urge acts of nonviolent civil disobedience. In all of these protests throughout the remainder of 2003, the antiwar coalitions were composed of people from all walks of life. On October 25 more than 100,000 marched in Washington and other cities carrying signs reading "No Blood for Oil" and "Bring Them Home Alive," reflecting the movement's concern for saving soldiers' lives. Protests were clearly directed at government policies, not the individuals ordered to carry them out. The big question facing peace activists was what to do now that the war was underway and how they could bring an end to it (**Document 9**). What kind of peace action would be necessary to end this conflict?

Throughout 2004 and 2005, antiwar demonstrations continued, with the largest crowds gathering at places such as New York City, San Francisco, and Washington, D.C. Although numerous arrests were made, what made these antiwar rallies remarkable was the discipline and adherence to the principle of nonviolent civil disobedience. As the number of American soldiers killed in action mounted, the American Friends Service Committee initiated its own novel protest that was then copied by other antiwar groups. Called "False Pretenses," AFSC first introduced the idea of a memorial by placing 500 pairs of boots at the Federal Building Plaza in Chicago to symbolize graphically the number of soldiers killed at that point in the war. Other antiwar activists built mock coffins and stretched out on busy roads. During the 2004 GOP Presidential Convention in Manhattan, hundreds of demonstrators carried coffins down 7th Avenue. During the convention one member of Code Pink disrupted Vice President Dick Cheney's speech. Jodie Evans, co-founder of Code Pink, was forcibly removed from the convention floor when she showed off her pink slip with anti-Bush slogans on it.

Perhaps even more dramatic were the efforts of the antiwar group Grandmothers Against the War (**Document 10**), a local, responsive coalition in New York. On October 17, 2005, a number of determined grandmothers attempted to enlist in the military at New York City's Times Square recruiting station. When they were refused entry into the station, they then sat down and 17 of them, ranging in age from 49 to 90, were promptly arrested. At their arraignment one of the protestors, 65-year-old Eva-Lee Baird, called her arrest "a badge of honor."

One of the unique aspects of the twenty-first-century peace movement has been the online international antiwar community. Many of the antiwar actions have been successful in their efforts to establish grassroots mobilization efforts. While it may be too early to assess the full impact of their efforts because of the continuation of the war, there have been some signs of an impact based on how the mobilization now takes place. One example of this new type of decentralized networks, or, as social theorists call them, heterarchies, is the Web-based antiwar network, WHY WAR? It provides news and analysis along with strategies to political activists. Another popular group, United for Peace and Justice, encourages student activism by offering updates as to what other student activists are doing around the nation. There are also sites where veterans encourage each other to participate in campaigns to bring the soldiers home. Among these online organizations are Veterans for Common Sense, Operation Truth, and Iraq Veterans against the War.

Other active groups include Peaceful Tomorrows, founded by family members of 9/11 victims in order to encourage nonviolent solutions to the problem of terrorism. The coalition called ANSWER consists of hundreds of organizations and individuals transcending both national and interest-group boundaries by focusing on common interests including world peace, respect for the environment, and workers' and human rights. Both online peace organizing and traditional antiwar groups continue their efforts to call for an end to the conflicts in Iraq and Afghanistan.

Although the war in Iraq has occupied most of peace activists' time and attention in the first decade of the new century, the promotion of human rights and social justice still remains an important part of their agenda. One issue of concern was the increasing problem of genocide in the Darfur region of the Sudan. The Sudanese government was accused of sponsoring militias responsible for killing, raping, and abusing thousands of non-Arabs living in the region, thus leading students to initiate a new effort at divestiture. The enormity of the crisis in the Sudan led to a national student movement beginning in 2005, which, similar to the divestment movement of the 1980s, was aimed at universities and major corporations.

Colleges proved fertile ground for the divestment wakeup call. Student activists questioned how higher-education money managers, whose primary goal is to look for the best returns on investment, were conducting their policies. When it became public knowledge that almost seventy-two percent of college investments paid little attention to matters involving political and social justice, students began creating campus chapters to address the matter. National umbrella groups like Students Taking Action Now on Darfur, which originated at Georgetown University, and the Sudan Divestment Task Force, formed at the University of California at Los Angeles, placed tremendous pressure on colleges and universities to reconsider their investments. In response, numerous college officials made a series of investment-policy changes. In April 2005, for instance, due to student pressure, Harvard University divested stock in the China National Petroleum Corporation, a business partner of the Sudanese government. Harvard owned an estimated $4.3 million in shares in PetroChina. In 2006, Harvard also withdrew almost $8.3 million in holdings in another Chinese oil company, Sinopec (**Document 11**).

Harvard's actions led other institutions of higher learning to follow suit. Among them were Brown, Stanford, Yale, Amherst, Dartmouth, Smith, and Swarthmore. In March 2006 the University of California system decided to divest shares of nine public companies with connections to the Sudanese government. Such action was also undertaken by the University of Pennsylvania, Princeton University, and Williams College.

The latest divestment movement bases its appeal on a rather traditional strategy: investigative research aimed at persuasion in the name of nonviolent direct action. Student groups like the Sudan Divestment Task Force did most of the research that led to colleges reconsidering their investment policies. Two student leaders, Adam Sterling at UCLA and Daniel Millenson at Brandeis, were instrumental in arousing student awareness. But rather than using events like rallies, they opted, instead, to wear business suits and present reports to colleges across the country. They also carefully targeted those companies that were the worst offenders.

From the environmental and antinuclear campaigns of the 1970s and 1980s to the present war in Iraq and the tragedies confronting the people of North Africa, the peace movement has continued to make its voice heard on pressing issues of war and human rights. The freeze campaign provided pacifists and their legions a modicum of hope. The peace movement nearly collapsed during the first Gulf War, and yet the movement against the second Iraq War has been the largest ever. Even before that war was launched in March 2003, veteran peace activist and noted historian Howard Zinn cautioned the nation about a conflict that would supposedly rid it of the trauma of America's longest war (Vietnam) and reestablish the nation's military might (**Document 12**).

The ongoing conflicts in Afghanistan and Iraq have brought disillusionment and dismay to the American public and continuous challenges from the peace movement. Most noteworthy is the variety of people who have joined the call for peace: antiglobalization activists, traditional peace organizations, Internet groups, churches and other religious organizations, trade unions, and many other organizations from mainstream America. It has cut across all socioeconomic and political lines. Many of the protestors against the current war, moreover, reflect the movement's internationalization.

At the same time, a more global view guides people in local struggles for social justice, thus many college students remain steadfast in their efforts to convince their own universities to adopt policies that do not support sweatshop labor in Asia or oppressive regimes in North Africa. Supporters of peace seek not only an end to the bloodshed and fighting in the Middle East but also a world in which basic human rights and social justice are accorded to each and every individual. In their view you cannot have one without the other.

Document 1: **Indians of all Tribes**
Proclamation to the Great White Father
(1969)

In order to call attention to their cause, the organization of Indians of All Tribes occupied the abandoned federal penitentiary on Alcatraz Island in San Francisco Bay. Determined activists stayed for months in order to illustrate the strength of Native American culture and the depth of Indian poverty (Native Americans were the poorest group in the American population). Here is the declaration of liberation they issued.

We, the Native Americans, re-claim the land known as Alcatraz island in the name of all American Indians by right of discovery. We wish to be fair and honorable in our dealing with the Caucasian inhabitants of this land, and thereby offer the following treaty:

We will purchase Alcatraz island for twenty-four dollars in glass beads and red cloth, a precedent set down by the white man's purchase of a similar island about 300 years ago. We know that $24 in trade goods for these 16 acres is more than what was paid when Manhattan was sold, but we know that land values have risen over the years. Our offer of $1.24 per acres is greater than the 47 cents per acre the white man is now paying California Indians for their land....

... We will further guide the inhabitants in the proper way of living. We will offer them our religion, our education, our life-ways, in order to help them achieve our level of civilization and thus raise them and all their white brothers up from their savage and unhappy state. We offer this treaty in good faith and wish to be fair and honorable in our dealing with all white men.

We feel that this so called Alcatraz island is more than suitable for an Indian Reservation, as determined by the white man's own standards. By this we mean that this place resembles most Indian Reservations in that:

It is isolated from modern facilities and without adequate means of transportation.

It has no fresh running water.

It has no adequate sanitation facilities.

There are no oil or mineral rights.

There is no industry and so unemployment is very great.

There is no health care facility.

The soil is rocky and non-productive and the land does not support game.

There are no educational facilities.

The population has always exceeded the land base.

The population has always been held prisoners and kept dependent upon others.

Further, it would be fitting and symbolic that ships from all over the world, entering the Golden Gate, would first see Indian land, and thus be reminded of the true history of this nation. The tiny island would be a symbol of the great land once ruled by free and noble Indians. . . .

In the name of all Indians, therefore, we claim this island for our Indian nations, for these reasons, we feel this claim is just and proper, and that this land should rightfully be granted to us as long as the rivers shall flow and sun shall shine.

Indians of All Tribes

———————

Source: http://siouxme.com/lodge/aim_69.html (accessed April 1, 2009)

QUESTIONS

1. What is the significance of the historical references with which this document begins?

2. In this proclamation/treaty what did the Indians of All Tribes mean in the words "thus raise them and all their white brothers up from their savage and unhappy state"?

3. What was the point of listing the ways in which Alcatraz resembled Indian reservations in the United States?

Document 2: Cathy Wolff
Reflections on the Seabrook Occupation **(1977)**

The Clamshell Alliance was established in response to the state of New Hampshire's plan to build a nuclear power plant in the town of Seabrook. The Alliance adopted the principle of nonviolence and held a series of occupations on the construction site. At one such occupation in April 1977, close to 1,500 protestors were arrested and taken to several armories throughout the state, where they remained incarcerated for two weeks. These are the words of one of the participants.

*T*he National Guardsman stood with his feet slightly apart, his hands behind his back; separated from me by a table barricade in the Somersworth Armory....

While I spoke with the young guardsman, other nuclear opponents in the armory sang a song about love. We sang for three hours, protesting a decision to physically break up our affinity groups, the basic unit of strength of the Seabrook nuke site occupation....

It was the fourth day we had been held in the cement-floor armory; more than 200 of us crowded onto a space the size of a basketball court....

On that fourth day of incarceration, a middle-aged occupier from Philadelphia also talked with a guard: "If the people of Germany had banded together and physically tried to halt construction of Hitler's crematories, perhaps they would never have been built. We consider the threat of nuclear power to be as great, if not greater, than Nazi Germany. That's why we occupied the Seabrook site."

Other people spoke with the silent guardsmen about the difference of their organization and ours. The Guard and much of our society is based on a hierarchy of order-giving and taking. But the people in the armories and the Clamshell Alliance believe that everyone must be involved in making the decisions that affect their lives, including decisions about nuclear power.

We have no officers; we follow no orders. We discuss, for hours sometimes, what to do until we reach a consensus everyone can live with. It's a little like town meetings.

Throughout the two-week ordeal in the five New Hampshire armories, we tried to let guardsmen know we considered them as fellow human beings, not enemies. The radiation and cost of suicidal nuclear

power will hit them and their families as hard as us. We gave them literature on atomic power and suggested books they should read....

Hopefully, the guards realized we were not a band of terrorists or
rich kids looking for a thrill. I'm sure they realized that being locked
up for two weeks was not a picnic and none of us wanted to be there
any more than they did. But most important, I hope some of the
guards now will begin to think about nuclear power, if they haven't
already, and realize that utilities and the federal government have not
been upfront about the danger, cost and alternatives of nukes.

Source: Cathy Wolff, "No Nuke of the North: Reflections on the Seabrook
Occupation," *WIN* (June 1977): 36–37.

QUESTIONS

1. What type of decision making did the protestors at Seabrook conduct?
2. How did the "Clams" distinguish their concept of democracy from
   that of the guardsmen?
3. What inherent dangers did the protestors see in the construction
   of nuclear power plants?

Document 3:   Physicians for Social Responsibility
Civil Defense in the Nuclear Age (1982)

At the height of the Nuclear Freeze Movement of the early 1980s, members of
Physicians for Social Responsibility pushed government leaders to eliminate
the threat posed by nuclear weapons. Based on biological, environmental,
and other health concerns, Dr. Jennifer Leaning offered compelling testimony before members of the U.S. Congress of what would occur to humankind
and society if a nuclear war were to occur. Her point was that there really are
no effective civil defense measures to undertake in case of a nuclear attack.

Introduction

$\mathcal{F}$or a few brief years in the 1950s, during the height of the cold
war, civil defense programs were introduced in a military setting as

the United States became concerned about Soviet nuclear capabilities and sought measures to protect the U.S. population from nuclear attack. The efficacy of air raid drills and home bomb shelters came into question, however, as U.S. military strategists learned more about the thermal, blast, and radiation effects of these weapons from above and underground testing; as technological developments in the speed of delivery systems reduced options for population response; and as the doctrine of mutual assured destruction [MAD], became the accepted mechanism for ensuring nuclear stability....

Now, again in response to developments in weapons systems, civil defense has re-entered the arena of national debate, promoted with a more explicit strategic rationale than ever. The weapons are more lethal, the scenarios more brazen, and the world peace more tenuous.... In the setting of nuclear war, however, a circumstance which engulfs us all in devastation of unprecedented scale, we submit that civil defense cannot ensure conditions for post-attack survival....

The Post-Attack World

The people who remain will not recognize their world when they emerge from the shelters. Many familiar natural landmarks and most man-made ones will have been destroyed. The urban areas, home to most Americans, will be in rubble, and little will be left to draw people into the highly radioactive dust of what were once the downtown centers of life. Fires and blast effects may have destroyed or damaged much of the rural environment. Radioactive contamination of the land and water will present an incessant, uncertain hazard.

Meeting needs for shelter, food and water will be paramount. Shelters may still have to be used as home, since most of the nation's housing stock will have been destroyed. Destruction of the petroleum and much of the coal industries may force dependence on wood for fuel. Building even rudimentary housing and foraging for wood takes energy. Food supplies will be very low. Food production will depend on many uncertainties, including availability of seed, extent of soil contamination, and season of the year.

Sanitary conditions will be primitive. Sewage and water systems will for the most part have been destroyed and makeshift ones may be inadequate. Millions of decomposing corpses from the attack and shelter period will require immediate burial or cremation. Insects, comparatively resistant to radiation and released from the constraints of their pre-attack predators (all of whom share radiation sensitivities more equivalent to human thresholds) will multiply.

Food Supply

Whether and for how long there will be enough food to support the population remaining after a nuclear war on the United States depends in part on the estimated population size. If crisis relocation is as effective as claimed, approximately 145 million people will survive the immediate effects and they will persist into the shelter period. Food supply in the United States depends on three main factors: production, processing, and distribution. A marked imbalance between production and population characterizes U.S. agriculture.... Almost 80 percent of the good processing capacity of the country is located in high risk areas and would be destroyed in the war. Similar destruction of the distribution network (transportation systems and managerial personnel) can be anticipated....

Currently about 6 percent of the U.S. population is involved in agricultural production. Regardless of what extent a remnant of skilled farmers may survive the attack, the majority of the population will have had little experience with farming. People will be disoriented, hungry, perhaps ill from radiation and disease. The work required to prepare and plant fields may be beyond the capability of many.

For... these reasons, the yield cannot be expected to compare with the pre-attack world. Estimates of production in the first several years after attack are beyond the scope of this discussion, but it is clear from the variables mentioned that problems with food production and distribution may exert significant negative constraints on population survival.... Living as they did on the margins of existence, two successive failures of the potato crop in 1816 and 1847 spelled death for close to 25 percent of the Irish population. The starkness of the view needs no recourse to more conjectural possibilities, such as whether depletion of ozone or injection of atmosphere dust will make crop production in North America for the succeeding 5 to 20 years completely impossible. In this way, persistent famine could be seen to characterize the post-attack world.

Infectious Disease and Epidemics

The incidence and relative virulence of infectious disease will increase enormously in the years after the nuclear attack. Change in characteristics of both host and environment may lead to morbidity and mortality rates rarely before recorded. Environmental conditions post attack will create conditions for the abundant spread of disease: (1) crowding, during the shelter period and thereafter because of inadequate housing stock; (2) inadequate ventilation; (3) destruction of sanitary systems with accumulation of sewage and waste; (4) absence of refrigeration leading to food spoilage; (5) the presence of millions of corpses; (6) exuberant overgrowth of insects. The population that remains will in turn be able to offer only reduced resistance to disease. The complex interactive effects of stress, malnutrition, and lingering radiation will weaken human immune system and physiological defense mechanisms to the point where people may succumb to disease of previously low virulence. . . .

In the setting of the post-attack world, erosion of host defenses and environmental changes fostering the spread of endemic and epidemic disease may combine to create a potential mortality crisis of severe proportions. Public health and medical measures will be virtually nonexistent. Most medical centers will have been consumed in the attack. No vaccines or antibiotics will be available beyond those stockpiled, since the pharmaceutical industry will have been destroyed. Strict rationing of antibiotics and vaccines will be necessary. . . . Without supportive and intensive medical care, they can do little to combat some of the more dangerous bacterial diseases, and against most viral diseases are largely ineffective. . . .

Under these conditions, estimates of plague incidence approach 12 percent of the population, with half of those contracting the disease dying. Within the first year after the attack, total deaths from all communicable diseases are estimated at 20 to 25 percent of the immediate post-attack population. Those at the extremes of the age spectrum, the very old and the very young, will probably succumb first to the ravages of disease. Virulent diseases such as plague, however, will strike everyone, and these effects on the age structure of the population are less easy to predict.

The cumulative mortality from infectious disease in the post attack world merits further careful study. What is known from examining the historical record may have somber application to this setting: death rates among societies living at the margins of agricultural production (and such is at best a characterization of post-attack America) "show a remarkable tendency to recurrent, sudden dramatic peaks that reach levels as high as 150 or 300, or even 500,000 . . . the intensity and frequency of the peaks controlled the size of agricultural societies. Furthermore, "historical experience suggests that something like

120 to 150 years are needed for human populations to stabilize their response to drastic new infections."

Conclusion

As an element of military offensive strategy, civil defense in the nuclear age serves to delude Federal officials and a few members of the populace into thinking that nuclear war can be waged with relative impunity. As a public health program, current civil defense plans fall short of evaluating issues of feasibility, medical care, and long-term health consequences. The demography of the post-attack world, when evaluated in light of the factors affecting survivability, does not support bright predictions of outcome....

To evaluate ... we must stretch our understanding of what existence may or may not mean for those of us who might survive. Our cities in rubble, our land burned and contaminated, our friends and relatives gone, future grimly foreshortened by prospects of famine and disease. Civil defense cannot change what the weapons can do.

If, after considered evaluation, it is seen that civil defense cannot protect the elements of our life and society we deem essential, then perhaps we need to call for an entirely different approach to the problem of nuclear war. If we begin with the understanding that nuclear war is not in any humane or civilized sense survivable, the path becomes clear: civil defense planning for nuclear war is delusionary behavior and should not be encouraged. All our efforts must be directed at prevention.

Source: Reproduced from U.S. Congress, Senate, Committee on Foreign Relations, Sub-committee on Arms Control, Oceans, International Operations, and Environment. United States and Soviet civil defense programs. Hearings, 97th Cong. 2d sess., March 16 and 31, 1982. Washington, DC: U.S. Government Printing Office 1982, pp. 93–111.

QUESTIONS

1. Summarize briefly what a post-attack world would look like, according to Dr. Leaning.
2. How useful would civil defense measures be in such a world?
3. What do you think PSR wanted the government to do in response to testimony such as this?

Document 4: American Friends Service Committee
U.S. Investments in South Africa (1985)

The American Friends Service Committee (AFSC) was one of the more established groups to take on the issue of divestment. In the 1980s, as the movement against apartheid picked up steam in the United States, the AFSC applied its philosophy of nonviolence to actions aimed at improving the lives of black people in South Africa, who made up the majority of the population. This press release is from the AFSC's Portland (OR) Area Program Office.

$\mathcal{R}$ecent demonstrations by the Free South Africa Movement and numerous anti-apartheid groups around the country, along with pending legislation at the national and state levels, have put the question of U.S. investments in the forefront of pubic debate on South Africa.

This increased attention to South Africa has also brought an increase in activity on the part of the South African government and its lobbies. The government and its closely affiliated private lobbying foundations spend millions of dollars annually to counter divestment and other efforts aimed at bringing pressure on the South African government. . . .

The AFSC has been engaged in issues of Southern Africa for over three decades. It sent a multi-racial fact-finding delegation to South Africa and front-line states in 1980. That group met with a broad range of community, church, government and business people—some working to change the system and others working to maintain the status quo. Since then, individuals have traveled to South Africa, facilitating a constant exchange of information. These exchanges have resulted in the following findings:

When the argument is made that Blacks in South Africa will suffer first and most from economic sanctions or corporate withdrawal, one must first of all listen to *who* is making the argument. For example, one of the black South Africans frequently quoted as a critic of apartheid but in favor of continued investments is Chief Gatsha Buthelezi. As chief of the Kwazulu "homeland" and employee of the South African government, he can hardly be considered an objective observer. Numerous other black South Africans who are not beholden to the government, including Nobel Peace Prize winner Bishop Tutu and Dr. Allan Boesak, resident of the World Alliance of Reformed Churches, have spoken out in favor of economic pressure on the government.

Less than 1% of all black South Africans are employed by U.S. companies. The great majority of black South Africans are so far outside the mainstream economy that they would be marginally affected by corporate withdrawal. As one black South African woman put it: "When you are already lying on the floor, you don't have far to fall."

The purpose of divestment actions is not to create "economic chaos" in South Africa. It is widely recognized that it would take considerable amount of corporate withdrawal and time for the economy to be disrupted in any real way. The purpose of economic sanctions of any kind is to send a *strong, clear message* to the South African government that it must begin *now* to negotiate with the legitimate black leaders (Nelson Mandela and others who have been imprisoned for years) of the disenfranchised majority, both on the grievances which have prompted school boycotts and outbreaks of violence, as well as the ongoing denial of power-sharing to the black majority....

Source: American Friends Service Committee Press Release, January 25, 1985, Portland Area Program Office, http://AFSC.org (accessed February 15, 2009).

QUESTIONS

1. How did the AFSC's program of "liberation pacifism" extend to the problem of apartheid in south Africa?
2. According to this document why would the program of divestment not bring "economic chaos" to South Africans, especially the dispossessed? How was this document intended to challenge the U.S. government's position on the matter?
3. How did critics of apartheid see economics and human rights as being related to peace?

Document 5: ACT-UP
Why We Fight (1988)

Faced with the growing epidemic of AIDS (acquired immune deficiency syndrome), ACT-UP was formed in 1987 to launch a concerted campaign to call pubic attention to the crisis. The excerpted speech below by Vito

Russo, co-founder of ACT-UP and author of *The Celluloid Closet* (1981), was delivered at ACT-UP demonstrations in Albany, New York, on May 9, 1988, and at the Department of Health and Human Services, Washington, D.C., on October 9, 1988.

A friend of mine in New York City has a half-fare transit card, which means that you get on buses and subways for half price. And the other day, when he showed his card to the token attendant, the attendant asked what his disability was and he said, I have AIDS. And the attendant said, no you don't, if you had AIDS, you'd be home dying. And so, I wanted to speak out today as a person with AIDS who is not dying. . . .

So, if I'm dying from anything, I'm dying from homophobia. If I'm dying from anything, I'm dying from racism. If I'm dying from anything, it's from indifference and red tape, because these are the things that are preventing an end to the crisis. . . . And, especially, if I'm dying from anything, I'm dying from the sensationalism of newspapers and magazines and television shows, which are interested in me, as a human interest story—only as long as I'm willing to be a helpless victim, but not if I'm fighting for my life.

If I'm dying from anything—I'm dying from the fact that not enough rich, white, heterosexual men have gotten AIDS for anybody to give a ____. You know, living with AIDS in this country is like living in the twilight zone. Living with AIDS is like living through a war which is happening only for those people who happen to be in the trenches. Every time a shell explodes, you look around and you discover that you've lost more of your friends, but nobody else notices. It isn't happening to them. They're walking the street as though we weren't living through some sort of nightmare. And only you can hear the screams of the people who are dying and their cries for help. No one else seems to be noticing.

And it's worse than a war, because during a war people are united in a shared experience. This war has not united us, it's divided us. It's separated those of us with AIDS and those of us who fight for people with AIDS from the rest of the population.

Two and a half years ago, I picked up *Life* magazine, and I read an editorial which said, "it's time to pay attention, because this disease is now beginning to strike the rest of us." It was as if I wasn't the one holding the magazine in my hand. And since then, nothing has changed to alter the perception that AIDS is not happening to the real people in this country. . . .

If it is true that gay men and IV drug users are the populations at risk for this disease, then we have a right to demand that education and prevention be targeted specifically to these people. And it is not happening. We are being allowed to die, while low risk populations are being panicked—not educated, panicked—into believing that we deserve to die.

Why are we here together today? We're here because it is happening to us, and we do give a ____. And if there were more of us AIDS wouldn't be what it is at this moment in history. It's more than just a disease, which ignorant people have turned into an excuse to exercise the bigotry they have always felt.

It is more than a horror story, exploited by the tabloids. AIDS is really a test of us, as a people. When future generations ask what we did in this crisis, we're going to have to tell them that we were out here today. And we have to leave the legacy to those generations of people who will come after us.

Someday, the AIDS crisis will be over. Remember that. And when that day comes—when that day has come and gone, there'll be people alive on this earth—gay people and straight people, men and women, black and white, who will hear the story that once there was a terrible disease in this country and all over the world, and that a brave group of people stood up and fought and, in some cases, gave their lives, so that other people might live and be free. . . .

Source: http:/www.actupny.org/documents/whfight.html (accessed April 1, 2009)

QUESTIONS

1. Why do you think the AIDS epidemic was being ignored by most citizens?
2. Why was it important for Vito Russo to deliver this speech and why do you think he compared his campaign to war in the trenches?
3. How did this nonviolent protest highlight the continuing struggle for social justice in the United States?

Document 6: Sharon Hostetler
Old Commitments, New Directions (1993)

Sharon Hostetler, a member of Witness for Peace, recounts the events of April 1983 and later when thirty members of the Carolina Interfaith Task Force on Central America witnessed an attack on a tobacco farm in northern Nicaragua by the contras. Between 1983 and 1993 Witness for Peace organized some 253 delegations that sent 4,500 people to see the war in Nicaragua firsthand. The organization maintained the longest nonviolent presence in a war zone in U.S. history. In this essay, Hostetler reflects on how Witness for Peace attempted to save lives and prevent physical destruction.

*O*ur commitments are deep; they are rooted in our hearts where we ponder the pain and injustices we see reflected in the eyes of a people who have suffered for centuries the results of U.S. policies which have waged war on the poor. Thousands of us have come to Nicaragua since the beginning of Witness for Peace in 1983. We came to bear witness and to respond by going into a war zone to say "no" to an immoral policy. . . .

Our commitments found expression in nonviolent actions directed at stopping the war and changing our government's foreign policy toward Nicaragua. We accompanied people in cooperatives and communities when they predicted imminent attacks. We traveled roads that often held the threat of ambushes and land mines. We accompanied priests and nuns who knew that to continue their mission could mean death. We drove an ambulance in an area where it was not safe for a Nicaraguan to drive. We chartered a small fishing boat and headed out to the Pacific Ocean to confront a U.S. warship, protesting that Nicaragua was not a threat to the security of the United States. We set out on a mission of peace on the beautiful San Juan River knowing that contra soldiers had orders to fire on any boat that passed beyond a certain point. We vowed that we were willing to risk our lives for peace as many had risked their lives for war.

Our deep commitments were not a guarantee of success. We were not able to stop the suffering, death and destruction that the U.S. policy of low-intensity warfare imposed on the Nicaraguan people. The U.S. Congress continued funding the contras until the Arias Central American Peace Plan was signed by the five Central American presidents. We were not successful in stopping the economic embargo or the blocking of loans from international lending agencies. Those policies changed only after the U.S. massively intervened in the 1990 elections and ensured the election of "our" candidate.

After the elections, one of our partners declared: "Witness for Peace needs to reflect on the true meaning of peace. The military war is over, but there is still violence—unemployment, poverty, and instability. Is this peace? Witness for Peace needs to reflect on the actual U.S. policy toward this poor country and educate the people in the U.S. about its effects on the people of Nicaragua. . . . "

Source: Sharon Hostetler, "Witness for Peace," *Witness for Peace Newsletter* 10, no. 2 (Summer 1993): 4–5.

QUESTIONS

1. How did Witness for Peace expand its humanitarian efforts for justice beyond the call for ending the violent war?
2. How did these nonviolent protestors risk their lives in the name of peace and justice?
3. According to Hostetler, what is the real meaning of peace?

Document 7: Jeff Paterson
Public Statement (1990)

Although the Persian Gulf War was a decisive military victory for the United States and its coalition forces, there were a number of American military personnel who registered their objections to it. During the buildup and the war itself in 1990–1991 more than 2,000 active-duty members and reservists applied for conscientious objector status. Sixty of them were court-martialed for refusing to deploy overseas. Three cities in California—San Francisco, Berkeley, and Oakland—declared themselves sanctuaries for Gulf War objectors. Here Corporal Paterson explains why he refused to serve in combat.

My name is Jeff Paterson.

I'm a CPL in the USMC.

I have served 3 yr., 10 mo. in the military with a relatively clean record, have received various awards, and have consistently received above average job proficiency and conduct ratings from my superiors.

I have seven months left to serve before my End of Active Service Date. My MOS (military occupation specialty) is that of a Field Artillery Fire Direction Controller, however, for the past two years I have been able to keep myself posted as a supply clerk to reduce the internal conflicts within myself. The recent moves by our government in the Persian Gulf has [sic] made my attempt to fulfill the remainder of my contract in a benign way impossible.

As we speak tens of thousands of servicemen are being mobilized to defend for the first time in American memory a blatantly imperialistic economic interest stripped of the State Department's beloved specter of international communism. Although the U.S. is facing off against a truly despicable man in Saddam Hussein, the reality is that U.S. foreign policy created this monster.

It was the U.S. who tacitly endorsed the Iraqi invasion of Iran ten years ago.

It was the U.S. and West Germany who sold Hussein chemical weapons throughout the war.

It was the U.S. who remained silent when Hussein used these weapons on his own populations. . . .

Although there are great differences in this interventionist policy and that of U.S. support for the death squad regimes in El Salvador and Guatemala, there is the underlining motive of corporate profit throughout. Unfortunately the American people have fell [sic] for a big lie—that corporate interests are always in the best interests of the people, this is rarely true. What is the equation that balances human lives and corporate profits?

In my opinion no such equation exists, except in the minds of those that are preparing to fight this war.

The United States has no moral ground to stand on in the Persian Gulf.

We created this monster and pointed him in this direction. . . .

I cannot and will not be a pawn in America's power plays for profits and oil in the middle east. I will resist my scheduled departure, tentatively Sunday, by immediately filing for conscientious objector status, and physically refusing to board the plane. And of course if I am drug out into the Saudi desert, I will refuse to fight.

Source: Fax by Jeff Paterson of the U.S. Marine Corps, released at press conference on August 16, 1990, Staughton Lynd and Alice Lynd, eds. *Nonviolence in America: A Documentary History.* Maryknoll, NY: Orbis Books, 1998, pp. 481–482.

QUESTIONS

1. What are the objections to this war raised by Paterson?
2. If Saddam Hussein is a "truly despicable man" in Paterson's eyes, why was he unwilling to fight against him?
3. Is there a contradiction in the actions of people like Paterson who volunteer for the military and then refuse to fight? Does he make a valid case for being a conscientious objector?

Document 8: Joanne Landy, Thomas Harrison, and Jennifer Scarlott
We Oppose Both Saddam Hussein and the U.S. War on Iraq **(2003)**

The September 11, 2001, attacks on the World Trade Center and the Pentagon emboldened the Bush Administration to undertake a hawkish approach to military intervention in both Afghanistan and Iraq. Although the military response in Afghanistan was largely supported by the American populace, intervention in Iraq was greeted with much more skepticism. The authors of this document, distributed prior to the "Shock and Awe" campaign in April 2003, were the co-directors of the Campaign for Peace and Democracy. Signed by thousands of Americans, primarily activists and intellectuals, this petition represents the increasingly important role the Internet plays in mobilizing a new type of "imagined community" based on peace and justice.

$\mathcal{W}$e oppose the impending U.S.-led war on Iraq, which threatens to inflict vast suffering and destruction, while exacerbating rather than resolving threats to regional and global peace. Saddam Hussein is a tyrant who should be removed from power, both for the good of the Iraqi people and for the security of neighboring countries. However, it is up to the Iraqi people themselves to oust Saddam Hussein, dismantle his police state regime, and democratize their country. People in the United State can be of immense help in this effort—not by supporting military intervention, but by building a strong peace movement and working to ensure that our government pursues a consistently democratic and just foreign policy.

We do not believe that the goal of the approaching war against Iraq is to bring democracy to the Iraqis, nor that it will produce this result. Instead, the Bush administration's aim is to expand and solidify U.S. predominance in the Middle East, at the cost of tens of thousands of civilian lives if necessary. This war is about U.S. political, military and economic power, about seizing control of oilfields and about strengthening the United States as the enforcer of an inhumane global status quo.…

Indeed, the U.S. could address these problems [terrorism and weapons of mass destruction] only by doing the *opposite* of what it is doing today—that is by:

Renouncing the use of military intervention…and withdrawing U.S. troops from the Middle East.…

Opposing, and ending U.S. complicity in, all forms of terrorism worldwide—not just by Al Qaeda, Palestinian suicide bombers and Chechen hostage takers, but also by Colombian paramilitaries, the Israeli military in the Occupied Territories and Russian counterinsurgency forces in Chechnya.

Ending the cruel sanctions on Iraq, which inflict massive harm on the civilian population.

Supporting the right of national self-determination for all peoples in the Middle East, including the Kurds, Palestinians and Israeli Jews. Ending one-sided support for Israel in the Palestinian-Israeli conflict.

Taking unilateral steps toward renouncing weapons of mass destruction, including nuclear weapons, and vigorously promoting international disarmament treaties.

…Initiating a major foreign aid program directed at popular rather than corporate needs.

These initiatives, taken together, would constitute a truly *democratic* foreign policy. Only such a policy could begin to reverse the mistrust and outright hatred felt by so much of the world's population toward the U.S.…

Weapons of mass destruction endanger us all and must be eliminated. But a war against Iraq is not the answer. War threatens massive harm to Iraqi civilians, will add to the ranks of terrorists throughout the Muslim world, and will encourage international bullies to pursue further acts of aggression. Everyone is legitimately concerned about terrorism; however, the path to genuine security involves promoting democracy, social justice and respect for the right of self-determination along with disarmament, weapons-free-zones and inspections. Of all the countries in the world, the United States possesses by far the most powerful arsenal of weapons of mass destruction. If the U.S. were to initiate a democratic foreign policy and take serious steps toward disarmament, it would be able to encourage global disarmament as well as regional demilitarization in the Middle East. . . .

Ordinary Iraqis, and people everywhere, need to know that there is *another* America, made up of those who both recognize the urgent need for democratic change in the Middle East and reject our government's militaristic and imperial foreign policy. By signing this statement we declare our intention to work for a new democratic U.S. foreign policy. That means helping to rein in the war-makers and building the most powerful antiwar movement possible, and at the same time forging links of solidarity and concrete support for democratic forces in Iraq and throughout the Middle East.

We refuse to accept the inevitability of war on Iraq despite the enormous military juggernaut that has been put in place, and we declare our commitment to work with others in this country and abroad to avert it. And if war should start, we will do all in our power to end it immediately.

Source: Timothy Patrick McCarthy and John McMillan, eds. *The Radical Reader: A Documentary History of the American Radical Tradition.* New York: The New Press, 2003, pp. 681–685.

QUESTIONS

1. In what ways did the authors of this petition promote the goals of peace and social justice above military intervention in Iraq?
2. How were their arguments both similar to and different from those who opposed the 1991 war against Saddam Hussein?
3. What new "democratic" U.S. foreign policy did the authors of this petition envision? According to this statement how is the U.S. acting as the "enforcer of an inhumane global status quo" by going to war against Saddam Hussein?

Document 9: David Cortright
What We Do Now: An Agenda for Peace (2003)

David Cortright, an academician, policy analyst, and president of the Fourth Freedom Forum, has published a number of scholarly works on soldiers in the military and the peace movement. In this essay published in *The Nation* shortly after the war began in Iraq, Cortright sets forth an alternative security policy for the United States. His solution is based on multilateralism—the collaboration of many nations to achieve security and peace.

What the Antiwar Movement Wants

*P*rotect the innocent. The United States should provide massive humanitarian assistance and economic aid for the Iraqi people and other vulnerable populations in the region. We should support the reconstruction and development of Iraq. This assistance should be administered by civilian agencies, not the Pentagon. We should also demand, or if necessary provide, an accurate accounting of the civilian dead.

Support our men and women in the armed forces. We regret that their Commander in Chief has sent them on an ill-advised and unnecessary mission, but we respect and thank them for their service. We urge special support for the families of service members and reservists who have been sent to the Persian Gulf. We call for greater efforts to address the medical problems that will result from service in the gulf. More than 167,000 veterans are currently on disability as a result of their service in the first Gulf War. We condemn the cuts in veterans' benefits approved by the Republican-controlled Congress and call for increased availability of medical care and other benefits for veterans.

Bring home the troops. We urge the withdrawal of American military forces from Iraq as soon as possible. We oppose the creation of any long-term or permanent U.S. military bases in Iraq.

No war or military threats against Iran. We oppose any attempt to coerce or threaten Iran with military attack. It is no secret that extremists in Washington and Israel favor a military strike against Iran as the next phase in the "war on terror." This would be a further catastrophe for the cause of peace and must be vigorously resisted.

No war for oil. We oppose any U.S. effort to seize control of Iraqi oil or to demand a percentage of Iraqi oil revenues. Ownership of Iraqi oil should remain with the Iraqi people. Iraq was the first Arab nation to nationalize its petroleum resources, and it must be allowed to retain control over this wealth to rebuild its economy and society.

Peace in the Middle East. The United States should give active support to a genuine peace process between Israel and the Palestinians. We should pressure both sides to accept a peace settlement that ends the violence and creates two sovereign and viable states.

Support for regional disarmament. The Gulf War cease-fire resolution of 1991 specified that the disarmament of Iraq was to be the first step toward the creation in the Middle East of a "zone free from weapons of mass destruction." The elimination of weapons of mass destruction in Iraq should thus lead to their elimination throughout the region.

There Are Alternatives

Our response to war and military occupation in Iraq must also include a longer-term vision of an alternative U.S. security policy. The Bush Administration claims that the deadly nexus of terrorism and weapons of mass destruction requires a radical new foreign policy of military pre-emption and the unilateral assertion of American technological power. This is the policy being implemented in Iraq. We must offer an alternative vision, one that takes seriously the terrorism and proliferation threat but that provides a safer, less costly and ultimately more successful strategy for countering these dangers.

The outlines of our alternative strategy are visible in the policy proposals we have suggested in the current debate over Iraq. We support the disarmament of Iraq, North Korea and other nations regarded by the international community as potential proliferators. We favor vigorous UN weapons inspections to verify disarmament. We call on our government to work diplomatically through the UN Security Council. We endorse targeted sanctions (restrictions on the finances and travel of designated elites, and arms embargoes) and other means of containing recalcitrant states. We endorse lifting sanctions and providing incentives as means of inducing compliance. We support the international campaign against terrorism and urge greater cooperative efforts to prosecute and cut off the funding of those responsible for the September 11 attacks.

At the same time, we recognize that disarmament ultimately must be universal. The disarmament of Iraq must be tied to regional disarmament, which in turn must be linked to global disarmament. The double standard of the United States and other nuclear states, in which we propose to keep these deadliest of weapons, indefinitely while denying them to the rest of the world, cannot endure. The Nuclear Nonproliferation Treaty of 1968 was based on a bargain—the nuclear powers' agreeing to pursue disarmament in exchange for the rest of the world's renouncing the nuclear option. The longer the United States and its nuclear partners refuse their obligation to disarm, the greater the likelihood that the nonproliferation regime will collapse. The only true security against nuclear dangers is an enforceable ban on *all* nuclear weapons. Chemical and biological weapons are already banned. The far greater danger of nuclear weapons also must be subject to universal prohibition.

The Regulation of Force

A global prohibition against all weapons of mass destruction is the best protection against the danger of terrorists' acquiring and using them. In effect, the disarmament obligations being imposed on Iraq must be applied to the entire world. All nuclear, chemical and biological weapons and long-range missiles should be banned everywhere, by all nations. This is the path to a safer and more secure future.

This is not a pacifist vision that eschews all uses of military force. The threat of force is sometimes a necessary component of coercive diplomacy. In some circumstances the actual use of force—in a targeted and narrow fashion, with authorization from the UN Security Council or regional security bodies—may be necessary. In contrast with the policy of the Bush Administration, however, the proposed approach would allow the threat or use of force only as a last resort, when all other peaceful diplomatic means have been exhausted, and only with the explicit authorization of the Security Council or regional security organizations. In no circumstance would the United States or any other nation have the right to mount a military invasion to overthrow another government for the ostensible purpose of achieving disarmament. Rather, the United States would respect the Charter of the UN and would strive to achieve disarmament and settle the differences among nations through peaceful diplomatic means.

Our immediate challenge in implementing these short- and long-term objectives is to change the political direction and leadership of the United States. In the upcoming political debates we must devote our energies to building support for our alternative foreign-policy vision and creating a mass political constituency that can hold candidates accountable to this vision. Our chances of preventing future military disasters depend in the short run on removing the Bush Administration from office and electing a new political leadership dedicated to international cooperation and peace. This is a formidable political challenge. It will be extremely difficult to accomplish by November 2004. We must begin to organize for this challenge now, however, and we must remain committed to this objective into the future, planning now for the additional election cycles that will probably be necessary to realize our goals. We must also recognize the enormity of the challenge we face in diminishing the unelected power of the national security establishment, which functions as a shadow government regardless of who is in office. These great challenges will be met only by a sustained, massive citizens' movement dedicated to the long-term challenge of fundamentally reshaping America's role in the world. The work begins now, as the military invasion of Iraq continues. We have no time to mourn. A lifetime of organizing and education lies ahead.

Source: David Cortright, "What Can We Do Now: An Agenda for Peace," *The Nation* (April 21, 2003).

QUESTIONS

1. What alternative strategies does the author recommend in lieu of preemptive militarism?
2. What are Cortright's ideas about how to rid the world of weapons of mass destruction?
3. What is the most pressing political action the peace movement in the United States must take to ensure an end to the Iraq war and all future wars? How can this be accomplished?

Document 10: *Statement of the Antiwar Grannies (October 17, 2005).*

Grandmothers Against the War was founded by then 76-year-old Joan Wile in 2003. This group of courageous and determined women staged a number of daring protests from demonstrating in front of the Armed Forces Recruiting Center in Times Square in New York to marching in front of the White House and the Pentagon. Their actions gained them national attention. Below is their explanation of why they sought to enlist in the armed services.

*W*e are grandmothers heartbroken over the huge loss of life and limb in Iraq. We feel it is our patriotic duty to enlist in the United States military today in order to replace our grandchildren who have been deployed there far too long and are anxious to come home now while they are still alive and whole. By this action, we are not supporting the use of military force in Iraq—in fact, we are totally against it. But inasmuch as it exists, our goal in joining up is only to protect young people from further death and maiming.

We grandmothers have all the privilege of living long lives and are willing to put ourselves in harm's way so that our own and other people's grandchildren will have a chance to enjoy full lives as we have.

We believe these young men and women are being used as cannon fodder in an illegal and totally unjustified war against a nation which posed no threat to us. They were sent there on a web of lies and deceit resulting in untold harm to them and countless innocent Iraqi people.

We hope that by enlisting today we can help bring about the early end of this immoral occupation and the return of our brave young people to their homes and families . . . now.

Source: Joan Wile, _Grandmothers Against the War: Getting off our Fannies and Standing Up for Peace._ New York: Citadel Press, 2008, p. 15.

QUESTIONS

1. What made these grandmothers take the steps they did to protest the war?
2. Would their actions be likely to have attracted public sympathy? Why or why not?
3. Do you agree with their characterization of the war in Iraq as illegal, immoral, and unjustified?

Document 11: Harvard Darfur Action Group
Divestment as a Tool to End Genocide (2007)

As the genocide in Darfur came to light, students organized to get their colleges and universities to divest from companies that did business with the government of Sudan. A group organized by students at Harvard, the Harvard Darfur Action Group, was one of many chapters that formed a national organization called STAND: Student Anti-Genocide Coalition. Their goals included raising awareness of the genocide taking place in the Sudan, waging campaigns to help end it, and supporting displaced citizens. Here they explain the reasoning behind the tactic of divestment.

*G*enocide and divestment: Since the genocide in Darfur began in 2003, the world has attempted to exert pressure on the Sudanese government with minimal success. The Sudanese government relies heavily on foreign investment to fund its ongoing genocide. In addition, the Sudanese Government has shown itself to be responsive to financial pressure in the past. Given this particular confluence of factors, Darfur presents a special case in which institutions can influence the Government of Sudan by pressuring the companies that are funding the genocidal campaign to sell ("divest") shares that they own in the companies operating in the Sudan...

What is divestment? Divestment is the process of selling shares of a company in which Harvard University is invested. This tool can be used as a moral statement that Harvard does not support the actions of the company that is financially complicit in a genocidal regime. Harvard University has an endowment managed by Harvard Corporation invested in both domestic and international companies from a range of industries. Due to a United States Executive Order, no US corporations are able to invest directly in the Sudan; however, some of Harvard's investments are in foreign corporations that are engaged in business with the Government of Sudan. These are the companies that are considered for possible divestment.

Harvard's role: Harvard University can make a statement that it will not be morally complicit in the companies' affairs by withdrawing its funds from those companies. As a result, this action or the mere threat of divestment will encourage the companies to engage with the Government of Sudan to end the genocide or cause them to withdraw operations and significant profit margins from Khartoum.

Hasn't Harvard University already divested? Yes, over the past two years, the University has pursued ad-hoc divestment from its shares in Petrochina and Sinopec, citing in the case of Petrochina that "there is a compelling case for action in these special circumstances, in light of the terrible situation still unfolding in Darfur and the leading role played by PetroChina's parent company in the Sudanese oil industry, which is so important to the Sudanese regime." However, a targeted model would be more a more appropriate response to the most egregious companies operating in Sudan. The model is well-researched and road-tested, with other universities and the State of California having already implemented the model.

What is targeted divestment? Targeted divestment affects only companies that meet very stringent criteria; companies that (1) have a business relationship with the government of Sudan or are involved in a government-sponsored project and, (2) impart minimal benefit to Sudanese civilians, and (3) have demonstrated no substantial corporate governance policy regarding the Darfur situation and (4) fail to respond to attempts at shareholder engagement

Has Harvard University ever divested this thoroughly in the past? Yes, Harvard University divested during both the South African Apartheid and from tobacco industries. In 1984, the University divested from companies that received the lowest ratings in the Sullivan Principles until the end of Apartheid, and the University divested from all companies in the tobacco industry indefinitely.

Source: http://www.harvarddivest.com/whydivest.html (accessed May 30, 2009)

QUESTIONS

1. Why were these students convinced that divestment could help to end the genocide in Sudan?
2. What did they mean by "targeted divestment"? What was the purpose of defining this in a limited way?
3. How is this movement an extension of earlier peace activists' efforts regarding social justice?

Document 12:   Howard Zinn
Terrorism and War (2002)

Howard Zinn is best known for his work, *A People's History of the United States* (1980). Before the Vietnam War he was very active in the civil rights movement, participating in protest marches in the south. During the Vietnam War he traveled to Hanoi as part of an antiwar protest group. His commitment to peace and justice developed out of his own World War II experiences as a bombardier pilot. Here he discusses how the shadow of the Vietnam War affected views of the Iraq War.

A number of people have speculated that the Bush administration is trying to kick the "Vietnam syndrome" in this war, to give greater legitimacy to U.S. militarism.

The Vietnam syndrome is an interesting phenomenon. Presumably the Vietnam syndrome refers to the fact that we fought a long war in Vietnam, which turned into a more and more unpopular war that the American people finally did not support. As a result, the American government had to withdraw ignominiously but obviously with the determination not to allow this defeat to be repeated again or to stand as a sign of the weakness of the American empire. So, the notion of a Vietnam syndrome became bandied about, this fear of engaging in a war that the American people would not support.

I think the ghost of Vietnam still remains. Americans are generally reluctant to go to war until the president goes into action and then the media go into action and they create an atmosphere in which war seems justified. The *New York Times* had an article asking if the United States was getting into "another Vietnam" in Afghanistan. And the *Times* ran a very interesting letter from a former officer at the American Embassy in Vietnam about the announcement that the U.S. government was sending more "advisers" into Afghanistan. He asked, "Are we now in for the same kind of subterfuge until we have another six-figure number of combat troops searching the caves of Afghanistan—with perhaps an equally distressing consequence?" And now the United States is sending "advisers," including eighty-five U.S. Special Forces training officers who have been "dispatched to help battle an Islamic insurgency," to the Philippines. The *Boston Globe* wrote that "[t]o Americans who remember the origins of the U.S. war in Vietnam, there is something unnerving about the news that the Pentagon is sending 660 military advisers to help Philippine armed forces overcome the radical Islamic group known as Abu Sayyaf."

So, immediately after the Vietnam War, the U.S. government methodically set about trying to eliminate the Vietnam syndrome, that is, trying to make wars palatable once again, as they had been after World War II. For many people, war was no longer acceptable, and the government had to do something to make war acceptable again.

The Gulf War was a more serious attempt to undo the Vietnam syndrome. Unlike the Mayaguez affair or the invasion of Grenada, the Gulf War was a full-scale military assault. The government took great pains to make sure that it did not have the same result as the war in Vietnam, that is, the building up of an antiwar movement. Although Iraq was really a fifth-rate military power, the U.S. government exaggerated the military strength of Iraq in a propaganda campaign designed to show that Saddam Hussein is really a formidable foe; if we defeat Iraq, we have done something important. And the Bush administration makes sure that the press is not allowed to see what is happening, because they are horrified by the fact that during the Vietnam War the press began to report the atrocities we were committing. Then they decide we have to end this war quickly, so after an air campaign and a short ground campaign, the Iraqi forces crumble very quickly, and the United States declares victory.

In fact, right after the U.S. defeats Iraq, Bush says specifically in a radio address, "The specter of Vietnam has been buried forever in the desert sands of the Arabian Peninsula." A wonderfully poetic statement by this president. So presumably the Vietnam syndrome is buried, which means that the American people will now accept war. I think there is some truth to this. The American people did support the Gulf War. By 1991, the Vietnam War was fifteen years behind us, and the American people generally believed the propaganda that we had gone to war to save Kuwait.

But we were not really allowed to think about the real issues behind the American war on Iraq. We are not allowed to think about what was behind the so-called sympathy for Kuwait. We are not allowed to think about oil. When legislation giving President Bush authorization to go into Iraq was being debated in the Senate, some young people on the balcony chanted, "No blood for oil!" Of course, the protesters were immediately hustled out of the Senate chamber. The American people were not supposed to think about oil as a basis for the war.

So, yes, the American people mostly believed the administration's arguments about the need to act against this tyrant Saddam Hussein, and therefore Bush had some basis for saying that the Vietnam syndrome had been buried. But I don't think it's completely true. I think there is still a memory of Vietnam in the American population, which cannot be put away. And whenever we engage in war, there always is a question: "Will this be another Vietnam?" That question does come up in the press, and people do think about it.

I think Abraham Lincoln was right. You can fool some of the people all of the time, and you can fool all of the people some of the time. But you can't fool all of the people all of the time. People in the United States woke up to what was happening to blacks in the South, and the civil rights movement became a national movement. People woke up to what was happening in Vietnam, and we had a great national antiwar movement.

So never think that because of the polls or the news anchors, they're going to have it their way and people will always be fooled.

Source: Howard, Zinn. *Terrorism and War.* New York: Seven Stones Press, 2002, pp. 104–110.

QUESTIONS

1. Briefly explain why the U.S. government wanted to get rid of the "Vietnam Syndrome."
2. What were the variety of concerns about Iraq becoming "another Vietnam"? In hindsight, does this seem a useful comparison?
3. What does Zinn think was really at stake in the war(s) on Iraq?

Conclusion

The struggle for peace and justice represents the best in the American democratic tradition. The documents in this collection highlight the editors' thesis that the organized peace effort and its allied components vigorously worked for a better America and more just world. While often accused of being unpatriotic, peace and justice activists in fact often encouraged leaders and policymakers to live up to the traditions established more than two hundred years ago. In urging an end to war and imperialism, economic inequality, and racial and gender discrimination, among other reforms, these tireless advocates did their best to create a better world for future generations.

Advocates for peace and justice relied heavily on their consciences and their convictions to guide them, often in the face of great obstacles. Quite often their vision was scorned and derided, and at various times in our history they were beaten or imprisoned. Such treatment itself is troubling in a society that prides itself on freedom of thought and expression. But even in the face of stiff resistance and threats of physical violence, even death, peace and justice activists continued their efforts to make the U.S. and the world a better place in which to live and prosper.

The documents also illustrate that the struggle for peace and justice is based on far more than a naive vision of a world without war; advocates themselves have continuously extended their analysis of society to encompass far more than simply opposing war and armaments. Struggles against slavery, support for women's equality and the rights of working people,

---

challenges to westward expansion, which nearly decimated native peoples, campaigns to end racial discrimination and segregation, save the environment, challenge the mistreatment of gays, and champion divestment are also part of the larger story of movements for peace and justice in American history. They have not only criticized government policy but in many instances, as in Benjamin Rush's plan for a federal-level department of peace, offered concrete alternatives.

Peace and justice advocates' determination to address structural violence as well as war remains one of the great contributions of peace as reform in America. They have self-consciously injected a dose of idealism to counter entrenched institutions such as militarism and social injustice. In our coauthored textbook *A History of the American Peace Movement from Colonial Times to the Present,* we asked where would American society be today if it were not for the efforts of peace and justice advocates in the abolitionist and civil rights crusades? The writings of John Woolman, William Lloyd Garrison, Frederick Douglass, Angelina Grimké, Bayard Rustin, Ida B. Wells, Langston Hughes, James Baldwin, and Martin Luther King, Jr., clearly illustrate the connection between peace and social justice. How far along would the women's rights and feminist movements be if it were not for the contributions of peace activists who criticized the inherent structural violence in American society that caused women to be treated as second-class citizens? One only has to look at the sentiments expressed in the views of Sojourner Truth, the Seneca Falls declaration, Julia Ward Howe, Charlotta Bass, Barbara Deming, and the statement of the National Organization for Women to understand how troubling this issue was for those who wanted to make America an equal and just society. Where would we be today were it not for those courageous individuals who practiced the act of nonviolence in the face of serious entrenched bureaucratic resistance and oppressive rule? Individuals like Anthony Benezet, Bayard Rustin, A.J. Muste, Martin Luther King, Jr., Albert Bigelow, Jessie Wallace Hughan, Cesar Chavez, and the antiwar grannies, among others, are shining examples of American citizens who used their acts of conscience in the name of peace and freedom. The movement has had its theorists, too, developing ideas about the causes of war and how to use nonviolence and civil disobedience to counter war and injustice. The writings of Henry David Thoreau, Richard Gregg, and Martin Luther King, Jr., continue to be read by those who seek alternatives to violence. What about those who linked peace to the cause of labor in the name of justice, such as Elihu Burritt, William Dean Howells, Eugene Debs, A.J. Muste, Joel Seidman, and Angelo Herndon? Clearly their words and actions were important in promoting workers' rights. How about William James's notion of an army of workers for domestic development as an alternative to war as an outlet for aggression? The call for national service other than military, currently in vogue, is a reminder of what James believed could be accomplished. Lastly, what about the numerous individuals and organizations who protested wars throughout our history as well as the development of weapons of mass destruction? The views conveyed by Dr. Benjamin Rush, Noah Worcester, Charles Sumner, Mark Twain, David Starr Jordan, Jane Addams, Randolph Bourne, Devere Allen, Women Strike for Peace, Vietnam Veterans Against the War, Physicians for Social Responsibility, among others, remind us that this has been a long struggle to which many dedicated and brilliant writers and activists have given voice.

In some instances their message was heard, as they helped to bring an end to the Mexican War and later the Vietnam War, and to get nuclear test ban treaties and missile reductions approved. They sincerely believed that they presented the more realistic alternative for the preservation of humankind than did the government and the military. It is also worth noting that many of the changes we take for granted—an end to slavery and segregation, recognition of labor unions, respect for the rights of Native Americans, concern for the natural environment, greater equality for women, and a movement away from reliance on a doomsday scenario—were largely attributable to these courageous advocates for peace and social justice.

Simply put, so long as there is economic and social injustice at home and military conflicts overseas, the peace movement will continue to promote alternatives. Based on the historical record and the written documents selected for discussion in this book, the efforts of those peace and justice proponents should not be forgotten. Their role in shaping American society deserves our attention. They have done much to merit our respect in their efforts to convince America to live up to its ideals.

Photos

Photo 1: Nineteenth Century Antiwar Postcard. Papers of Elihu Burritt (Courtesy of Swarthmore College Peace Collection).

For the People, pages 311–322

Universal Military Training
A Debate:

Henry L. West   v.   Charles T. Hallinan

of the

**National
Security
League**

of the

**American Union
Against
Militarism**

"God help us if we should prove as weak as we are rich!"
—*Mr. West, p. 4.*

Photo 2:   World War I Pamphlet Cover of American Union Against Militarism.
Records of American Union Against Militarism (Courtesy of Swarthmore College
Peace Collection).

Photo 3: Peace and Disarmament Parade in New York City, 1916. General/Misc. Portraits Collection (Courtesy of Swarthmore College Peace Collection).

Photo 4: 1931 Peace and Disarmament Demonstration. Papers of Katherine Devereaux Blake (Courtesy of Swarthmore College Peace Collection).

Photo 5: July 12, 1935 Peace Demonstration in Massachusetts. Misc. Events, Demonstrations (Courtesy of Swarthmore College Peace Collection).

Photo 6: Brookwood Labor Players Tour Bus (Archives of Labor and Urban Affairs, Wayne State University).

Photo 7: World War II Civilian Public Service Camp [Possibly Coshocton, PA.]. Personal Papers of Civilian Public Service Camps (Courtesy of Swarthmore College Peace Collection).

Photo 8: Richard Gregg speaking at a Civilian Public Service Camp during World War II. General/Misc. Portraits Collection (Courtesy of Swarthmore College Peace Collection).

Photo 9: 1946 Protest calling for Amnesty for imprisoned war objectors. Records of Committee for Amnesty for All Objectors to War and Conscription (Courtesy of Swarthmore College Peace Collection).

Photo 10: Bayard Rustin teaching at School of Nonviolence. Papers of Bayard Rustin (Courtesy of Swarthmore College Peace Collection).

Photo 11: Journey of Reconciliation, The First Freedom Ride, Richmond, Virginia, April 1947. Records of Congress of Racial Equality (Courtesy of Swarthmore College Peace Collection).

Photo 12: 1950s Anti-Hydrogen Bomb peace display in shop window. General/ Misc. Portraits Collection (Courtesy of Swarthmore College Peace Collection).

Photo 13: 1956 Civil Defense protest in New York City. General/Misc. Portraits Collection (Courtesy of Swarthmore College Peace Collection.

Photo 14: Anti-Vietnam War Protest in Nation's Capitol. Papers of Clergy and Laity Concerned about Vietnam (Courtesy of Swarthmore College Peace Collection).

Photo 15: A.J. Muste Memorial Float, 1967 Peace demonstration. General/Misc. Portraits Collection (Courtesy of Swarthmore College Peace Collection).

Photo 16: Philip and Daniel Berrigan burning draft records during 1968 peace protest. General/Misc. Portraits Collection (Courtesy of Swarthmore College Peace Collection).

Photo 17: Late 1970s Civil Disobedience Protest at the Pentagon. Records of Mobilization for Survival (Courtesy of Swarthmore College Peace Collection).

Photo 18: Seabrook, New Hampshire, Clamshell Alliance Project. Records of Clamshell Alliance (Courtesy of Swarthmore College Peace Collection).

Photo 19: BOOTS 2007 Anti-Iraq War Demonstration, Washington, D.C. Photo Courtesy of Diane Lent.

References

Abernathy, Ralph David. *And the Walls Came Tumbling Down: An Autobiography.* New York: Harper & Row, 1989.

Adams, Judith Porter. ed. *Peacework: Oral Histories of Women Peace Activists.* Boston: G.K. Hall, 1992.

Addams, Jane. *Peace and Bread in Time of War.* New York: Macmillan Co., 1922.

Allen, Devere. *The Fight for Peace.* 2 vols. New York: Macmillan, 1931. Reprint, New York: Garland Publishing, 1971.

Allen, Devere. ed. *Pacifism in the Modern World.* Garden City, NY: Doubleday, Doran, 1929.

Alonso, Harriet Hyman. *Peace as a Women's Issue: A History of the U.S. Movement for World Peace and Women's Rights.* Syracuse, NY: Syracuse University Press, 1993.

Alonso, Harriet Hyman. *Growing Up Abolitionist: The Story of the Garrison Children.* Amherst: University of Massachusetts Press, 2002.

Alpers, Benjamin. *Dictators, Democracy, and American Public Culture: Envisioning the Totalitarian Enemy, 1920s–1950s.* Chapel Hill: University of North Carolina Press, 2003.

Anderson, Carol. *Eyes off the Prize: The UN and the African American Struggle for Human Rights, 1944–1955.* New York: Cambridge University Press, 2003.

Anderson, Jervis B. *A. Philip Randolph: A Biographical Portrait* New York: Harcourt Brace Jovanovich, 1972.

Anderson, Jervis B. *Bayard Rustin: Troubles I've Seen.* New York: HarperCollins, 1997.

Anderson, Terry H. *The Movement and the Sixties: Protest in America from Greensboro to Wounded Knee.* New York: Oxford University Press, 1995.

Arsenault, Raymond. *Freedom Riders: 1961 and the Struggle for Racial Justice.* New York: Oxford University Press, 2006.

For the People, pages 323–339
Copyright © 2009 by Information Age Publishing

Avrich, Paul. *The Haymarket Tragedy*. Princeton, NJ: Princeton University Press, 1984.

Bacevich, Andrew. ed. *The Long War: A New History of U.S. National Security Policy since World War II*. New York: Columbia University Press, 2007.

Barber, Lucy. *Marching on Washington: the Forging of an American Political Tradition*. Berkeley: University of California Press, 2002.

Bay, Mia. *To Tell the Truth Freely: The Life of Ida B. Wells*. New York: Hill & Wang, 2008.

Beacon, Margaret Hope. *One Woman's Passion for Peace and Freedom: The Life of Mildred Scott Olmstead*. Syracuse, NY: Syracuse University Press, 1993.

Beinart, Peter. *The Good fight: Why Liberals—and Only Liberals—Can Win the War on Terror and Make America Great Again*. New York: HarperCollins, 2006.

Beisner, Robert. *Twelve Against Empire: The Anti-Imperialists, 1898–1900*. New York: McGraw-Hill, 1968.

Bennett, Scott H. *Radical Pacifism: The War Resisters League and Gandhian Nonviolence in America, 1915–1963*. Syracuse, NY: Syracuse University Press, 2003.

Berrigan, Philip. *No More Strangers*. New York: Macmillan & Co., 1965.

Bess, Michael. *Realism, Utopia, and the Mushroom Cloud: Four Activist Intellectuals and the Strategies for Peace, 1945–1989*. Chicago: University of Chicago Press, 2003.

Bills, Scott. *Kent State/May 4: Echoes Through a Decade*. Kent, OH: Kent State University Press, 1988.

Blackwell, Joyce. *No Peace without Freedom: Race and the Women's International League for Peace and Freedom, 1915–1975* Carbondale: Southern Illinois University Press, 2004.

Blau, Justine. *Betty Friedan: Feminist*. New York: Chelsea House Publishers, 1990.

Bloom, Alexander, & Breines, Wini. eds. *Takin' It to the Streets: A Sixties Reader*. New York: Oxford University Press, 1995.

Blum, Edward J. *W.E.B. Du Bois, American Prophet*. Philadelphia: University of Pennsylvania Press, 2007.

Bolt, Ernest C. *Ballots Before Bullets: The War Referendum Approach to Peace in America, 1914–1941*. Charlottesville: University of Virginia Press, 1977.

Bondurant, Joan. *Conquest of Violence: The Gandhian Philosophy of Conflict*. Princeton, NJ: Princeton University Press, 1988.

Booth, Ken, & Wright, Moorehead. eds. *American Thinking about Peace and War*. New York: Barnes & Noble, 1978.

Boyer, Paul. *By the Bomb's Early Light: Thought and Culture at the Dawn of the Atomic Age*. Chapel Hill: University of North Carolina Press, 1994.

Branch, Taylor. *Parting the Waters: America in the King Years, 1954–63*. New York: Simon & Schuster, 1988.

Breines, Wini. *Community and Organization in the New Left, 1962–1968*. New Brunswick, NJ: Rutgers University Press, 1989.

Brinkley, Alan. *The End of Reform: New Deal Liberalism in Recession and War.* New York: Knopf, 1995.

Brinkley, Douglas. *Rosa Parks.* New York. Penguin, 2000.

Brinton, Howard H. *The Peace Testimony of the Society of Friends.* Philadelphia: American Friends Service Committee, 1958.

Brock, Peter. *Pacifism in the United States: From the Colonial Era to the First World War.* Princeton, NJ: Princeton University Press, 1968.

Brock, Peter. ed. *Liberty and Conscience: A Documentary History of the Experiences of Conscientious Objectors in America through the Civil War.* New York: Oxford University Press, 2002.

Brock, Peter, & Young, Nigel. *Twentieth Century Pacifism.* Syracuse, NY: Syracuse University Press, 1999.

Brown, Victoria Bissell. *The Education of Jane Addams.* Philadelphia: University of Pennsylvania Press, 2004.

Buhle, Mari Jo, Buhle, Paul, & Georgakas, Dan. eds. *Encyclopedia of the American Left* Urbana: University of Illinois Press, 1992.

Buhle, Paul. *Marxism in the United States: Remapping the History of the American Left.* rev. ed. New York: Verso, 1991.

Calloway, Colin G. ed. *Our Hearts Fell to the Ground: Plains Indians View of How the West was Lost.* Boston: Bedford/St. Martins, 1996.

Campbell, Kenneth. *A Tail of Two Quagmires: Iraq, Vietnam, and the Hard Lessons of War.* Boulder, CO.: Paradigm Publishers, 2007.

Cancian, Francesca, & Gibson, James W. eds. *Making War/Making Peace: the Social Foundations of Violent Conflict.* Belmont, CA: Wadsworth Publishing Co., 1990.

Carson, Clayborne. *In Struggle: SNCC and the Black Awakening of the 1960s.* Cambridge, MA: Harvard University Press, 1981.

Carson, Clayborne, et al.. eds. *The Autobiography of Martin Luther King, Jr.* New York: Warner Books, 1988.

Caute, David. *The Great Fear: The Anti-Communist Purge under Truman and Eisenhower.* New York: Simon & Schuster, 1978.

Ceplair, Larry. *The Public Years of Sarah and Angelina Grimke : Selected Writings, 1835–1839.* New York: Columbia University Press, 1989.

Chambers, John Whiteclay II. *The Eagle and the Dove: The American Peace Movement and United States Foreign Policy, 1900–1922.* Syracuse, NY: Syracuse University Press, 1991.

Chambers, John Whiteclay II. *To Raise an Army: The Draft Comes to Modern America.* New York: Free Press, 1987.

Chappell, David L. *Inside Agitators: White Southerners in the Civil Rights Movement.* Baltimore: Johns Hopkins University Press, 1994.

Chatfield, Charles. *For Peace and Justice: Pacifism in America, 1914–1941.* Knoxville: University of Tennessee Press, 1971.

Chatfield, Charles. ed. *Peace Movements in America.* New York: Schocken Books, 1973.

Chatfield, Charles, with Kleidman, Robert. *The American Peace Movement: Ideals and Activism.* New York: Twayne Publishers, 1992.

Chatfield, Charles. ed. *Devere Allen: Life and Writings.* New York: Garland Publishers, 1976.

Chatfield, Charles, & Ilukhina, Ruzanna, eds. *Peace/Mir: An Anthology of Historical Alternatives to War.* Syracuse, NY: Syracuse University Press, 1993.

Chmielewski, Wendy, Kern, Louis, & Klee-Hartzell, Marilyn. eds., *Women in Spiritual and Communitarian Societies in the U.S.* Syracuse, NY: Syracuse University Press, 1993.

Cohen, Robert. *When the Old Left was Young: Student Radicals and America's First Mass Student Movement, 1929–1941.* New York: Oxford University Press, 1993.

Colaiaco, James A. *Martin Luther King, Jr.: Apostle of Militant Nonviolence.* Basingstoke, UK: Macmillan, 1993.

Conlin, Jospeh R. *American Anti-war Movements.* Beverly Hills, CA: Glencoe Press, 1968.

Cook, Blanche W, Chatfield, Charles, & Cooper, Sandi. eds. *The Garland Library of War and Peace: A Collection of 360 Titles Bound in 328 Volumes.* New York: Garland Publishing, 1971.

Cooney, Robert, & Michalowski, Helen. eds. *The Power of the People: Active Nonviolence in the United States.* Philadelphia: New Society Publishers, 1987.

Cortright, David. *Peace Works: The Citizen's Role in Ending the Cold War.* Boulder, CO: Westview Press, 1993.

Cortright, David. *Peace: A History of Movement and Ideas.* New York: Cambridge University Press, 2008.

Cotrell, Robert H. *Roger Nash Baldwin and the American Civil Liberties Union.* New York: Columbia University Press, 2000.

Cousins, Norman. *Who Speaks for Man.* New York: Macmillan & Co., 1953.

Craig, John M. *Lucia Ames Mead (1856–1936) and the American Peace Movement.* Lewiston, NY: Edwin Mellen Press, 1990.

Craig, Robert H. *Religion and Radical Politics: An Alternative Christian Tradition in the United States.* Philadelphia: Temple University Press, 1992.

Crawford, Neta C., & Klotz, Audi. eds., *How Sanctions Work: Lessons from South Africa.* New York: St. Martin's Press, 1999.

Crittenden, Ann. *Sanctuary: A Story of American Conscience and Law.* New York: Weidenfeld & Nicholson, 1988.

Curran, Thomas F. *Soldiers of Peace: Civil War Pacifism and the Postwar Radical Peace Movement.* New York: Fordham University Press, 2003.

Curti, Merle. *Peace or War: The American Struggle, 1636–1936.* New York: W.W. Norton & Co., 1936.

Curti, Merle. *The American Peace Crusade, 1815–1860.* Durham, NC: Duke University Press, 1929.

Curti, Merle. *The Learned Blacksmith: The Letters and Journals of Elihu Burritt.* New York: Garland Publishing, revised, 1972.

Danner, Mark. *Torture and Truth: America, Abu Ghraib, and the War on Terror.* New York: New York Review of Books, 2004.

Davis, Allen F. *American Heroine: The Life and Legend of Jane Addams.* New York: Oxford University Press, 1973.

Dawes, James. *The Language of War: Literature and Culture in the U.S. from the Civil War Through World War II.* Cambridge, MA: Harvard University Press, 2002.

Dawley, Alan. *Changing the World: American Progressives in War and Revolution.* Princeton, NJ: Princeton University Press, 2003.

Day, Dorothy. *Loaves and Fishes.* New York: Harper & Row, 1963.

Day, Mark. *Forty Acres: Cesar Chavez and the Farm Workers.* New York: Praeger, 1971.

DeBenedetti, Charles. *The Origins of the Modern American Peace Movement, 1915–1929.* Millwood, NY: KTO Press, 1978.

DeBenedetti, Charles. *The Peace Reform in American History.* Bloomington: Indiana University Press, 1980.

DeBenedetti, Charles. ed. *Peace Heroes in Twentieth Century America.* Bloomington: Indiana University Press, 1986.

DeBenedetti, Charles, with Chatfield, Charles. *An American Ordeal: The Antiwar Movement of the Vietnam Era.* Syracuse, NY: Syracuse University Press, 1990.

Debs, Eugene. *Walls and Bars.* Chicago: Charles H. Kerr Co., 1927.

D'Elia, Dennis. "Benjamin Rush: Philosopher of the American Revolution," *Transactions of the American Philosophical Society 64, part 5.* Philadelphia: American Philosophical Society, 1974.

Debo, Angie. *And Still the Waters Run: The Betrayal of Five Civilized Tribes.* Princeton, NJ: Princeton University Press, 1973.

Dellinger, David. *From Yale to Jail: Life of a Moral Dissenter.* New York: Pantheon, 1993.

D'Emilio, John. *Lost Prophet: The Life and Times of Bayard Rustin.* New York: Free Press, 2003.

Dennis, Matthew. *Cultivating a Landscape of Peace.* Ithaca, NY: Cornell University Press, 1993.

Denisoff, R. Serge. *Songs of Protest, War and Peace: A Bibliography and Discography.* Santa Barbara: ABC-CLIO, 1973.

Denisoff, R. Serge. *Great Day Coming: Folk Music and the American Left.* Urbana: University of Illinois Press, 1971.

Dodge, David Low. *War Inconsistent with the Religion of Jesus Christ.* New York: Garland Publishers, reprint, 1971.

Doenecke, Justus D. *Storm on the Horizon: The Challenge to American Intervention, 1939–1941.* New York: Rowman & Littlefield, 2000.

Doenecke, Justus D. *The Battle Against Intervention, 1939–1941.* Malabar, FL: Krieger Publishing Co., 1997.

Dowling, John. *War/Peace: Film Guide*. Chicago: World Without War Publications, 1980.

Dray, Philip. *At the Hands of Persons Unknown: The Lynching of Black America*. New York: Random House, 2002.

Dubofsky, Melvyn. *We Shall Be All: A History of the Industrial Workers of the World*. Chicago: Quadrangle Books, 1969.

Dudziak, Mary. *Cold War Civil Rights: Race and the Image of American Democracy*. Princeton, NJ: Princeton University Press, 2000.

Du Bois, Ellen Carol. *Feminism and Suffrage: The Emergence of an Independent Women's Movement in America, 1848–1869*. Ithaca, NY: Cornell University Press, 1978.

Dunbar, Anthony P. *Against the Grain: Southern Radicals and Prophets, 1929–1959*. Charlottesville: University Press of Virginia, 1981.

Eagan, Eileen. *Class, Culture and the Classroom: The Student Peace Movement of the 1930s*. Philadelphia: Temple University Press, 1981.

Early, Frances H. *A World Without War: How U.S. Feminists and Pacifists Resisted World War I*. Syracuse, NY: Syracuse University Press, 1997.

Eddy, Sherwood, & Page, Kirby. *Creative Pioneers*. New York: Association Press, 1937.

Ekirch, Arthur A. Jr. *The Civilian and the Military*. New York: Oxford University Press, 1956.

Ekirch, Arthur A. Jr. ed. *Voices in Dissent: An Anthology of Individualist Thought in The United States*. New York: The Citadel Press, 1964.

Eller, Cynthia. *Conscientious Objectors and the Second World War: Moral and Religious Arguments in Support of Pacifism*. New York: Praeger, 1991.

Epstein, Barbara. *Political Protest and Cultural Revolution: Nonviolent Direct Action in the 1970s and 1980s*. Berkeley: University of California Press, 1991.

Evans, Sara. *Born for Liberty: A History of Women in America*. New York: Simon & Schuster, 1997.

Evans, Sara. Personal Politics: The Roots of Women's Liberation in the Civil Rights Movement and the New Left. New York: Vintage Books, 1980.

Fairclough, Adam. *To Redeem the Soul of America: The Southern Christian Leadership Conference and Martin Luther King, Jr.* Athens: University of Georgia Press, 2001.

Farmer, James. *Lay Bare the Heart: An Autobiography of the Civil Rights Movement*. New York: Arbor, 1985.

Farrell, John C. *Beloved Lady: A History of Jane Addams' Ideas on Reform and Peace*. Baltimore: Johns Hopkins University Press, 1967.

Farrell, James J. *The Spirit of the Sixties: Making Postwar Radicalism*. New York: Routledge, 1997.

Fass, Paula. *The Damned and the Beautiful: American Youth in the 1920s*. New York: Oxford University Press, 1997.

Fey, Harold E. ed. *Kirby Page, Social Evangelist: The Autobiography of a 20th Century Peace Prophet*. Nyack, NY: FOR Press, 1975.

Ferber, Michael, & Lynd, Staughton. *The Resistance.* Boston: Beacon press, 1971.

Fink, Leon. *Workingmen's Democracy: The Knights of Labor and American Politics.* Urbana: University of Illinois Press, 1983.

Finn, James. ed. *Protest, Pacifism and Politics.* New York: Random House, 1967.

Fischer, Marilyn, Nackenoff, Carol, & Chmielewski, Wendy. eds. *Jane Addams and the Practice of Democracy.* Urbana: University of Illinois Press, 2008.

Fisher, James Terrance. *The Catholic Counterculture in America, 1933–1962.* Chapel Hill: University of North Carolina Press, 1989.

Flexner, Eleanor. *A Century of Struggle: The Women's Rights Movement in the United States.* Cambridge, MA: Belknap Press, reprint 1996.

Fosdick, Harry Emerson. *The Living of These Days.* New York: Harper Bros., 1956.

Fosdick, Raymond P. *Chronicle of a Generation: An Autobiography.* New York: Harper Bros., 1958.

Foley, Michael S. *Confronting the War Machine: Draft Resistance during the Vietnam War.* Chapel Hill: University of North Carolina Press, 2003.

Foster, Carrie A. *The Women and the Warriors: The U.S. Section of the Women's International League for Peace and Freedom, 1915–1946.* Syracuse, NY: Syracuse University Press, 1996.

Fox, Richard Wrightman. *Reinhold Niebuhr: A Biography.* San Francisco: Harper & Row, 1987.

Freeberg, Ernest. *Democracy's Prisoner: Eugene V. Debs, the Great War, and the Right to Dissent.* Cambridge, MA: Harvard University Press, 2008.

Friedan, Betty. *The Feminine Mystique.* New York: W.W. Norton & Co., 1963.

Friedland, Michael B. *Lift Up Your Voice Like a Trumpet: White Clergy and the Civil Rights and Anti-war Movements, 1954–1973.* Chapel Hill: University of North Carolina Press, 1998.

Gara, Larry. *War Resistance in Historical Perspective.* New York: War Resisters League, 1989.

Garrison, Dee. *Bracing for Armageddon: Why Civil Defense Never Worked.* New York: Oxford University Press, 2006.

Garrow, David J. *Bearing the Cross: Martin Luther King Jr., and the Southern Christian Leadership Conference.* New York: Vintage, 1993.

Giffen, Frederick C. *Six Who Protested: Radical Opposition to the First World War.* Port Washington, NY: Kennikat Press, 1976.

Gilbert, Marc Jason, Ed. *The Vietnam War on Campus: Other Voices, More Distant Drums.* Westport, Conn.: Praeger, 2001.

Gitlin, Todd. *The Sixties: Years of Hope, Days of Rage.* New York: Bantam Books, 1987.

Glen, John M. *Highlander: No Ordinary School.* Knoxville: University of Tennessee Press, 1996.

Gobat, Michel. *Confronting the American Dream: Nicaragua Under U.S. Imperial Rule.* Durham, NC: Duke University Press, 2005.

Goldsby, Jacqueline. *A Spectacular Secret: Lynching in American Life and Literature.* Chicago: University of Chicago Press, 2006.

Gosse, Van. *Where the Boys Are: Cuba, Cold War America and the Making of the New Left.* New York: Verso, 1993.

Goosen, Rachael Waltner. *Women Against the Good War: Conscientious Objection and Gender on the American Home Front, 1941–1947.* Chapel Hill: University of North Carolina Press.

Gray, Francine du Plessix. *Divine Disobedience: Profiles in Catholic Radicalism.* New York; Knopf, 1970.

Gregg, Richard B. *The Power of Nonviolence.* Nyack, NY: Fellowship of Reconciliation, 1959.

Gronowicz, Anthony. ed. *Oswald Garrison Villard: The Dilemma of the Absolute Pacifist in Two World Wars.* New York: Garland Publishing, 1983.

Hall, Mitchell. *Because of Their Faith: CALCAV and Religious Opposition to the Vietnam War.* New York: Columbia University Press, 1990.

Hall, Simon. *Peace and Freedom: The Civil Rights and Anti-war Movements in the 1960s.* Philadelphia: University of Pennsylvania Press, 2005.

Heineman, Kenneth J. *Campus Wars: The Peace Movement at American State Universities in the Vietnam Era.* New York: New York University Press, 1993.

Hentoff, Nat. *Peace Agitator: The Story of A.J. Muste.* New York: Macmillan & Co., 1963.

Herman, Sondra R. *Eleven Against War: Studies in American Internationalist Thought, 1898–1921.* Stanford, CA: Hoover Institution Press, 1969.

Herring, George C. *America's Longest War: The United States and Vietnam, 1950–1975.* New York: McGraw-Hill, 1996.

Hershberger, Guy F. *War, Peace, and Non-resistance.* Scottdale, PA: Herald Press, 1953.

Hershberger, Mary. *Traveling to Vietnam: American Peace Activists and the War.* Syracuse, NY: Syracuse University Press, 1998.

Hill, Lance. *The Deacons for Defense: Armed Resistance and the Civil Rights Movement.* Chapel Hill: University of North Carolina Press, 2004.

Hirst, Margaret. *The Quakers in Peace and War.* New York: George H. Doran, 1923.

Holmes, John Haynes, and Lawrence, Reginald. *If this Be Treason.* New York: Macmillan & Co., 1935.

Holmes, John Haynes. *I Speak for Myself.* New York: Harper Bros., 1959.

Holsworth, Robert D. *Let Your Life Speak: A Study of Politics, Religion and Anti-nuclear Weapons Activism.* Madison: University of Wisconsin Press, 1989.

Horne, Gerald. *Communist Front? The Civil Rights Congress, 1946–1956.* Rutherford, NJ: Farleigh Dickinson University Press, 1987.

Horne, Gerald. *Black and Red: W.E.B. DuBois and the Afro-American Response to the Cold War, 1944–1963.* Albany: State University of New York Press, 1986.

Hostetter, David L. *Movement Matters: American Antiapartheid Activism and the Rise of Multicultural Politics.* New York: Routledge, 2006.

Howlett, Charles F. *The American Peace Movement: References and Resources.* Boston: G.K. Hall & Co., 1991.

Howlett, Charles F. *Troubled Philosopher: John Dewey and the Struggle for World Peace.* Port Washington, NY: Kennikat Press, 1977.

Howlett, Charles F. *Brookwood Labor College and the Struggle for Peace and Justice in America.* Lewiston, NY: Edwin Mellen Press, 1993.

Howlett, Charles F., & Lieberman, Robbie. *A History of the American Peace Movement from Colonial Times to the Present.* Lewiston, NY: Edwin Mellen Press, 2008.

Hughan, Jesssie Wallace. *Three Decades of War Resistance.* New York: War Resisters League, 1942.

Hull, William I. *The New Peace Movement.* Boston: World Peace Foundation, 1912.

Hunt, Andrew E. *The Turning: A History of Vietnam Veterans Against the War.* New York: New York University Press, 1999.

Hunt, Andrew E. *David Dellinger: The Life and Times of a Non-violent Revolutionary.* New York: New York University Press, 2006.

Hymowitz, Carol, & Weissman, Michaele. *A History of Women in America.* New York: Bantam Books, 1984.

Isserman, Maurice. *If I Had a Hammer: The Death of the Old Left and the Birth of the New Left.* New York: Basic Books, 1987.

Jackson, Thomas F. *From Civil Rights to Human Rights: Martin Luther King, Jr. and the Struggle for Economic Justice.* Philadelphia: University of Pennsylvania Press, 2006.

James, Sydney V. *A People Among People: Quaker Benevolence in 18th Century America.* Cambridge, MA: Harvard University Press, 1963.

Jennings, Francis. *The Founders of America: How Indians Discovered the Land; Pioneered in it; and Created Great Classical Civilizations: How They Were Plunged into a Dark Age by Invasion and Conquest; and How They are Reviving.* New York: W. W. Norton & Co., 1994.

Johnpoll, Bernard. K. *Pacifist's Progress: Norman Thomas and the Decline of American Socialism.* Chicago: Quadrangle Books, 1970.

Johnson, Chalmers. *The Sorrows of Empire: Militarism, Secrecy, and the End of the Republic.* New York: Metropolitan Books, 2004.

Johnson, Robert David. *The Peace Progressives and American Foreign Relations.* Cambridge, MA: Harvard University Press, 1995.

Jones, Mary Hoxie. *Swords into Ploughshares: An Account of the American Friends Service Committee, 1917–1937.* New York: Macmllan & Co., 1937.

Jones, Rufus. *The Quakers in the American Colonies.* New York: W.W. Norton & Co., 1962.

Jordan, David Starr. *The Days of Man.* New York: World Book, 1922.

Josephson, Harold. ed. *Biographical Dictionary of Modern Peace Leaders.* Westport, CT: Greenwood Press, 1985.

Juhnke, James C., & Hunter, Carol M. *The Missing Peace: The Search for Nonviolent Alternatives in United States History.* Kitchner, ON, Canada: Pandora Press, 2001.

Katz, Milton. *Ban the Bomb: A History of SANE, the Committee for a Sane Nuclear Policy.* Westport, CT: Praeger, 1986.

Keetley, Dawn, & Pettegrew, John. eds. *Public Women, Public Words: a Documentary History of American Feminism.* New York: Rowman & Littlefield, 2005.

Kelley, Robin D. G. *Hammer and Hoe: Alabama Communists During the Great Depression.* Chapel Hill: University of North Carolina Press, 1990.

Kelley, Robin D. G. *Race Rebels: Culture, Politics, and the Black Working Class.* New York: Free Press, 1996.

Kennedy, David M. *Over Here: The First World War and American Society.* New York: Oxford University Press, 1980.

Kennedy, Kathleen. *Disloyal Mothers and Scurrilous Citizens: Women and Subversion During World War I.* Bloomington: Indiana University Press, 1999.

King, Martin Luther, Jr. *Stride Toward Freedom.* New York: Holt, Rinehart and Winston, 1958.

King, Martin Luther, Jr. *Why We Can't Wait.* New York: New American Library, 1964.

Kleidman, Robert. *Organizing for Peace: Neutrality, the Test Ban, and the Freeze.* Syracuse, NY: Syracuse University Press, 1993.

Klejment, Anne. *The Berrigans: A Bibliography of Published Works by Daniel, Philip, and Elizabeth McAlister Berrigan.* New York: Garland Publishing, 1979.

Knight, Louise W. *Citizen: Jane Addams and the Struggle for Democracy.* Chicago: University of Chicago Press, 2005.

Kohn, Stephen M. *Jailed for Peace: The History of American Draft Law Violators, 1658–1985.* Westport, CT: Praeger, 1986.

Kosek, Joseph Kip. *Acts of Conscience: Christian Nonviolence and Modern American Democracy.* New York: Columbia University Press, 2009.

Kramer, Larry. *Reports from the Holocaust: The Making of an AIDS Activist.* New York: St. Martin's Press, 1989.

Kuehl, Warren F. *Seeking World Order: The United States and International Organization to 1920.* Nashville, TN: Vanderbilt University Press, 1969.

Kutulas, Judy. *The Long War: the Intellectual People's Front and Anti-Stalinism, 1930–1940.* Durham, NC: Duke University Press, 1995.

Ladd, William. *The Essays of Philanthropos on Peace and War.* New York: Garland Publishing, reprint, 1971.

Lembcke, Jerry. *The Spitting Image, Myth, Memory and the Legacy of Vietnam.* New York: New York University Press, 1998.

Lepore, Jill. *In the Name of War: King Philip's War and the Origins of American Identity.* New York: Knopf, 1998.

Levine, Daniel. *Jane Addams and the Liberal Tradition.* Madison: Wisconsin Historical Society Press, 1971.

Levine, Daniel. *Bayard Rustin and the Civil rights Movement.* New Brunswick, NJ: Rutgers University Press, 2000.

Lewis, David Levering. *W.E.B. DuBois: The fight for Equality and the American Century, 1919–1963.* New York: Henry Holt & Co., 2000.

Lewis, John. *Walking with the Wind: A Memoir of the Movement.* Fort Washington, PA: Harvest Books, 1999.

Lieberman, Robbie. *The Strangest Dream: Communism, Anticommunism and the U.S. Peace Movement, 1945–1963.* Syracuse, NY: Syracuse University Press, 2000.

Lieberman, Robbie, & Lang, Clarence. eds. *Anticommunism and the African American Freedom Movement: "Another Side of the Story."* New York: Palgrave McMillan, 2009.

Loeb, Paul Rogat. *Generation at the Crossroads: Apathy and Action on the American Campus.* New Brunswick, NJ: Rutgers University Press, 1994.

Lofland, John. *Polite Protestors: The American Peace Movement of the 1980s.* Syracuse, NY: Syracuse University Press, 1993.

Lowe, Ben. *Imagining Peace: A History of Early English Pacifist Ideas: 1340–1560.* University Park, PA.: Pennsylvania State University Press, 1997.

Lynd, Alice. ed. *We Won't Go: Personal Accounts of War Objectors.* Boston: Beacon Press 1968.

Lynd, Staughton, & Lynd, Alice. eds. *Nonviolence in America: A Documentary History.* Maryknoll, NY: Orbis Books, 1998.

Marchand, C. Roland. *The American Peace Movement and Social Reform. 1898–1918.* Princeton, NJ: Princeton University Press, 1972.

Margulies, Joseph. *Guantanamo and the Abuse of Presidential Power.* New York: Simon & Schuster, 2007.

Markowitz, Norman D. *The Rise and Fall of the People's Century: Henry A. Wallace and American Liberalism, 1941–1948.* New York: Free Press, 1973

Martin, Robert F. *Howard Kester and the Struggle for Social Justice in the South, 1904–1977.* Charlottesville: University of Virginia Press, 1991.

McCarthy, Timothy Patrick, & McMillian, John, eds. *The Radical Reader: A Documentary History of the American Radical Tradition.* New York: The New Press, 2003.

McCoy, Alfred W. *A Question of Torture: CIA Interrogation from the Cold War to the War on Terror.* New York: Metropolitan Books, 2006.

McKanan, Dan. *Identifying the Image of God: Radical Christians and Non-violent Power in the Antebellum United States.* New York: Oxford University Press, 2002.

McMurray, Linda O. *To Keep the Waters Troubled.* New York: Oxford University Press, 1998.

McNeal, Patricia. *American Catholic Peace Movements, 1928–1972.* New York: Arno Press, 1978.

McNeal, Patricia. *Harder than War: Catholic Peacemaking in Twentieth Century America.* New Brunswick, NJ: Rutgers University Press, 1992.

Mead, Lucia Ames. *Swords into Ploughshares*. New York: G.P. Putnam's Sons, 1912.

Meier, August, & Rudwick, Elliott. *Along the Color Line: Explorations in the Black Experience*. Urbana: University of Illinois Press, 1976.

Meier, August, & Rudwick, Elliott. *CORE: A Study in the Civil rights Movement, 1942–1968*. New York: Oxford University Press, 1973.

Mekeel, Arthur J. *The Relation of the Quakers to the American Revolution*. Washington, D.C.: Public Affairs Press, 1979.

Meriwether, James H. *Proudly We Can Be Africans: Black Americans and Africa, 1935–1961*. Chapel Hill: University of North Carolina Press, 2002.

Miller, Christian T. *Blood Money: Wasted Billions, Lost Lives, and Corporate Greed in Iraq*. New York: Little, Brown, 2006.

Miller, James. *"Democracy in the Streets": From Port Huron to the Siege of Chicago*. New York: Simon & Schuster, 1987.

Miller, Robert Moats. *American Protestantism and Social Issues, 1919–1939*. Chapel Hill: University of North Carolina Press, 1958.

Miller, William Robert. *Nonviolence: A Christian Interpretation*. New York: Association Press, 1964.

Mills, C. Wright. *The Causes of World War Three*. Armonk, NY: M.E. Sharpe, 1985.

Mills, C. Wright. *The Power Elite*. New York: Oxford University Press, 1999.

Mollin, Marian. *Radical Pacifism in Modern America*. Philadelphia: University of Pennsylvania Press, 2006.

Mortizen, Julius. *The Peace Movement of America*. New York: G.P. Putnam's Sons, 1912.

Morris, Aldon D. *The Origins of the Civil Rights Movement: Black Communities Organizing for Change*. New York: Free Press, 1984.

Moser, Richard. *The New Winter Soldiers: GI and Veteran Dissent During the Vietnam Era*. New Brunswick, NJ: Rutgers University Press, 1996.

Moskos, Charles C., & Chambers II, John Whiteclay. eds. *The New Conscientious Objection: From Sacred to Secular Resistance*. New York: Oxford University Press, 1993.

Murphy, Paul. *World War I and the Origins of Civil Liberties in the United States*. New York: W.W. Norton & Co., 1979.

Muste, A.J. *Nonviolence in an Aggressive World*. New York: Harper Bros., 1940.

Nash, Gary. *Quakers and Politics: Pennsylvania, 1682–1736*. Princeton, NJ: Princeton University Press, 1968.

Nelson, John K. *The Peace Prophets: American Pacifist Thought, 1919–1941*. Chapel Hill: University of North Carolina Press, 1967.

Nelson, Keith L., ed. *The Impact of War on American Life: The Twentieth-Century Experience*. New York: Holt, Rinehart & Winston, 1971.

Oakes, Guy. *The Imaginary War: Civil Defense and American Cold War Culture*. New York: Oxford University Press, 1994.

Oropeza, Lorena. *Raze Si! Guerra No! Chicano Protest and Patriotism During the Viet Nam War Era.* Berkeley: University of California Press, 2005.

Packer, George. *The Assassins' Gate: America in Iraq.* New York: Farrar, Straus, & Giroux, 2005.

Patterson, David S. *Toward a Warless World: The Travail of the American Peace Movement, 1887–1914.* Bloomington: Indiana University Press, 1976.

Patterson, David S. *The Search for a Negotiated Peace: Women's Activism and Citizen Diplomacy in World War I.* New York: Routledge, 2008.

Payne, Charles M. *I've Got the Light of Freedom: The Organizing Tradition and the Mississippi Freedom Struggle.* Berkeley: University of California Press, 1995.

Peck, James. *Freedom Ride.* New York: Simon & Schuster, 1962.

Peck, James. *We Who Would Not Kill.* New York: Lyle Stuart, 1958.

Perry, Lewis. *Radical Abolitionism: Anarchy and the Government of God in Antislavery Thought.* Knoxville: University of Tennessee Press, 1995.

Perry, Ralph Barton. *The Thought and Character of William James.* Cambridge, MA: Harvard University Press, 1948.

Peterson, H.C., & Fite, Gilbert. *Opponents of War, 1917–1918.* Seattle: University of Washington Press, 1957.

Pfeffer, Paula F. *A Philip Randolph: Pioneer of the Civil Rights Movement.* Baton Rouge: Louisiana State University Press, 1990.

Phelps, Christina Stokes. *The Anglo-American Peace Movement in the Mid-Nineteenth Century.* New York: Columbia University Press, 1930.

Pickett, Clarence E. *For More than Bread.* Boston; Little, Brown & Co., 1953.

Piehl, Mel. *Breaking Bread: The Catholic Worker and the Origin of Catholic Radicalism in America.* Philadelphia: Temple University Press, 1982.

Plummer, Brenda Gayle. *Rising Wind: Black Americans and U.S. Foreign Affairs, 1935–1960.* Chapel Hill: University of North Carolina Press, 1996.

Polner, Murray & O'Grady, Jim. *Disarmed and Dangerous: The Radical Lives and Times of Daniel and Philip Berrigan.* New York: Basic Books, 1997.

Polner, Murray, & Woods, Thomas E., Jr. eds. *We Who Dared To Say No to War: American Antiwar Writing from 1812 to Now.* New York: Basic Books, 2008.

Powers, Roger S., & Vogele, William B. eds. *Protest, Power, and Change: An Encyclopedia of Non-violent Action from ACT-UP to Women's Suffrage.* New York: Garland Publishing, 1997.

Raines, Howell, ed. *My Soul Is Rested: Movement Days in the Deep South Remembered.* New York: G.P. Putnam Sons., 1977.

Randall, Mercedes M. *Improper Bostonian: Emily Greene Balch.* New York: Twayne, 1964.

Ransby, Barbara. *Ella Baker and the Black Freedom Movement: A Radical Democratic Vision.* Chapel Hill: University of North Carolina Press, 2003.

Reardon, Betty. *Sexism and the War System.* New York: Teachers College Press, 1985.

Ricks, Thomas. *Fiasco: The American Military Adventure in Iraq.* New York: Penguin Books, 2006.

Roberts, Nancy. *Dorothy Day and the Catholic Worker.* Albany: State University of New York Press, 1984.

Robinson, Jo Ann Gibson. *The Montgomery Bus Boycott and the Women Who started It: The Memoir of Jo Ann Gibson Robinson.* Edited by David Garrow. Knoxville; University of Tennessee Press, 1987.

Robinson, Jo Ann O. *Abraham Went Out: A Biography of A.J. Muste.* Philadelphia: Temple University Press, 1981.

Rochester, Stuart. *American Liberal Disillusionment in the Wake of World War I.* University Park: Pennsylvania State University Press, 1977.

Rossinow, Doug. *The Politics of Authenticity: Liberalism, Christianity, and the New Left in America.* New York: Columbia University Press, 1999.

Rotberg, Robert I. *A Leadership for Peace: How Edwin Ginn Tried to Change the World.* Stanford, CA.: Stanford University Press, 2006.

Royster, J.J. *Southern Horrors and Other Writings.* New York: Bedford, St. Martins, 1997.

Rupp, Leila. *Worlds of Women: The Making of an International Women's Movement.* Princeton, NJ: Princeton University Press, 1997.

Rustin, Bayard. *Down the Line: The Collected Writings of Bayard Rustin.* Chicago: Quadrangle Books, 1971.

Ryan, Claes, G. *America the Virtuous: The Crisis of Democracy and the Quest for Empire.* New Brunswick, NJ: Transaction Books, 2003.

Saar, Erik, & Novak, Viveca. *Inside the Wire: A Military Soldier's Eyewitness Account of Life at Guantanamo.* New York: Penguin Books, 2005.

Salvatore, Nick. *Eugene V. Debs: Citizen and Socialist.* Urbana University of Illinois Press, 2007.

Schecter, Patricia A. *Ida B. Wells-Barnett and American Reform, 1880–1930.* Chapel Hill: University of North Carolina Press, 2001.

Schell, Jonathan. The Fate of the Earth. New York: Knopf, 1982.

Schell, Jonathan. *The Unconquerable World: Power, Nonviolence, and the Will of the People.* New York: Metropolitan Books, 2003.

Schissel, Lillian. ed. *Conscience in America: A Documentary History of Conscientious Objection in America, 1657–1957.* New York: E.P. Dutton & Co., 1968.

Schlabach, Theron, & Hughes, Richard, T. eds. *Proclaim Peace: Christian Pacifism from Unexpected Quarters.* Urbana: University of Illinois Press, 1997.

Schott, Linda. *Reconstructing Women's Thoughts: the Women's International League for Peace and Freedom before World War II.* Stanford, CA: Stanford University Press, 1997.

Schrecker, Ellen. *No Ivory Tower: McCarthyism and the University.* New York: Oxford University Press, 1986.

Schrecker, Ellen. *Many Are the Crimes: McCarthyism in America.* Boston: Little, Brown & Co., 1998.

Seidler, Murray. *Norman Thomas: Respectable Rebel.* Syracuse, NY: Syracuse University Press, 1967.

Sharp, Gene. *The Politics of Nonviolent Action.* Boston: Sargent, 1973.

Sibley, Mulford Q., & Jacob, Philip E. *Conscription of Conscience*. Ithaca, NY: Cornell University Press, 1952.

Sibley, Mulford Q. ed. *The Quiet Battle: Writings on the Theory and Practice of Nonviolent Resistance*. Boston: Beacon Pres, 1963.

Sklar, Kathryn Kish. ed., *Women's Rights Emerges within the Antislavery Movement, 1830–1870*. Boston: Bedford/St. Martins, 2000.

Small, Melvin. *Antiwarriors: The Vietnam War and the Battle for America's Hearts and Minds*. Wilmington, DE: Scholarly Resources, 2002.

Small, Melvin, & Hoover, William D. eds. *Give Peace a Chance: Exploring the Vietnam Antiwar Movement*. Syracuse, NY: Syracuse University Press, 1992.

Smith, Christian. *Resisting Reagan: The U.S. Central American Peace Movement*. Chicago: University of Chicago Press, 1996.

Smith, Clive Stafford. *Eight O'Clock Ferry to the Windward Side: Seeking Justice in Guantanamo Bay*. New York: Nation Books, 2007.

Smith, E. Timothy. *Opposition Beyond the Water's Edge: Liberal Internationalists, Pacifists, and Containment, 1945–1953*. Westport, CT: Greenwood Press, 1999.

Smith, Jackie & Johnson, Hank. eds. *Globalization and Resistance: Transnational Dimensions of Social Movements*. New York: Rowman & Littlefield, 2002.

Spock, Benjamin. *Decent and Indecent: Our Personal and Political Behavior*. New York: Fawcett Crest, 1971.

Stauffer, Jon. *The Black Hearts of Men: Radical Abolitionism and the Transformation of Race*. Cambridge, MA: Harvard University Press, 2002.

Stevenson, Lilian. *Towards a Christian International: the Story of the International Fellowship of Reconciliation*. New York: Fellowship of Reconciliation, 1936.

Stone, Geoffrey R. *Perilous Times: Free Speech in Wartime From the Sedition Act of 1798 to the War on Terrorism*. Chicago: University of Chicago Press, 2004.

Sullivan, Michael. *American Adventurism Abroad*. Boston: Wiley-Blackwell, 2007.

Sumner, Charles. *Address on War*. New York: Garland Publishing, reprint, 1971.

Swanberg, W.A. *Norman Thomas: The Last Idealist*. New York: Scribner's Sons, 1976.

Swerdlow, Amy. *Women Strike for Peace: Traditional Motherhood and Radical Politics in the 1960s*. Chicago: University of Chicago Press, 1993.

Taylor, Cynthia. *A. Philip Randolph: The Religious Journey of an African American Labor Leader*. New York: New York University Press, 2006.

Taylor, Ronald B. *Chavez and the Farm Workers*. Boston: Beacon Press, 1975.

Theoharis, Jeanne, & Woodard, Komozi, eds. *Groundwork: Local Black Freedom Movements in America*. New York: NYU Press, 2005.

Thomas, Norman. *A Socialist's Faith*. Port Washington, NY: Kennikat Press, 1971.

Tolis, Peter. *Elihu Burritt: Crusader for Brotherhood*. Hamden, CT: Shoestring Press, 1968.

Tolles, Frederick, & Gordon, Alderfer E. eds. *The Witness of William Penn*. New York: Macmillan & Co., 1957.

Tolles, Frederick, & Gordon, Alderfer E.. *Quakers and the Atlantic Culture.* New York: Macmillan & Co., 1960.

Tracy, James. *Direct Action: Radical Pacifism from the Union eight to the Chicago Seven.* Chicago: University of Chicago Press, 1996.

Trueblood, Benjamin F. *The Federation of the World.* New York: Garland Publishing, reprint 1971.

Vaughn, Stephen. *Holding Fast the Inner Lines: Democracy, Nationalism, and the Committee on Public Information.* Chapel Hill: University of North Carolina Press, 1980.

Von Eschen, Penny. *Race against Empire: Black Americans and Anticolonialism, 1937–1957.* Ithaca, NY: Cornell University Press, 1997.

Wall, Joseph Frazier. *Andrew Carnegie.* New York: Oxford University Press, 1970.

Wallace, Paul A. *The White Roots of Peace.* Port Washington, NY: Kennikat Press, 1946.

Wallis, Jill. *Valiant for Peace: A History of the Fellowship of Reconciliation, 1914–1989.* London: Fellowship of Reconciliation, 1991.

Wallis, Jim. *God's Politics: Why the Right Gets It Wrong and the Left Doesn't Get It.* San Francisco: HarperOne, 2005.

Wank, Solomon. ed. *Doves and Diplomats: Foreign Offices and Peace Movements in Europe and America in the Twentieth Century.* Westport, CT: Greenwood Press, 1978.

Warren, Heather A. *Theologians of a New World Order: Reinhold Niebuhr and the Christian Realists, 1920–1948.* New York: Oxford University Press, 1997.

Weber, Karl. Ed., *I.F. Stone, The Best of I.F. Stone.* New York: Public Affairs, 2006.

Webber, David R., ed. *Civil Disobedience in America: A Documentary History.* Ithaca, NY: Cornell University Press, 1978.

Weddle, Meredith B. *Walking in the Way of Peace: Quaker Pacifism in the Seventeenth Century.* New York: Oxford University Press, 2001.

Weinberg, Arthur, & Weinberg, Lila. eds. *Instead of Violence.* Boston: Beacon Press, 1963.

Wells, Tom. *The War Within: America's Battle over Vietnam.* Berkeley: University of California Press, 1994.

White, Ronald C., Jr. *Liberty and Justice for All: Racial Reform and the Social Gospel, 1877–1925.* San Francisco: Harper & Row, 1990.

Wittner, Lawrence. *Rebels Against War: The American Peace Movement, 1933–1983.* Philadelphia: Temple University Press, 1984.

Wittner, Lawrence. *The Struggle Against the Bomb,* 3 Vols. Stanford, CA: Stanford University Press, 1993–2003.

Wittner, Lawrence. *Confronting the Bomb: A Short History of the World Nuclear Disarmament Movement.* Stanford, CA: Stanford University Press, 2009.

Worcester, Noah. *A Solemn Review of the Custom of War: Showing that War is the Effect of a Popular Delusion and Proposing a Remedy.* New York: Garland Publishing, reprint, 1971.

Young, Robert J.C. *Postcolonialism: An Historical Introduction.* Malden, MA: Blackwell, 2001.

Zahn. Gordon. *Another Part of the War: The Camp Simon Story.* Amherst: University of Massachusetts Press, 1979.

Zaroulis, Nancy, & Sullivan, Gerald. *Who Spoke Up? American Protest Against the War in Vietnam, 1963–1975.* New York: Holt, Rinehart, & Winston, 1984.

Zeigler, Valerie H. *The Advocates of Peace in Antebellum America.* Bloomington: University of Indiana Press, 1992.

Zinn, Howard. *A Peoples' History of the United States: 1492 to the Present.* New York: HarperCollins, 2003.

Zwick, Jim. *Mark Twain's Weapons of Satire: Anti-Imperialist Writings on the Philippine-American War.* Syracuse, NY: Syracuse University Press, 1992.

Index

For the People, pages 341–351

C

Calder, Nigel, 265

Calhoun, John C., 33

Campaign for Peace and Democracy, 294

Camp Upton (Long Island), 96

Capote, Truman, 210

Carnegie, Andrew, 86

    United States Steel Corp., 87

    "A League of Peace" (doc), 103

Carnegie Endowment for International Peace (CEIP), 86–88, 140

Carolina Interfaith Task Force, 291

Cass, Lewis, 27

Castro, Fidel, 209–210, 218

Carter, Jimmy, 267

Cather, Willa, 128

Catholic Association for International Peace, 140

Catholic Peace Fellowship (CPF), 217–218

Catholic Worker Movement, 179

"Catonsville Nine", 216

    "Statement" (doc), 248

Catt, Carrie Chapman, 92

Cayuga Tribe, 1

Central Intelligence Agency (CIA), 171 & *passim*

Charles, King II, 4

Chatfield, Charles, 140

Chavez, Cesar, 219–220, 308

    "Letter from Delano" (doc), 258

Cherokee Removal Act (1830)

    Trail of Tears, 27

    Worcester v. Georgia, 27–28

Chivington, J.M.

    Sand Creek Massacre, 58

Church of Peace Union, 88

Civil Rights Movement, 176 & *passim*

Civil War (1861–1865), 34–35, 53–54

Civilian Conservation Corps (CCC), 89

Civilian Public Service Camps (CPS), 167 & ff., 186

Clamshell Alliance, 263–264

    "Reflections" (doc), 281

Clark, John Bates, 88

Clarke, John Henrik, 210

Clergy and Laity Concerned about Vietnam (CALCAV), 217

Cleveland, Grover, 87

Coddington, Marion, 174

CODEPINK for Peace, 275–276

Cohen, Ben, 275

Cold War, 171 & ff.

Collins, Larry, 265

Committee for a Sane Nuclear Policy (SANE), 179 & ff.

Committee for Non-violent Action (CNVA), 172 & ff.

Committee of Friends of Indian Affairs, 59

Communist Party, 138 & *passim*

Congress on Racial Equality (CORE), 170–171 & *passim*

Conscientious Objectors, 2 & *passim*

    "Statement of Conscientious Objectors" (doc), 119

    "Why We Refuse to Register" (doc), 186

Contras, 272–273

Cortright, David, 296–300

Cotton, John, 3–4

Cousins, Norman, 180

Cremer, Randal, 60

Crosby, Ernest Howard, 63, 182

Custer, GEN George A., 58

Curti, Merle, 26, 33

D

Dallas, Meredith, 169

Darfur, Sudan, 277–278

    "Divestment as a Tool" (doc), 301

LaVergne, TN USA
20 October 2009
161510LV00002B/25/P